CRITICAL THINKING

THESE THOUGHTS BELONG TO:

Sara Miller McCune founded SAGE Publishing in 1965 to support the dissemination of usable knowledge and educate a global community. SAGE publishes more than 1000 journals and over 800 new books each year, spanning a wide range of subject areas. Our growing selection of library products includes archives, data, case studies and video. SAGE remains majority owned by our founder and after her lifetime will become owned by a charitable trust that secures the company's continued independence.

Los Angeles | London | New Delhi | Singapore | Washington DC | Melbourne

CRITICAL THINKING

TOM CHATFIELD

YOUR GUIDE TO EFFECTIVE ARGUMENT, SUCCESSFUL ANALYSIS & INDEPENDENT STUDY

Los Angeles | London | New Delhi
Singapore | Washington DC | Melbourne

Los Angeles | London | New Delhi
Singapore | Washington DC | Melbourne

SAGE Publications Ltd
1 Oliver's Yard
55 City Road
London EC1Y 1SP

SAGE Publications Inc.
2455 Teller Road
Thousand Oaks, California 91320

SAGE Publications India Pvt Ltd
B 1/I 1 Mohan Cooperative Industrial Area
Mathura Road
New Delhi 110 044

SAGE Publications Asia-Pacific Pte Ltd
3 Church Street
#10-04 Samsung Hub
Singapore 049483

Editor: Mila Steele
Editorial assistant: John Nightingale
Assistant editor, digital: Chloe Statham
Production editor: Ian Antcliff
Marketing manager: Catherine Slinn
Cover & illustrations: Shaun Mercier
Typeset by: C&M Digitals (P) Ltd, Chennai, India
Printed in the UK
& Handwriting Stunt Double!

First published 2018

Library of Congress Control Number: **2017941645**

British Library Cataloguing in Publication data

A catalogue record for this book is available from the British Library

ISBN 978-1-4739-4713-9
ISBN 978-1-4739-4714-6 (pbk)

At SAGE we take sustainability seriously. Most of our products are printed in the UK using FSC papers and boards. When we print overseas we ensure sustainable papers are used as measured by the PREPS grading system. We undertake an annual audit to monitor our sustainability.

CONTENTS

THANKS AND ACKNOWLEDGEMENTS

First, if you're reading this – thank you, and I hope you enjoy the book. Please do share any thoughts, comments, queries, corrections or objections with both me and other readers via the hashtag #TalkCriticalThinking – or look me up online and get in touch.

Second, a book like this doesn't happen without the help, decency and skill of a lot of people. Writing it has not been easy, and it couldn't have happened without them.

My darling wife, Cat, and children – Toby and Clio – have both been a constant support and put up with me locking myself in my office for many, many days of writing. Thank you for everything, with all my love.

It is a remarkable privilege to be published by SAGE, and to have found good friends there as well as colleagues: Ziyad, Kiren, Martha, Katie, Mark, and many others with whom I have spent some of the happiest and most stimulating times of my recent years. My editor, Mila Steele, has been expert, enthused and tolerant throughout – and not a little brilliant. This beautiful design is nothing to do with me, and everything to do with the talents of Ian Antcliff (production manager) and Shaun Mercier (creative designer). And none of this would have happened without the passion and friendship of Ziyad Marar in particular. I hope I have justified your belief in me.

The Oxford Internet Institute provided an academic home and sanctum to me for much of the writing process, and I am especially grateful to Vicky Nash for making my time there both possible and pleasurable, and to Luciano Floridi for works and words that inspired my thinking. Oxford itself was a second home to me, thanks to the generosity of Judith and Lawrence Freedman, to whom I owe a great debt of friendship and gratitude.

I have been privileged over the last few years to enjoy friendships and conversations with people who inspire me. Nigel Warburton in particular has been a generous friend and role model, both in person and on paper. Colleagues I am proud to know through the School of Life in London continue to enrich my thinking and feeling life – Roman Krznaric, Philippa Perry and John-Paul Flintoff – while others, including Julian Baggini, Jules Evans, Jonathan Rowson and David Edmonds, have given more than they might realize through their work and examples.

Last but not least, my agent Jon Elek has advised, supported and backed me since the beginning, and I hope he enjoys this latest enthused foray into words and ideas. It has certainly been a pleasure to write it.

WELCOME TO THE BOOK!

WHAT THIS BOOK WILL HELP YOU TO DO

Welcome! Whether you are reading this book for work or pleasure, as part of your studies or as an extension of your professional skills, there are two obvious ways in which critical thinking skills are likely to be important and useful.

1 Helping you to become a selective and critically engaged consumer of other people's work and sources of information.
2 Helping you to produce better work yourself, and to express your knowledge and ideas more clearly and effectively.

As a discipline, critical thinking traditionally places a great deal of emphasis on these ideas, in connection with learning to engage critically with arguments and explanations: with the ways in which both you and others seek to explain how things came to be the way they are, and why certain beliefs and courses of action are reasonable.

All of this remains important – but I am also interested in two further areas in which a critically informed approach is becoming more and more significant:

3 Helping you to manage your own time and attention effectively, while becoming more aware of the ways in which thinking itself tends to be biased or flawed.
4 Helping you to be a more confident and critically engaged user of digital information systems, ranging from search engines to websites to social media and beyond.

Like the first two uses of critical thinking listed above, these areas are closely connected.

The moment we begin to study or explore any question or topic today, we are likely to be using a digital device. We type a search query into our smartphone, look up an article on Wikipedia, browse online news and views, search a database of journals, download a lecturer's presentations, hunt on social media for help and inspiration, and so on.

Even before we start typing, clicking or interacting, we are deluged by streams of information about whatever is currently trending or being shared: status updates, news, headlines and comment, disinformation and rumour, the trivial jostling alongside the profound. We gather, reshape and create information ourselves – from media to code, from text to mathematical models. And, increasingly, information systems autonomously create outcomes that shape our world – from artificial intelligence drawing on big data to billions of networked devices tracking our every action.

I struggled with this while writing this book!

Both the significance and sheer volume of this information make the question of how we engage with it a vital one. How can we make the most of the astonishing resources at our fingertips while retaining a sense of control and understanding? How, moreover, can we make the most of the human capacity for reasoning and creativity in an age where technologies like big data and artificial intelligence are encroaching on ever-more areas of expertise?

We need to be equipped to think as critically as possible about thinking itself if we are to succeed in this context – and we need strategies for taking full advantage of our unprecedented interconnectivity through technology, rather than simply finding ourselves swept along by its momentum.

Metacognition: thinking about thinking itself; the higher-order skills that allow you to successfully keep on learning, improving and adapting.

Critical thinking skills are not just about learning information: they're part of **metacognition**, meaning the higher-order skills that equip us to adapt and to continue learning throughout our lives. Given the sheer pace of technological change, and the fact that many of the fields within which people will be working in a few decades' time don't yet exist, I can think of few more valuable capacities to put at the heart of education and work in the 21st century.

This book is divided into two halves. The first half roughly corresponds to points (1) and (2) in my list, setting out what it means to be a critically engaged reader of others' work and confident in applying the principles of reasoning to your own. The second half turns to points (3) and (4), looking at the ways in which all of our thinking tends to be biased in predictable ways – and what it means to make allowances for these biases in a 21st-century environment suffused with information technology.

Definitions like this are set aside from the main text throughout the book — to help you master key terms.

THINKING CRITICALLY FOR YOURSELF

In the spirit of critical thinking, please don't assume that everything I say is the last word on anything – or that you're obliged to agree with it. Disagree, debate, enquire and question as much as you like. Just make sure you *understand* exactly what it is you disagree with in the first place; try to work out exactly *why* you disagree; and then ask *what* a better explanation might look like.

SMART STUDY: Throughout the book you'll see sections like this, highlighting the connection between critical thinking and study skills, with suggestions on how you might apply them practically to your own work.

THINKING CRITICALLY ONLINE

You're very welcome to share thoughts with me directly about this book on social media at @TomChatfield – and to discuss it both with me and other readers via the hashtag #TalkCriticalThinking. You'll also find online resources such as videos flagged up throughout the book, all easy to find on YouTube and Vimeo channels with the #TalkCriticalThinking hashtag.

THINK ABOUT THIS: Each chapter has one or two questions set out like this, as a prompt for reflection. There's no right or wrong involved. But you'll get the most out of the book if you embrace these opportunities to pause, clear your mind and ask yourself what you think and believe. Here's one question to start you off: what are you hoping to get out of this book – and why? ....

Don't be afraid to write outside the box.

WHAT IS CRITICAL THINKING (AND WHY DOES IT MATTER)?

FIVE THINGS YOU'LL LEARN IN THIS CHAPTER

1 The difference between *critical* and *uncritical thinking*
2 Practical advice for applying *scepticism* in your work
3 Smart *study tips* on managing your time and attention
4 Why you need to watch out for *confirmation bias*
5 Five key techniques for your *critical thinking toolkit*

THE OPPOSITE OF UNCRITICAL THINKING

The word 'critical' isn't the friendliest of terms. If I'm being critical of you, you may say: Why can't you be more supportive? Why are you criticizing me? People don't tend to like being criticized, or react to it well.

Critical thinking is different. It doesn't mean being critical in the sense of being negative or offering criticism. It's much more interesting (and positive) than this. As a starting point, let's approach it as the opposite of something we are all guilty of sometimes – **uncritical thinking** – in which we take things at face value without pausing to consider whether this is sensible or justified.

Uncritical thinking: automatically believing what you read or are told without pausing to ask whether it is accurate, true or reasonable

Take a look at this email, which arrived in my inbox on 9 July 2013:

> Hello,
>
> I'm writing this with tears in my eyes,My family and I came down here in Manila,Philippines on a short holiday unfortunately we got mugged at the hotel park where we stayed,all cash,wallet,credit card and phones were taken away,but luckily for us we still have our passport back in our hotel room...We've been to the consulate here and the Police but they're not helping issues at all...Our flight is leaving in a couple hours time from now but we're having problems settling our hotel bills.
>
> We're very sorry if we are inconveniencing you, but we have only few people to run to now. We will be indeed very grateful if we can get a quick loan of (£2,450 GBP) from you. this will enable us sort our bills and get our sorry self back home. We will appreciate whatever you can afford in assisting us with via western union. We promise to refund it in full as soon as we return. let us know if you can be of any assistance. Please, let us know soonest. Thanks so much.
>
> Thanks
> David

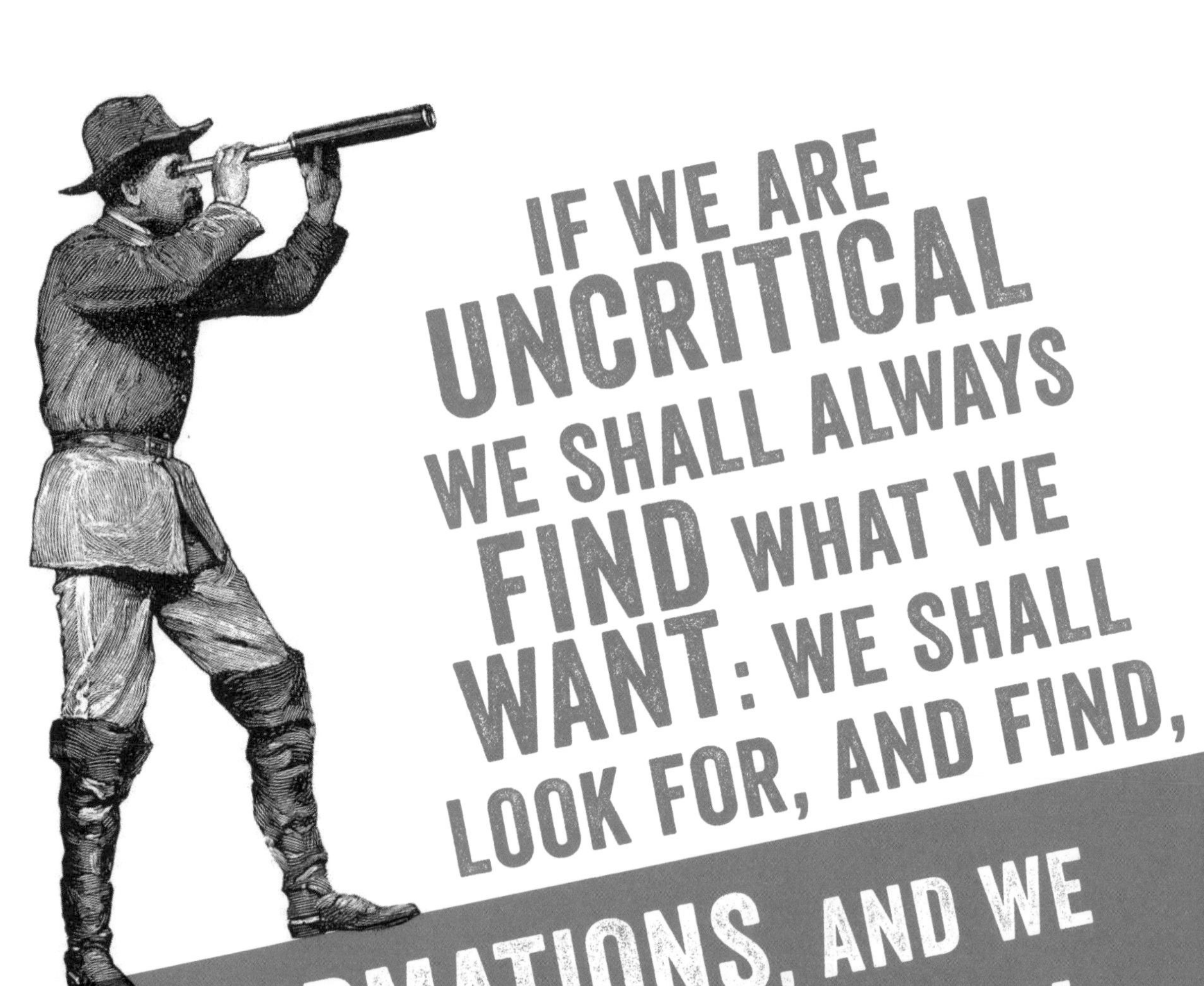

IF WE ARE UNCRITICAL WE SHALL ALWAYS FIND WHAT WE WANT: WE SHALL LOOK FOR, AND FIND, CONFIRMATIONS, AND WE SHALL LOOK AWAY FROM, AND NOT SEE, WHATEVER MIGHT BE DANGEROUS TO OUR PET THEORIES.

KARL POPPER

#TalkCriticalThinking

An uncritical reading of this email would simply accept all of its claims. It was sent from my friend David's personal email address. It was July. Perhaps he was on holiday with his family; perhaps he had got into trouble and desperately needed my help. I must help him at once!

This kind of instant, uncritical response would almost certainly get me into trouble. What I needed to do was to pause, step back and think critically for a moment.

First, I read the email again, carefully. Did this sound like my friend: a writer, editor, experienced traveller, someone unlikely to panic? No. The message didn't really read like something written by him. It had odd turns of phrase – 'get our sorry self back home' – and mistakes in punctuation, spacing, grammar and capitalization that David wouldn't have made even if he were upset: 'at the hotel park where we stayed,all cash,wallet,credit card and phones were taken away,but luckily…'.

Also, would he really have emailed me and asked for money like this, even in an emergency? Again, not likely. He would have put things differently, provided more context and concrete details; he would have been in touch with family and closer friends than me.

How could I check? If this was a fake message, it suggested his email had been hacked or spoofed: that someone else was behind it. I launched Google and copied the first line of the email into inverted commas – 'I'm writing this with tears in my eyes' – looking for other examples of the precise phrase online.

Sure enough, plenty came up. Try it yourself: it's a genuine scam email. At the time of writing this chapter, in 2017, I found 21,500 results, the earliest dating back to 2010. One of the top results was a September 2012 news story from Forbes, exploring what I discovered was known as 'the grandparent scam' – because it's most likely to fool older, inexperienced computer users.

'The scam works because it has urgency', noted the article's author, finance expert John Wasik: 'It's an emotional appeal that preys upon lonely moments in which we feel totally vulnerable.'[1] In other words, it's a scam deliberately designed to provoke uncritical thinking: an instant, urgent reaction driven by strong emotion.

Having explored the scam email to my satisfaction online, I quickly sent a text message to my friend, David, explaining that I thought his email address had been compromised, and double-checking that he and his family were OK. He replied, slightly wearily, to say that they were fine – and that I was the tenth person to text him in the last hour to check he wasn't in trouble in the Philippines. In fact, he was at home in Surrey.

This really did happen – although it's targetted 'phishing' that gets most people today.

The kind of critical thinking I engaged in after receiving this email comes easily to most people, so long as they have some experience of the internet and email. It's a vital survival mechanism for a world in which things aren't always as they seem. Without even noticing it, most of us apply a series of critical filters to our thinking about things like unusual emails. They go something like this:

- Is this somehow unusual, out of the ordinary, unexpected or odd?
- If so, it's time to pause, pay attention and ask a few careful questions.
- Who and where did this message come from?
- Why was it sent?
- Is the person sending it who they claim to be?
- Do I believe what the message is saying?

- If I don't believe it, what might be the hidden intentions behind it?
- What reliable sources can I use to check what is really going on?
- Finally – once I've done all this – what actions should I take?

Of course, most people with any experience of email or technology don't need to go through these steps when looking at a suspicious message. Instead, they simply ask:

- Does this look like a legitimate message – or is it just spam?

This is because, at least when it comes to spam email, most of us are old hands at critical engagement. We've seen hundreds, if not thousands, of spam messages. We know what's going on. We've developed some useful habits and assumptions and short cuts. We're hardened spam critics without even knowing it. This is an important point that we'll return to: if you've handled similar situations many times, and they're not dominated by random noise, you're likely to have developed some meaningful expertise and intuitions. It's when things are strange and new – when you don't have any expertise or information to contextualize them – that your instant reactions are most likely to be misguided.

We engage in critical thinking, or benefit from the lessons of previous critical thought, all the time without being aware of it. If we took everything at face value, we wouldn't get very far in life: we would be deceived, bewildered, manipulated, confused. Imagine if you believed everything you were told by everyone, everything that you saw and heard and read in every advert, every politician's claim.

The art of critical thinking isn't about changing human nature, or pretending we can or should act entirely rationally all the time. It's about learning to recognize our own – and others' – limitations; and knowing when to pause, think again and reach for the right questions in order to work out what is really going on.

Critical thinking: setting out actively to understand what is really going on by using reasoning, evaluating evidence and thinking carefully about the process of thinking itself

Here, then, is my definition of the kind of **critical thinking** we are going to be working towards. When we are thinking critically, we are setting out actively to understand what is going on by using reasoning, evaluating evidence and thinking carefully about the process of thinking itself.

SCEPTICISM AND OBJECTIVITY

Now that we've introduced the idea of critical thinking, try to think critically about each of the eight claims below. Are they reasonable and reliable, or should you think twice before accepting them? Why?

1 They say it's probably the best beer in the world? It must be great: I'll buy some. ....

2 She wrote the world's leading psychology textbook: her views on psychology must be worth taking seriously. ....

3 She wrote the world's leading psychology textbook: her views on the PlayStation 4 must be worth taking seriously. ....

The TROUBLE with having an OPEN MIND, OF COURSE, is that PEOPLE will insist on coming along and trying to put things in it.

Terry Pratchett

#TalkCriticalThinking

4 French fries are delicious. I'm going to eat them all the time. ....

5 My friend has hurt his leg and is lying close to me, in pain: I must rush and help him right now. ....

6 My friend has hurt his leg and is lying on the other side of that busy road, in pain: I must rush and help him right now. ....

7 The video my friend posted on Facebook is really funny. I'm going to click 'like'. ....

8 The video my friend posted on Facebook is pathetic. I'm going to post an insulting personal comment. ....

Scepticism: not automatically accepting something you hear, read or see as true

Statement (1) – that I should buy something which claims to be the best beer in the world – is a piece of uncritical thinking that needs to be viewed with **scepticism**. Scepticism means refusing to take something at face value, and instead asking questions about its reliability. In this case, sceptical reflection should lead us to realize that this is an advertising slogan, and thus unlikely to embody an expert assessment of every beer in the world.

Statement (2) – in which I suggest that a leading psychologist is likely to know about psychology – is not so suspicious. It seems reasonable to take an expert psychologist's views on psychology seriously, although there may be a follow-up question I need to ask about her particular areas of expertise. When it comes to statement (3) and the same psychologist's views on the PlayStation 4, however, being an expert in one field doesn't necessarily mean she knows anything about games consoles. We should think twice before accepting this.

As for the other four statements, from (5) to (8), you'll notice that what they have in common is that they express rapid judgements about something I am planning to do. I'm going to eat French fries all the time, help a friend, click a 'like' button, make a rude comment. Rapid judgements are sometimes necessary. But they also reflect instant emotional responses that may turn out, upon reflection, to be a bad idea. Rushing out into traffic to help our friend may simply end up hurting both of us; posting an offensive comment online may cause lasting offence to someone else – or give us a bad reputation.

Objectivity: trying to understand something from a more neutral perspective, rather than relying on a single opinion or the first piece of information that comes to hand

Critical thinking skills usually involve trying to grasp a situation as **objectively** as possible: setting aside our own immediate feelings and preferences, and trying to identify the relevant facts. Objectivity and scepticism are related ideas. Both of them involve a commitment to finding out as best you can what is actually going on, rather than automatically accepting the first piece of information you encounter.

Both objectivity and scepticism are also possible only to a degree. You can never be entirely objective, and you can never distrust absolutely everything you think you know. Thinking is always rooted in who you are, what you have experienced and what you feel. The trick is reaching an accommodation with this: knowing yourself better and practising techniques that help you understand the world as carefully and realistically as possible.

The eight examples I gave above don't divide neatly into two categories of 'yes, this is reasonable and reliable' or 'no, this is completely unreasonable and unreliable'. Instead, they exist on a spectrum of reliability, ranging from highly unreliable to pretty trustworthy. Most of the claims that we encounter in real life are like this. It's not a question of simply accepting or rejecting them – it's about *how* we should judge them.

In the case of both professional and academic work, it's also about asking about the ways in which different materials may or may not be useful or important. Much like a police investigation, if we are trying to find out what is really going on we need to consider a number of possibilities and use a range of different sources, rather than relying on our immediate feelings or what is in front of us.

This advice might sound so obvious that it's barely worth putting in a textbook, yet you would be amazed at how often all of us – and I include myself in this – form a judgement based on a quick reaction to whatever information is instantly available, or what we feel, rather than even trying to find out whether there is more we need to know.

SMART STUDY: Becoming a better sceptic in four questions

Scepticism entails refusing to take things at face value. You can start practising it in life, work and study by asking four simple questions whenever you need to think twice:

- Why should I trust this claim?
- Why does the person making this claim believe it – or want me to believe it?
- What else has been said, written or reported about this?
- Do I know enough to answer all of the above questions confidently?

If the answer to this final question is 'no', you need to face the fact that you don't know enough to make an informed decision, and you must go in search of more information.

THE BATTLE AGAINST BIAS

If objectivity and scepticism entail trying to understand things as they actually are, then **bias** represents their opposite – looking at things in a way that is entirely dominated by a particular prejudice or perspective. There are many different kinds of bias, and we will explore them in detail later in the book, but all of them fall under the same general definition: approaching something in a one-sided way that distorts your understanding.

Bias: approaching something in a one-sided way that creates a distorted account of the way things actually are

If, for example, I am madly in love with you, I may be biased in my assessment of your skills as a conversationalist or the quality of your jokes. Even if I'm not in love with you, the fact that you're really ridiculously good-looking may bias me towards giving you a job or claiming you sang beautifully in an amateur production of *Phantom of the Opera*. Similarly, if I'm trying to sell you a car, I may emphasize the car's good points and try to cover up its bad ones.

At this point, it's worth making a distinction between two categories of bias: **conscious bias** and **unconscious bias**. Here are a couple of examples; see if you can tell them apart:

Conscious bias: when someone deliberately presents a one-sided view of something, or explicitly holds a one-sided opinion about something

Unconscious bias: when someone's opinions or decisions are distorted by factors that they are not even aware of

	CONSCIOUS	UNCONSCIOUS
1 The prime minister's spokesperson insisted that the prime minister had acted in good faith and from the best of intentions – unlike his cowardly critics.	○	○
2 Voters across the country tended to prefer the taller and the more conventionally good-looking of two candidates when they compared both photographs.	○	○

Example (1) is a case of conscious bias: the prime minister's spokesperson is knowingly and deliberately trying to present the prime minister in the best possible way while implying that his critics are cowardly. Example (2) is a case of unconscious bias. Voters tended to prefer the taller and better-looking of two candidates when shown photographs, but they may not even be aware that this is a factor in their preferences – it can affect their judgement without them consciously noticing what is going on.

Unconscious biases can be harder to deal with than conscious biases. If someone actively expresses a biased perspective – arguing, for example, that they would never choose to vote for a woman over a man – then it is relatively easy to identify and to challenge this bias (changing their minds is quite another thing). If, however, a bias is unconscious, it can be extremely difficult even to identify, let alone to challenge, it. For example, someone may not think of themselves as sexist in any way, yet still frequently act in accordance with sexist assumptions they don't even acknowledge.

Just as total objectivity is impossible, none of us can ever be entirely without biases – and we wouldn't wish to get rid of them all. The challenge is to become more aware of them, and to find ways of minimizing the distortions caused by the more troubling ones. We'll be exploring this in more detail in the second half of this book.

THINK ABOUT THIS: What unconscious biases do you most often see in the people around you? Might any of these also affect your own judgement? ....
....
....
....
....
....

Slow down: critical thinking cannot happen in a rush. Before you do anything else, you need to take the time to engage your slow, considering mind rather than relying on instinct

What You See Is All There Is: a phrase used by psychologist Daniel Kahneman to describe the human tendency to pay attention only to what is immediately obvious, and to neglect the hidden complexities that exist in most situations

FAST AND SLOW THINKING

Most of the time, we rely on general intuitions about what to do, say and think. We wouldn't be able to function if we had to think hard about every single action and decision in our daily lives. We do, however, have the ability to pause and to think more deliberately about some things – and it's this 'slow', considered thinking that we develop when we improve our critical thinking skills (and that we can then use as the basis for making better rapid decisions). That's why the first and most important rule of critical thinking is about speed: **slow down**.

In his book *Thinking, Fast and Slow*,[2] the psychologist Daniel Kahneman offers a useful phrase to describe the problem of relying too much on first impressions, feelings and the information we happen to have in front of us. He calls this problem WYSIATI, a not-so-snappy acronym that stands for **What You See Is All There Is**.

This phrase describes something that almost all of us do all the time in everyday life: we form a judgement based on what we know, without pausing to consider whether we actually know enough to justify such a judgement.

If you develop a deep dislike of someone you work with because they have one unpleasant habit – picking their nose constantly, say – this may be a case of assuming that one thing you happen to have noticed means you understand what kind of a person they are. Similarly, if you only read just one article about a particular subject and then assume you can confidently analyse it – if, for example, you write an essay about Daniel Kahneman based on a single Wikipedia entry – you are using the most easily available information as if it were all you needed to know.

Do the above errors sound obvious and easy to avoid? Have a think about this:

> How meaningful do you think it is to study a couple of hugely successful technology companies, like Apple and Google, in order to find out what makes technology companies successful?

The answer is: it's not necessarily very meaningful. You might find this surprising. Many people would think that looking at the world's most successful organizations is a perfect approach to understanding success. Indeed, plenty of people have indeed made successful careers precisely out of this kind of business analysis. Yet there is a problem with this kind of thinking. When you look only at successful companies, you are looking at a tiny and extremely lucky fraction of all the companies that exist or that once existed.

Literally thousands!

For every giant like Apple, there are thousands of smaller and less successful companies. For each of these, there are thousands of companies that no longer exist because they failed. For each of these, there are thousands of potential companies that never even made it to day one. For almost any 'principle for success' you come up with, based on looking at Apple and Google, it's likely that thousands of unsuccessful companies also adhered to exactly the same principle. It's just that you don't see these companies, because you are only aware of the tiny percentage of companies that happen to be hugely successful.

This is known as **survivorship bias** – one of a host of unconscious biases that can distort almost everyone's thinking and decision-making. As the name suggests, this bias involves forming a general judgement by looking only at successful outcomes, and completely ignoring failures. Successes are rare, but striking; failures are numerous, but almost invisible. People thus tend to act as though a small number of famous successes are all that matters – when in fact they represent a mere fraction of cases.

Survivorship bias: the tendency only to think about successful examples of something, failing to consider the bigger picture in which the vast majority of all cases are failures

When conducting experiments and assessing research, being able to minimize bias of all kinds is a vital skill. When reading, writing and speaking critically, it's equally vital to be as aware as possible of potential sources of bias in both other people's and your own thinking.

There are many forms of unconscious bias, but perhaps the most important form it takes as an obstacle to critical thinking is **confirmation bias**. Confirmation bias describes the near-universal human tendency to use new information only to confirm existing beliefs, rather than to challenge them. If you only remember one kind of bias to watch out for, make it this.

Confirmation bias: the universal human tendency to use new information only to confirm existing beliefs, rather than seeking to improve and clarify your understanding

Confirmation bias is the enemy of objectivity and scepticism. It's the kind of thinking in which someone treats their existing assumptions as sacred, rather than as something to be tested, improved and, if necessary, abandoned in the face of new evidence. Confirmation bias is the difference between looking at fossilized dinosaur bones and saying 'I know that the world was created 6,000 years ago by God; He obviously created these to test us' and saying 'Here is something that cannot satisfactorily be explained if the world was created 6,000 years ago; I wonder what a better explanation might be?'[3]

It is also impossible to entirely avoid this kind of bias. We all bring assumptions with us wherever we go; we cannot be sceptical of everything. We can, however, train ourselves to be more alert. Here is an example for you to explore. Try to think sceptically and to identify how confirmation bias may be getting in the way of critical engagement in this scenario, taken from a fictional student research project:

> An extended macro-economic investigation brings some fascinating news that bears upon my research project exploring weather conditions and economic output: in two leading global economies, rain in one summer month appears to have successfully predicted increased productivity over the last two years!

Although the result may sound impressive, someone who is combing through large amounts of information looking for any kind of relationship between weather and the economy is likely to eventually find something – especially if they pluck out one particular month in just two countries. This is the nature of looking for confirmation: you allow yourself to ignore all those occasions on which there is no evidence. Think of the person who points to a particular piece of good luck as evidence that they are blessed – ignoring all those other occasions on which they were not lucky (not to mention all the other people just like them who have been unlucky).

Critical thinking does not argue that there is no place for tradition or belief, or that we can understand or explain everything. But it does demand that we set out to test what we think we know, and the boundaries of what we do not. It is, in other words, opposed to **dogmatism** – the laying down of certain principles as both absolutely true and immune to scrutiny – whether this dogmatism is practised by priests, scientists or politicians.

Dogmatism: the claim that certain principles or ideas are both absolutely true and immune to any form of critical scrutiny or discussion

ALLOCATING YOUR ATTENTION

The phrase 'pay attention' is surprisingly accurate. Our attention is a limited resource: not just because there are only so many hours in the day, but also because it takes a great deal of effort (and practice) to pay focused attention to something. Truly paying attention doesn't just mean concentrating – it means noticing, engaging, grasping something with your mind. Slow, focused thinking is difficult. It's tiring. It involves using up a resource that is in limited supply.

Being honest with yourself about when and whether your mind is wandering is an important skill – as is knowing what kind of working conditions and preparation put you in the best frame of mind for attending effectively. When I was an undergraduate, I worked mostly from the desk in my room. By the time I was a postgraduate, I had started to use libraries far more – not so much for the books as for the effect that the space had on my level of attention and commitment to my work. It helped me shut out distractions.

The enemy of attention is **distraction**, and this is a word you'll surely have heard a great deal about in the context of technology. Perhaps you have checked social media or your email inbox already while reading this book, or have them open in a browser tab or on your device? How long can you manage to pay careful attention to a single text or idea?

Attention vs distraction: the art of allocating not just time but focused engagement to the task in front of you, while shutting out other tasks and irrelevant information

Dealing with distraction and spending time wisely is one of the single greatest challenges for anyone studying today – and that's before you get to the question of what materials deserve your precious attention in the first place. What should you read, watch, listen to and do, given just how much is out there – and how little time you have?

As with everything else in this book, the answer isn't superhuman willpower: it's about strategy, planning and habits. You'll need to decide in advance which materials deserve close reading in order to grasp the key ideas – and which simply need scanning. Having a strategy for how best to spend your precious time and energy is one of the most important practical steps you can take towards better thinking.

Really does matter – when, how, where you work.

SMART STUDY: Ten tips for managing your time and attention

Taking control of your time and attention is more important than ever in the context of always-on technologies and the sheer volume of information that's out there. Here is a top-ten list of study techniques to help lessen distraction in your working life:

1 Create a calm, uncluttered workspace – and log out of social media
2 Put your phone into 'do not disturb' mode (or turn it off) for an hour of focus
3 Write out memory cards with the key points and terms summarized
4 Make mind maps on paper – scribble and scrawl by hand to help open up ideas
5 Use digital tools like MindView to map your thinking too
6 Use browser extensions like Concentrate to shut out distractions
7 Set up study groups with friends to bring multiple perspectives together
8 Look into mentoring and being mentored by other students
9 Buy at least one core textbook to keep and to annotate as you work through it
10 Experiment: try to find what space and setup best suits your own work style

YOUR TOOLKIT FOR CRITICAL THINKING

Now that we have introduced it in some detail, how confident are you in your abilities to think critically? Try these five questions, scoring yourself in each case out of ten, where ten represents total confidence and zero represents no confidence at all.

1 I am able to pay close, detailed attention to information and ideas ______/10
2 I can summarize and explain information I've come across ______/10
3 I easily understand others' points of view and why they believe what they do ______/10
4 I can clearly express my own point of view ______/10
5 I am willing to change my mind and modify my beliefs when I learn new things ______/10

Total score: ______/50

If your total is over 40, congratulations: you're either very confident, very critically adept in your thinking already, or both. If you scored below 20, never mind – you may lack confidence now, but practice and focus have the ability to transform your attitude. Now try these five questions, exploring your thinking in the context of study and research:

1 I am able to compare and to evaluate multiple sources of information ______/10
2 I can locate and research sources of relevant information by myself ______/10
3 I can clearly summarize and explain others' work, including its limitations ______/10
4 I am able to justify my own conclusions and to outline the evidence behind them ______/10
5 I am aware of and able to explain to others the limitations of my knowledge ______/10

Total score: ______/50

Again, you should end up with a total score out of 50. For most people, this second score will be lower than the first. My first five questions were about thinking skills in general; the second five relate more specifically to study, reading and writing – turning general skills into something specifically related to work.

If you scored over 40 in total this second time, I'm impressed. If you scored below ten – well, that's what this book is all about. I'll ask you to do this same self-assessment again during the course of this book. If you've worked through it carefully, you should see a huge improvement.

> **THINK ABOUT THIS:** Look back over your answers above. Where are your own particular strengths and weaknesses? Take a few minutes to interrogate yourself honestly. ....

Reflecting on your own thinking is an important element of becoming a more effective thinker. It can also be extremely difficult. Even the most brilliant thinkers aren't actively engaged in critical thinking most of the time; even they suffer from the same vulnerabilities and fallibilities that affect us all. Improvement is often a matter of insight, honesty and good habits rather than sudden inspiration.

Reasoning: thinking about things in a sensible or logical way, and then presenting this thinking so as to permit meaningful debate, disagreement and collaboration

This is why critical thinking is best thought of as a set of techniques rather than something you either can or cannot do. What we need is to develop and keep practising a particular set of skills: a toolkit for critical engagement. There are five key techniques that we will be developing during the course of this book, all related in their way to the art of **reasoning** – thinking about things in a sensible or logical way, and then presenting this thinking to others in a way that permits meaningful debate, disagreement, comparison and collaboration.

SMART STUDY: Five key techniques for critical thinking

Learning to understand and to evaluate reasoning (Chapters 1–4): reasoning entails providing convincing, rigorous support for a claim or belief, or offering a convincing explanation for something. It's this business of providing, comparing and criticizing chains of reasoning that allows us to test different arguments and ideas meaningfully, rather than simply accepting or rejecting them based on how we feel. Confidently evaluating reasoning is a vital study skill, and means ensuring that we understand precisely what someone is claiming – and why. Throughout any process of critical thinking, you will find yourself returning to a deceptively simple question: 'Is this a reasonable thing to say or to believe?'

Learning to understand and to evaluate evidence (Chapters 5 and 6): evidence is information gathered to support a point of view or to offer a particular account of the way things are. It comes in many forms, and sifting through these is one of the greatest challenges of most programmes of study. Understanding evidence involves: finding useful and relevant materials; recognizing the conventions of the many different kinds of source you'll encounter; and knowing how to extract from them the information you need. It also involves assessing just how far any source is reliable and relevant.

Learning to understand and to account for bias (Chapters 7–10): people and sources are all biased in their own ways – as are you. There's no such thing as a perfectly objective perspective, but understanding the ways in which you bring particular biases to your work is just as important as accounting for others' biases. You'll learn how to spot them, how to make allowances for them, and how to reframe concepts and questions in order to make them less vulnerable to distortion.

Becoming a critically engaged user of technology (Chapter 11): from reading and writing to researching, discussing and collaborating, digital information systems touch almost every part of our personal and professional lives. Chapter 11 deals with what it means to be a confident, critically engaged user of technology. Throughout the other chapters, you will find opportunities to explore ideas online, and reflections on the particular significance of topics and themes in a digital age. You can also use the hashtag #TalkCriticalThinking at any time to share thoughts and comment with other readers and the author.

Developing a clear, confident approach to reading and writing (Chapters 6 and 12): reading others' writing closely and critically is closely connected to developing clarity and confidence in your own work. The final chapter in each half of the book looks at what it means to read and to write well – and how you can develop effective structures, habits and practices to support this. By the end of this book, you will have gained skills that allow you to explain your ideas with precision and force; to engage with others' work clearly and helpfully; and to keep on improving and clarifying your own thinking.

WHAT IS CRITICAL THINKING FOR?

Consider these rival accounts of the Earth's position in the universe. Tick off the account you think is best, and jot down why.

- The Earth is a flat disc carried on the back of a giant tortoise..... ○
  ....
  ....
- The Earth is a giant egg laid long ago by a massive bird........... ○
  ....
  ....
- The Earth is a sphere located at the centre of the universe..... ○
  ....
  ....
- The Earth is a rocky planet orbiting our sun, Sol, in the Milky Way galaxy... ○
  ....
  ....

Obviously, the last account is the best. But why? Because none of the first three accounts can satisfactorily explain many of the things we know about the Earth. We have plenty of images taken from aircraft and satellites clearly showing the planet's curvature; we have amassed huge amounts of information about the movement of the planets and stars in the universe around us. Stories about flat discs, tortoises and giant eggs may once have been sufficient to explain what people knew – but they are no longer the best account we have for addressing the sum total of our knowledge.

The last account, however – that the Earth is a rocky planet orbiting our sun – fits in with the best current information we have. It does not require us to deny what we know or to make special excuses. Moreover, it is precise enough that we can test it rigorously.

This doesn't mean we now know everything or that we are entirely correct in a way that nobody has ever been before. Quite the opposite. Our understanding will continue to change as we learn new things, and it is the task of critical thinking to keep challenging us to come up with better explanations.

This is an important point: rigorous critical thinking means not only explaining why we believe something to be the case, but also being obliged to change our minds when our knowledge about the world changes. In this sense, it is related to a **purpose** that it shares with all scientific and philosophical investigations: searching for the best account we can currently offer of the way things actually are.

The purpose of critical thinking: critical thinking helps us to search for the best account we can find of the way things actually are

This is how progress works, if and when it works: we attempt to find a clear and precise account of the way things are, then we test our thinking not by seeking confirmation, but by looking for things we still cannot explain. It is those things we cannot explain that point the way forward; that sketch the outlines of new theories and ideas which may, in their turn, push back the frontier of human ignorance a little further.

SUMMARY

Uncritical thinking entails automatically believing what you read or are told without pausing to ask whether it is accurate, true or reasonable.

Critical thinking means actively setting out to understand what is really going on, by carefully evaluating information, ideas and arguments – and thinking carefully about the process of thinking itself.

Underlying critical thinking are the connected principles of scepticism and objectivity:

- **Scepticism** entails not automatically accepting that something you hear, read or see should be taken at face value.
- **Objectivity** means trying to identify the facts of a situation as seen from the outside, rather than relying only on your own – or someone else's – particular feelings or point of view.

There is no such thing as perfect objectivity – you will always bring your experiences and perspective with you – but it is possible to know yourself better, and to practise using tools and techniques for seeing things more clearly. This includes dealing with the difficulties of **bias**, which comes in two general forms:

- **Conscious bias** is when someone deliberately presents a very one-sided view of something, or explicitly holds a one-sided opinion about something.
- **Unconscious bias** is when someone's opinions or decisions are distorted by factors that they are not even aware of.

In particular, it's important to be alert to the problem of **confirmation bias**: the universal human tendency to use new information only to confirm what you already believe, rather than seeking to improve and clarify your understanding.

It's vital to **allocate your attention** effectively if you want to think critically – and to remember that the first rule of critical engagement is to **slow down**, and to set aside your first impressions and prejudices.

Critical thinking is best thought of as a set of techniques rather than something you either can or cannot do. Improving your critical thinking means developing and practising a particular set of skills: your **toolkit** for critical engagement. These tools will help you:

- understand and evaluate reasoning.
- understand and evaluate evidence.
- understand and account for bias.
- develop clear, confident, critical writing.
- become a critically engaged user of technology.

When we think critically, we are searching for the **best account** we can currently offer of the way things actually are – and this means being obliged to change our minds when facts and reason demand that we do.

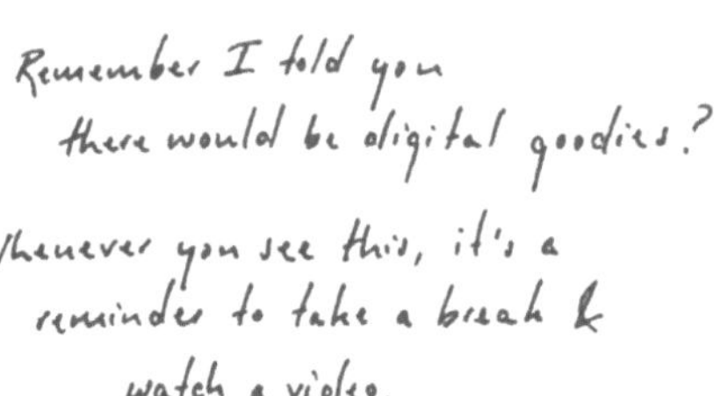

Remember I told you there would be digital goodies?
Whenever you see this, it's a reminder to take a break & watch a video.

Also — try my critical thinking Buzzfeed quizzes!

Now watch the video 'What is critical thinking (and why should I care)?' It's on YouTube. Tell me what you think via #TalkCriticalThinking

Need a break? Try a Buzzfeed quiz and test what you (think you) know. They're at buzzfeed.com/tomchatfield

PART I

THE ART AND SCIENCE OF BEING REASONABLE

UNDERSTANDING THE REASONS BEHIND THINGS

Why does reasoning matter (and how can you spot an argument)?

↓

How do you spell out the reasoning behind an argument?

↓

How do you draw out a logical conclusion from your premises?

↓

How do you draw out a probable conclusion from your premises?

↓

How can you select and test the best explanation of something?

↓

How should you assess evidence and plan your reading strategy?

All about how reasoned arguments matter in your work — & everything else you do.

DON'T RAISE YOUR VOICE, IMPROVE YOUR ARGUMENT.

DESMOND TUTU

#TALKCRITICALTHINKING

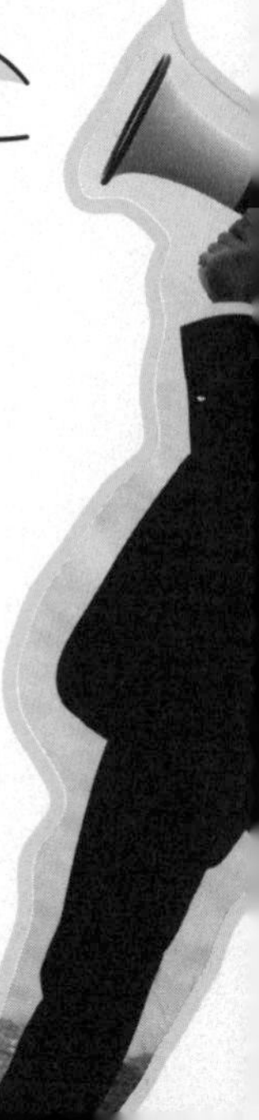

FIVE THINGS YOU'LL LEARN IN THIS CHAPTER

1 The significance of *reasoning* in work and research
2 How to identify *arguments* and their *conclusions*
3 How to improve your ability to create *clear descriptions*, *summaries* and *examples*
4 How to tell the difference between *arguments* and *explanations*
5 How to distinguish between *better* and *worse explanations*

We have defined critical thinking as the opposite of uncritical thinking. Rather than automatically believing what you read or are told, it entails pausing and carefully evaluating what is really going on. When we think critically, we are searching for the best account we can currently offer of the way things actually are. This involves two related questions:

- **Why** we should accept something as true, and...
- ...**How** things came to be the way they are.

Another way of putting this is that we are interested in identifying and making good arguments, coming up with reasonable explanations – and rejecting bad examples of both.

Critical-thinking books often place a great deal of emphasis on arguments – and we'll explore why in this chapter – but they are far from the whole story. We also need to be able to think critically about other kinds of communication and expression – and to be especially alert to the kind of reasoning that lies behind explanations, theories and the scientific method of investigation.

WHAT IS AN ARGUMENT? PERSUASION THROUGH REASONING

Why does reasoning matter so much? To answer this, let's first look at something different: assertions. Here is an **assertion** about keeping animals as pets:

Assertion: a statement of fact or belief, provided without support or justification

> It is wrong to keep animals as pets.

An assertion is a statement of fact or belief, provided without support or justification. It's also something that, on its own, does little other than impart information.

By contrast, an argument does something more useful. Consider this line of argument about keeping animals as pets:

> It is wrong to keep animals as pets, because this means they are not free and cannot lead dignified lives. All living creatures deserve the dignity of freedom.

Now, we are looking not only at a claim about the way things are, but also at a line of reasoning seeking to justify this claim. This attempt to provide reasonable justification for a particular conclusion is important. When someone asserts that 'it is wrong to keep animals as pets', we have no way of knowing why they think this. They might have an amazingly convincing reason that would change our lives if we heard it. They might simply be saying it because their mother used to say it. We don't know. As soon as they make an argument, however, we can start to do all kinds of interesting things. We can:

- Gain a fuller understanding of their view of the situation.
- Work out whether or not we agree with their reasoning.
- Compare different arguments to see whether something else is more convincing.
- Investigate to see whether they have ignored important information or ideas.
- Debate with them and attempt to change their minds – or change our own.

When someone makes an argument, they are attempting to persuade you that you should accept a particular conclusion – and they are doing so by presenting a series of other propositions that (they claim) support it. Here, then, is a working definition of an argument in critical thinking: an **argument** is an attempt to persuade you of the truth of a particular conclusion using reasoning.

Argument: an attempt to persuade someone through reasoning that they should agree with a particular conclusion

We can break this down into two key elements:

- You are presented with a line of reasoning that…
- …seeks to convince you to accept a particular conclusion.

Conclusion: the final point that someone making an argument is trying to convince you of

The **conclusion** of an argument is its final point: the point that everything else leads towards. One argument's conclusion can be the starting point of another; but each argument only has one final conclusion.

Below are three different ways in which I might talk to you about a job you are looking to fill. Only one of them is an argument in the sense I've just described: presenting both a conclusion and a line of reasoning. Try to identify which one:

		YES	NO
1	Hi! My name is Tom, and I'm the right man for this job!............	◯	◯
2	I'm the right person for the job. I'm the best qualified and I'm available now..........	◯	◯
3	I have plenty of work experience from around the world; I'm a great worker..........	◯	◯

Let's go through them in order, seeing whether they have both reasoning and a conclusion:

(1) This definitely has a conclusion – 'I'm the right man for this job!' – but no reasoning is provided to support it. I may have provided a cheerful introduction, but I haven't offered any reasons in support of my conclusion: I have simply asserted it.
(2) This has both reasoning and a conclusion: it may sound informal, but it still counts as an argument. The first sentence provides our conclusion – 'I'm the right person for the job'; while the second sentence provides two reasons supporting it – 'I'm the best qualified' and 'I'm available now'.
(3) This presents what you might think of as a line of reasoning – 'I have plenty of work experience' – but there is no explicit attempt to link it to a conclusion, or indeed to persuade you. I'm simply making an assertion about my experience and abilities.

Note, however, that if this third example came in the context of a general conversation about jobs, you might decide that what I would like you to conclude is so evident that my words *do* count as an argument. If, for example, you had just said 'I really need a new employee with global experience' and I instantly replied 'I have plenty of work experience from around the world', then the conclusion I wanted to convince you of would be obvious enough for this to qualify as an argument. In other words, explicitly presenting a line of reasoning may be enough for something to qualify as an argument, if the concusion is self-evident from the context.

In other words:
Beware of evaluating things outside of context.

In real life, it can be quite an art to identify whether an argument is being made. For each of the examples below, try to identify whether an argument is being made or not. If one is, tick, and pick out what reasoning and conclusion is being presented:

	YES	NO
1 Come on in, the water's lovely!..	◯	◯
2 Beware of the dog: he's angry and might bite your hand...........	◯	◯
3 You wouldn't want to meet my brother when he has a hangover	◯	◯

Although (1) sounds informal – 'come on in, the water's lovely!' – it does qualify as an argument once we spell it out. It's an effort to persuade you of the conclusion that you should come into the water, using the reasoning that the water is lovely. As to whether you find this convincing – you may want to dip a toe in to test the temperature before diving.

Example (2) also contains an argument. It's an effort to persuade you of the conclusion that you should beware of the dog, using the reasoning that he is angry and might bite you. Again, the informality of the tone means we need to paraphrase things to be clear about what is going on.

Finally, example (3) is not an argument, although it sounds similar to one: 'You wouldn't want to meet my brother when he has a hangover.' No attempt at persuading you of a conclusion is taking place: you are simply being told some information about my brother that you may choose to believe, or not.

If, instead, I had said 'my brother has a hangover: you should just ignore him because he's bound to be in a bad mood', then this would count as an argument because I would be trying to persuade you of a conclusion (that you should ignore my brother) using reasoning (that he has a hangover and is bound to be in a bad mood).

SPOTTING ARGUMENTS BY SEARCHING FOR A CONCLUSION

You may have noticed that, in each of the examples above, I began analysing all of them by **searching for a conclusion**. This may sound like doing things backwards, but – as we will explore in more detail in the next chapter – this is the most useful way to begin when trying to work out whether you are dealing with an argument. Tick off any you believe are arguments and note why.

Searching for a conclusion: when you're trying to work out whether someone is making an argument, begin by seeing if there is a particular conclusion they want to convince you of

Look at the three passages below and try using conclusion-spotting as a technique to help you determine whether they are arguments or not Tick off any you believe are arguments and note why.

1 You should definitely let me look after your cat while you're on holiday. I love cats. And cats love me. I have lots of cats at home and know how to look after them. I have 12 cats, and I talk to them all the time. I'm a real cat expert.......................... ◯
....
....

2 For a surprisingly large number of clinical trials, scientists cannot reproduce the original result when a study is repeated. This suggests that something may be seriously wrong with the system of peer review and publication around clinical trials..........

....

....

3 I have a large number of friends who work in the finance industry: horrid people, insecure profession. But we do go out for some excellent dinners...

....

....

Example (1) is an argument. Here, the conclusion comes in the first sentence: 'you should definitely let me look after your cat while you're on holiday.' The rest of the paragraph then provides some reasoning as to why you should accept this conclusion – the fact that I love cats, have lots of cats and know how to look after them – alongside some less relevant (and frankly alarming) information about my cat-related habits.

Example (2) is also an argument. The first sentence sets out a line of reasoning around the fact that scientists cannot repeat the results of some clinical trials. The second sentence presents a conclusion supported by this line of reasoning – that something may be wrong with peer review and publication. Spotting the conclusion allows us to work backwards and see that the first sentence comes before it, and that an argument is being made.

Example (3) is not an argument. The ideas presented do not fit in any particular order, and one is not the conclusion of a line of thought suggested by another. It may very well be the case that I have reached the conclusion that finance is an 'insecure profession' – but in this case it is simply asserted, without any reasoning in support.

Language is slippery. V. few consistent rules. More like conventions.

In real life, you will be dealing with longer and more confusing arguments than these examples – making it useful, as in the case of reasoning, to bear in mind a number of indicator words that point towards a conclusion. There is no firm rule about using indicator words, and sometimes there will not be any. Often, however, a final conclusion will either be indicated by words like 'because' and 'since' or will appear prominently at either the start or end of a piece of writing.

Now try reading the following passage. Does it contain an argument, complete with reasoning and conclusion? If so, see if you can spot any indicator words that show where each is to be found.

> Expenditure on early childhood education varies greatly from country to country. By some measures, the UK spends more than any other country on this first educational stage – but then drops behind when it comes to primary and secondary education. Given that there is a lack of direct evidence around the impact of spending on educational outcomes, and that evidence-based policymaking is especially important in the educational space, detailed comparative research into the impact of spending on attainment at each level across different countries would thus make a valuable topic for rigorous investigation.

Close reading is vital for teasing out the key points being made here. As the phrase 'given that' indicates, the main reasoning of this argument is that 'there is a notable lack of direct evidence around the impact of spending on educational outcomes' and that 'evidence-based policymaking is especially important in the educational space' – while, as the word 'thus' indicates, its conclusion is that 'detailed comparative research into the impact of spending

Any human power can be resisted and changed by human Beings.

Ursula K. Le Guin

#TalkCriticalThinking

on attainment at each level across different countries would thus make a valuable topic for rigorous investigation'.

Did you come up with the same analysis? If not, don't worry. Arguments aren't always easy to spot – and doing so means paying as much attention to what *isn't* an argument as to what *is* one. In the next sections, we're going to look at several key types of **non-arguments** – types of writing that do not count as arguments, because they don't involve trying to persuade you of a conclusion through reasoning.

Non-argument: any element of a piece of writing that does not attempt to persuade you of a conclusion through reasoning, and thus doesn't qualify as part of an argument

SMART STUDY: spotting the words that indicate conclusions and reasoning.

Certain words and phrases often indicate where an argument's reasoning and its conclusion are.

When trying to identify a line of reasoning, look for phrases such as 'given that,' 'based upon', 'considering', 'since', 'because' and other words that mobilize information in support of an idea rather than simply presenting it as fact. When trying to spot a conclusion, look for indicator words and phrases like 'thus' 'therefore', 'and so', 'overall', 'which shows that'.

WHAT ISN'T AN ARGUMENT? INFORMATION WITHOUT REASONING

We've said that an argument means using reasoning to support a particular conclusion. If this is not taking place, something other than an argument is being presented.

When we are presented with information but no explicit reasoning, the crucial question is how far we believe this information to be **accurate** and **relevant** to the particular topic we are engaging with. This section explores four different types of information that we commonly find in writing and speech:

- Descriptions.
- Summaries.
- Opinions and beliefs.
- Clarifications and illustrations.

Descriptions

Consider the following statements. Are any of them arguments?

		YES	NO
1	According to the World Health Organization, the world's leading cause of death is coronary heart disease.	○	○
2	My grandfather died of coronary heart disease at the age of 90.	○	○
3	Coronary heart disease affects more men than women.	○	○

Description: simply reporting information without any attempt at evaluating, commenting on or using the information to persuade

As you probably guessed, none of the statements above is an argument. Instead, they are **descriptions**: they report information about something, but they don't perform any kind of reasoning – and nor do they pass judgement on or analyse the information they contain.

You might think that saying 'coronary heart disease affects more men than women' does include some kind of reasoning or evaluation. But even this simply provides descriptive information. I am not telling you what I think. I am simply passing on information.

A **good description** aims to provide clear information without introducing any evaluation, reasoning or persuasion: its purpose is to convey relevant information as clearly and neutrally as possible. Compare the following two descriptions.

WHICH IS BETTER?

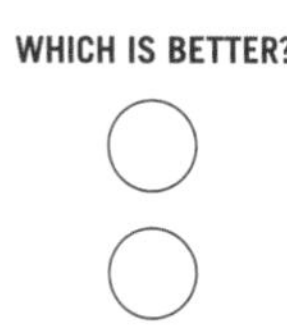

1 A lot of people in our experiment found it difficult to work out what was going on.
2 Eight out of the ten subjects in our experiment found the instructions they were given sufficiently unclear that they failed to perform the tasks correctly.

Both of the sentences above describe the same thing, but it's clear that the second sentence is a better description than the first. It is more detailed, more precise and clearer: it offers a more useful record of what happened. Paying close attention and writing detailed, useful descriptions is quite an art – not least because it means deciding what is worth paying attention to in the first place.

In the example above, it is useful to know that eight out of ten people found the instructions they were given unclear. It would be even more useful to know exactly what each of them found unclear within the instructions. It would probably not, however, be useful to know what colour clothes they were each wearing, or how tall they were. In any situation, there are an almost infinite number of things we could choose to describe – and so the question of what it is most relevant to include and exclude is of the utmost importance.

When reading or writing a description yourself, try to bear these questions in mind:

- What was the person writing this description in a position to know?
- What within this description is useful or relevant to what I want to know?
- What other details have been left out that might be useful or important?
- Is the description precise and clear, or is it vague, unclear or exaggerated?

What does 'good' description mean in different contexts? Science, journalism, literature, record-keeping…

Summaries

Here's an extended example of a particular kind of description often used in academic work and research:

> The experiment entailed dividing 100 volunteers into two groups of 50. The groups were selected at random in advance using a random number generator, and allocated to two different rooms in which they would sit an identical test. Half an hour was allowed for completing the test, which consisted of 30 multiple-choice questions based on correctly identifying the next symbol in a sequence. The first group was permitted, before sitting the test, to eat as many freshly baked cookies as they wished from five trays placed in the room. The second group had identical trays of cookies placed in their room, but were told that they could not eat until they had finished. Overall, those who were allowed to eat immediately averaged 75 per cent correct results in the test compared to 55 per cent among those who were not allowed to eat until the end.

This passage is a **summary**, in this case of a fictional experiment (based very loosely on a real psychological experiment conducted by Baumeister, Bratslavsky, Muraven and Tice at Case Western Reserve University in 1998).[4] Like any description, it conveys information without offering analysis or reasoning; but the particular skill of writing a summary is, as briefly as possible, to cover all the main points in an area.

Summary: a brief outline of key information, often setting out the main points covered in a longer piece of work

Being able to write and to read this kind of description closely is a surprisingly important and difficult skill. It means thinking and writing clearly – and identifying what the key points are within a longer piece of work. It also involves ensuring we do not unthinkingly introduce biases, arguments, opinions and other extraneous material into our work at a point where we are simply trying to provide information. Compare the summary above to this very different account:

> The experiment entailed dividing 100 volunteers into two groups of 50 that we ended up thinking of as the 'greedy' and the 'hungry' groups. Each group was forced to sit an identical and extremely boring test. I'm not sure all of them understood it, and am worried that the results might be invalid given how many of them seemed to crash the system or get stuck and not bother finishing. Anyway, the first group ate lots of cookies which we had put on a table while the others didn't, and it was amazing what a difference this made; being hungry is clearly bad for the brain, although actually the best performer was in the 'hungry' group. Then again, I think they cheated and stole a cookie or two before the time was up.

This is a pretty poor summary of an experiment compared to the first version (although I will admit that it's a livelier read). It's confused and confusing in terms of structure. It doesn't tell us everything we need to know to get a clear picture of what happened. It mixes things like opinion and evaluation in with the description ('being hungry is clearly bad for the brain'). And it contains irrelevant details, like speculation about whether one person stole cookies, while missing out key information – such as what the overall results were.

A **good summary** carefully and clearly sets out relevant information – and covers all the key points as briefly as possible, while introducing nothing that is irrelevant or confusing. When reading or writing a summary, ask yourself:

- What is the purpose of this summary?
- What are the key points needed to understand what is going on?
- Is there any irrelevant detail that can be left out – or some essential information that needs to be added – in order to make this as concise and clear as possible?

Opinions and beliefs

If I tell you what someone else thinks, then I am simply reporting a piece of information. If, during the course of a public debate, a politician says 'I believe that immigration is the greatest crisis facing this country today', everyone who has watched the debate is equally in a position to describe what the politician said. Reporting their opinion – by saying 'the minister stated during the debate that immigration is the greatest crisis facing our country' – is just another kind of description.

If, however, I share my own opinion or belief, then I am doing something different. I am describing something that nobody else has access to: what is taking place inside my own mind. Consider these three statements. Each one, in its way, presents an **opinion** or **belief**, offering information about one person's view of the world:

Opinion or **belief**: presents someone's point of view without offering reasoning. Opinions tend to be personal judgements based on facts; while beliefs tend to be convictions based on morality, faith or cultural context

	OPINION	BELIEF
1 Governments are morally obliged to lead the fight against heart disease.	○	○
2 Heart disease is a terrible thing.	○	○
3 Your diet is awful: you ought to stop eating so much bacon!	○	○

The first example doesn't contain the words 'I think that', but it's clear on reading it closely that saying 'governments are morally obliged to lead the fight against heart disease' is not simply a neutral description of something the speaker has noticed. It's not like saying 'there is a lot of heart disease in the world': it presents a particular individual's view about the way things ought to be.

The second statement, 'heart disease is a terrible thing', is more obviously a statement of belief. You might think that it's true, but what matters is that, in this particular case, it is presented without any particular reasoning being offered. We are simply being informed that this is what the speaker thinks about heart disease.

The last of my three examples is an opinion directly addressed to someone else, saying what I think they ought to do – 'your diet is awful: you ought to stop eating so much bacon!' We can classify this as a piece of **advice** or a **warning**: a special kind of opinion that describes not only someone's point of view, but their point of view about what ought to be done.

Advice and **warnings:** opinions about what someone should, or should not, do

In the real world, we spend much of our time dealing with beliefs and opinions – and expressing our own. We only tend to offer reasoning for our point of view occasionally; and even when we do, we are often not so much trying to persuade someone else that we are correct, as seeking to explain why we did something or believe something. When encountering an opinion or a belief, ask yourself:

- Does this seem like a reasonable view for someone to hold?
- What effect is holding such a belief or opinion likely to have?
- What different opinions or beliefs is it possible to hold, or are held by others?

Clarifications and illustrations

Clarifications and illustrations are often used to help us understand ideas and arguments. Here is an example of each – read them closely and see if you can tell them apart:

		CLARIFICATION	IIUSTRATION
1	By coronary heart disease, I mean a group of diseases that involve reduced blood flow to the muscles of the heart itself, resulting from the narrowing of the coronary arteries.	○	○
2	Cultures all around the world celebrate dancing in public. In China, many couples used to perform publicly in parks to ballroom dancing music played through loudspeakers.	○	○

The first is an example of a **clarification**: it takes a phrase or an idea (in this case, coronary heart disease) and clarifies what is meant when this phrase is used. The second is an **illustration**. Having made a point – that cultures all around the world celebrate dancing in public – a specific example of the point is supplied in order to show how the point may apply in a particular instance.

Clarification: spells out what is meant by a particular phrase, idea or line of thought

Illustration: provides a particular instance of a general point

A clarification may sound similar to supplying the definition of a word or concept, but it can also apply to a more general explanation of what an author is interested in or means. For example, if I am writing an essay about research ethics in sociology, I might begin by clarifying my focus:

> Research ethics is a contentious field. For the purposes of this essay, I will largely be referring to research ethics within the field of sociology; this is not to suggest that many other fields do not face their own version of these challenges.

We can think of illustrations as a special kind of clarification: a particular example is used to illustrate what is meant by a larger idea. In my essay on research ethics, I might use a particular case to illustrate a general principle:

> Before starting any research, you must obtain ethics approval in the form of written confirmation from your department – bearing in mind that standards can vary from country to country. One recent piece of research involving questionnaires about intimate sexual behaviour was successfully approved in Australia, but had to be substantially rewritten before it could be approved in America.

An illustration may simply sound like a posh term for an example – and in many ways it is – but it puts a useful emphasis on the fact that not every example can illustrate a general point effectively, and that a good example is one selected for both its relevance and its usefulness in clarifying a larger point.

EXPLANATIONS: THE BUSINESS OF REASONING BACKWARDS

Explanation: suggests the reason or reasons that something came to be the way it is

Explanations can be difficult to distinguish from arguments, because both of them offer reasons in support of something. While an argument attempts to persuade you that a particular conclusion is true through reasoning, however, an **explanation** takes it for granted that something is true – and then sets out to explain how or why it happened.

In a sense, explanations are an inversion of arguments: they reason backwards from a conclusion that is assumed to be true, and are interested in persuading the audience that their answer to the question 'why did this thing happen?' is the best available.

Although they don't behave like formal arguments, properly reasoned explanations are both a vital form of reasoning and a major element of most scientific and philosophical research. Most worth-while enquiries will at some point entail the question 'why?' – why the world is like it is, why one thing happened rather than another, why someone did something. Here's a simple example of an explanation:

> I stopped eating lots of bacon because I was worried about my heart.

Even though this includes the word 'because', I am not trying to persuade you of the fact that I have stopped eating lots of bacon. Instead, I have begun with a statement of fact that I expect you to accept as true – 'I stopped eating lots of bacon' – and have then offered an explanation of how that fact came to be: 'because I was worried about my heart'.

Is my explanation the whole truth? Almost certainly not. The reasons behind even an apparently simple decision are likely to be more complex than I can express in a single sentence. Why did I become worried about my heart? Why did this make me stop eating bacon in particular? What other factors are involved? A 'why' invariably involves further 'whys'.

Another way of putting this is that explanations are stories – and there are always more stories to be told. They're one of the most contested and slippery ways we can use our reasoning because, so far as the person offering an explanation is concerned, what they are saying is often so obvious it is barely distin-guishable from straightforward description – and yet someone else might disagree entirely. Consider the following three examples: are these explanations or arguments?

	EXPLANATION	ARGUMENT
1 Tom read on the British Heart Foundation website that healthy eating and staying active help keep your heart healthy. As a result, he decided to change his diet and to go jogging twice a week.	○	○

2 Her husband no longer eats butter or drinks full-fat milk. She showed him a picture of clogged arteries which frightened him into changing his eating habits.

3 I go running twice a week because it helps me keep my life feeling balanced.

In the first example above, I am offering an explanation rather than an argument because I am not trying to persuade you that something is true. I am simply reporting as a fact the information that Tom is now going jogging twice a week, and that the explanation for this is the fact that he read about staying active on the British Heart Foundation website.

In the second example, it's the same story again. It is presented as a fact that her husband no longer eats butter or drinks full-fat milk – and the explanation for this is that he was shown a picture of clogged arteries which frightened him into changing his habits.

Finally, the third example offers in a single sentence an explanation of why I go running twice a week: because it helps me keep my life feeling balanced. You may or may not believe what I am saying; if you wish to offer a rival explanation, however, you'll need to produce some pretty compelling evidence.

So they were all explanations — bit of a trick question.

One reason that explanations can be tricky to tell apart from arguments is that they have a similar structure, and use similar words, like 'because' and 'since'. If you're trying to distinguish between them, ask:

- Is someone trying to persuade me that something is true (argument) or simply trying to inform me why something is the way that it is (explanation)?
- Is the thing for which reasons are being offered a completed event in the past that is presented as a fact (explanation) or a possibility that I am being asked to agree with (argument)?

Explanations are significant in critical thinking, and it's a mistake to treat them as less complex than arguments. Deciding between rival explanations is one of the most important everyday critical thinking tasks most people face – and one that often demands evidence-based investigation. In Chapter 5, we'll look at this kind of investigation in more detail. For now, here are two general principles for comparing the quality of explanations:

- A good explanation is able to account for all the evidence in a particular case, and does not simply ignore inconvenient facts.
- A good explanation is economical: it has no unnecessary steps or assumptions. In general, a simpler explanation that accounts for all the facts is preferable to a more complex explanation that does the same.

Imagine that I have just been caught driving too fast by the police, and you are required to decide between the following four explanations:

BEST EXPLANATION

1 I was driving too fast because I didn't notice my speed had crept up.

2 I was driving too fast because I have a fast car and love driving it fast.

3 I was driving too fast because I'm dashing to see my sick mother.

4 I was driving too fast because my speedometer is faulty.

Determining which of these is most reasonable requires further investigation, and here is some information from a police report presenting the results of this:

> Upon inspection, the car's speedometer turned out to be working perfectly; a phone call revealed that the driver's mother was perfectly healthy; and a search of the police database revealed that it was not his first time being caught speeding.

At this point, you might decide that the second explanation – I was driving too fast because I have a fast car and love driving it fast – is the best fit. This doesn't mean it is definitely correct; but it does mean that I would need to come up with something else that explained all the facts more efficiently and effectively if I wanted to change your mind (or that of the police).

SMART STUDY: Six key types of content

Here is a list of the six different kinds of information and expression we have looked at in this chapter, with a brief summary for each. We have looked at four types of information presented without reasoning:

Description: reporting information in a direct and straightforward way

Summary: providing a brief outline of key information

Opinion: presenting a judgement without providing reasoning

Belief: presenting a judgement without providing reasoning

Clarification: spelling out or demonstrating a particular concept

Illustration: spelling out or demonstrating a particular concept

And we have also looked at two types of information presented with reasoning:

Argument: persuasion through reasoning in support of a conclusion

Explanation: reasoning backwards from something assumed to be true

Between them, these six classes of content describe most of what is likely to be relevant and meaningful within a piece of work you are studying or writing yourself – these will need to be carefully distinguished from irrelevant and extraneous materials.

Try to classify each example below as either a description, summary, opinion or belief, clarification or illustration, argument, or explanation. There are only two arguments, and at least one example of every other type of content we've covered:

1 An odd number of participants means that someone will always be left out when picking two balanced teams: five people means two teams of two and one person left out; seven people means two teams of three and one left out; and so on.
2 My cake burned to a crisp because I accidentally left it in the oven for 13 hours.
3 The IKEA wardrobe gently collapsed as I stepped back to admire my handiwork; it was almost majestic to behold its gravitationally induced self-disassembly.
4 Here is how I built the wardrobe: first, I threw away the instructions; second, I fitted all the round bits into the little holes; third, I screwed together everything that looked like it needed screwing; fourth, I hit all the remaining parts with a hammer.
5 It's immoral to buy incredibly cheap clothing on the high street.
6 It's immoral to buy incredibly cheap clothing: people work long hours for terrible pay in overcrowded factories in order to produce it.
7 The clothing we buy is only incredibly cheap because the people making it are paid so little.
8 He ran rapidly and gracefully out of the water because he had a crab attached to his face.

9 You ought to buy copies of this book for all your friends: it is excellent value and will almost certainly make them all cleverer.

10 I only wrote the previous example because I was running out of ideas.

It isn't easy to think up engaging examples...

DESCRIPTION #: .... **SUMMARY #:** ....

OPINION #: .... **BELIEF #:** ....

CLARIFICATION #: .... **ILLUSTRATION #:** ....

ARGUMENT #: .... **EXPLANATION #:** ....

The two arguments are: (6), which attempts to persuade you that it's immoral to buy cheap clothing, using the reasoning that the people who make it work in terrible conditions; and (9), which attempts to persuade you that you should buy this book for your friends, using the reasoning that it is excellent value and will make them cleverer. Whether either of these constitutes a good argument is something for you to ponder.

Among the rest, (1) is an illustration: a general point is made, about someone always being left out when you pick teams from an odd number, and then illustrations are provided of particular cases that show how it works. Then (2) is an explanation: I am explaining why it is that my cake burned to a crisp. Next, (3) is a simple description (of a wardrobe collapsing), while (4) offers a summary outlining the process by which I built the wardrobe so badly, and (5) is an opinion or belief – it's probably most accurate to call it an opinion about the immorality of cheap clothing, likely to be based on underlying beliefs about what is right and wrong.

As we've already seen, (6) is an argument – notice that it takes the opinion expressed in (5) and turns it into an argument by expressing reasons to support that point of view, while (7) is an explanation on the same theme – it simply seeks to explain the fact that the clothing we buy is incredibly cheap. Finally, (10) is also an explanation, providing an account of why it is that I wrote the previous example.

Overall, how many did you correctly identify out of ten? If it was fewer than seven, I'd recommend you look briefly again over the ones you found most difficult.

THINK ABOUT THIS: Can you think of other kinds of information offered without attempts at persuasion beyond those listed in this chapter? How might you classify them? ....

....

....

....

....

....

WHAT ISN'T AN ARGUMENT? PERSUASION WITHOUT REASONING

While arguments are an attempt to persuade us of something using reasoning, **rhetoric** is an attempt to persuade us by other means. Rhetoric is a general term for the art of persuasive speaking or writing, dating back to the ancient Roman and Greek world. A great variety of rhetorical techniques are deployed by speakers and authors, with the intention of bringing their audience around to a particular conclusion or point of view. We'll examine rhetoric in depth in Chapter 7 – for now, it's worth running through a few of its basic features.

Rhetoric: the attempt to persuade by appealing to emotions rather than to reason

In practice, most of the arguments (and the non-arguments) we encounter in real life will have some rhetorical elements around them. Rhetoric isn't inherently a bad thing, but we need to pay very close attention to how the **style** in which something is written and presented can affect our thinking in ways that have nothing to do with reasoning.

Style: describes the way something is written: its words, phrases and the structures of its language. Different topics and audiences require very different styles

Everyone writes in a different style, and there are different styles appropriate to different subjects. When we are writing a message to friends, we use different words and phrases than if we are writing to our parents. If you were writing a story, a lyric or a poem, you would do very different things with language than if you were writing an essay or describing a scientific experiment.

'whatever cannot be said clearly is probably not being thought clearly either.' – Peter Singer

In general, academic writing requires a style that is as clear as possible: that says exactly what you mean and that is not confusing. Difficulty is an inevitable feature of academic disciplines that demand specialist terms and high-level understanding. Unfortunately, some academic writing can also be needlessly difficult itself – either in terms of its structure and vocabulary, or the length and complexity of its sentences.

This lack of clarity can itself be a rhetorical manipulation: a way of conveying that you are an expert and that only experts are able to deal with the complexities of your subject. In general, it's a good idea to be wary of very difficult writing. It may be concealing a lack of precision, understanding, evidence – or simply the fear that expressing something too clearly devalues expertise. Then again, even the use of rational and reasonable language can itself be a persuasive technique ('I am a serious scientist: you can trust me'). One of the first things you need to do when looking at any piece of writing is to ask:

- What style of writing is this?
- What are the intentions behind this style: how does the author want me to feel?
- Is there actual reasoning behind what's being presented, or am I being asked to accept it on other grounds?

Here are examples of just a few rhetorical techniques. In each case, how might you describe the particular manipulation I'm using to try to make my case?

1. You look great today! So professional, so powerful. You should let me come and work with you, given that you're such a brilliant leader and entrepreneur.
2. It's time for a change: for something new and for someone fresh and keen in your workplace – and that someone is me.
3. I'm fending off job offers from a dozen potential employers right now – but it's you I really want to work for. What do you say?
4. If you don't give me a job, I really don't know what I'm going to do – I've got nothing. You are my only hope. Please.
5. If you don't take someone like me on in the current business climate, your company will fail; just see if it doesn't. You're in trouble and you need my help.
6. I've worked with some major-league disruptors in the disintermediation space. I know how to radically rethink verticals and horizontals. I can add real value.

In order, these examples embody:

1 **Flattery**: praising someone in order to get them to do what you want.
2 **Appeal to novelty**: saying that something is new and so it must be good.
3 **Appeal to popularity**: saying that something is popular, so it must be good.
4 **Appeal to sympathy**: playing on the heartstrings.
5 **Appeal to fear**: trying to frighten someone into agreement.
6 **Jargon**: using fancy, largely meaningless words in order to sound smart.

There's plenty more where this came from. When it comes to critical thinking, you need to recognize as far as possible the rhetorical elements of any text you are engaging with – and then to disentangle the underlying reasoning from the materials surrounding it.

Let's take a look at an emotive piece of writing, sentence by sentence. Can you see where the author is attempting to persuade you using emotional appeals and rhetorical devices rather than reasoning?

> (1) The world of business is crazy! (2) Everyone is always talking about disruption, new ideas and new technology. (3) They say artificial intelligence is going to put half of the world's workers out of a job. (4) But I don't believe it. (5) I think that we are going to end up with a world where everything we do involves smart machines, but these smart machines allow us to find all kinds of interesting new work. (6) After all, people have always been afraid of new technology. (7) Just look at the Luddites, smashing up cotton mills during the Industrial Revolution back at the start of the 19th century. (8) Yet everybody didn't stop working. (9) They just couldn't imagine what all the new kinds of work would look like – until technology created it.

Sentence (1) is pure rhetoric: 'the world of business is crazy!' This is emotional language, complete with an exclamation mark for emphasis. It's trying to get you on the author's side, to create the expectation that you're about to hear some zany stuff about the world of tech, and to create an informal rapport with the author.

Sentence (2) is also rhetorical rather than an attempt to provide reasoning or make an argument: 'everyone is always talking about disruption' we are told, which is unlikely literally to be true. The author is using **exaggeration** to set the stage: in this case, to suggest that 'everyone' is 'always' saying one thing, but that you are about to be presented with an exciting alternative point of view.

Exaggeration: over-stating the case, often as a rhetorical tactic; like over-generalization, this is a way of making a far bigger claim than is actually the case

Sentences (3) and (4) deliberately contrast what 'they say' with the fact that 'I don't believe it'. This is conversational language, designed to create a sense of drama and engagement – so that by the time we finally get to sentence (5) and find out what 'I think', we are ready to start nodding our heads even though we have as yet seen no reasoning or evidence. Sentence (5) contains the concluding idea that the author wants you to believe – although it's only after you get to the end of the passage that you are likely to work this out

As often happens in everyday prose, the reasoning in support of this conclusion is presented after rather than before that conclusion (it can be more rhetorically effective to start with your conclusion, and then to justify it). 'After all' begins sentence (6), before telling us that people have 'always been afraid of new technology' – a piece of reasoning expressed in the form of an **over-generalization**.

Over-generalization: suggesting that something is more generally true than it actually is, often as a rhetorical tactic; making a far broader claim than is the case in reality

Sentences (7) and (8) further support the conclusion by inviting us to 'look at the Luddites' in the 19th century – making the assumption that the way things were 200 years ago is

ONE

FIRST AND FOREMOST:
SLOW DOWN.
CUT YOURSELF SOME SLACK!
DOES WHAT'S IN FRONT OF YOU
MATTER AND REQUIRE
DEEP THOUGHT?
IF SO, PAUSE.
IT DESERVES A STRATEGY.
IF NOT, DON'T WORRY TOO MUCH.
GET ON WITH IT. GET IT OUT THE WAY.

#TalkCriticalThinking

automatically relevant to the way things are today. This isn't a strong form of reasoning: the example may or may not be relevant, but we need further details if we are to be convinced. It is, however, lively and engaging. Finally, sentence (9) offers the observation that people in the early 19th century 'couldn't imagine what all the new kinds of work would look like' – which is hardly surprising.

Overall, we might strip away the rhetoric and express the ideas at the heart of this example like this: 'People have always feared new technology. For example, the Luddites in the 19th century couldn't imagine the opportunities new technology would create. But their fear was misguided. And the same is true today when it comes to fears around technology and jobs.' This is a less exciting piece of prose – but it's far easier to engage with its strengths and weaknesses as an argument. This process of stripping down and clarification is the focus of our next chapter, and the foundation of critical engagement with others' ideas.

THINK ABOUT THIS: What are the main differences in your writing style between everyday communication – email, messages, status updates – and formal academic writing? Why do these differences exist? ....

....

....

....

....

....

SUMMARY

An **assertion** is a statement of fact or belief, provided without support or justification.

An **argument** is an attempt to persuade someone through reasoning that they should agree with a particular conclusion. You can split this into two key elements when identifying arguments:

- **Reasoning** is being used to...
- ...make the case for a particular **conclusion**.

Arguments are important for critical thinking. By providing reasoning, seeking to justify a particular claim, arguments allow us to work out whether or not we agree with this reasoning – and to compare different arguments in order to see which one we find most convincing.

When you're trying to work out whether someone is making an argument, it's often best to begin by seeing if you can **find a conclusion** that they're trying to prove.

It's important to distinguish between arguments and attempts at **persuasion without reasoning**. **Rhetoric** is the attempt to persuade by making an emotional appeal rather than by using reasoning. Paying close attention to writing **style** is important when reading critically: don't be deceived by vagueness, exaggeration or difficulty.

Much of the time, you will also encounter **information without persuasion**. It's important to be able to identify and evaluate this material separately from arguments. There are four types of information without persuasion:

1 **Descriptions** simply report information without evaluation or comment.
2 A **summary** provides a brief outline of key information, often setting out the main points covered in a longer piece of work.
3 An opinion or belief presents someone's point of view without offering reasoning. **Opinions** tend to be personal judgements based on facts; while **beliefs** tend to be convictions based on morality, faith or cultural context.
4 A **clarification** spells out what is meant by a particular phrase, idea or line of thought, while an **illustration** offers a particular instance of a general point.

Finally, **explanations** are a special form of reasoning that works backwards from a claim about the world – telling the story of how this thing came to be.

An explanation suggests the reasons that something came to be the way it is. The **best explanations** are able (1) to explain all the available evidence in (2) as simple a way as possible.

Now watch the video 'Why should I bother to reason with other people?' It's on YouTube. Tell me what you think via #TalkCriticalThinking

For spelling out what you think, taking nothing for granted.

SPELLING OUT ARGUMENTS AND ASSUMPTIONS

A.k.A. PROVE You know What You're Talking About.

Why does reasoning matter (and how can you spot an argument)?

↓

How do you spell out the reasoning behind an argument?

How do you draw out a logical conclusion from your premises?

How do you draw out a probable conclusion from your premises?

How can you select and test the best explanation of something?

How should you assess evidence and plan your reading strategy?

THERE IS ALWAYS A WELL-KNOWN SOLUTION TO EVERY HUMAN PROBLEM – NEAT, PLAUSIBLE, AND WRONG.

H.L. MENCKEN

#TalkCriticalThinking

FIVE THINGS YOU'LL LEARN IN THIS CHAPTER

1 How to *reconstruct* someone else's argument in standard form
2 How to spot *premises* and *conclusions*
3 How to spell out *assumptions*
4 The importance of being charitable towards *others' arguments*
5 How to tell the difference between *linked* and *independent premises*

Assuming an argument is being made, what exactly is its author claiming – using what reasoning? To return to the analogy of developing a toolkit for critical thinking, answering these questions is like getting to grips with a complicated piece of machinery. We need to be able to take something apart and identify its different components if we want to fully understand it. This is known as **reconstructing** an argument.

Reconstructing an argument: identifying all its different parts, then spelling these out clearly in a standard form that allows us to see exactly how they work

Over the course of this chapter, we will build up a recipe for reconstructing any argument. The skills involved apply to more than just arguments: they are used whenever we are trying to get to the bottom of someone else's thinking, and to spell out the key ideas and assumptions at play in a piece of writing or evidence. You can use them when thinking about explanations, and indeed any act of reasoning – so long as you don't let your own assumptions prevent you from seeing what someone else is trying to say.

PREMISES AND CONCLUSIONS: THE STANDARD FORM

Appropriately enough, the most common approach to setting out an argument clearly is known as **standard form**. Here's an example of a simple argument expressed first in a paragraph of ordinary writing, and then in standard form:

> There are no copies of the textbook that you need in the library: this means that you won't be able to borrow a copy from there.

Premise 1: The library does not have any copies of the textbook that you need.

Conclusion: **You cannot borrow a copy of the textbook that you need from the library.**

Standard form means rewriting an argument so that:

1 The **conclusion** is set out clearly at the bottom.
2 The reasoning leading to the conclusion is set out clearly above it in the form of numbered **premises**.

Premise: a claim presented by an argument in support of its conclusion

Conclusion: the final proposition in any argument, supported by its premises

A premise is the most basic building block of an argument. Many different premises can be linked together into a chain of reasoning to support a conclusion – or, as in the example above, just one premise can sometimes be enough to support a conclusion on its own.

An argument can have many premises, but it can have only one final conclusion. The conclusion of one argument can form the premise of another: what defines a conclusion is simply its place at the end of an argument. In a sense, all arguments are just a collection of propositions within which one is supported by all the rest. This is made clear when we use standard form. Every proposition has its own numbered line, and these lead in sequence to the final conclusion. When an argument is successful, the progression between them is like a smooth stroll up a flight of steps.

Often, we encounter arguments in everyday life as a jumble of propositions, rather than a neatly structured sequence of premises followed by a conclusion. Below is an example of a more complex argument, set out in ordinary language first and then in standard form:

> If I don't know how to tell apart different types of variables, I will definitely fail my statistics exam. Unfortunately, I don't even really know what a variable is, let alone how to tell different types apart. I am doomed to fail my exam!

Premise 1: Knowing how to tell apart different variables is essential to passing my statistics exam.

Premise 2: I do not know how to tell apart different types of variables.

Conclusion: **I will fail my statistics exam.**

Notice that in setting out this argument in standard form, I have rephrased and clarified the two premises compared to their original language. The second sentence of the original – 'Unfortunately, I don't even really know what a variable is, let alone how to tell different types apart' – contains emotional information that is irrelevant to the process of reasoning.

Once we have accepted the premise that 'knowing how to tell apart different variables is essential to passing my exam', the only relevant information for the purposes of this argument becomes whether or not I can tell variables apart. If I cannot tell them apart, I will fail – which is the conclusion that the argument is seeking to justify. The information 'unfortunately, I don't even really know what a variable is…' is **extraneous** to the argument, so I should leave it out of my reconstruction.

Extraneous material: information that is not relevant to the argument and should be left out as we carefully clarify each premise and conclusion by rewriting them

Try rewriting the example below in standard form, eliminating extraneous material in the process. It's an argument with three premises, leading to a single conclusion.

> Listen up! We must set off by 5pm at the latest. The river crossing is only open until 6pm. We need to use that river crossing – and we are one hour's travel away.

Write them out below:

Premise 1: ....

....

Premise 2: ....

....

Premise 3: ....

....

Conclusion: ....

....

How did you do? Compare your version to my one, below. Did you put the premises in a different order to me? Did you separate all three in the same way as I have done? In this particular case, the sequence of the premises is not the most important thing. What matters is that the combination of three separate premises comes together to provide reasoning in support of one particular conclusion.

Premise 1:	We need to use the river crossing.
Premise 2:	We are one hour's travel away from the river crossing.
Premise 3:	The river crossing is only open until 6pm.
Conclusion:	**We need to set off by 5pm at the latest.**

There is one further thing we can add to aid our understanding here. In order to reconstruct this argument in as much detail as possible, we can fill in a missing piece of the reasoning: a step in the argument that has been **assumed** rather than spelled out. As often happens in arguments, the author has taken some information for granted – and we can only fully investigate their reasoning if we spell out what they are inviting us to assume.

Assumption: something relevant to an argument that has been taken for granted by the person presenting it, rather than spelled out

Can you see what assumption is being made in the middle of this argument? It's something so obvious that you might not think it's even worth noting. I have added it in, below, next to the heading 'Conclusion 1':

Premise 1:	We need to use the river crossing.
Premise 2:	We are one hour's travel away from the river crossing.
Conclusion 1:	**We need to set off at least one hour before the crossing shuts.**
Premise 3:	The river crossing is only open until 6pm.
Conclusion 2:	**We need to set off by 5pm at the latest.**

Notice that I have put this assumption in the form of an intermediate conclusion into my reasoning. The first two premises suggest this conclusion, which I then re-use as a new premise in combination with the third premise. An argument can only have one final conclusion, but it can have many intermediate conclusions along the way.

An intermediate conclusion is a conclusion arrived at during the course of an argument; it is then used as a premise for building towards the final conclusion, which is the very last thing that the argument is attempting to prove.

Before we finish this introductory section, let's look at one of the great advantages of using the standard form for argument – the fact that it allows us, easily, to compare different points of view and, once we have set them out clearly, to spot which is better or more reasonable. Imagine that there are a dozen of us in a group facing the scenario above: we all need to use a river crossing which is only open till 6pm and we are debating what we should do next. Someone else in the group shouts:

> We need to get going right now! It would be terrible if we missed the crossing; we really need to use it. It is only open until 6pm. It takes an hour to get there and it's 2pm already. Time is flying past. I can't bear the thought of us failing to get across: it would be a disaster. There's no time to lose – we need to get moving right now!

Just as we did above, let's reconstruct this argument by disregarding the extraneous material, clarifying the language, setting out the conclusion at the end, and then listing the individual premises in order. Once we do all this, we end up with the following:

Premise 1: We need to use the river crossing.

Premise 2: We are one hour's travel away from the river crossing.

Conclusion 1: **We need to set off at least one hour before the crossing shuts.**

Premise 3: The river crossing is only open until 6pm.

Conclusion 2: **We need to set off by 5pm at the latest.**

Premise 4: It is currently 2pm.

Conclusion 3: **We need to set off right now in order to use the river crossing. [WRONG!]**

Now that we have done this, we can see that the final conclusion suggested in this particular argument – 'we need to set off right now' – is not supported by the reasoning that comes before it. We will analyse the details of testing arguments in more detail later. Some of the time, however, successful reconstruction does most of the work for us: as soon as we have successfully reconstructed someone else's argument in full detail, it becomes clear whether or not it makes sense.

If all this seems very cumbersome, don't worry. I'm not suggesting that you need to set out every argument you encounter in standard form. Above all, familiarizing yourself with standard form can help you think about: how precisely arguments work; what it means to take them apart and make the best possible use of them; and how often it is that unstated assumptions need spelling out if we are to fully grasp what is going on.

SMART STUDY: What's the point of reconstructing an argument?

Writing out someone else's argument in standard form is hard work. It's also not something you are going to do for everything you read. So why bother? Here are four practical reasons:

1. Actively spelling out someone else's argument in logical steps is one of the best ways of ensuring you understand it all the way through yourself.
2. Spelling out something in logical steps with no extraneous material often reveals flaws or gaps in someone's reasoning that would otherwise have remained hidden.
3. Reconstructing an argument forces us to identify the key assumptions that it relies on, but that might not have been made explicit, and we can then analyse these in turn.
4. Getting into the habit of doing all of the above is one of the best ways of becoming more confident (and successful) at making convincing, reasonable arguments yourself.

RECONSTRUCTING EXTENDED ARGUMENTS

Arguments rarely exist in splendid isolation. The conclusion of one argument is often used as a premise in another argument, just as one of its premises may have been taken from another argument in turn. Consider this simple example:

Premise 1: My friend Bob is either in the library or in the pub.

Premise 2: Bob is not in the library.

Conclusion: **Bob is in the pub.**

I have concluded on the basis of two initial premises that my friend Bob is in the pub. This could be my final conclusion, and I might then head off to the pub to join him. Alternatively, I could re-use my old final conclusion as an intermediate conclusion in an extended argument. My intermediate conclusion now has a double life: it has become one of the premises for a new stage in the overall argument.

An **extended argument** is one in which the final conclusion is supported by one or more premises that are themselves intermediate conclusions, supported by previous premises.

Extended argument: an argument whose final conclusion is supported by one or more premises that are themselves intermediate conclusions, supported by previous premises

To see what this means in practice, here is one way to extend my original argument:

Premise 1: My friend Bob is either in the library or in the pub.

Premise 2: Bob is not in the library.

Conclusion 1: **Bob is in the pub.**

Premise 3: There is no phone reception in the pub.

Conclusion 2: **Bob has no phone reception.**

My initial conclusion that 'Bob is in the pub' has now become an intermediate conclusion within an extended argument. When used in combination with a new premise – 'there is no phone reception in the pub' – this leads me to a new final conclusion: 'Bob has no phone reception'.

I don't have to stop with just one intermediate conclusion. I can continue my reasoning further, taking my second conclusion – that 'Bob has no phone reception' – as one of the premises for a further stage of argument:

Premise 1: My friend Bob is either in the library or in the pub.

Premise 2: Bob is not in the library.

Conclusion 1: **Bob is in the pub.**

Premise 3: There is no phone reception in the pub.

Conclusion 2: **Bob has no phone reception.**

Premise 4: Bob's mother is trying to get hold of him on his phone.

Conclusion 3: **Bob's mother will not succeed in getting hold of him by phone.**

Hopefully, you get the idea by this point. How might this extended argument look as an ordinary piece of writing? Here is one possibility, written in an informal way:

> Bob is always in the library or the pub at this time of day – and I know that he isn't in the library. His mum is trying to get hold of him on the phone, but the pub is a total dead spot for phone reception. So I guess there's no way they will get to speak.

Time for you to try one. Below is a new extended argument, based on a typical research project into teamwork. I have started off the reconstruction process by filling in the first premise beneath it. Try to complete the rest in the space provided.

> Our research suggests that teams with clearly defined roles and expectations outperform those with more fluid structures. When a team has a fluid structure, it shows that debate and delegation are difficult. By contrast, clearly defined roles and expectations facilitate debate and delegation. Given that arranging team training in order to clearly define roles and expectations is affordable, and there are no other obviously effective alternatives at a similar cost, we would recommend this training as a budgetary priority for firms in the sector.

Premise 1: When a team has a fluid structure, debate and delegation are difficult.

Premise 2: ....

....

Conclusion 1: ....

....

Premise 3: ....

....

Premise 4: ....

....

Conclusion 2: ....

....

How did you do? Below is a completed version of that argument in standard form.

All clear to you when you first read the example?

Premise 1:	When a team has a fluid structure, debate and delegation are difficult.
Premise 2:	Clearly defined roles and expectations facilitate debate and delegation.
Conclusion 1:	**Teams with clearly defined roles and expectations outperform those with more fluid structures at debate and delegation.**
Premise 3:	Team training to clearly define roles and expectations is affordable.
Premise 4:	There are no other obvious effective alternatives at a similar cost.
Conclusion 2:	**Team training to clearly define roles and expectations is an affordable, effective option for improving performance at debate and delegation.**

The language used in this argument is relatively cumbersome, but its structure is straightforward. Conclusion 1 – the intermediate conclusion – comes in the first sentence, but other than that all the points flow in order. For comparison, take a look at exactly the same argument set out in a less logical way, with some additional information introduced:

> Team training to clearly define roles and expectations is extremely affordable, according to our research. We believe that it should be a budgetary priority. When a team has a fluid structure, debate and delegation are difficult. Members report far greater stress and difficulty in communication. Much better experiences of debate and delegation come when roles and expectations are clearly defined. There are no obvious effective alternatives to team training, of the type suggested above, available at a similar cost. Teams with clearly defined roles and expectations outperform those with more fluid structures. This is unsurprising, in light of the above.

Here, the very same extended argument is being expressed much less clearly. Carefully tracing the steps in an author's reasoning is all the more important in such cases – as is bearing in mind the flow of your own arguments when you are writing. As often in critical thinking, you'll find that the skills of close reading and comprehension directly translate into making you a better writer and thinker.

THE TRUTH IS ALWAYS SOMETHING THAT IS TOLD, NOT SOMETHING THAT IS KNOWN. IF THERE WERE NO SPEAKING OR WRITING, THERE WOULD BE NO TRUTH.

SUSAN SONTAG

#TalkCriticalThinking

THINK ABOUT THIS: What are the main differences between ordinary writing and writing an argument out in standard form? What might you be able to learn in your writing from thinking about standard form and the structure of arguments?

A STEP-BY-STEP GUIDE TO RECONSTRUCTING ARGUMENTS

Now that we've introduced the standard form and extended arguments, let's look in more detail at the process of reconstruction. I have divided it into five steps:

1. Apply the **principle of charity**.
2. Identify the **final conclusion** (and write it down at the bottom).
3. Identify the **explicit premises** (and write them down in order above).
4. Identify any **implicit premises** (and insert them where they are needed).
5. Distinguish between **linked** and **independent** premises.

1 Apply the principle of charity

The first principle to bear in mind when reconstructing someone else's argument is to keep an open mind and not to let your own feelings, beliefs or expertise get in the way. In particular, we should begin by assuming that someone is:

- Telling the truth rather than aiming to deceive us
- Sufficiently well informed to know what they are talking about
- Presenting a coherent and reasonable account.

In other words, our default position should be one of generosity towards someone else's perspective when we are reconstructing their argument: something that philosophers often call the **principle of charity**.[5]

Principle of charity: the assumption that someone else is truthful and reasonable, and that their argument deserves stating in its strongest form

The principle of charity requires us to begin with the assumption that someone else is truthful and reasonable, reconstruct their argument in its strongest form. Why should we do this? The answer isn't that we should always be nice to other people. In fact, it's the reverse: if we want to subject someone else's point of view to as vigorous an analysis as possible, we need first of all to grasp their point of view in its strongest form. This is the only way we can then hope to either come up with a really robust argument for a different point of view or be certain that we have the best possible reasons for agreeing with them. Imagine that a friend makes this argument to me:

> I have seen the latest accounts at the company you work for and they don't look good. Sales have declined and profits are the lowest they have been for five years. I would suggest that you are unlikely to get a good bonus this year.

There are a number of different ways I could respond to this. I could say:

> (1) I don't believe you: you're just trying to make trouble. You've never forgiven me for that incident on our trip to Latvia.

Or I could say:

> (2) You don't understand what you're talking about. You're claiming that profits can exactly predict everyone's bonuses every time. That's just crazy.

Or I could think to myself:

> (3) Hmm... The fact that you've seen the accounts, and that they show sales declining and low profits, does suggest that bonuses might not be good this year. It looks like I shouldn't base my plans on getting a big bonus.

Response (1) – 'I don't believe you: you're just trying to make trouble...' – is dominated by **prejudice**. In it, I have decided not to take my friend's argument seriously without bothering to consider the evidence.

Prejudice: holding a belief without consideration of the evidence for or against it; deciding in advance of hearing an argument what you believe to be the case

Meanwhile, in response (2) – 'You're claiming that profits can exactly predict everyone's bonuses every time...' – I am putting words into my friend's mouth. She didn't actually argue that profits can exactly predict bonuses: I am setting up this claim as a **straw man** so that I can dismiss her position more easily. It's tempting to do this when we disagree with people, but it means we miss out on the opportunity to either learn from them or come up with the best possible response (straw men are designed for one thing only: burning).

Straw man: an absurd simplification of someone else's position that is obviously wrong or stupid, and that is only expressed so that it can easily be defeated

Finally, response (3) – 'It looks like I shouldn't base my plans on getting a big bonus...' – embodies the most charitable interpretation of my friend's argument. It assumes she is truthful, reasonable and well informed. Compared to the first two responses, this last reaction is most likely to prove useful: it allows me to make the best possible use of potentially important information, and to check out a potentially alarming scenario.

In the real world, complex arguments will always tend to have strong points and weak points. Often, people who disagree with one another will each attack the weakest point of their opponent's argument, looking for an easy victory. The problem with this is that attacking only the weakest point of someone else's argument is unlikely to change their mind, or to change the minds of anyone else who agrees with them.

If we wish, genuinely, to challenge what other people think, we need to engage with the very strongest version of their arguments. Otherwise, by attacking straw men or picking only on their weakest points, we are likely only to reinforce existing beliefs – and to allow ourselves to get away with weak or underhanded forms of argument.

SMART STUDY: Why be charitable towards other people's arguments?

It may seem strange to suggest that you should be as generous as possible to other people's points of view, especially if you think they are likely to be wrong. Yet this is a vital skill, for three reasons:

1. Beginning with the assumption that someone is truthful, informed and reasonable ensures that you don't simply dismiss their views through prejudice.
2. Understanding someone else's argument in its strongest form is the best way of analysing it as rigorously as possible – and learning as much as you can from it.
3. If you do wish to come up with the strongest possible objection to an argument, or to change someone else's mind, you need to understand the most convincing features of what they and others like them say, rather than simply attacking their weakest points.

2 Identify the final conclusion

When reconstructing an argument, we almost always begin with the end: the final conclusion. Why? First, because identifying a conclusion tends to be one of the most important ways through which we recognize that an argument is being made in the first place. Second, because no matter how many premises may be involved or how long the chain of reasoning, every argument only has one final conclusion. Once we have determined this, we can safely tease out the chain of reasoning leading to it.

Correctly identifying conclusions is a question of close reading and practice rather than a precise science, but there are some general questions we can ask ourselves to help spot a final conclusion:

- What is the author ultimately trying to prove?
- What is the message you are expected to take away from reading this?
- Is a final decision, verdict or recommendation being offered?
- Is a particular point being repeated or emphasized?

Try to identify and underline the final conclusion for each of these arguments:

1 I love eating pies. My friend Bob is organizing a competition to see who can eat the most pies. Because I love pies, I should have a great time taking part.
2 If there were intelligent aliens out there in the universe, they would have sent us some kind of clear message by now. Since we haven't received any kind of message like that, there can't be any intelligent aliens out there.
3 Insomnia is extremely difficult to treat. There is some evidence that cognitive behavioural therapy (CBT) can improve sleep quality for sufferers. We should watch CBT trials in the field closely, given that it's important to pay close attention to any possible therapeutic treatment for this difficult condition.

In the first example, the conclusion comes at the end: I should have a great time taking part in my friend's pie-eating competition. In the second example, the conclusion also comes at the end: there can't be any intelligent aliens out there. In the third example, the final conclusion comes in the first part of the last sentence – we should watch CBT trials in the field of insomnia closely – followed by a premise that supports it. Here is a slightly more complex example. Can you find the final conclusion?

> The experiment was a failure. I was testing to see if rabbits preferred lettuce or carrots. But I had forgotten to lock the door of the hutch and all the rabbits ran away without eating either the lettuce or the carrots. I didn't get any results and I'm too embarrassed to write up what actually went on. Some experiment!

The final conclusion, here, comes in the first sentence: *the experiment was a failure*. If you wanted to express this paragraph more formally, you might shift this to the end, together with an indicator word at the start: 'Thus, the experiment was a failure'. Make sure, however, that you remove all indicator words as part of the process of clarification when writing something out in standard form.

3 Identify the explicit premises

Once we have identified the final conclusion, we can begin listing the premises provided by the author. Separating out premises from extraneous material can be difficult, depending on how clearly an argument is expressed, not least because a premise can be a very simple or basic piece of information. In general, use these guidelines to help you hunt out individual premises:

- Work backwards from the conclusion: what are the key points that support it?
- Ignore emotion and repetition: what matters is whether something counts as part of a process of reasoning, not what it may tell us about the author's feelings.

- The most basic fact or assertion can be a premise: ask, is it just there to provide a background piece of context, or is it actively used to build up the author's case?

We call the premises that someone has provided themselves the **explicit premises**: this covers everything an author or a speaker has decided to spell out in support of their conclusion. As we will see in the next section, this is in contrast to those things they have left unsaid and have instead left to be assumed.

Explicit premises: all the claims that someone has set out in support of their conclusion

For each of the following arguments, I have written out the final conclusion in standard form but left a blank space next to the premises. Try filling these out with a clear statement of each premise that has been provided.

> Politicians' personal lives should be kept private. What they do in the privacy of their own homes has no impact on how good they are at their jobs. As long as something has no impact on their work, we have no need to know about it.

Premise 1: ....

....

Premise 2: ....

....

Conclusion: **Politicians' personal lives should be private.**

> My sister is amazing. She can type at, like, a hundred words a minute. She reads loads of books, all the time. She always gets full marks in tests: top marks, no problem, easy. My sister has got to be one of the smartest people in the country.

Premise 1: ....

....

Premise 2: ....

....

Premise 3: ....

....

Conclusion: **My sister is one of the smartest people in the country**.

In the first example, not much more is required than slightly rephrasing the second and third sentences. For our first premise, we can say 'What politicians do in the privacy of their homes has no impact on how well they do their jobs'. For the second, we can say 'We have no need to know about something that has no impact on how well politicians do their jobs'.

In the second example, there is more need to rephrase and clarify the language. Here, the first three premises might look like this when written out as clearly as possible:

Premise 1: My sister can type at a hundred words a minute.

Premise 2: My sister reads a lot of books.

Premise 3: My sister always gets full marks in tests.

Conclusion: **My sister is one of the smartest people in the country.**

The exact way you rephrase things is up to you, but it is useful to be internally consistent in your phrasing so that key concepts are repeated in similar terms between premises, making the logic of the argument easier to follow.

4 Identify any implicit premises

Implicit premises are not spelled out by the person stating an argument, but are assumed as part of their reasoning and need to be included in reconstruction

Often, once we have identified the explicit premises that someone has provided in support of a conclusion, we will find that something crucial in the argument has been left **implicit**: it has been taken for granted but not actually stated. Spelling out the implicit premises on which an argument relies is just as important as listing the premises that are provided if the argument is to be fully reconstructed. Consider this example:

> The new teacher at my daughter's school is in a same-sex relationship. They should never have employed her.

First, let's write out the conclusion and the explicit premise in standard form:

Premise 1: The new teacher at my daughter's school is in a same-sex relationship.

Conclusion: **This person should not have been employed as a teacher at the school.**

Can you see what missing, implicit premise needs to be inserted between the first premise and the conclusion to spell out this argument?

Premise 1: The new teacher at my daughter's school is in a same-sex relationship.

Premise 2: [Implicit] People in a same-sex relationship are unfit to work as teachers.

Conclusion: **This person should not have been employed as a teacher at the school.**

Why is it important to spell this out? As with every other aspect of reconstructing an argument, we do this so that we understand as precisely as possible what is being claimed – something that then allows us to analyse it critically with as much precision as possible.

In this case, once we have spelled out the implicit premise, we can see that a controversial and objectionable assumption – that people in a same-sex relationship are unfit to work as teachers – is central to the argument being made.

At times, an assumption will be so obvious that it won't seem worth mentioning; at other times, it may be extremely important to identify and dispute something that the person making an argument took for granted. In general, it is necessary to spell out an assumption when it provides an unstated but necessary element of an argument's reasoning. Consider the following four examples. What are the implicit premises or conclusions that are being assumed in each of these cases?

1 You should slow down: the road has sharp corners ahead..........

....

....

....

2 Yum! I hear that the Prince of Wales is a big fan of this particular marmalade..........

....

....

....

3 There is nothing wrong with breaking wind in public: it's perfectly natural..........

....

....

....

4 She is going to fail her degree: I never see her at lectures..
....
....
....

Think carefully for yourself before looking at my answers, below. For each, I've commented on whether the assumption is likely to prove important or not. Do you agree?

1 *It is a good idea to slow down if a road has sharp corners. If you don't do this, you might come off the road.* [Probably so obvious that it isn't worth mentioning, although someone driving too fast may need reminding of these reasons]
2 *Things that the Prince of Wales likes are good. Therefore this marmalade is good.* [Perhaps worth mentioning: once we have spelled this out, it becomes far easier to see how we might argue against this position or find it unconvincing. What is so special about the Prince of Wales's taste in marmalade?]
3 *There is nothing wrong with doing things that are perfectly natural.* [Definitely worth spelling out: once we look closely at this assumption, we can find several problems with it. For example, is it also OK to urinate in public because it's 'natural'? And what does and does not count as 'natural' anyway: wearing clothes, writing?]
4 *If I haven't seen someone at lectures, this means that they are not going to lectures. If you do not go to lectures then you are not going to pass your degree.* [Probably worth spelling out: looking more closely at these assumptions might lead us to change or be more specific in our thinking. Can we be entirely certain that not seeing someone means that they are not going to lectures, or that doing this definitely means failing their degree?]

Here's a final example, below, of an argument expressed first in ordinary prose and then in standard form. I have filled out all the explicit premises and the final conclusion already. It's your job to fill in the relevant implicit information.

> A book says that tall people are more confident than shorter people. I'm much taller than you: no wonder I find it easier to ask someone out on a date!

Premise 1: This book says that tall people are more confident than short people.

Premise 2: [Implicit] ....
....

Premise 3: [Implicit] ....
....

Conclusion 1: **Tall people are more confident than short people.**

Premise 4: I am taller than you.

Conclusion 2: **[Implicit]** ....
....

Premise 5: [Implicit] ....
....

Conclusion 3: **I find it easier than you do to ask someone out on a date.**

Here's my version, below, with the missing steps of the argument filled in:

Premise 1:	This book says that tall people are more confident than shorter people.
Premise 2:	This book accurately describes the way things are.
Premise 3:	I'm accurately describing what the book says.
Conclusion 1:	**Tall people are more confident than shorter people.**
Premise 4:	I am taller than you.
Conclusion 2:	**[Implicit] I am more confident than you.**
Premise 5:	[Implicit] Being more confident makes it easier to ask someone out.
Conclusion 3:	**I find it easier than you do to ask someone out on a date.**

In this particular case, it is probably worth spelling out Premise 2 and Premise 3 – that this book accurately describes the way things are, and that I'm accurately describing the book – because the argument not only relies on both of these things being true, but also seems particularly vulnerable to scepticism at this point.

Is it likely that a book actually says something this simple, or that I'm reporting it entirely accurately? Perhaps not. On balance, the truth is likely to be a little more complicated – and it's precisely by spelling out assumptions like this that we can move towards a more nuanced account (or a counter-argument of our own).

5 Distinguish between linked and independent premises

Linked premises: support a conclusion when taken together, but not individually

Independent premises: support a conclusion individually and don't rely upon each other

As you may have noticed in the examples above, some premises only provide support for a conclusion when they are **linked** together, while others **independently** provide some support. Here's an argument involving two linked premises, expressed in ordinary prose with (P1) and (P2) used to mark the two premises and (C) to show the conclusion:

> (P1) The chemical only reacts at this temperature in the presence of a catalyst. (P2) There is currently no catalyst present, so (C) it cannot react at this temperature.

Here, by contrast, is an argument on a similar theme involving two independent premises:

> (P1) The chemical doesn't react when I apply heat. (P2) The chemical doesn't react when I increase the pressure. (C) I may need a catalyst to help the reaction.

In the first instance, neither premise supports the conclusion when taken on its own: if you read either one without the other, there is no argument. This means that they are linked, because it is only when they are taken together that they support the conclusion.

In the second example, both (P1) and (P2) independently provide some support for the conclusion. The argument is stronger as a result of having two premises, but it would still function as an argument with just one of them, even if it would be less convincing.

It's possible to draw diagrams of arguments that show the relationships between linked and independent premises, but for most purposes it is simpler, and more important, to ensure that you can distinguish between:

- Which premises must be taken together in order to support a conclusion (linked) and
- Which premises support a conclusion without relying on any others (independent).

Here is a longer example for you to consider, including both linked and independent premises. Can you see which is which?

> (P1) All successful athletes combine effective training with natural ability. (P2) My sister wants to be a successful athlete and (P3) she has managed to stick to an effective training programme. (P4) She's tall, muscular and seems to have a great deal of natural flexibility and co-ordination. (P5) Her coach says she has great potential. (C1) That suggests she really is a natural. (C2) So I reckon she has a decent chance of making it all the way.

Here, premises (P4) and (P5) work independently to support (C1) – my sister being tall and muscular, and her coach saying she has great potential, both suggest she has natural talent. The rest of the premises are linked together. If it is the case that (P1) all athletes combine effective training with natural ability – and (P2) my sister wants to succeed as an athlete – then (P3) combined with (C1) supports the final conclusion (C2). She has a decent chance of making it, because she both trains effectively and has natural ability.

You'll notice that I haven't written out this reconstruction in as lengthy a form as the earlier examples. Practically speaking, unless an argument is very complex, it is often easier to note premises and conclusions like this, making sure you spell out implicit assumptions and rephrase to clarify as needed.

SMART STUDY: Ensuring you don't confuse the two types of premise

Arguments can use a combination of both linked and independent premises, but each works very differently:

- Linked premises rely on one another, so an argument using them fails if even one linked premise is faulty. The relationship between linked premises is typically one of 'IF BOTH X AND Y, THEN Z'. For example, '*If both a warning light is on and we know it is not a test, then we should evacuate the lab.*'
- Independent premises reinforce one another, but, although an argument is weakened if one or more is faulty, it does not automatically fail. The relationship between independent premises is typically one of 'IF X, THEN PERHAPS Z; IF Y, THEN PERHAPS Z'. For example, '*If there is a smell of burning, then perhaps we should evacuate the lab; if there are unexplained noises coming from inside the test chamber, then perhaps we should evacuate the lab.*'

Being alert to this difference allows you to distinguish between an argument that fails when it has a faulty premise and one that is just weakened. Be sure that, in your own work, you know whether you're presenting independent premises that support a conclusion individually, or linked premises that need to be taken together. This will help you to stay on top of your own arguments and to deliver a conclusion with confidence.

A FEW FURTHER WORDS ABOUT ASSUMPTIONS

We can't talk about anything without making assumptions. If you think hard enough, there is no end to the assumptions you can list behind any claim or argument. Imagine we are standing together in a kitchen and I say this to you:

> Don't touch that pan – it's hot!

This seems so obvious it is hardly worth analysing. Yet the shared assumptions required for us to communicate successfully are considerable. I am assuming that:

- A hot pan will burn you if you touch it.
- You don't want to get burned.
- You are able to understand the meaning of my words in English.
- You trust me to be telling the truth.
- The pan really is hot and I'm not simply confused.

Is any of this worth spelling out? Probably not. If, however, I'm talking to my 2-year-old son, I will work hard to explain several of the assumptions above, because he doesn't yet know enough to take all these things for granted. Similarly, if you are talking to someone in a language that's foreign to you, or from a different culture, you may find that certain things you usually take for granted need to be spelled out in order for you to successfully communicate.

Here's an example in the kind of prose you might find in a newspaper article about the global economy. What key assumptions are being made here?

> The financial crisis of 2008 was fuelled by bad loans in the US housing market, and the financial derivatives based on these loans. When the housing bubble burst, massive losses associated with the derivatives wiped trillions off the global economy. Today, lessons have been learned around both loans and derivatives, and so we will not see a repeat of the circumstances of 2008, thus making us safe from crises on a similarly massive scale, even though lesser global recessions may still occur.

As so often with arguments, it's useful first of all to locate the final conclusion, so we can see what is being claimed. In this case, the author wishes us to conclude that the world is safe from future financial crises on the scale of 2008. Now we can ask – what reasoning is provided to support this? The argument is that the 2008 crisis was caused by bad loans and derivatives based on these loans, and that, because lessons have now been learned around both loans and derivatives, a similarly massive crisis won't come again. What relevant reasoning is being assumed but not spelled out? Here are the two most important implicit premises:

1 The lessons learned around loans and derivatives are sufficient to ensure that the circumstances of 2008 will never be repeated.
2 The only way that a financial crisis as massive as the 2008 crisis can occur is through a repeat of the circumstances of that crisis.

We can now rewrite the argument in ordinary prose, adding in these assumptions along the way. I have underlined the inserted assumptions, below:

> The financial crisis of 2008 was fuelled by bad loans in the US housing market, and the financial derivatives based on these loans. When the housing bubble burst, massive losses associated with the derivatives wiped trillions off the global economy. Today, lessons have been learned around both loans and derivatives that are sufficient to ensure we will avoid any such mistakes in future. So we will not see a repeat of the circumstances of 2008, because the only way that a financial crisis as massive as that in 2008 can occur is through a repeat of its circumstances; this thus makes us safe from crises on a similarly massive scale…

Not a full reconstruction: sometimes it's enough to just spell out key assumptions.

I would say that it is very much worth explaining these assumptions, because both of them are open to questioning. Is it really true that the circumstances of 2008 will never be repeated? Perhaps. But it's hardly a certainty. Is it also true that the only way a massive financial crisis can occur is through those circumstances? Almost certainly not.

SMART STUDY: A practical guide to challenging assumptions

Every single argument relies on assumptions, and learning to spell out the ones that matter is important for getting to grips with ideas and research in any field. To help you do this, try asking these five questions whenever you're struggling to work out whether you should accept someone's claims at face value:

1 Is this argument moving too simplistically from the particular to the general, or assuming that one thing must be like another without a good reason?
2 Is an assumption being made about one thing being the cause of another when, in fact, this is not obviously true?
3 Are any particular beliefs about what is right and wrong, or natural and unnatural, being used to support a conclusion without being made explicit?
4 Does this argument assume that the future must follow the same pattern as the past without providing evidence or considering differences in circumstances?
5 Has what you're reading begun by assuming the thing it is supposed to be proving?

PUTTING IT ALL TOGETHER

We have looked at a method for reconstructing arguments in five steps:

1 Apply the principle of charity
2 Identify the conclusion
3 Identify the explicit premises
4 Spell out any relevant assumptions
5 Distinguish between linked and independent premises.

Here's an example to help you put this into practice. First, read the paragraph below. I have marked up premises and conclusions in brackets:

> For the purposes of my research project, I developed an initial theory about student work habits. Unfortunately, (P1) it is not possible to obtain any good quality data about student work habits. This means that (C1) I cannot meaningfully test my theory. Given that (P3) a theory which cannot meaningfully be tested is unsuitable for a research project, it has become clear that (C3) I need to abandon this particular theory.

Now we are going to put this into standard form. In the argument box below, I have provided a structure with some elements filled in and some left blank. Try to fill in all the blanks, beginning with the final conclusion and working back from there. Note that a couple of the steps you need to clarify are implicit rather than explicit.

Premise 1: [Implicit] ....

....

Premise 2: It is impossible to obtain good quality data about student work habits.

Conclusion 1: ....

....

Premise 3: [Implicit] ....

....

Conclusion 2: ....

....

Premise 4: ....

....

Conclusion 3: **I need to abandon my theory about student work habits.**

How did you do? Probably the most difficult thing about this exercise is correctly identifying the relevant assumptions in the passage. There are two key points which are assumed rather than explicitly stated. First, that meaningfully testing a theory requires good data; and second, that an unsuitable theory needs to be abandoned. Spelling both of these things out allows the entire extended argument to flow.

Premise 1:	[Implicit] Meaningfully testing a theory requires good quality data.
Premise 2:	It is impossible to obtain good quality data about student work habits.
Conclusion 1:	**I cannot meaningfully test my theory about student work habits.**
Premise 3:	[Implicit] A theory that cannot meaningfully be tested is unsuitable for a research project.
Conclusion 2:	**My theory about student work habits is unsuitable for a research project.**
Premise 4:	A theory that is unsuitable for a research project needs to be abandoned.
Conclusion 3:	**I need to abandon my theory about student work habits.**

Here's another example. This time it's a more confusing piece of writing to analyse, full of extraneous material – you'll need to paraphrase and simplify it considerably. I have started you off with the first premise: one I have summed up as 'protection from unwanted intrusions is a vital part of privacy'. Remember, also, to apply the principle of charity: try to state as clearly as possible the strongest version of the point being made.

> One of the great debates in technology at the moment concerns data and privacy. Only last week I found myself shouting at a computer scientist who couldn't accept that I do not want an algorithm scanning my email in order to show me 'relevant' adverts. Privacy is not simply a question of whether or not other people know what I'm doing. Privacy is also a question of how I can protect myself from unwelcome intrusions like email adverts, spam emails and so forth – of which there are far too many. This kind of protection is a vital part of privacy. In my opinion, technology companies know far too much about us and should be legally forbidden from intruding on us like they do. This is what the rule of law should be about: obliging all companies to respect rights like personal privacy, rather than letting them get away with bombarding us with unwanted intrusions.

Premise 1: Protection from unwanted intrusions is a vital part of privacy.

Premise 2: ....

....

Premise 3: ....

....

Conclusion: ....

....

This isn't easy, and you may well come up with something different to my solution. Phrasing things differently doesn't matter so long as you have made things as clear as possible, and tried to come up with as charitable and coherent a version of the argument as you can. Are we being too generous to the author by making things this clear and explicit? Perhaps. But this is the best way for us to engage with their position as fully as possible, and to learn as much from it ourselves as we can.

Premise 1: Protection from unwanted intrusions is a vital part of privacy.

Premise 2: Technology companies expose us to far too many unwanted intrusions.

Premise 3: The rule of law should oblige all companies to respect our privacy.

Conclusion: **Technology companies should be obliged by law to stop exposing us to unwanted intrusions.**

Are you starting to feel confident about using the standard form to set out arguments? Here's a different kind of exercise. I'm not going to provide an example. Instead, I want you to write briefly in the space below an argument you disagree with in the form of a few sentences. Once you've done this, write it out in standard form, making sure to apply the principle of charity rather than setting up a straw man.

An argument I disagree with is..

....

....

....

....

....

....

The same argument can be set out in standard form like this..

....

....

....

....

....

....

....

....

Do you feel any different about such an argument having set it out like this? Are its flaws more obvious or its merits harder to ignore? Now, hopefully, you're ready to begin assessing reasoning in detail.

Why might a smart, sensible person, totally disagree with you?

Practically speaking, careful reconstruction will often make the flaws in an argument obvious, or suggest where its weaknesses may lie. There are, however, different forms of reasoning that each have their own features, and specific techniques for evaluation that need to be learned. We'll be covering these over the next three chapters, together with the related topics of evidence and proof.

TWO

CONSERVE MENTAL ENERGY. BUILD HABITS AND A WORKING ENVIRONMENT THAT HELP YOU FOCUS. THIS MEANS NOT HAVING EMAIL OR SOCIAL MEDIA OPEN IN THE BACKGROUND. DEAL WITH EMAIL IN FOCUSED BURSTS. DON'T LET OTHERS DICTATE YOUR TIME AND ATTENTION.

#TalkCriticalThinking

THINK ABOUT THIS: How does it make you feel to set out a position that you disagree with like this? Does it have any impact on what you think or believe, or on how you might choose to argue with someone who believes differently to you? ....

....

....

....

....

....

SUMMARY

Reconstructing an argument means identifying all its different parts, then setting these out clearly in a standard form that allows us to see exactly how they work.

Standard form means rewriting an argument so that:

- The **conclusion** is set out clearly at the bottom.
- The reasoning leading to the conclusion is set out clearly above it in the form of numbered premises.

A **premise** is the most basic building block of an argument. Many different premises can be linked together into a chain of reasoning to support a conclusion.

Extraneous material is information that is not relevant to the argument, and that should be left out as we carefully **clarify** each premise and conclusion by rewriting them.

An **assumption** is something relevant to an argument that has been taken for granted by the person presenting it, rather than spelled out.

An **extended argument** is one in which the final conclusion is supported by one or more premises that are themselves supported by previous premises.

An **intermediate conclusion** is a conclusion arrived at during the course of an argument; it is then used as a premise for building towards the final conclusion.

The **final conclusion** comes at the end of an extended argument: it is the final thing that the person making the argument is attempting to persuade you of.

Prejudice means holding a belief without consideration of the evidence for or against it, or deciding in advance of reading an argument what you believe to be the case.

A **straw man** is an absurd simplification of someone else's position that is obviously wrong or stupid – and that is only expressed so that it can easily be defeated.

The **process of reconstruction** can be divided into five steps:

1 Apply the **principle of charity**. This requires us to begin with the assumption that someone else is truthful and reasonable, and to try to reconstruct their argument in its strongest form.
2 Identify the **final conclusion** (and write it down at the bottom) – conclusion indicator words such as 'because', 'since', 'thus' and 'so' may help us to work out what is going on in an argument by indicating where the final conclusion is. Final conclusions also often appear at either the very start or very end of a piece of writing.

3 Identify the **explicit premises** (and write them down in order above the final conclusion) – these are all the claims that someone has set out in support of their conclusion.
4 Identify any **implicit premises** or **implicit conclusions** (and put them where they are needed) – these are not spelled out by the person stating an argument, but are **assumed** as part of their reasoning and need to be included in reconstruction.
5 Ensure you know which premises are **linked** (they need to be taken together to support a conclusion) and which are **independent** (they work on their own).

Following this reconstruction, you are ready to **evaluate** the reasoning on display, paying careful attention to the different types of reasoning in use.

Now watch the video 'The astonishing importance of challenging assumptions'. It's on YouTube. Tell me what you think via #TalkCriticalThinking

THINK

REASONING WITH LOGIC*ALLY* AND CERTAINTY

It's how to successfully challenge other people's conclusions!

Why does reasoning matter (and how can you spot an argument)?

↓

How do you spell out the reasoning behind an argument?

How do you draw out a logical conclusion from your premises?

How do you draw out a probable conclusion from your premises?

How can you select and test the best explanation of something?

How should you assess evidence and plan your reading strategy?

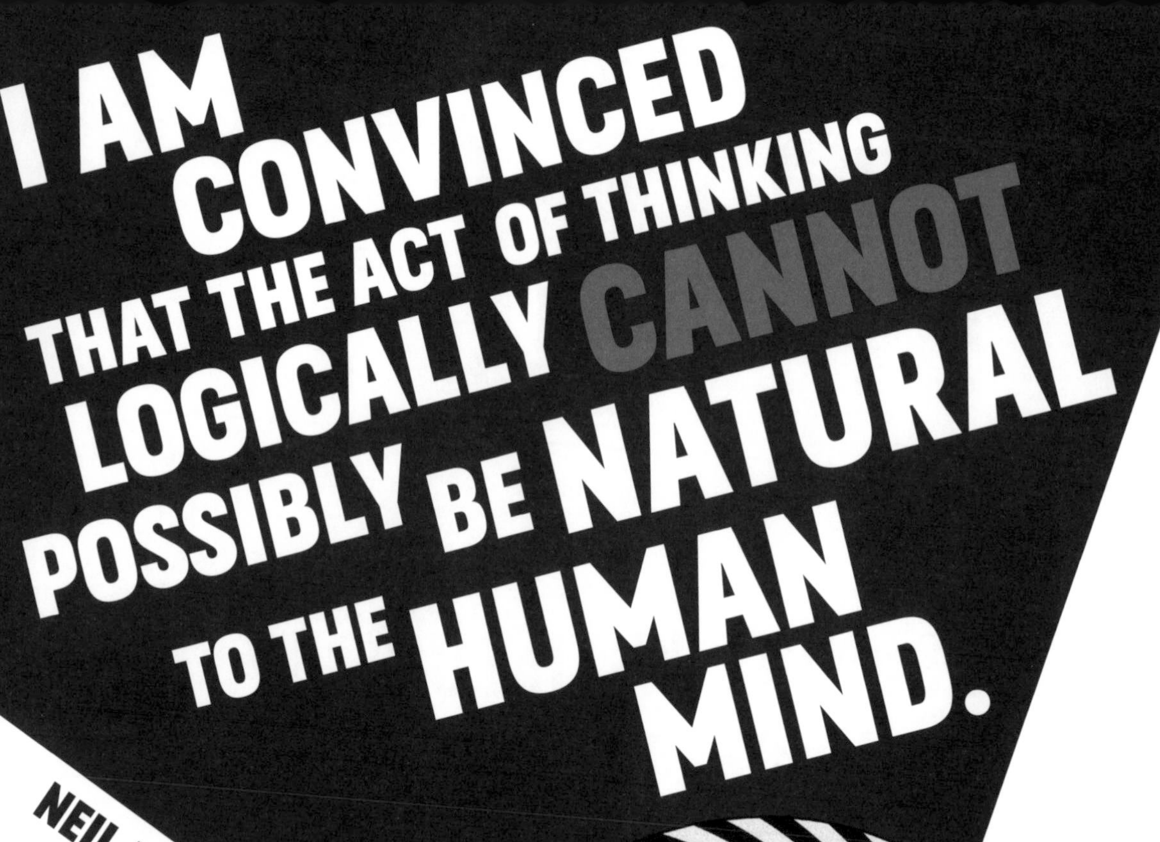

I AM
CONVINCED
THAT THE ACT OF THINKING
LOGICALLY CANNOT
POSSIBLY BE NATURAL
TO THE HUMAN
MIND.
NEIL DEGRASSE TYSON

#TalkCriticalThinking

FIVE THINGS YOU'LL LEARN IN THIS CHAPTER

1 How to draw out a *logical conclusion* from your premises
2 What happens when a conclusion doesn't follow from its *premises*
3 How to *identify* when an argument's conclusion *must be true*
4 How logic is based on *necessary* and *sufficient conditions*
5 Common confusions in *reasoning out* a *conclusion*

This is the first of three chapters engaging with three different types of reasoning: deduction, induction and abduction. These correspond approximately to logic, probability and explanations in the flow diagram for this half of the book. Although each has a chapter of its own, these differing types of reasoning are not opposed or exclusive ways of thinking. One does not trump the other, and it's a mistake to ask which is 'better'. Between them, they describe a range of different ways in which we can seek, reasonably, to think about the world.

In this chapter, we will begin by exploring **deductive reasoning**, and the related concept of **deductive proof**. Deduction is all about the structure of arguments: what it means to correctly put together the information in front of you. If you spot a flaw in deduction, it means that someone has structured their argument incorrectly and drawn conclusions that their premises do not support. In terms of an essay or a research project, it's all about carefully structuring your reasoning so that you don't arrive at incorrect or unsupported conclusions.

Deductive reasoning: spelling out whatever conclusion follows logically from your premises, without reference to any external information

Deductive proof is a matter of logical certainty. If it is true that every healthy baby has an innate capacity for language, and if it is true you have a healthy baby, then it must also be true that your baby has an innate capacity for language.

Deductive proof: demonstrating that a particular conclusion logically follows from certain premises, and that this conclusion must be true if these premises are true

When it comes to the logical structure of arguments, correctly using deductive reasoning guarantees something special: that the truth of your premises will be preserved in your conclusions. For this reason, deductive reason is sometimes called **truth-preserving**.

Truth-preserving: when used correctly, deductive reasoning is guaranteed to preserve the truth of its premises in its conclusion (just so long as they're true in the first place)

INTRODUCING DEDUCTIVE REASONING

Here is an example of **deductive** reasoning in action:

Premise 1: All fish live in water.

Premise 2: I am a fish.

Conclusion: **I live in water.**

This may sound like nonsense, but the conclusion follows perfectly logically from its two premises. If it is true that all fish live in water, and if it is true that I am a fish, it is inevitably true that I must live in water. The conclusion is right there, ready for us to deduce it – hence the term deduction.

When we engage in deductive reasoning, we are not bringing any additional information to bear on a situation: we are simply drawing out a conclusion that is already implicit in our premises. Similarly, assessing someone's deductive reasoning doesn't tell us anything about whether what they claim is true or not. It just tells us whether the logical structure of their argument makes sense, or whether something has gone wrong on this structural level.

Deduction sounds a bit like detective work, and for good reason: it entails looking very closely at the information in front of you and then teasing out exactly what it implies. Here are a few examples. In each case, use your powers of deduction to spell out the logical conclusion that the information leads to:

1 I can't stand any kind of physical activity. Sailing is a physical activity, so................................

....

2 There is no such thing as a magnetic plastic. My plate is plastic, so..

....

3 Anyone ignoring me while speaking on their phone is irritating. You are ignoring me while speaking on your phone, so..

....

The logical conclusion of each of these is that: (1) I can't stand sailing (because it's a physical activity); (2) My plate is not magnetic (because there is no such thing as magnetic plastic); and (3) You are irritating me (because you are ignoring me while speaking on your phone).

How did you do? Here's a more complex example, with blank lines for you to fill in at the end:

> A combination of poor diet and inactivity in elderly patients leads to memory loss. George (not his real name) is inactive and eats a poor diet. Barbara (not her real name) is inactive but eats well. Thus, we predict that..
>
> ....
>
> ....
>
> ....

The correct conclusion is that 'George will suffer from memory loss owing to his poor diet and inactivity'. Notice that there is no mention of Barbara. This is because we don't have enough information to predict what will happen to her. All that our premises tell us is that both poor diet and inactivity lead to memory loss. Someone who is inactive but eats well doesn't fit into this category, and so we have nothing further to say about them. If you mentioned Barbara when completing the example, you were introducing an assumption that isn't actually contained in the premises – a common error in deductive reasoning.

VALID AND INVALID ARGUMENTS

Logic and truth are two distinct things. In the first example in this chapter, the fact that one of the premises is obviously false – I am definitely not a fish – makes no difference to the structure of the argument being a perfectly logical piece of deductive reasoning. If all fish live in water, and I am a fish, then it logically follows that I must live in water. Here's another perfectly structured deductive argument:

Premise 1:	All Blahs live in Bloop.
Premise 2:	I am a Blah.
Conclusion:	**I live in Bloop.**

Valid reasoning: correctly applying deductive reasoning in drawing out the logical conclusion of your premises

Invalid reasoning: incorrectly applying deductive reasoning, so that your conclusion does not logically follow from your premises

There is no such thing as a Blah or a place to live known as Bloop, but this makes no difference to the deductive force of the argument. Deductive reasoning is not directly concerned with truth: it is simply concerned with **validity**, which means the question of whether a particular conclusion inevitably follows from its premises. If the structure of an argument is such that its conclusion must follow from its premises, then that argument is **valid**. If, by contrast, its conclusion does not follow from its premises, then the argument is **invalid**.

Here is another perfectly valid piece of deductive reasoning, expressed in ordinary prose:

All men who wear glasses are sexy. I wear glasses. Therefore, I am sexy.

The conclusion – that I am sexy – follows logically and inevitably from the premises. If all men who wear glasses are sexy, and I wear glasses, then it must follow that I am indeed sexy. My argument is valid, even if the truth of my premises is open to debate. By contrast, here is a piece of invalid reasoning based on the same premises:

> All men who wear glasses are sexy. I wear glasses. Therefore, I am a man.

This conclusion – that I am a man – does not follow logically and inevitably from my premises. It may happen to be true that I am a man, but this is neither here nor there so far as deduction is concerned. My argument doesn't work on a structural level: I have failed to correctly deduce what my premises imply, instead leaping to an **unwarranted** conclusion.

Unwarranted: a conclusion that is not supported by the argument

Much of the time, you can use a combination of common sense and close reading to work out whether the form of an argument is valid or invalid. Here are a few examples. Are the arguments below deductively valid or invalid?

		VALID	INVALID
1	All students must register if they wish to attend the workshop. I wish to attend the workshop. Therefore, I must register.	○	○
2	There is no such thing as a purple monkey. This creature is purple, so it can't be a monkey.	○	○
3	Purple monkeys are difficult to spot. This creature is difficult to spot, so it must be a purple monkey.	○	○
4	We always need the permission of human volunteers if our experiments on them are to be ethical. We do not yet have permission from these subjects, so we cannot yet experiment on them in an ethical manner.	○	○
5	We always need the permission of human volunteers if our experiments on them are to be ethical. We do not yet have permission from these subjects, so we can only experiment on them if they don't know what we are doing.	○	○

Number (1) is clearly valid. Number (2) is also valid, although it takes a little more thought to see why: if there is no such thing as a monkey that is purple, it logically follows that anything which is purple cannot be a monkey. Number (3) is invalid, because saying that purple monkeys are difficult to spot does not imply that 'anything that is difficult to spot must be a purple monkey'. There may be countless other things that are also hard to spot (chameleons, tiny objects that are very far away, brown monkeys sitting on brown trees).

Number (4) is a valid argument. Its premises are lengthier than our first examples, but its form is straightforward: if we always need someone's permission to do something, then we cannot do that thing if we do not have their permission.

Finally, number (5) is invalid. It involves the kind of slippery thinking that people often use in order to justify a course of action, but this shifting of meanings has no place in valid reasoning. If we always need someone's permission to do something ethically, then we cannot do that thing ethically without their permission – full stop. Trying to provide an excuse for doing so is not valid. The conclusion is unwarranted: the given premises do not support it.

SMART STUDY: How evasion creates invalid arguments

One of the most useful practical reasons for thinking about validity is that it allows us to spot situations in which someone is trying to get away with drawing an unwarranted conclusion from their premises, via a hidden assumption that they would rather not spell out.

In the final example above – 'We always need the permission of human volunteers if our experiments on them are to be ethical. We do not yet have permission from these subjects, so we can only experiment on them if they don't know what we are doing' – thinking rigorously about validity exposes the fact that the author is concealing an alarming assumption beneath their explicit argument: that, so long as someone doesn't know what we are doing, we can get away with acting unethically towards them.

Assessing sources closely for validity means insisting that people cannot pull off this kind of evasion. If someone wishes to present a claim as the logical outcome of their argument, it's our job to insist that their argument is honest and explicit. Don't be afraid to challenge invalid claims wherever you find them: it's an integral part of honest thought and research.

Invalid doesn't mean untrue — it means not serving as proof.

NECESSARY AND SUFFICIENT CONDITIONS

Necessary condition: must be met if something is to be true, but cannot by itself guarantee the truth of that thing

Sufficient condition: one that, if met, does guarantee the truth of something

One of the most fundamental ways in which concepts can be logically connected is through **necessary** and **sufficient** conditions. Here is an example of each:

> In order for me to be a successful student, it is necessary for me to work hard.
>
> This exam has a pass mark of 50, so my score of 52 is sufficient to pass.

A necessary condition is something that must be true in order for another thing to be true, but where the truth of the first thing does not guarantee the second. I must work hard if I want to succeed, but working hard doesn't guarantee success. A sufficient condition, by contrast, can guarantee that something is true. If I score 52 in an exam with a pass mark of 50, this does indeed guarantee that I have passed. Here are a number of conditions that are **necessary but not sufficient** for me to stream a movie on my iPhone:

> My iPhone needs to have a sufficiently fast data connection.
>
> I need to have access to some kind of streaming service.
>
> My iPhone needs to be sufficiently charged.
>
> My iPhone needs to be switched on and unlocked.

These conditions are necessary because, if even one of them is not met, I cannot stream a movie. Yet they are not sufficient because, even if these four things are true, I am not guaranteed to be able to stream a movie. All of the above could be true, yet my screen could be smashed and broken; or my phone could be paralysed by malware; and so on. Identifying and distinguishing between necessary and sufficient conditions is vital in logic. In general:

> Failing to meet a necessary condition means that THING X cannot be true. But…
>
> …meeting any number of necessary conditions still can't guarantee that THING X is true. But…
>
> …the moment that any sufficient condition is met, this does guarantee that THING X is true.

TEACHING IS SUCCESSFUL ONLY AS IT CAUSES PEOPLE TO THINK FOR THEMSELVES.

WHAT THE TEACHER THINKS MATTERS LITTLE.

ALICE MOORE HUBBARD

TalkCriticalThinking

Here's a particular example:

Being alive is a necessary condition for being a parent. But...

...just because you are alive does not guarantee that you are a parent. But...

...having one or more children is sufficient to guarantee that you are a parent. So...

...if you have one or more children, you are guaranteed to be a parent.

Here is another example in the same form, with gaps for you to fill in:

Not eating any dairy products is a necessary condition for being a vegan. But...

...just because you do not ______________________________ does not guarantee that you are _____________. But...

...not eating or using any animal products whatsoever is sufficient to guarantee that you are _____________ . So,...

...if you _______________________________________ then you are guaranteed to be ________________ .

How did you do? Here's what it should say:

Just because you do not eat any dairy products does not guarantee that you are a vegan. But not eating or using any animal products whatsoever is sufficient to guarantee that you are a vegan. So, if you do not eat or use any animal products whatsoever, then you are guaranteed to be a vegan.

As we'll see in the next section, our ability to connect ideas in terms of 'if' and 'then' is the foundation of our ability to structure an argument logically – while it's our tendency to confuse necessary with sufficient conditions that produces many of the most common errors in everyday logic.

As we'll also see, defining sufficient conditions in real life is extremely tricky. The Vegan Society defines veganism as 'a way of living which seeks to exclude, as far as is possible and practicable, all forms of exploitation of, and cruelty to, animals for food, clothing or any other purpose'. This is a definition that is deliberately left open to some interpretation, given the great difficulty of tracking the ingredients and production process of every single product you use. Deduction may look neat, but pinning down the truth of every component part in its logic is an extraordinarily tricky business.[6]

THINK ABOUT THIS: Try to think of some necessary conditions for performing everyday tasks: preparing food, travelling, shopping, communicating with others. Can you think of any sufficient conditions for performing tasks in everyday life? ....

....

....

....

....

....

TWO TYPES OF VALID AND INVALID REASONING

Common sense and close reading go a long way when you're assessing arguments, but sometimes it's important to understand things on a more fundamental level – and to have in the back of your mind a sense of the general logical forms that valid arguments take.

I've been using the word **logic** and **logically** a lot in this chapter, and you probably have a decent sense of what they mean. We use the word 'logical' informally to describe something that makes sense, and 'illogical' to describe something that doesn't. These everyday senses come pretty close to the formal definition of logic: the principles and methods used to distinguish between correct and incorrect reasoning.

Logic: the study of the principles distinguishing correct from incorrect reasoning

Logic can also be thought of as the science of validity. By correctly structuring a deductive argument, we are spelling out the logical implications of our premises. We do not add any additional information: we simply make logical (that is, correct) deductions on the basis of what we already know. Valid arguments are logical; invalid arguments are defective in their logic.[7]

Really worth getting the hang of this.

Understanding the logic of valid arguments means looking at their form rather than their content. This isn't a logic textbook, and so I have covered a fuller range of logical arguments in an extra section at the end of the book, while restricting myself in this chapter to introducing the two most basic forms of valid argument, together with the forms of invalid argument that correspond to them.[8]

Affirming the antecedent versus affirming the consequent

Affirming the antecedent: a valid form of argument in which, because one thing is said always to follow from another, the truth of the first guarantees the second is also true

Affirming the antecedent is a valid logical argument that has the following general form – meaning that any argument at all which correctly follows this form must be valid

Premise 1: If A, then B.

Premise 2: A.

Conclusion: **Therefore, B.**

What does this mean? First, it asserts that one thing always follows from another (thing A is sufficient to guarantee thing B). Second, it affirms that, because the first thing has happened, the second thing must therefore be true. This becomes clear when we fill in A and B with something specific:

Premise 1: If it is raining, then I will use my umbrella.

Premise 2: It is raining.

Conclusion: **Therefore, I will use my umbrella.**

Formal fallacy: an invalid form of argument representing an error in logic, meaning that arguments in this form cannot be relied on to arrive at valid conclusions

To reiterate: any argument that has this form must be valid. If B follows from A, then whenever A is the case, we can say with certainty that B must also be the case.

Affirming the consequent: an invalid argument which mistakenly assumes that, when one thing always follows from another, the truth of the second also guarantees the first

Affirming the antecedent needs to be carefully distinguished from a similar but invalid form of argument – something we call a **formal fallacy**, because the form of the argument is itself false and illogical. This is the fallacy of **affirming the consequent** and it takes this form:

Premise 1: If A, then B.

Premise 2: B.

Conclusion: **Therefore, A.**

Here is the fallacy in concrete form:

Premise 1:	If it is raining, then I will use my umbrella.
Premise 2:	I am using my umbrella.
Conclusion:	**Therefore, it is raining.**

This is an invalid argument because its conclusion does not inevitably follow from its premises. It may or may not be true that, if I am using my umbrella, it is raining – but my stated premises do not allow us to deduce this. B is necessarily true if A is true, but B does not guarantee A. A further example makes it clear what is wrong with this kind of fallacy:

> If I were conducting a secret affair with the president of the United States, the president would not mention my name publicly. The president has never mentioned my name publicly; therefore, I am conducting a secret affair with the president.

Clearly, there are many more likely explanations for the fact that the president has never mentioned my name. In making this mistake, I have confused necessary and sufficient conditions: I have mistaken something that would necessarily be true in the event of a certain conclusion with something that guarantees the same conclusion. My name not being mentioned might necessarily be true if I were having an affair with the president, but it is far from being sufficient to guarantee this conclusion.

Denying the consequent versus denying the antecedent

Denying the consequent: a valid form of argument in which, because one thing is said always to follow from another, the fact that the second isn't true also guarantees the first isn't true

Denying the consequent is a valid argument in the following general form:

Premise 1:	If A, then B.
Premise:	Not B.
Conclusion:	**Therefore, not A.**

We are once again saying that one thing will always follow from another, but we are then affirming that the second of these things has not happened, and thus that the first thing cannot have happened either. A is sufficient to guarantee B, which means that the absence of B must be sufficient to guarantee the absence of A.

Premise 1:	If it is raining, then I will use my umbrella.
Premise 2:	I am not using my umbrella.
Conclusion:	**Therefore, it is not raining.**

Denying the antecedent: an invalid argument which mistakenly assumes that, when one thing always follows from another, the fact that the first isn't true also guarantees the second isn't true

Any argument with this form must be valid, for reasons that mirror our initial 'affirming' form of argument. If B inevitably follows from A, and if we know that B is not the case, then A cannot be the case either. If I use my umbrella every time it rains, and I then tell you that I am not using my umbrella, you can validly conclude that it cannot be raining.

There is another invalid form of argument that corresponds to denying the consequent: a formal fallacy known as **denying the antecedent**. It takes this form:

Premise 1:	If A, then B.
Premise 2:	Not A.
Conclusion:	**Therefore, not B.**

Here is the fallacy in concrete form:

Premise 1:	If it is raining, then there will be clouds in the sky.
Premise 2:	It is not raining.
Conclusion:	**Therefore, there will not be clouds in the sky.**

The problem with this particular example is that, while the absence of clouds does logically mean that it cannot be raining – because we have said that there will inevitably be clouds if it is raining – the absence of rain does not logically imply the absence of clouds. Clouds are a necessary condition for rain, but not a sufficient one. Once again, it is the confusion of necessary for sufficient conditions that creates the fallacy.

SMART STUDY: When fallacies confuse 'if' with 'if, and only if'

Both types of fallacious argument I've listed are based on the same kind of confusion: the idea that these two sentences mean the same thing:

> The subject's leg will move upwards if we hit the reflex spot.
>
> The subject's leg will move upwards if, and only if, we hit the reflex spot.

Put like this, the error seems ridiculous: there are obviously thousands of reasons why someone's leg might jerk upwards in addition to being hit in the reflex spot. At other times, however, it is dangerously easy to act as though 'if' means 'if, and only if'. For example:

> Our research suggests that, if someone is highly intelligent, they are also likely to be of above-average wealth. This supports the theory of wealth denoting high natural ability.

Some people might find the above argument forceful, but its form is fallacious: there are many things other than high intelligence that are associated with wealth.

If we were to say that '*research suggests that if, and only if, someone is highly intelligent then they are also likely to be of above-average wealth*', then it would make sense to say that wealth denotes intelligence – but this is no longer a convincing description of reality. Instead, it shows the kind of confusion associated with logical fallacies: failing to realize that describing a tendency ('the highly intelligent are more likely to be wealthy') is very different indeed from discovering a rule ('all of the wealthy are intelligent).

THINK ABOUT THIS: Under what circumstances do you think valid arguments are most important, and under what circumstances might making a valid argument miss the point or not fit the facts? ....

....

....

....

....

....

THREE

IF IN DOUBT, WAIT. LEAVE THOSE DIFFICULT MESSAGES FOR A FEW DAYS, EVEN A WEEK, AND SUDDENLY WHAT YOU NEED TO SAY WILL FEEL MUCH CLEARER. DOING SOMETHING IS NOT NECESSARILY BETTER THAN DOING NOTHING.

#TalkCriticalThinking

SOUND AND UNSOUND ARGUMENTS

We have said that validity is entirely separate from truth: an argument can be perfectly valid while being based on lies or made-up nonsense. However, validity has an important relationship with truth, because every valid deductive argument is truth-preserving. Its validity means that it will successfully preserve the truth of all its premises, allowing us to draw true conclusions – so long as our premises are also true. If the premises of a valid deductive argument are true, then its conclusion must also be true.

We call a deductive argument that is both valid and has true premises a **sound** argument. By contrast, an **unsound** argument is one that does not satisfy these conditions: either because it is invalid (all invalid arguments are automatically also unsound), or because it is valid but its premises are untrue, meaning its conclusion cannot be relied on.

Sound: a deductive argument that is both valid and has true premises, meaning its conclusion must also be true

Unsound: an argument that does not meet the standard of soundness, either because it is invalid or because one or more of its premises is untrue, or both

Let's look at an everyday example of assessing an argument for soundness, and how it might apply to an essay or a textbook. Consider the following two premises:

> If you want to conduct a literature review for your research, you must only make use of completely unbiased sources. But all sources are biased in one way or another.

Both of these statements may seem perfectly reasonable. Yet, when we apply deductive reasoning, they lead us to a conclusion that makes little sense. Here are the premises set out in standard form, followed by the underlying form of the argument in brackets:

Premise 1:	If you want to write a literature review, then you should only make use of completely unbiased sources. (If A, then B)
Premise 2:	There are no unbiased sources for you to use. (Not B)
Conclusion:	**You cannot write a literature review. (Therefore, not A)**

This conclusion is logically implicit in the premises themselves: it is a valid argument, conforming to the second form we looked at, 'denying the consequent'. Once we spell this out, however, we also need to decide whether we believe this to be a sound argument. Here, the conclusion which our premises lead us to should, hopefully, make us think twice about the truthfulness of our premises. What do you think might be going wrong with these?

In this particular case, the problem lies in the assertion that 'you should only make use of completely unbiased sources'. You can reasonably claim that all sources are biased in *some* sense, but this doesn't mean that you cannot use them. It simply means that you need to be sensitive to their different potential biases. Our premise is not true. In the light of this insight, we might rewrite our argument along these lines:

> If you want to conduct a literature review for your research, you must be aware of any bias in your sources. All sources are potentially biased in one way or another. Therefore, when conducting a literature review you must consider potential biases in every source.

This is more likely to be a sound argument: it has a valid form and its premises are true. At least, its premises feel pretty convincing. Now that we are in the realm of truth as well as logical validity, we face questions of judgement and likelihood as well as those of logical correctness. Are you 100 per cent convinced of the truth of the statement 'you must be aware of any bias in your sources'? Are there some sources of bias that you don't need to be aware of, or some circumstances in which this doesn't apply? Does being published in a leading scientific journal count as a kind of bias?

These are questions that point us towards the uncertainties of the world beyond our descriptions of it, and our inability to know many things for sure. They are not questions that can be resolved simply by looking at the form of our arguments – and addressing them entails the second type of reasoning at play in critical thinking, and the topic of the next chapter: inductive reasoning.

THINK ABOUT THIS: Can you think of a deductive argument in common use that is valid but unsound? What kind of premises can we be certain are true? What kinds of deductive argument may never be sound, because their premises can't be proven as true? ....

....

....

....

....

....

SUMMARY

Deductive proof means demonstrating that a particular conclusion logically follows from certain premises, and that this conclusion must be true if these premises are true.

When applying **deductive reasoning**, you are looking at the structure of an argument and drawing out a logical conclusion that is implicit in your premises.

Logic is the study of the principles distinguishing correct from incorrect reasoning, and its building blocks are the ideas of necessary and sufficient conditions:

- **Necessary** conditions need to be met in order for something to be true, but they cannot guarantee its truth. However, if any of the necessary conditions are not met, then something is guaranteed not to be true.
- **Sufficient** conditions do guarantee the truth of something. If the sufficient conditions for something are met, then it is guaranteed to be true.

We have looked in detail at **two general valid forms** of deductive reasoning:

- Affirming the antecedent – If A then B. A. So, B.
  If it is sunny, I get hot. It is sunny. So I am hot.
- Denying the consequent – If A then B. Not B. So, not A.
  If it is sunny, I get hot. I am not hot. So it cannot be sunny.

We have also looked at **two fallacious (logically invalid) forms** of argument, both of which result from the mistaken assumption that something which is necessarily true is also sufficient to guarantee the truth of a conclusion:

- Affirming the antecedent – If A then B. B. So, A.
  If it is sunny, I feel happy. I feel happy. So it must be sunny.
- Denying the antecedent – If A then B. Not A. So, not B.
  If it is sunny, I feel happy. It is not sunny. So I cannot feel happy.

Overall, we have established that:

- **Valid reasoning** correctly draws out a logical conclusion from its premises.
- **Invalid reasoning** means a conclusion does not logically follow from its premises.
- A **sound argument** is both valid and has true premises, meaning its conclusion must also be true.
- An **unsound** argument does not meet the standard of soundness, either because it is invalid or because one or more of its premises is untrue, or both. Thus, you cannot rely on its conclusion being true.

Now watch the video 'Why logic is a really great thing, until it isn't'. It's on YouTube. Tell me what you think via #TalkCriticalThinking

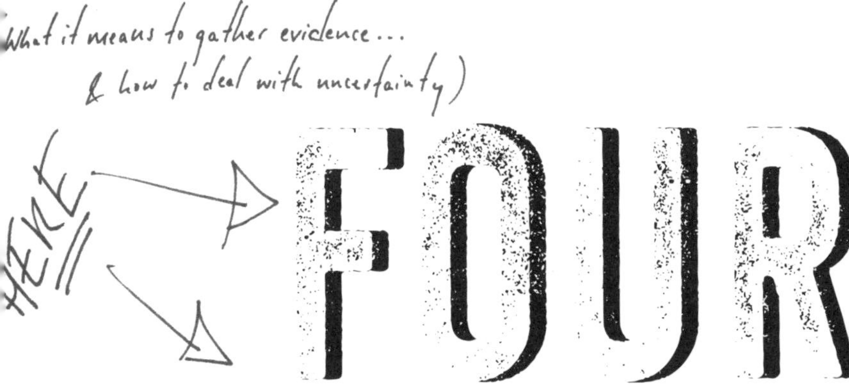

REASONING WITH OBSERVATION AND UNCERTAINTY

Why does reasoning matter (and how can you spot an argument)?

↓

How do you spell out the reasoning behind an argument?

↓

How do you draw out a logical conclusion from your premises?

↓

How do you draw out a probable conclusion from your premises?

↓

How can you select and test the best explanation of something?

↓

How should you assess evidence and plan your reading strategy?

To be prepared against surprise is to be trained.
To be prepared for surprise is to be educated.
James P. Carse
a
b
c
d
f
g
#TalkCriticalThinking

FIVE THINGS YOU'LL LEARN IN THIS CHAPTER

1. How *inductive reasoning* applies to *evidence* and *research*
2. How to assess the *strength* of an *inductive argument*
3. How to understand *probability* and *rational expectation*
4. How to make *good use of samples* in your work
5. The significance of *black swan events* and *falsification*

In the previous chapter, we looked at rigorously examining the form of an argument through deductive reasoning. We were interested in drawing out the conclusions implicit in our premises. So far, so logical. If a deductive argument has both true premises and a valid form, it is sound: its conclusion must also be true.

As soon as we start looking for patterns, causes and consequences within everyday experience and evidence, however, we run up against a problem. In real life, there is very little that we can be 100 per cent certain about. Deduction is all very well but before we can apply its logic we first need to make assertions about the world. And this brings us towards a second, equally important form of reasoning: reasoning on the basis of observation and extrapolation rather than pure logic.

Although we rarely consciously think about it, small leaps of faith occur every time we assume that tomorrow will be like today, that one thing will follow the same pattern as another, or that the same observation will be true of different people or places. This brings us to **inductive reasoning** – the business of seeking good reasons to believe something in the absence of logical certainty.

Inductive reasoning: a form of reasoning in which premises strongly support a conclusion, but where we can never be absolutely certain that it is true

ARGUMENT BY INDUCTION

The word **induction** comes from the Latin verb *inducere*, meaning 'to lead into'. When we reason inductively, we are looking to see where our premises might lead us. We are making generalizations, inferring future events from past ones and asking what is most likely to be true, rather than dealing in absolutes.

Some people don't like the phrase 'inductive reasoning' and prefer to talk about **ampliative reasoning**, because this offers a more explicit reminder that it is a form of reasoning where your conclusion is an 'amplification' of your premises. The two phrases, however, mean exactly the same thing – and, because induction is a more commonly used term, I'm going to stick with it.[9] Here is a simple example of an inductive argument:

Ampliative reasoning: another way of describing inductive reasoning – intended to show that such reasoning works by 'amplifying' premises into a broader conclusion

> There has never been a female president of the United States. So, the next president of the United States will almost certainly be a man as well.

Do you find this argument convincing? The first premise is certainly true – at least at the time of writing, in 2017, there had never yet been a female US president – which means that whether you are convinced or not depends on how far you agree that the conclusion is a reasonable generalization based on this observation.

Notice that the key question here is *how far* you agree with the idea that the past is a good guide to the future in this case. When deploying inductive reasoning, we are always dealing with degrees of confidence rather than certainty. An inductive argument cannot be valid in the way that a deductive argument is logically valid. When someone makes an inductive argument, they are trying to persuade us to accept their particular account as the best one available. But they are not, and cannot be, proving something beyond all doubt.

Ranking inductive arguments: determining which arguments are more or less convincing relative to one another

In practice, this means that when comparing inductive arguments we often **rank** them in relation to one another rather than coming up with an absolute assessment. Consider the following inductive arguments. Can you rank them in order, from least convincing to most convincing?

1 There has never been a female US president – and this suggests there will never be a female US president. ◯
2 There has never been a female US president – and this suggests the next president will not be female either. ◯
3 There has never been a female US president – but all things change and, at some point, there eventually will be. ◯
4 There has never been a female US president – but the time is ripe for change sooner rather than later and there will be one within the next decade. ◯

I would say that the most convincing of these arguments is (3), which argues that at some point there will be a female president. This prediction must be more likely than (4), which offers a more specific version of the same scenario: not only will there be a female president, but she will arrive within the next decade.

This is one firm rule to bear in mind when assessing the relative likelihood of different possibilities. When one scenario is a subset of another ('having a female president within a decade' is a subset of 'having a female president at any point in the future' because it's a more specific version of the same prediction), the more specific scenario will always be less likely than the less specific scenario.

Similarly, it's clear on a close reading that example (1) – the argument that there will never be a female president – is a more specific, and thus less likely, subset of the possibility outlined in (2). The prediction that 'the next president definitely won't be female' must be more likely than the prediction that 'no president will ever be female', because making a definitive prediction about all possible future presidents (that they won't be female) means making a prediction about a far greater number of future events than a prediction that involves only the next president.

Beyond this, it's a question of judgement as to which arguments are more convincing. My personal ranking, from least to most convincing, goes like this:

Least convincing: there will never be a female US president.
Slightly more convincing: there will be a female president within a decade.
Even more convincing: the next president will not be female.
Most convincing of all: there will at some point be a female US president.

Because we are in the realm of inductive reasoning, we are making extrapolations from the particular to the general. We cannot be certain about any of these predictions, but we can use a number of guidelines and techniques to help us assess them.

SMART STUDY: Putting induction in practical terms

Induction is a form of reasoning we apply hundreds of times each day without noticing. We do so every time we try to work out what is going to happen next, based on what has happened before. Induction comes so naturally that it can be difficult to think about critically. Here are four questions to help focus your thinking – and to bear in mind whenever you're looking for the best possible questions for a new piece of work or research:

- Inductive reasoning is at its strongest when we have good reasons to believe that we are seeing a well-established pattern with plenty of evidence in its favour.
- Inductive reasoning is at its weakest when there is little evidence, no clear pattern or a high degree of unpredictability, complexity or uncertainty.
- A more general scenario is always more likely than a more specific scenario that's a subset of the general one. It's inevitably more likely that 'a randomly selected passer-by is female' than that 'a randomly selected passer-by is female and has long hair'.
- When assessing inductive reasoning, ask: how far is what you know a good guide to what you don't know? To what degree is the future, in this situation, likely to resemble your knowledge of the past?

INTRODUCING INDUCTIVE FORCE

In general, when talking about how convincing (or not) an inductive argument is, we use the idea of **inductive strength** – also known as **inductive force**.

The greater the strength of an inductive argument, the more likely it is to be true. Where deductive arguments are either valid or invalid – one of two absolute possibilities – inductive arguments exist on a sliding scale of strength and weakness. While a valid deductive argument with true premises guarantees the truth of its conclusion, the best we can ever say about an inductive argument is that it is sufficiently strong for us to accept its conclusion as almost certainly true. Imagine I say this:

> Every single person I have ever met hates me. The next person I meet is going to hate me too.

My argument appears inductively strong on its own terms. If every single person I have ever met really does hate me, it seems quite likely that the next person I meet will hate me too. My opening premise, however, is almost certainly an exaggeration: at the least, you might think that a large number of people I have met are indifferent towards me.

We can thus say that this particular argument is **cogent**, but not **inductively forceful**. Its structure is perfectly reasonable, but its premise is not true. A cogent inductive argument resembles a valid deductive argument, in that both have a good structure but do not necessarily lead us to accept their conclusions. Similarly, an inductively forceful argument resembles a sound deductive argument because both conclusions are convincing.

Does this mean that deduction and induction have nothing to do with one another, or are somehow rivals in the realm of reason? Not at all. Let's revisit my opening example, about the gender of the next US president:

> There has never been a female president of the United States. So the next president of the United States will almost certainly be a man as well.

This is an inductive argument. Yet we can, if we wish, convert it into a deductive argument by carefully spelling out its underlying assumptions:

Premise 1:	There has never been a female US president.
Premise 2:	[Implicit] It is almost certain that the immediate future will repeat the same pattern as the past in this particular case.
Conclusion:	**The next US president will almost certainly be a man.**

Inductive strength or **inductive force**: a measure of how likely we believe an inductive argument is to be true

Cogent: an inductive argument that has a good structure, but whose conclusion we should not necessarily accept as true (similarly to a valid deductive argument)

Inductively forceful: an inductive argument that has both a good structure and true premises, and whose conclusion we thus have good reason to accept as true (similarly to a sound deductive argument, although without its certainty)

We have now converted our inductive argument into a perfectly valid deductive argument. Does this mean we have magically plucked logical certainty from uncertainty? No. We have simply turned our inductive inference into an explicit premise, spelling out the leap between observation and generalization. If we have done so correctly, we have potentially created a sound argument, but only if we can be entirely certain of the truth of our inductive leap (which of course we cannot).

In other words, we can create a valid deductive argument through clarifying the exact details of an inductive leap, but we can never create an argument we know to be sound. We can make our uncertainty explicit, but we cannot banish it. Here is an example for you to try. Can you turn this inductive argument into a deductive one by spelling out the inductive leap between its premise and conclusion?

Premise 1: Even the world's fastest computers and most advanced software are currently nowhere near replicating the intelligence of a small child, let alone a fully grown adult.

Premise 2: [Implicit] ....

....

....

....

Conclusion: **Computers will almost certainly never achieve human-level intelligence.**

How did you do – and do you find the resulting argument convincing? Once you've thought about it, try spelling out this second example in the same way:

Premise 1: Computer power and capabilities have been doubling around every two years for decades.

Premise 2: [Implicit] ....

....

....

....

Conclusion: **Within two decades, the capabilities of computers will almost certainly have overtaken those of humans.**

As you'll have noticed, the two different opening premises suggest two different patterns that may – or may not – provide an accurate basis of inductive amplification. Certainly, both cannot be true. In the first case, the implicit assumption goes along these lines: 'the fact that computers have not yet replicated even a small child's intelligence is almost certainly a good guide to the ultimate limitations of the level of intelligence it's possible to create in a computer'. In the second case, the implicit assumption is: 'the increases of the last few decades in computers' power and capabilities will almost certainly continue at the same rate over the next two decades'.

Which one should we believe? Both arguments are deductively valid, if written out carefully enough. But we cannot know whether either (or neither) is sound until we have definitive evidence. What we are left with is a cautious obligation to investigate the strength of each inductive claim – and to keep in mind the illusory nature of any certainty implied simply by being explicit.

Most seemingly sound arguments involve simplifications.

WE OURSELVES
CAN MAKE EXPERIENCE
VALUABLE
WHEN, BY IMAGINATION
AND REASON,
WE TURN IT

Eleanor Roosevelt

#TALKCRITICALTHINKING

INDUCTION AND EVERYDAY LANGUAGE

As the example at the end of the previous sections suggests, the words we use are extremely important when it comes to inductive reasoning, and a lot of everyday habits of speech can prevent us from weighing up different possibilities with proper precision. Consider the following example:

> Little children are always breaking fragile things. I have lots of breakable things in my house; so if you came round with your little children, they would break my things. I'm afraid you can't visit unless you leave your children with a babysitter.

This reads like a piece of valid deductive reasoning: its conclusion seems to follow logically from its premises. Yet when we think about the first premise – 'little children are always breaking fragile things' – it's clear that there are a couple of **implicit qualifying words** that need to be inserted if these deductions are to be based on an accurate inductive inference.

Implicit qualification: when a general statement is not literally intended, some implicit qualification needs to be assumed, indicating the frequency with which it applies

A more accurate statement might begin by saying 'Some little children are always breaking fragile things' – or that 'little children often break fragile things'. This is because it is not literally true that all little children are constantly breaking fragile things. What was meant, and could have been said instead, is something along these lines:

> Little children often break fragile things. I have lots of fragile things; if you come round with your little children, I'm worried that they might break them. So, how can we make it less likely that this will happen?

We do this kind of thing all the time in everyday language. Consider these unqualified statements, all of which also appear to make absolute claims:

1 You never help!
2 Young, male ex-cons with no education always end up back in jail.
3 People don't survive pancreatic cancer.
4 Computers will continue to double in power every two years.

In each case, a careful analysis should begin by getting rid of the pretence that these are universal statements about something that is always the case – and instead supply some qualifying words.

Before looking at my answers below, try it for yourself: re-read each of the three sentences above, supplying a qualification for each that spells out the level of probability involved. Here are my versions:

1 You **almost** never help!
2 **Many** young, male ex-cons with no education end up back in jail.
3 **Very few** people survive pancreatic cancer.
4 Computers **may** continue to double in power every two years **for some time**.

Something interesting happens once we start to spell out these elements of an inductive argument more precisely. By filling in the gaps in everyday speech and thinking, we start to identify uncertainties that we might wish to investigate further.

The absolute statement that 'young, male ex-cons with no education always end up back in jail' invites little debate or exploration, not to mention being false. But as soon as we qualify this by noting that this does apply to 'many' people in this group, we admit to both the uncertainties and the investigative opportunities surrounding this issue.

Similarly, spelling out the inherent uncertainty and limitations around a prediction like 'computers will continue to double in power every two years' opens the door to a debate around evidence, trends and limitations. Is there actually a pattern at all in the sense we originally thought? Perhaps there is something else going on here: a chance to test and to increase our knowledge about a complex, uncertain world.

SMART STUDY: Choosing and using qualifying words

Using the right qualifying words is one of the most important ways of signalling your knowledge of inductive reasoning, and its uncertainties, in your work. Here are four guidelines:

1 Be careful never to express absolute certainty in the conclusion of an inductive argument.
2 Always keep in mind a range of qualifying words, from least to most confident, to allow you to express inductive conclusions precisely in your writing.
3 For example:

 Extremely unlikely < unlikely < not that likely < possible < quite likely < probably < almost certainly.

4 Always be ready to make explicit the implicit qualifications you encounter in others' inductive arguments – don't make the mistake of taking apparent certainty literally.

THINK ABOUT THIS: Can you think of something that you believe which contains an implicit qualification that you don't usually acknowledge or examine? What might you assume is certain, that is only highly probable; or impossible, that is in fact only unlikely? ....

ADDRESSING UNCERTAINTY THROUGH PROBABILITY

We have said that an inductively forceful argument resembles a sound deductive argument: it is reasonable to accept it as true. But what does it mean to say that it is 'reasonable' to accept the conclusion of an inductive argument in the first place? Where and how do we draw the line between accepting something as true, or not? To address this, we need to turn to the concept of probability.

Probability is the study of how likely we believe something is to be true, or to occur. It's extremely useful because it allows us to deal with the uncertainties of the real world without simply throwing our hands up in the air and abandoning reasoned analysis.

Probability: the study of how likely something is to happen, or to be true

Probability allows us to compare and contrast the likelihood of different possibilities by assigning them a value on a numerical scale. In terms of probability, we say that something which is absolutely certain has a probability of one, and that something which is absolutely impossible has a probability of zero. Everything thus exists on a sliding scale between one and zero, with a half – or 0.5 in decimal terms – marking the exact middle. A simple diagram looks like this, complete with the kind of qualifying words we saw in the previous section:

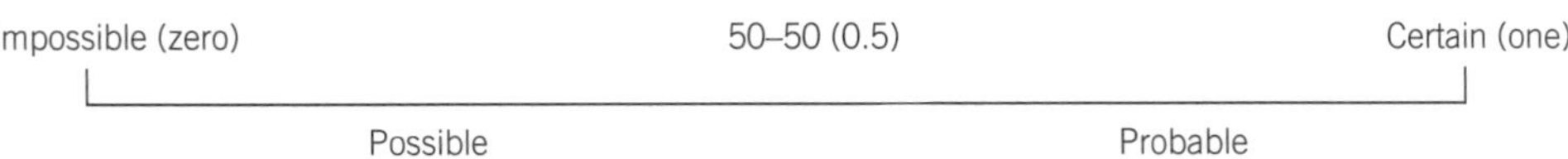

Something is more likely (than not) to be true if it has a probability greater than 0.5, meaning it will happen more than half the time. Something with a probability of less than 0.5 will happen less than half the time, and is more likely to be untrue than true.

Rational expectation: whatever it would be most reasonable to expect in a particular situation; this can be quite different to what somebody personally expects

We can use these numbers to talk about what it is, and isn't, reasonable to believe. Imagine that the chance of winning the top prize in a lottery is one in a million: that for every million tickets sold, there is just one winner. If you buy one lottery ticket, your **rational expectation** should thus be that 999,999 times out of a million you will not win the top prize. Another way of putting this is that your only reasonable expectation should be one of near-certain loss.

Importantly, how probable we believe something to be is often quite different to how probable it actually is. Imagine that a friend tells you they have bought one lottery ticket at a particular shop at a particular time, according to instructions they received in a dream where a talking penguin told them they were going to win the lottery. Their personal expectation is that they have purchased a winning ticket. This, however, makes no difference whatsoever to the rational expectation that someone in their position ought to have.

Probability doesn't care about perceptions: it's there to describe what it is actually most reasonable to expect in any given situation. It's also there to remind us that uncertainty is at least sometimes a quantifiable feature of the world, and that there are many different degrees of uncertainty: being unsure about something is not at all the same thing as knowing nothing.

How does this apply to induction? If there is a worse than 0.5 probability that an argument is false, then it is not inductively forceful: our rational expectation should be that it's more likely to be false than true. If there is a better than 0.5 probability it is true, then the argument is inductively forceful: it's more likely to be true than false. Sometimes we can calculate these odds precisely; sometimes it's a matter of estimation or investigation based on past experience or comparison to similar cases. Try it for yourself. In each of the following scenarios, do you find the argument inductively forceful or not?

	YES	NO
Every winter for 30 years my mother has gone somewhere warm on holiday. I guess she'll do the same thing once again this year.	○	○
On the day of my birthday, there has been a record high temperature for that month every year for the last three years. I guess it will happen again this year.	○	○

The first of these arguments seems inductively forceful. Unless there is some other information we don't know, it seems more likely than not that my mother will once again do something she has deliberately done every winter for 30 years. It's thus rational for you to assume she will do this. The second argument, however, is not inductively forceful. Three instances of a record temperature on a particular day do not make a fourth instance on that same day more likely than not. It's in the very nature of exceptional results that they are rare. The 'pattern' suggesting this assumption is most likely simply to be coincidence.

SMART STUDY: Making sure you're not fooled by probability

It's important to get to grips with probability, both because it offers a way of thinking carefully about uncertainty and because it doesn't come naturally to most people. Before you go any further, spend some time thinking through these key points:

- If there is no connection between two different events, then their individual probabilities can have no effect on one another. One fair coin toss has an equal chance of coming up heads or tails. So does the next toss. And the next. The previous result can be completely ignored when it comes to thinking about the next one.

- This doesn't apply if you are thinking about the probability of several things all turning out a certain way. In this situation, the probability of the end result comes from multiplying each individual event's probability. Every extra factor reduces the likelihood of them all turning out a particular way. One fair coin toss has an equal chance of coming up heads or tails. Two coin tosses have a one-in-four chance of coming up heads and heads. Three tosses have a one-in-eight chance of coming up heads, heads and heads.
- The more precise a result you're looking for, the less likely it is to happen. For example, it is less likely that every subject sitting a test will get full marks than it is that half the subjects will get full marks, which is less likely than one person doing so.
- Similarly, a more specific scenario is always less likely to happen than a general scenario which encompasses that specific scenario. It is, for example, inevitably less likely that someone chosen from a crowd at random owns a blue car than that they own any car.
- Just because something seems striking to a human observer doesn't make it remarkable. Six sixes are exactly as likely to come up as any other dice throw: the fact that they attract more attention has no effect upon this.
- Coincidences only seem astonishing because we ignore those millions upon millions of daily events that don't strike us as astonishing. Rare and unlikely things happen all the time.

MAKING USE OF SAMPLES

Induction is a process of generalization. It moves from the particular to the general, and this makes the concept of **sampling** important. A sample consists of some particular cases you are examining in order to make generalizations about a larger shared feature, trend or regularity.

Sample: the particular cases you are using to stand for the entire category about which you wish to make an inductive generalization

If I'm investigating feline behaviour, I might use my pet cat, Basil, to stand for cats in general – and I might make an inductive argument along the following lines. Is this a weak or a strong inductive argument?

	WEAK	STRONG
My pet cat, Basil, is very shy and will only let himself be stroked by people he knows. Therefore, cats are shy animals and will only let people they know stroke them.	○	○

This is not a very strong inductive argument, because there is only a single cat in my sample. In research, the letter **n** is often used to denote sample size, in the form **n = 1** for a sample of one, **n = 100** for a sample of 100, and so on. Because one is the smallest possible sample size, the phrase **n = 1** has become a kind of shorthand for the fact that an anecdote involving a single instance will almost inevitably produce a weak inductive argument.

n = 1: a sample size of one indicates an anecdote rather than a serious investigation; any inductive argument based on a single instance is likely to be very weak

If someone tells you 'my uncle smoked every day of his life, and he lived to the age of 90: how can it be bad for you?' then the correct (if impolite) answer is that basing this conclusion on a sample size of one is an extraordinarily bad way to think about health issues.

So far as cats are concerned, my argument would be much stronger if it were based on a larger sample. In general, it is true to say that:

- The larger the sample, the more reliable it tends to be as a representation of the whole. Inductive arguments based on small samples are likely to be far weaker than those based on large samples.

I wish that I did actually do this...

It is not enough, however, simply to use a large sample and assume this makes your assessments correct. Imagine that I run a website that's all about coffee. I want to know how many people prefer coffee to tea, so I put a survey on the site under the title 'Tom's Big Coffee Survey', inviting people to click and answer a few questions about their beverage preferences. Here is a summary of my results:

> In a recent survey of over 2000 people, an astonishing 80 per cent named coffee as their favourite hot drink – over four times as many as prefer tea – and over half named it as their favourite among all drinks, beating even alcoholic beverages. Coffee is officially the biggest drink in the country!

Representative samples closely resemble the larger group about which claims are being made, while unrepresentative samples fail to do so

Can you see what might be wrong with my making these claims? The problem is that I run a website that's all about coffee. Although over 2000 people responded, every single one of these responses comes from *someone who both visited a specialist coffee website and then decided to participate in a survey about coffee.*

Randomized sample: one selected at random from across a field of study, with no particular element misleadingly over-represented

Is this particular group of people likely to represent the views of the population as a whole? No. My claim that coffee is 'officially' the biggest drink in the country is ridiculous. All I can legitimately claim is that 'coffee appears to be the biggest drink among readers of my coffee website who decided to take part in a survey about coffee'. This is because I have used an **unrepresentative sample** – one that, while quite large, is a poor representation of the overall population I'm making claims about.

A good sample should be as **representative** as possible, meaning that it closely resembles the larger group about which general claims are being made. This brings us to the most important question of all: how can we ensure we are using a representative sample?

Sampling bias: biases introduced by imperfect methods of selecting a sample

There's no easy answer to this, partly because no sample is ever perfectly representative. In general, the best samples are both as large as possible and successfully **randomized** from across the entire field of study, meaning that the sample is randomly selected from all possible cases of interest, using a method that does not bias the results.

Observational error: errors due to the accuracy of your measuring system, usually reported as ±X, where X is the potential difference between measured and actual values

Because no sample is ever perfectly representative, it's important to remain aware of both potential sources of **sampling bias** and the degrees of error involved in your investigation. Errors are inevitable in all samples and measurements, and are not the same thing as mistakes.

The **observational error** relates to the accuracy of your measuring system, and is usually expressed in the form 'plus or minus X' where X is the potential difference between measured and actual values. For example, if you are using a set of scales you know to be accurate to within ten grams, your results should be reported as '±10g' – and should never be reported to apparent fractions of a gram, which might give a false idea of accuracy.

Take it slowly – this stuff isn't easy.

Margin of error: an expression of the degree to which results based on a sample are likely to differ from those of the overall population

The **margin of error** is more complex and expresses the greatest expected difference between the results you've obtained from your sample and the results you might have got had you been able to test the entire population. Typically, this takes the form of '±X with a confidence level of Y%', meaning 'if we kept on repeating this test, then Y% of the time the results from our sample would be within X of the entire population's results'. For example, if you reported that a survey in your research had a margin of error of '±5% with a confidence level of 80%', this means that you believe your results would fall within 5 per cent of the total population's results 80 per cent of the time.

Potential sources of sampling bias to be avoided – or to be aware of in others' investigations – include:

- **Self-selection**: setting up your sample in such a way that a certain type of participant effectively selects themselves. For instance, the kind of person most likely to fill in a detailed survey may differ substantially from the population at large.
- **Specific area selection**: selecting your sample so that one particular area is over-represented. For example, conducting research into global urban population trends based only on statistics gathered in London and New York.
- **Exclusion**: selecting your sample in a way that disproportionately excludes certain elements. For instance, conducting a wildlife survey only during daylight hours might exclude nocturnal animals.
- **Pre-screening**: conducting your sample selection via an initial method that is likely to select only a certain kind of participant – for example, only advertising for volunteers to participate in a health trial in hospital waiting rooms.
- **Survivorship**: a sample that considers only successes can be highly biased if failures are also relevant. For instance, an investigation of business debts that looked only at companies with more than ten years of accounts would entirely ignore all companies that had failed within a shorter period.

Each of the following examples has at least one major problem in its sampling methodology. Try to identify the problem in each case:

1 To test pollution in a lake, I took 20 water samples at different times of day from one spot on the beach next to my lab. ....
2 To test pollution in a lake, I took three water samples from three different locations spaced throughout the site. ....
3 In order to find out whether literacy was in decline, I included my questionnaire about reading habits with every copy of a monthly political magazine. ....
4 My first major experiment about motivation levels in the general population involved a cohort of 50 student volunteers from Harvard Business School. ....

In the first example, taking every sample from a single spot makes them less likely to be representative of the entire lake – even though it's a good idea to take 20, and to take them at different times of day.

In the second example, it's a good idea to take samples from three different locations – but three is a very small number of samples to use in order to represent an entire lake.

In the third example, including a questionnaire about literacy in a monthly magazine is likely to get responses from people who are unrepresentative of the population as a whole: the kind of people who not only read a monthly political magazine but also take the time to respond to literacy surveys.

The final example too is unlikely to represent the general population accurately, because the kind of people who are both studying at Harvard Business School and volunteer to take part in experiments seem likely to be more motivated than the population as a whole – and also likely to represent a narrower spectrum of traits such as age, wealth and education.

Here's an improved sampling methodology for each of the three studies (the first and second examples being taken from the same one):

1+2 To test pollution in a lake, we took samples each day over the course of a year from 50 randomly selected sites across the lake at a variety of depths.

3 In order to investigate whether literacy was in decline, I gathered comparable data from the last 50 years across a representative sample of 100 schools.

4 My first major experiment about motivation levels in the general population involved a telephone poll conducted across a representative sample of 500 adults.

None of the above techniques are perfect, but they all represent an improvement and make it more likely that inductive inferences will meaningfully apply to the whole.

SMART STUDY: Picking a representative sample in four steps

Picking a representative sample means considering as fully as possible the variations that exist within whatever population you're studying, or the range of circumstances you're examining. Understanding the basic principles of successful, methodical sampling is vital for social scientists, and extremely useful for everyone else. In general, good sample design will:

- Establish as thoroughly and accurately as possible the specifics of the target population: without this, there is no way of knowing what variations you need to represent.
- Determine an appropriate sample size: in general, a larger sample size is better, but the exact size you need depends on how confident you need to be in your result, the level of variability within the population you're studying, the margin of error in your measurements and the proportion of the population displaying whatever attribute you're interested in (there are plenty of good online tools for calculating sample sizes).
- Determine an appropriate sampling method: this depends on what you're studying and on what resources you have at your disposal; all methods have their limitations, and range from relatively simple 'convenience' samples based on volunteers or case studies to more complex 'multi-stage' samples based on dividing a population into clusters, and then selecting clusters at random for close examination.
- Consider whether results need weighting: this entails giving more weight to certain results within your sample in order to better reflect the overall situation: for example, giving adults twice the weight of children in a piece of research exploring transit costs, on the basis that adults' tickets cost twice as much as children's tickets.[10]

THE PROBLEM OF INDUCTION

The best an inductive argument can ever do is suggest that something is very, very likely. This can be confusing, because most of the time we work on the basis that very, very likely things are effectively certain. Consider this famous example of an inductive argument:

> Every day for millions of years, the sun has risen. Thus, the sun will rise tomorrow morning.

As the 18th-century philosopher David Hume pointed out,[11] all of us believe that the sun will rise tomorrow: we act as though this had a probability of one. Yet this apparent fact is something we cannot prove with absolute certainty, any more than I can say something like this with absolute certainty:

> I have been alive every day for the last 10,000 days; thus, I will always be alive.

Some day, I will die. Or – to put it in truly rigorous inductive terms – it is much, much more likely that I will die at some point than that I will live forever. Similarly, a day will almost certainly come when the sun itself no longer exists. Hopefully, this will happen many millions of years from now. Yet, it could also be tomorrow.

We can put this another way, by noting that, although it will always be a perfectly valid deductive argument to say – 'For millions of years, the sun has risen; every single day in the future will conform to this pattern; so the sun will always rise' – at a certain point, this will cease to be a sound deductive argument. Eventually, the premise that the sun's future will eternally resemble its past will cease to be true.

The fact that something happened in the past cannot guarantee that it will happen in the future, no matter how many times it has happened, is sometimes known as **the problem of induction**. It is theoretically possible that I might never die, or that the sun might exist for ever and ever. It's just very, very, very, very unlikely, based on our current understanding of the universe.

The problem of induction: no matter how likely we believe something to be, an inductive argument can never actually prove it to be true

To this, you might reasonably say: this is just a made-up problem for philosophers to talk about. Nobody – not even philosophers – actually talk about the world like this! We do not say, 'the sun is very likely to rise tomorrow, but there is a tiny chance the world might end'. I do not say, 'I will almost certainly meet you at Starbucks tomorrow at 2pm, apart from the small chance that I die or am incapacitated before then'.

Even in science and research, the same is true. We say, 'the flame heats the water' – not 'the flame is very likely to heat the water based on past experience'. We accept countless things as facts based on experience and consensus without feeling the need to constantly invoke probability. Why, then, does it matter that inductive reasoning is always concerned with probability rather than certainty? There are at least two important ways in which remembering this can make us better thinkers, researchers and writers:

- It helps us realize that many things we take for granted are not necessarily the whole truth, and that everyday thinking often ignores or under-estimates the uncertainties of the world.
- It allows us to avoid a misleading method of research that simply involves seeking confirmation of an idea, and instead to think rigorously about how likely something is to be true – and how we might most thoroughly test this through **falsification**.

Falsification: the contradiction of something previously accepted as true or obvious

INDUCTION AND FALSIFICATION

Here is a famous example of the way in which inductive reasoning can lead us into error – the error of overconfidence when using past experience as a basis for general conclusions:

> Every swan ever observed has been white. Therefore, all swans are white.

Counter-example: an example whose discovery makes it necessary to rethink a particular position, because it directly contradicts a generalization previously believed to be true

This was believed to be true for many centuries in Europe – until the exploration of Australia, at which point a black species of swans was first glimpsed by Europeans (in 1697, during a Dutch voyage along its west coast). The sample of swans available to Europeans did not, it turned out, accurately represent the entire global population of swans. The global swan population actually existed across a wider range of possibilities than had previously been imagined.[12]

It only takes one strong **counter-example** like this to falsify an inductive line of reasoning. Here, the discovery of a black species of swan demanded changes to all existing European beliefs around

FOUR

KNOW YOUR LIMITS. DON'T PRETEND TO KNOW WHAT YOU DON'T KNOW. PRACTICE SAYING: I DON'T KNOW, I HAVEN'T READ THAT, I NEED TO FIND OUT MORE. SEEK OUT OTHERS' EXPERTISE. BUT REMEMBER: EXPERTISE IS ALWAYS SPECIFIC.

#TalkCriticalThinking

what a swan was After 1697, it became necessary to replace the earlier generalization with something along these lines:

> Every European swan ever observed has been white. Therefore, all European swans can be assumed to be white. But we now know that there are black swans, in Australia. Therefore, being white seems not to be a defining characteristic of all swans, only of European swans.

In this example, both the strengths and weaknesses of inductive reasoning are evident. The weakness is summed up by the phrase a **black swan**, which is now used to describe anything that lies so far outside previous experience and assumptions that it shows that a generalization previously thought to be true cannot be the case. The 2008 financial crisis was labelled a black swan by some in the finance industry, because it was something that lay entirely outside the expectations created by their previous experience.

Black swan event: an event that defies both previous experience and expectations based on that experience, making it almost impossible to predict

The strength of a rigorous approach to inductive reasoning lies in the fact that even a black swan event can be learned from – and that, as when Europeans rethought their definition of a swan after 1697, we can use new evidence to produce a better description of the way things are.

Indeed, we can go further than this and argue that – given that inductive methods can never leave us in a position of absolute certainty – the most valuable kind of inductive reasoning actively sets out to invite falsification rather than seek confirmation.

Why is seeking falsification better than confirmation? Because evidence can be found to support any theory at all, whether it is correct or not. If I am determined to prove that all swans are white, I can point to a million white swans while ignoring anything that contradicts my belief. If a Dutch explorer returns from Australia with tales of black swan-like birds, I can simply laugh and dismiss his reports, saying that everyone knows swans are white. After all, I have personally seen one million white swans.

If, however, I am genuinely interested in coming up with the best possible account of what a swan is, the possible discovery of a black swan represents a wonderful opportunity for improving my concept of swans – because it falsifies an existing account of the way things are, creating the opportunity for me to come up with a new account that corresponds more closely with the real world.

THINK ABOUT THIS: What other examples of black swan events can you think of from history or from your own experience? When has new information completely falsified something that people had simply assumed to be true? ....

....

....

....

....

....

Bearing in mind that the most important evidence you can gather is that which potentially falsifies a theory, here's a famous puzzle for you to try. Imagine there are four playing cards in a row in front of you. Each of them has a single patch of colour on one side and a number on the other – but you can only see the upturned sides. You are allowed to turn over as many or as few of the cards as you like in order to find out whether this particular rule applies to all of these cards:

> If a card has an even number on one side, then it must have the colour yellow on the opposite side.

The upturned sides of the four cards show an eight, a three, a yellow patch and a grey patch – as in the diagram below. *What card or cards must you turn over in order to test this rule, using the fewest steps possible?*

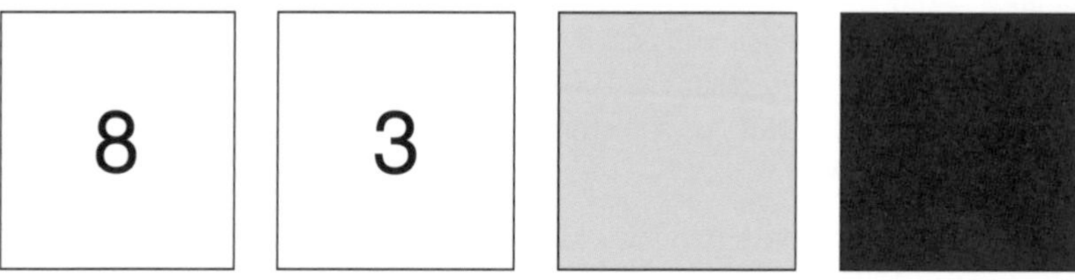

Before I tell you the answer, it's worth mentioning that when it was first devised as an experiment in 1966 around 90 per cent of people got this puzzle wrong. It's called the Wason Selection Task after the cognitive psychologist Peter Cathcart Wason, who designed it to explore the ways in which people struggle with logical reasoning.[13]

If this is the first time you've attempted this puzzle, and haven't yet looked at the answer, here is a hint: you need to turn over exactly two cards in order to test the rule, one showing a colour, one showing a number. Does this match your answer? If not, go back and think again before reading the next paragraph.

Ready? The answer is that you need to turn over the card showing the eight, and the grey card. Why? Because these are the only two cards capable of falsifying the rule.

We have said that a card with an even number on it will be yellow on the other side. Three is not an even number, so the card with the three on cannot test the rule: the rule doesn't say anything about odd numbers also having yellow on the other side.

Similarly, no matter what number is on the other side of the yellow card, it cannot falsify the rule. If the number is even, then the rule holds; but if the number is odd, we simply have an example of an odd number that also has yellow on the other side.

The other two cards can falsify the rule, however, and so we need to test them both. If the eight has anything other than yellow on its back, the rule is falsified – so we must turn it over to see. And if the grey card has an even number on its back, the rule is also falsified – because even numbers are not allowed to have any colour other than yellow on their backs.

The Wason Selection Task is both a tricky logic problem and an exercise in gathering evidence to test a theory. In this, it's a useful starting point for both thinking about induction and what it means to move beyond straightforward induction towards scientific notions of theories and proof: the subject of our next chapter.

SUMMARY

When applying **inductive reasoning**, you are dealing with degrees of certainty rather than absolutes; you are looking for reasons that suggest a conclusion is likely to be true. Inductive reasoning is sometimes known as **ampliative reasoning**, to spell out the fact that its conclusions are an 'amplification' of its premises:

- One important skill is **ranking** inductive arguments according to how convincing they are.
- In general, good inductive reasoning is based on well-established patterns with consistent supporting evidence, while weaker inductive reasoning results from poor evidence, no clear patterns, or a high degree of unpredictability and complexity.

When talking about how convincing an inductive argument is, we use the idea of **inductive strength**, also known as **inductive force**:

- A **cogent** inductive argument is one that has a good structure, but whose conclusion we should not necessarily accept as true, because we are unsure about the truth of its premises (similar to a valid deductive argument).
- An **inductively forceful** argument is one that has both a good structure and premises we accept as true, meaning we also have good reasons to accept its conclusion as true (similar to a sound deductive argument, although without its certainty).

Inductive reasoning requires us to spell out the **implicit qualifications** in a premise: when a general statement is not literally true, we need to indicate whether it applies to a few, most or some cases; or often, sometimes, or infrequently.

Probability is the study of how likely something is to happen or to be true:

- Probability is usually expressed on a scale between zero and one, where a zero probability is entirely impossible and a probability of one is a certainty. A probability of 0.5 is equally likely to happen or not, while values above 0.5 are more likely than not and values below 0.5 are less likely.
- Assessing **rational expectation** is a key question around inductive arguments. Rational expectation asks: assuming the premises are true, is it more reasonable for you to expect an inductive argument's conclusion to be true or false?

Making use of **samples** is a vital part of inductive reasoning. A sample consists of the particular cases you are examining in order to make larger generalizations:

- In general, the larger the sample, the better. A sample tends to be expressed in research through the letter **n**, where **n = 1** indicates a sample of one – an anecdote based on a single instance.
- A **representative sample** is one that closely resembles the larger group it is taken from, while an **unrepresentative sample** is one that does not. Inductions based on an unrepresentative sample are likely to be distorted compared to reality.
- A successfully **randomized sample** is one of the best ways of escaping bias in sampling, and means selecting elements of the sample at random from across the entire field of study, with no particular element misleadingly over-represented.
- Because no sample is ever perfectly representative, it's important to be aware of the **margin of error** (the chance that the result from a survey is the same as in the overall population) and **observational error** (the accuracy of your measuring system).

The **problem of induction** describes the fact that, no matter how likely we believe something to be, no inductive argument can ever actually be **confirmed** – it can only seek **refutation** and **counter-examples**:

- **Falsification** is an important investigative process for inductive reasoning, because a single **counter-example** can prove that an inductive line of reasoning is false – while no amount of positive instances can ever actually confirm one.
- A **black swan** is something that defies all previous experience, and the expectations based on that experience, making it almost impossible to predict.

Now watch the video 'The importance of proving people wrong'. It's on YouTube. Tell me what you think via #TalkCriticalThinking

DEVELOPING EXPLANATIONS AND THEORIES

Why does reasoning matter (and how can you spot an argument)?

↓

How do you spell out the reasoning behind an argument?

↓

How do you draw out a logical conclusion from your premises?

↓

How do you draw out a probable conclusion from your premises?

↓

How can you select and test the best explanation of something?

↓

How should you assess evidence and plan your reading strategy?

All about the scientific method

How it works. Why it matters.

Discovery commences with the awareness of anomaly.

Thomas Kuhn

#TalkCriticalThinking

FIVE THINGS YOU'LL LEARN IN THIS CHAPTER

1 How to tell the difference between *explanations, theories* and *hypotheses*
2 How to apply standards of *proof* and *significance*
3 How to distinguish between *correlation* and *causation*
4 How to analyse and apply the *scientific method*
5 How to *choose a research question* and develop your own ideas

In 1620, the polymathematical English philosopher Francis Bacon published a book entitled *Novum Organum Scientiarum* – Latin for 'the new instrument of science' – in which he argued that reasoning on the basis of established ideas and texts was insufficient for understanding the world. Instead, Bacon made the case for **empirical** thinking.[14]

Empiricism: a way of thinking about the world rooted in the precise observation of what you can verify with your own senses, and investigate through experience and observation

Empiricism means basing your knowledge on immediate experience. It entails the principled application of inductive reasoning: seeking strong justifications for conclusions based on careful observation and extrapolation. But it also entails a further form of reasoning that's essential to both the modern scientific method and to how we think about the world: developing theories about what trends, causes and laws lie behind things, and testing these theories by further observation.

The 17th century was a golden age for scientific discovery, seeing, among other things, Galileo's discovery of the planet Jupiter's moons, Newton's laws of motion and gravitation, William Harvey's work on the heart and the circulation of blood, Robert Boyle's foundational work in modern chemistry, Robert Hooke's microscopic observations of cells and tiny organisms, and the founding of the Royal Society in London. New observations and ways of thinking fed new ideas about the nature of the universe, and helped usher in what is widely known as the Scientific Revolution.

The kind of theorizing that accompanied these leaps in human understanding is sometimes known as **abductive reasoning** – meaning 'to lead away from'. This is a form of reasoning that seeks to find the best possible explanations for things: moving from specific evidence to a theory about why things are the way they are.[15]

Abductive reasoning: sometimes known as 'inference to the best explanation', this seeks to establish the best possible explanation for something believed to be true

INTRODUCING ABDUCTION

Once we have asserted some things we believe to be true, abductive reasoning asks the question: 'what is the most likely cause of these things?' Some people class abduction as a form of argument, and talk about 'abductive arguments', while others simply classify abduction as a form of reasoning. For the purposes of this book, I've treated abduction as a form of reasoned explanation.

Like induction, abduction deals with uncertainty and leaps of inference rather than pure logic. Where an inductive argument draws out what is claimed to be a reasonable generalization from its premises, however, abductive reasoning draws out what is claimed to be a reasonable explanation. You could say that abduction is a kind of rationally inspired guesswork – an intuitive leap based on the best evidence available, creating an explanatory model that can then be subjected both to deductive analysis and inductive prediction. Here is one of history's most famous examples of abduction in action:

> After dinner one warm evening, Isaac Newton went into the garden with a friend and sat drinking tea under the shade of some apple trees. Why, he wondered, did the apples falling from the tree always descend exactly at right angles to the ground? Why didn't they go sideways – or upwards? Why did they seem so determined to head directly towards the centre of the Earth?

This story, based on a 1752 account by the friend who was sitting with Newton that day, describes the moment when Newton's theory of gravity was apparently inspired by watching how apples fell from a tree.[16] What, Newton asked himself, might explain why every single object – apples included – fell directly towards the Earth, rather than at an angle towards it? Could it be that a mutual attraction existed between the Earth and apples, and indeed between all objects, based on some mysterious property of attraction contained within matter itself?

Like any scientist, Newton drew on the cumulative insights of many other minds!

Arriving at questions such as these took much more than watching fruit, of course. But Newton's ability to ask the right questions – and then to answer them in a rigorous yet astonishingly elegant manner – resulted in a theory far more powerful and accurate than anything that had come before it: one that would endure for centuries before being superseded.

Taking Newton's apple as an example, let's consider how the three different types of reasoning we have examined in the last few chapters might be applied to such a situation:

Deduction All objects that are denser than air fall directly downwards, towards the Earth. All apples are denser than air. So the apples in this tree will fall directly downwards, towards the Earth.

Induction All the apples I have ever seen falling from trees have fallen directly downwards to Earth. So, these apples will also almost certainly fall directly downwards to Earth.

Abduction The apples in this tree, like all other falling objects I've seen, are falling directly downwards to Earth. Why is this? Perhaps because the matter that makes up all objects – including apples and the Earth – itself generates a force that creates this attraction.

And here is a more general explanation of each form of reasoning:

Deduction The conclusion is a direct, logical consequence of the premises. If the argument is valid and the premises are true, then the argument is sound: the conclusion must also be true.

Induction The conclusion is supported by the premises, but cannot be proved to be true. If the argument is well structured and the premises are true, it is inductively forceful: it's reasonable to accept it as true.

Abduction We are seeking the best available explanation for the premises. If this is the simplest available explanation that fits in with all known facts, then it's reasonable to accept it (or to start testing it).

Notice that a sound deductive argument, a forceful inductive argument and a successful abductive explanation occupy common ground – they must fit in with what we know to be true, and they aspire towards further truths on its basis.

It all goes together!

Far from being divergent or opposed, our three modes of reasoning are intimately connected in any scientific investigation of the world. First, a theory or hypothesis is developed through an abductive leap. Second, deductive reasoning carefully analyses the logical implications of this theory. Third, inductive predictions are made that allow this theory and its consequences to be tested. Finally, the results of these tests are fed back into the model – leading to its adjustment, abandonment or adoption.

SMART STUDY: Applying abductive reasoning in eight simple steps

Every time you ask the question 'what is the best explanation for this?' you are applying abductive reasoning. Handling this effectively in essays and research can entail some or all of the following steps, which map out the structure of a basic research methodology. You can use the following frame as a kind of scaffolding for building a paper, section by section:

1 Begin with as precise an account as possible of something that needs explaining.
2 Suggest why it would be significant or interesting to explain this.
3 Present a possible explanation in the form of a theory or hypothesis.
4 Suggest either an experimental method or a non-experimental approach, drawing on diverse sources of evidence, suitable for testing your theory/hypothesis.
5 Investigate whether your explanation does manage to account for (or has successfully predicted) the evidence you have gathered.
6 Acknowledge whether any other explanation or explanations might more convincingly account for your evidence or results.
7 Acknowledge the limitations of your research.
8 Outline possible future investigations to further test and refine your theory – or to seek something different if it has proven unsuccessful.

A model research method

EXPLANATIONS, THEORIES AND HYPOTHESES

'Abduction' itself is a clumsy and uncommon word – with the unfortunate habit of sounding like something unfriendly aliens might do. In its place, you'll more often encounter terms like **explanations**, **theories** and **hypotheses**. These can sound intimidatingly formal, but in fact they're all variations on the same basic idea: trying, with various degrees of precision, to show why things are the way they are.

Explanation: any attempt, formally or informally, to explain something

Theory: a general explanation of the underlying nature of a phenomenon

Hypothesis: a precise, testable prediction designed to allow the rigorous investigation of a theory

An explanation is the most general term of all: it describes any attempt to explain something, whether informally or formally, badly or well. A theory is a larger and more abstract idea than an explanation: it tries to say something about the underlying nature of a particular phenomenon. Finally, a hypothesis is a precisely testable formulation of a theory, designed to allow you to investigate it in a rigorous and controlled way. Importantly, a scientific theory that has been tested and refined in this manner is not 'just' a theory in the ordinary sense of the word: it explains natural phenomena in a manner that is widely accepted, supported by detailed evidence and investigation, and that helps us predict and understand the results of future investigations. Here's an example of each one in practice:

Explanation	The planets orbit the sun because of gravity.
Theory	All matter is attracted towards other matter by gravitational force, in proportion to the quantity of matter involved.
Hypothesis	It will be possible to explain unexpected perturbations in the orbit of one of the planets in the solar system using Newton's theory of gravitation.

Scientific method: the systematic empirical investigation of the world through observation, experiment and measurement, together with the development, testing and reformulation of theories

Not all research relies on hypotheses – sometimes it is better to take a more open approach to exploring a research question – but formulating a testable hypothesis is an important skill in many fields, from medicine to psychology to anthropology to economics. Even philosophers come up with the occasional testable hypothesis.

In the best tests, we make a prediction that creates an opportunity for falsification, and we set out our method with enough clarity and transparency to allow others to attempt an independent replication of our results. These three ideas lie at the heart of the **scientific method**:

Null hypothesis: the exact opposite of the hypothesis you're testing – seeing whether you can falsify a null hypothesis is a common way of ensuring rigour in research

1 Replication: can the results we're basing our theory on be reproduced?
2 Prediction: what predictions can we make on the basis of this theory?
3 Falsification: what evidence is capable of falsifying this theory?

This commonly means making use of a **null hypothesis** in order to explicitly put an attempt at falsification at the heart of an investigation. A null hypothesis is the opposite of a particular hypothesis: it describes the thing you need to disprove if a hypothesis is to be accepted. In the case of our gravitational example, a null hypothesis might go like this:

> Unexpected perturbations in the orbit of one of the known planets in the solar system cannot be explained by Newton's theory of gravitation.

In 1846, the mathematician Urbain-Jean-Joseph Le Verrier contradicted this particular null hypothesis when he predicted both the size and location of a previously unknown planet based on his observations of Uranus's slightly perturbed orbit. Having made his prediction, he wrote to the Berlin Observatory with the details. A new planet, dubbed Neptune, was almost immediately discovered by the astronomer Johann Galle exactly where Le Verrier had said it would be – an astonishing triumph for mathematical prediction.

Newton's theory of gravitation had been demonstrated, in spectacular style, to be the best theory available for understanding the universe's laws of motion. In other words, although Newton's theory could never be confirmed as absolutely certain, it had proved itself to be by far the most robust functional account of the universe – one that had survived countless rigorous tests by scientists, and successfully predicted observations in a way no other theory could match.

Newton's theory led in due course to further and equally compelling predictions. As astronomers' Observations of the solar system continued to improve, it became clear that there were also slight anomalies in the orbit of the planet Mercury. This, surely, pointed towards the existence of another unknown planet, between Mercury and the Sun! For decades, mathematicians and astronomers looked for this object – dubbed Vulcan – as predicted by Newton's theory of gravitation.

Yet it was the null hypothesis that ultimately won. In 1915, a scientist called Albert Einstein stood in front of the Prussian Academy delivering a lecture on a new theory of gravitation, able to explain all the known data about Mercury's orbit without relying on a hidden, other planet.

Known as general relativity, Einstein's theory demolished centuries of growing certainty around the rightness of Newtonian physics – and ushered in a new theoretical era that itself demanded updating within a few decades, thanks to the insights of quantum electrodynamics and other relativistic delights.[17]

This is the point of working theories and falsification. The search for that which cannot be explained by what we currently know is what drives new knowledge – and ensures that those things we think we know have passed the best tests we can throw at them.

MOVING TOWARDS BETTER EXPLANATIONS

Abductive reasoning is sometimes defined as 'inference to the best explanation'.[18] But what defines one explanation as better than another? As we briefly explored in the second chapter, a good explanation should do two things:

- Successfully explain all the things that we already know
- Be as simple as possible while still explaining everything.

This in turn suggests that there are two key criteria we can use for challenging, and for choosing between, different lines of abductive reasoning:

- We can find new evidence that existing abductive reasoning cannot explain.
- We can come up with a simpler line of abductive reasoning that explains everything.

The way to do RESEARCH is to ATTACK the FACTS at the point of GREATEST ASTONISHMENT.

Celia Green

#TalkCriticalThinking

Compare the two following explanations for an unexpected result discovered during the course of an experiment conducted by two undergraduate researchers. According to the criteria above, which explanation might you use as a better model for applying abductive reasoning in your own work?

> In our study, users who self-identified as 'inexperienced with tablets and apps' were more prone to making simple errors during our first round of testing via a tablet-based app. This may be because consistently using software correctly in the case of a tablet-based app is dependent on a certain level of experience.

> In our study, users who self-identified as 'inexperienced with tablets and apps' were more prone to making simple errors during our first round of testing via a tablet-based app. This may be because such users are likely to have lower intellectual abilities than those with more experience, in turn making them more likely to commit simple errors in comparison to those whose greater experience suggests greater general intelligence.

Both explanations manage to account for the errors we're interested in, but the first one is better. This is because the second explanation involves more steps than the first.

Only one step is involved in the first explanation: that consistent performance on a tablet-based app is partly dependent on a certain level of experience using similar software and hardware. Compare this to the two connected steps involved in the second: that users who self-identify as inexperienced with tablets and apps have lower intellectual abilities than those who don't (the evidence itself does not tell us this, but we are asked to assume it); and that these lower intellectual abilities make such users more likely to commit simple errors.

Applying this principle of simplicity brings us back into the realm of probability. More things are being supposed by the second explanation than by the first – and in the absence of other information we can assume that two things both happening is less likely than just one thing happening.

Occam's razor: the principle that, when choosing between explanations, the simplest one is usually best – while more assumptions make something less likely to be true

This principle is sometimes known as **Occam's razor**, in honour of the 14th-century Franciscan friar William of Ockham, whose writing on logic led others to give his name to this 'principle of parsimony': the most reasonable explanation is never any more complex than is necessary.

Does this mean that we should now stop and accept our first explanation as final? No. Although we have explained all the information we began with, we know very little about the overall situation. A good explanation for some evidence is not necessarily a good explanation for all possible evidence. Before we accept an explanation, we thus need a high degree of confidence that there is:

- Neither a simpler explanation available, nor…
- …Some as-yet-unknown evidence likely to contradict our explanation.

What might you do to follow up in this particular case, in order to gather some evidence capable of either backing up or disproving our preferred explanation? There are several possibilities, but here is one suggestion:

> Our best current theory is that inexperienced tablet and app users made simple errors during our first round of testing because their lack of experience with similar software and hardware led to inconsistent performance. In order to investigate this further, we spoke to these users about their experience of the test, and whether adjusting its interface and presentation might help prevent simple errors.

And here is how you might report on a successful follow-up test:

> Inexperienced users were more prone to making errors during the course of our first experimental investigation. However, after the first steps of their instructions were rephrased to spell out more carefully how to use a simplified onscreen interface, these errors entirely vanished from subsequent test results. This strongly supports the theory that inexperience with tablets and apps led some users to make simple mistakes in the initial version of the experiment.

Did you have a different suggestion? If so, how might it have worked out in the same circumstances? Would it also have allowed you to test our theory satisfactorily?

THINK ABOUT THIS: What are some of the ways in which you apply abductive reasoning without really thinking about it: observing events, then assuming an explanation? Have there been any occasions when what you assumed to be the best explanation turned out to be incorrect? If so, why did you assume it was correct in the first place? ....
....
....
....
....
....

MOVING FROM EVIDENCE TO PROOF

Like inductive arguments, theories and explanations are always a matter of probability rather than certainty. Sometimes – as in court cases – a phrase like 'beyond reasonable doubt' may be enough for us to use as a rule of thumb. When it comes to more rigorous scientific explanations, however, it is often necessary to set a more precise **standard of proof** – a threshold that marks the dividing line between accepting and rejecting a theory.

Standard of proof: the threshold beyond which you have decided to accept something as proven, meaning you will not accept something as true if this standard is not met

In an experimental context, the concept of **statistical significance** is important. Including the word 'statistical' may make this sound abstract and mathematical, but in fact it describes a straightforward idea: the likelihood that a particular result could have occurred entirely by chance.

Statistical significance: the probability that a particular result was achieved entirely by chance, as opposed to having a noteworthy cause; setting a threshold for significance is the usual way of establishing a particular standard for proof in an experiment

As you'd expect, the less likely it is that something occurred by chance, the more likely it is that something real and noteworthy is going on. By contrast, a result that was likely to happen anyway proves very little. For example, someone telling you that their magic powder will protect you from abduction by aliens is probably not to be trusted, even if they observe that it has a 100 per cent success rate. Consider the following case:

> I have invented a dazzling smartphone app that allows me to predict the outcome of a coin toss while the coin is still in the air. Allow me to demonstrate. Take a coin out of your wallet and toss it. I will call the result the moment it leaves your hand and I promise that I will be correct! And I'll sell you the secret for ten million pounds.

How impressed would you be if you did as I said, tossed a coin, and I correctly predicted the outcome of ... 'heads!' ... the moment that the coin left your hand? Not very impressed, I imagine. After all, half the time I would get the correct result purely by luck.

In order to test my crazy claim about a magical smartphone app, you would need me to demonstrate a large number of correct predictions in a row. This is the simplest way for me to show that

I'm doing more than guessing – because, with every coin toss, it becomes more and more unlikely that I could keep on being correct simply through luck.

We can put this in terms of a hypothesis and a null hypothesis. The hypothesis you're exploring is that 'Tom's app can successfully predict the outcome of a coin toss every time'; and so the null hypothesis you are interested in disproving is 'Tom is simply guessing the result of a coin toss at random every time'.

How many times would you need me to correctly predict a coin toss before you accepted my magical app really worked? Five? Twenty? One thousand? We can explore this question by looking at how likely it is that I could continue to be correct purely through luck as more and more coins are tossed.

After the first coin toss, my chance of getting the correct result through luck is one in two: one-half. After the second, my chance of guessing both the first and the second results correctly through luck is one-half multiplied by a half – one quarter. After a third coin toss, my chance of guessing all three results correctly is now one in eight (we keep multiplying by one-half for each additional coin toss).

Here's a table showing the probability I am guessing correctly purely through luck up to ten tosses of a coin, expressed both as a fraction and as a decimal:

Number of tosses	Chance of guessing correctly each time through pure luck	Chance of guessing correctly through luck, expressed as a probability, where 1 = certain and 0 = impossible
1	1 in 2	0.5
2	1 in 4	0.25
3	1 in 8	0.125
4	1 in 16	0.0625
5	1 in 32	0.03125
6	1 in 64	0.015625
7	1 in 128	0.0078125
8	1 in 256	0.00390625
9	1 in 512	0.001953125
10	1 in 1024	0.0009765625

By the time I have reached ten correct predictions in a row, there is less than one chance in 1000 that I have been right every time simply through luck. At this point, you might decide that my magical app has met an impressive threshold for significance, and that you would like to own a copy at any cost.

p-value: the probability that an experiment's results came about through pure chance, expressed in the form of a decimal between one (certainty) and zero (impossibility)

Something is statistically significant if the probability that the results you're looking at were achieved simply by chance is lower than the level set in advance as your threshold for a belief: a level known in statistics as the **p-value** (short for probability-value). In the chart of coin tosses, the right-hand column gives the p-value for each outcome – the probability that this result arose purely by chance, on a scale between absolute certainty at one and total impossibility at zero.

Scientists often use a p-value of 0.05 as a threshold for research, meaning that for any result with a p-value lower than this, there is a better than 95 per cent chance that the results did not arise simply through chance.

Having 95 per cent confidence that your results are significant may sound very confident indeed, but it's worth remembering that this means that one experiment in every 20, with a 95 per cent chance of genuine results, is statistically likely to simply be lucky. People often forget this.

If you had set a p-value of 0.05 as the threshold for this particular test, how many correct coin tosses would it take me to reach this? Check the table. Four coin tosses isn't quite enough – the probability is 0.0625 – but by the time we reach five I have passed the 0.05 threshold. Assuming that you decided in advance on the much more demanding threshold of 0.001, how many throws would now be required? Check the table and see. It would take ten correct coin tosses in a row to achieve this level of significance. At this point, we might say:

> The results are significant at $p <= 0.001$.

This means that there is a better than one-in-a-thousand chance that the results are significant. Amazing! You'd better start raising that money. Unless, of course, you asked around and discovered that my friends and I had visited over 1000 people before we got to you, making similar claims every time about a coin-tossing app. Some cons actually work like this. Given sufficient reward, you can try something a thousand times with the hope of getting sufficiently lucky just once. In some circumstances, even a significance of better than one in 1000 may not be good enough.

CORRELATION AND CAUSATION

Assuming that the following claim is accurate, and based on accurate data, what do you make of it? Do you agree with it, or is there a reason to be cautious about this reasoning?

> The results of my analysis of economic productivity and high street spending patterns are clear. With a significance of better than $p = 0.05$ I have demonstrated a direct correlation between spending and productivity over the last decade, suggesting that how much people spend on the high street is heavily influenced by productivity – perhaps because, in a less productive economy, both consumer confidence and household finances are in a worse state.

Correlation: two trends that follow each other closely; the exact degree of correlation between two sets of information can be calculated through a variety of statistical methods

Causation: the assertion that one thing is the direct cause of another

As you may have guessed, the analysis above is nonsense. High street spending and productivity may be closely **correlated** – meaning that these two trends follow each other closely (literally, they are 'co-related') – but this does not demonstrate **causation** (meaning that one is actually caused by the other). What the paragraph above has demonstrated is the kind of wishful thinking that too often happens when someone notices a similarity between things – together with the extreme caution we should apply before asserting that things are directly **causally related**.

There is, for example, a close statistical relationship between new diagnoses of autism and sales of organic food in America. Just look at the graph below. As you can see, the two lines clearly represent two closely correlated variables. Does this mean that one causes the other? No. Most likely, it describes the fact that autism is diagnosed much more frequently than it used to be, thanks to far greater awareness of the condition, while eating organic food has grown increasingly popular as a lifestyle choice over the same period.

I can't prove that there is no causal link between autism diagnoses and organic food sales, any more than I can definitively prove that growing video game sales over the last four decades have caused the growth of India's population. I can, however, strongly suggest that there are better explanations for both these things – as well as plenty of evidence that cannot be explained by these particular theories of causation.

I can also strongly suggest that, especially given the ability of computers to search through vast amounts of data and draw graphs, it's almost laughably easy to find millions of highly correlated things that have no causal relationship whatsoever. Another favourite graph is below; the number of films in which Nicolas Cage appeared in a given year and the number of Americans who drowned by falling into a pool.

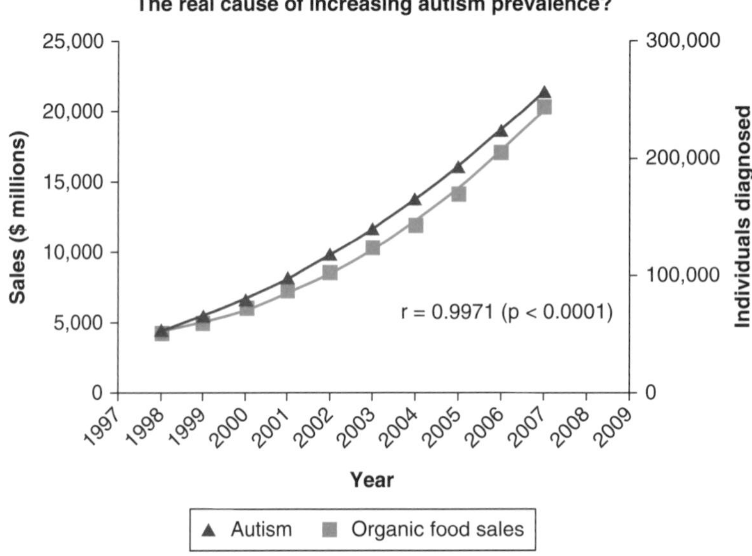

Sources: Organic Trade Association, 2011 Organic Industry Survey, US Department of Education, Office of Special Education Programs, Data Analysis System (DANS), OMB# 1820-0043: 'Children with Disabilities Receiving Special Education Under Part B of the Individuals with Disabilities Education Act'

Source: Spurious Correlations, tylervigen.com

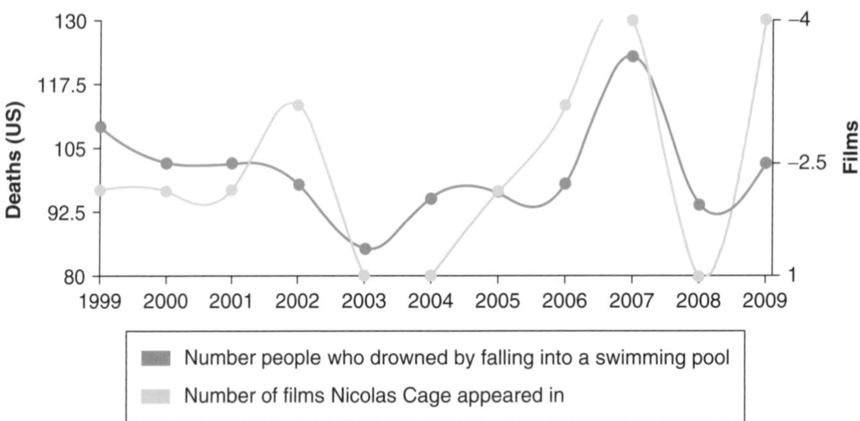

Source: Spurious Correlations, tylervigen.com

The Nicolas Cage/swimming pool example may sound too absurd to believe for a moment, but it's worth noting just how easy it is to look at any similar graph and to assume, without bothering to read the details, that the two variables shown must be related simply based on appearance. The impact of the image is instant and persuasive: you see only what somebody wants you to see, and not the thousands of other factors they have ignored before finding this correlation.

If the above examples still sound impossible to take seriously, you don't have to look very far through any news or current affairs resource to realize that, if one noteworthy thing happens after another, the first thing is often automatically treated as the cause of the second. Imagine reading this news article an hour after a speech by the British prime minister:

> Disappointed by the prime minister's weak stance on manufacturing, the markets fell sharply after she finished her speech.

It may be that the prime minister's speech did indeed directly cause the markets to fall. Then again, it may be that lots of very complicated factors control the rise and fall of markets, but that discussing these doesn't make a very engaging story. Now imagine that the markets rallied and rose sharply three hours after the article above came out. The same news source might now say this:

> After an initial fall, the markets rallied and rose sharply following the prime minister's speech, inspired by her calm consistency on manufacturing policy.

Is this any more likely to be true than the first analysis? No. It's an exercise in story-telling, based on an oversimplified and highly selective reading of a complex situation. But such exercises can be far more persuasive than a careful attempt to say what's really going on.

SMART STUDY: When correlation is not causation

It's very common to fall into the trap of equating causation with correlation: of seeing two variables that follow each other closely, or one thing following immediately on from another, and deciding that one must thus be the other's cause. Before you make any assumption of causation, ensure you have first ruled out all of these other possibilities:

1 **A third factor**: this is one of the most common sources of confusion around correlation, and it occurs when a third factor is the underlying cause of two other things that look closely related. For example, the price of your car and the size of your house may be closely correlated, but this doesn't mean that one has caused the other. Both are themselves probably caused by a third, underlying factor: your wealth.
2 **Advantage but not cause**: one thing does have a substantial influence on another, but it's not causal. For instance, it is not just a coincidence that lots of very tall people play professional basketball. Being very tall makes you more likely to succeed as a professional basketball player, while it's tough to succeed if you're short. Yet height is neither absolutely essential nor sufficient: most tall people aren't good at basketball, and becoming good requires plenty of other factors to be in place.
3 **Entwined cause and effect**: the relationship between two things may be real, but both elements may be continually affecting one another. For example, there is a close relationship between inflation and unemployment, but they are both causes and effects at the same time, that is, each continually affects the other.
4 **Pure chance**: plenty of things are correlated simply by chance, and no meaningful relationship of any kind exists between them. For instance, the number of different beers brewed in America has increased over the last decade, and so has national debt. But neither one is likely to have a meaningful relationship with the other.
5 **Statistical manipulation**: an apparently impressive correlation can be the result of the selective use of statistics, where only the data that shows a desired result is discussed. For example, a small sample of dieters who lost huge amounts of weight might be widely discussed in a diet company's promotional literature, while several other studies in which dieters didn't lose weight are never published.
6 **Confusing cause and effect**: it's possible for two things to be correlated, but for you to confuse which one is cause and which one is effect. For example, feeling depressed as a result of losing your job could be misidentified as its cause, rather than as a symptom ('you probably lost your job because you were sitting around full of negative thoughts').

Only when you're confident that none of the above applies should you consider suggesting direct causation – and your caution in doing this will set you apart from most writers, thinkers, students, and even a good number of researchers! When you do identify it, however, direct causation can yield a revolutionary insight: for example, the knowledge that malaria is directly caused by a parasite carried by certain mosquitos brings with it the possibility of combatting one of the world's greatest, avoidable causes of death.

For each of the four examples below, see if you can decide what relationship – if any – the correlation in question has with causation:

> Attending university has been shown to have a strong correlation with lifetime earnings. Clearly, a degree is worth the investment of your time and money: it is likely to help you earn far more money over the rest of your life.

> Being infested with lice is good for your health. In our village, healthy people tend to have lice all over their bodies, while sick people don't have any at all.

> We asked ten customers what they thought about our new customer service policy and they all replied that it significantly boosted their enjoyment of Tom's Luxury Gym Spa Palace. Our new policy is working brilliantly!

> Social deprivation has been shown to correlate strongly with a range of negative outcomes across the education system: from high rates of absenteeism to exclusions and poor exam performance. In fact, social deprivation is the leading cause of under-performance in education.

The first example is an argument that has frequently been made by politicians, among others: that a university education causes higher earnings. Yet this correlation may in fact imply *not* causation but other factors in play. It's possible that the kind of people who choose to go to university are also the kind of people who tend to make more money – curious, intelligent, ambitious, energetic – and would have done so even if they had not gone to university. Or both earning more money and going to university may be caused by being born into a relatively privileged, wealthy background. We'd need to investigate further before crediting any particular explanation.

The second example is a famous story taken from the New Hebrides, where it was traditionally believed that lice caused good health. If this sounds absurd, remember that the observation of a correlation was entirely correct. It was simply the case that everybody always had lice except when they were extremely ill, and the lice then left their sick bodies – leading local people to incorrectly conclude that lice helped keep people healthy.[19]

The third example is likely to involve some statistical manipulation. There may well be a causal relationship involving ten customers, but this is a small number to base such a definitive claim on, and it's wise to take such a self-serving survey with a pinch of salt.

The final example is more complex and is just the kind of thing that might crop up in the conclusion to an essay or a research project. It feels convincing that social deprivation would cause such things as poor exam performance, because pupils in more deprived households are more likely to lack various significant kinds of support and security. At the same time, this is a very broad trend, within which many complex factors interact. In other words, 'social deprivation' is not a concrete thing that directly affects educational outcomes, but rather a measure that is likely itself to correlate with specific factors that do have a causal relationship with educational outcomes. Higher social deprivation may correlate with a higher likelihood of attending worse-than-average schools, for example, which may then have a causal relationship with worse performance in exams. But even this relationship will be complex. Similarly, it's easy to talk about abstractions like poverty 'causing' certain outcomes, when in fact the causal relationship is anything but straightforward – no matter how clear-cut the correlation itself.

Doesn't mean no relationship or connection — just more to delve into.

THINK ABOUT THIS: Can you think of any occasions in the recent news, or your everyday life, when someone made an unsupported assumption about causation? Can you think of two things that are correlated because of a third, underlying factor causing them both? ....

CONDUCTING MEANINGFUL RESEARCH

Scientific and research methods have developed to include an impressive toolkit of techniques both for investigating the possibility of genuine causation and for carefully and precisely describing what is going on without falling into the trap of wrongly assuming causation. Depending on the circumstances of your own research, you'll need to be confident at applying both these skills:

- Recognizing the conditions under which it is possible to meaningfully suggest the presence or the absence of causation.
- Recognizing the conditions under which it is not appropriate to suggest causation, and in which detailed and suggestive accounts of what is actually going on are the most valuable form of research.

Typically, fields such as social science involve complex variables and causal relationships that cannot easily be studied in anything other than real-life situations, while fields such as medicine and biology can isolate and study many effects in rigorously controlled trials or in laboratory conditions. In each case, however, meaningful investigations and advances in knowledge are underpinned by meticulous information-gathering, testing, recording and investigation across a community of researchers.

Low-quality or misleading research, by contrast, often involves: isolated results that are not repeated or easily checked by others; the selective use of data; inadequate recording and testing during an investigation; or the desire to defend rather than to rigorously test a particular kind of explanation. Some of these general distinctions are set out below:

Good research tends to...	Flawed research tends to...
Be interested in establishing new knowledge or in rigorously testing existing knowledge	Be interested in seeking confirmation of a particular, favoured explanation
Be conducted openly and transparently within a community of practice	Be conducted secretively or in isolation
Invite replication by others, and the checking of all its raw results and analysis	Be difficult for others to replicate, or to check and analyse in its entirety
Thoroughly investigate an area in sufficient depth and detail	Rely on a superficial, selective or insufficiently detailed investigation
Aim at a fair and balanced account	Be overtly influenced by personal biases or other distorting pressures

The 'gold standard' for medical and much experimental research is the **randomized [placebo-] controlled trial** – usually abbreviated to **RCT** – meaning a trial in which subjects are allocated at random to a control group (who receive a **placebo**, which has no medical effects) and a **treatment group** (who receive the actual treatment). Ideally, such a trial would also be **double-blind**, with neither subjects nor experimenters knowing until the end who is receiving the placebo. This allows researchers to discount any bias that might otherwise arise from the expectations of either the participants or the researchers.

Control group	A group, usually selected at random from the overall sample, who do not receive any kind of experimental intervention and can thus provide a comparison to the treatment group to show what effect any active intervention has
Double-blind	A research trial in which neither the subjects nor the researchers know who is in the control group and who is in the treatment group
Placebo	A deliberately ineffective treatment, such as a sugar pill, supplied to a control group in order to give them the potential psychological benefits of thinking they are receiving a treatment, thus allowing researchers to rule out this psychological impact as a potential cause of any health effects
RCT	Short for a 'randomized controlled trial', in which subjects are allocated at random to a control group and to a treatment group (or groups)
Single-blind	A research trial in which the subjects do not know whether they are in the control group (in which case they are receiving a placebo) or the treatment group (in which case they are receiving the actual treatment)
Treatment group	A group of subjects who are receiving active treatment; the difference between their results and those of the control group, if any, should indicate any impact of the treatment

As these details suggest, the kind of experimental setup that allows us to confidently talk about causation is simply impossible to establish in many fields. In general, research across medicine and the 'harder' sciences tends to focus directly on experimentally assessing causation – or the lack of it – while projects and research across the social sciences are obliged to approach similar objectives more indirectly: through generating rigorous, detailed descriptions of complex human phenomena that then allow us to explore explanations, causes and the relationships between these phenomena.

It's important to note that there are more similarities than differences between these aspirations, which are rooted in the same scientific principles: that causation can never be proven with absolute certainty, but may be compellingly suggested when we find an economical explanation for a rigorous, substantial and reliable body of evidence.

SMART STUDY: Two types of research question

In general, there are two types of research question, both of which address different aspects of abductive reasoning. Make sure you know which you are asking, and why – and ensure that you have the skills and resources to answer your question meaningfully!

Descriptive questions are research questions that set up a detailed investigation into the nature of a particular phenomenon, trend or field. For example, 'What are the attitudes of students on campus towards the country's major political parties?'

Such questions can generate both **qualitative** (such as answers to survey questions or subjective evaluations by the researcher) and **quantitative** results (any statistical measure of different factors) – with the most important question being whether the information gathered constitutes a meaningful, robust and reliable exploration of your area of inquiry.

Qualitative research: exploratory research based on assessing the qualities or nature of something, rather than by measuring it

Quantitative data: research based on precisely quantifying a particular variable or variables in order to generate usable statistics

Explanatory questions are research questions that set up an investigation into the potential causes of a phenomenon. For example, 'What factors most influence the attitudes of students on campus towards the country's major political parties?' Addressing such questions adequately tends to require more resources, experience and time than in the case of descriptive questions, but provides the opportunity for lasting and socially significant insights into complex processes, events and circumstances.

It may be possible to conduct social science research through a testable hypothesis: that, for example, 'students on campus are likely to be more liberal than the country as a whole' or 'students on campus are likely to be most influenced in their political attitudes by their family background'. At the same time, experimental approaches to social science – for example, in fields such as psychology and economic decision-making – can suffer from the accusation that, precisely because these experiments occur in controlled situations rather than in an everyday social context, they do not realistically represent everyday behaviours.

There's no easy resolution to these tensions, but it's safe to say that questions of **feasibility** loom large at the start of most research projects. This entails asking whether a project can both plausibly be undertaken and produce credible insights. In particular, before embarking on any research project you should ensure that:

Feasibility: whether a proposed research question can meaningfully be addressed given the time, resources and information at your disposal

1. It is **possible to answer** your research question clearly and usefully in the first place.
2. Your question is sufficiently **focused** to be answerable given the time and resources available.
3. Your question is meaningfully answerable based on information that you are able either **to generate** or **to access**.

Satisfying these criteria is often a question of degree rather than a binary 'yes' or 'no'. How, for example, might you rank these three initial proposals for areas of research, in terms of feasibility?

	FEASIBILITY
This research project will investigate consumer attitudes towards leading online brands.	◯
This research project will analyse a range of factors associated with attendance and exclusions at local primary schools.	◯
This research project will examine local attitudes to the closure of the town's minor injuries unit.	◯

FIVE

BEWARE SUNK COSTS. ONCE YOU'VE PUT TIME, EFFORT, CASH OR CARE INTO SOMETHING, IT'S TEMPTING TO STICK WITH IT NO MATTER WHAT. DON'T. YOU'LL NEVER GET THAT BACK. BE BRUTAL – DON'T GET SHACKLED TO YOUR PAST.

#TalkCriticalThinking

Perhaps the least feasible of these projects is also the only one that deals directly in questions of causation: the analysis of factors associated with attendance and exclusion at local primary schools. Why is this the least feasible? Because of the quantity and complexity of the factors involved, the difficulties in reliably tracing any causal relationships, and the potential ethical sensitivity and access problems when it comes to primary schools.

After this, I would rank the research project investigating consumer attitudes towards leading online brands as reasonably feasible. This is a descriptive rather than an explanatory investigation, and one for which plenty of relevant data is likely to be available. The key difficulty will be narrowing it down and developing a suitably systematic and rigorous approach in such a broad and vaguely defined field.

Finally, the last project – examining local attitudes towards the closure of the town's minor injuries unit – seems the most feasible. The initial proposal is concrete, clearly defined and amenable to investigation through multiple approaches such as surveys, interviews and documentary research. It is also a descriptive rather than explanatory piece of research, although it may well lay the groundwork for subsequent explanatory investigations.

Especially in your own work, beware of any overconfidence in claiming causation, and of taking on a research area that is too broad, too vaguely defined or too lacking in reliable sources of information. Scientific research of all kinds proceeds cautiously from rigorous observation. While abductive reasoning may yield great leaps, these are only of use if they are able to withstand the scrutiny of a community of researchers, and measure up to what is actually taking place in the world.

You can still take on big questions – just do so rigorously!

SUMMARY

Also known as 'inference to the best explanation', **abductive reasoning** seeks to establish the best explanation for something believed to be true. The **best explanation** should:

- Successfully explain all the things that we already know, and
- Be as simple as possible while still explaining evidence.

This 'principle of parsimony' is sometimes known as **Occam's razor**: when choosing between explanations, the simplest one that explains everything is likely to be best, while increasing the number of assumptions makes something less likely to be true. Testing abductive explanations involves two kinds of investigation:

- Seeking new evidence that existing explanations cannot account for
- Seeking new, simpler explanations that still account for everything.

Discussing abductive reasoning involves explanations, theories and hypotheses:

- An **explanation** is any account of why something is the way it is.
- A scientific **theory** explains the underlying nature of a phenomenon in a robust, rigorous and evidence-based manner that is widely accepted by those studying the field.
- A **hypothesis** provides a specific, testable **prediction** based on a theory.
- A **null hypothesis** is the exact opposite of the hypothesis you're testing. Attempting to falsify a null hypothesis ensures a rigorous approach to research.

Moving from evidence to proof requires a rigorous **standard of proof** – a threshold beyond which you have decided to accept something as proven, and that allows you to specify this standard explicitly:

- **Statistical significance** describes the likelihood that a particular result could have occurred entirely by chance (as opposed to having a noteworthy cause).

- The **p-value** is a numerical expression of statistical significance, showing the probability that a result came about through chance on the standard probability scale between zero (impossible) and one (certainty).

A **correlation** between variables (when one closely follows the other) does not prove **causation** (meaning that one has caused the other). Attempting to successfully demonstrate causation is a central concern of the **scientific method**, as is being aware of false or misleading sources of correlation.

In general, the less rigorously you are able to scrutinize a theory's predictive power and find a means of testing its claims of causation, the more careful you should be in accepting it as the best working theory available.

Good research across both the 'hard' and social sciences is interested in creating new knowledge or testing existing knowledge, rather than seeking to confirm a pet theory. It is open, transparent and takes place within a community of practice, and aims to:

- Recognize the conditions under which it is possible to meaningfully suggest the presence or the absence of causation
- Recognize the conditions under which it is not appropriate to suggest causation, and in which detailed and suggestive accounts of what is actually going on are the most valuable form of research.

Now watch the video 'Your dangerous obsession with cause and effect'. It's on YouTube. Tell me what you think via #TalkCriticalThinking

In which the author will share a host of practical tips for handling sources and reading lists.

ASSESSING EVIDENCE AND PLANNING YOUR READING STRATEGY

Why does reasoning matter (and how can you spot an argument)?

↓

How do you spell out the reasoning behind an argument?

↓

How do you draw out a logical conclusion from your premises?

↓

How do you draw out a probable conclusion from your premises?

↓

How can you select and test the best explanation of something?

↓

How should you assess evidence and plan your reading strategy?

"THERE'S SO MUCH MORE TO A BOOK THAN JUST THE READING."

MAURICE SENDAK

#TALKCRITICALTHINKING

FIVE THINGS YOU'LL LEARN IN THIS CHAPTER

1 The difference between *primary* and *secondary sources*
2 How to evaluate sources for *reliability* and *relevance*
3 How to make a *longlist* and a *shortlist for your reading*
4 How to draw on different *reading techniques*
5 A method for *clear* and *comprehensive note-taking*

We have spent the first half of this book looking at reasoning: exploring what it means to offer good reasons in support of a conclusion, and to work rigorously with observations and theories in search of reasonable explanations.

Good reasoning does more than make sense on its own terms. For us to accept someone's reasoning, it must not only be coherent but also be connected to the world by firm **evidence** in the form of accurate, relevant information demonstrating the truthfulness of their claim. When we think critically, we are trying to see things as they actually are.

As well as being able to evaluate others' reasoning, you will need to examine their evidence closely in order to achieve this – while working your way confidently through a variety of resources in order to build up your own understanding. This chapter explores both parts of this process:

- Engaging critically with different sources of evidence
- Reading strategically and building your own understanding.

I've emphasized the process of critical reading here, as opposed to engaging with other media, but the skills involved apply beyond the written word. Anything and everything can be analysed critically if you have the right questions and context: from videos and music to events, performances, debates, images and software.

SMART STUDY: Seven questions worth asking about any source

Engaging critically with different kinds of source demands a range of skills specific to each medium and format, but there are also some general questions that it's useful to ask when you start to make use of any source in your work, and that will stand you in good stead as a critical consumer of others' work (and a more confident author of literature reviews):

1 What is the aim or agenda behind this?
2 What do those creating or curating this know, and what don't they know?
3 How far are any claims contained here either verified or replicated elsewhere?
4 What else might I need to know to check this out, or to find out more?
5 Is there reasoning on display here, or something else?
6 If reasoning is going on, what type is it and is it any good?
7 If reasoning is not going on, what is happening and why?

ENGAGING CRITICALLY WITH PRIMARY AND SECONDARY SOURCES

All study resources are typically divided into two categories, reflecting their distance from whatever is being investigated: primary and secondary.

Primary sources derive directly from the place, time or phenomenon under investigation. Depending on context, they might consist of raw experimental data, historical documents, eyewitness testimony, video or audio footage, photographs, archaeological artefacts, manufactured objects, human or animal remains, or chemical or material traces.

Primary sources are derived directly from the subject, period or phenomenon under investigation

Secondary sources are the product of someone else's work about a particular subject, period or phenomenon

Secondary sources are the product of someone else's work about or around an area of investigation. When you're using secondary sources, rather than directly investigating a phenomenon, you are looking at something someone else has produced about it: perhaps an article or a book, a film or podcast, a website, or a summary of research data.

Depending on context, something can be either a primary or secondary source. If I'm investigating the life of the German emperor Kaiser Wilhelm I, the Wikipedia entry on his life is very much a secondary source. If, however, I'm investigating the history of Wikipedia, exactly the same entry is a primary source. Consider the following four examples. In each case, is the source in question primary or secondary?

		PRIMARY	SECONDARY
1	I'm investigating possible predictors of acute respiratory failure in elderly patients, and am analysing hospital records to do this.	○	○
2	Her theory is that large mammals are more vulnerable to climate change than small ones, and she is drawing on biological science publications from across Europe.	○	○
3	Her theory is that large mammals are more vulnerable to climate change than small ones, and she is conducting a dig to explore the palaeontological evidence in Arizona.	○	○
4	I am studying American attitudes towards voting using a selection of reports written by polling organizations in the wake of the last presidential election.	○	○

The first and third examples here are of primary sources: hospital records and palaeontological evidence (evidence of ancient life, such as fossils) are both derived directly from the subjects being studied. The second and fourth examples, meanwhile, involve secondary sources: a variety of articles and reports written by other people who were investigating the same area.

Does this mean that the research involving primary sources is better, or more original, than the research involving secondary sources? No. It simply means that different questions apply to each, together with different opportunities and potential problems. When it comes to primary sources, we face questions such as these:

- How can you be sure that this evidence is **authentic**?
- How was this evidence **created**, and what impact might this process have had?
- How far is this particular evidence **representative** and **accurate**?
- How **relevant** is this evidence to the claim or argument you're interested in?

Secondary evidence can share some of these questions, but using it well also depends on the degree to which you understand the context of secondary research in a field – and how confidently you can judge both the expertise and the limitations of its creators. Key questions include:

- How far is this secondary source **reliable** and **reputable**?
- What **biases** and limitations might this particular source have?
- What's the **context**: how does this source fit in with other secondary sources?
- Is it **current** (up to date)?
- Have its findings been **replicated** elsewhere?
- What are considered to be the **authoritative** or **seminal** works in this area?

We'll work through these factors one at a time.

THINK ABOUT THIS: What kinds of source are you most, and least, comfortable analysing? Do you feel confident in your ability to think critically about primary materials? Do you feel able to disagree with secondary sources? What is one of the best secondary sources you've ever used, and what is one of the worst and least useful? Why? ....
....
....
....
....
....

Authenticity

Which of these primary sources is more likely to be **authentic**, meaning that it is exactly what it is claimed to be?

An original 1912 edition of a regional newspaper stored in a local library.

A black-and-white recording of a 1950s television show uploaded to YouTube.

The newspaper is very likely to be authentic: if you are handling an original copy that has been stored in a library, and you can verify for yourself its condition, date and content, then you can be almost certain that it is what you think it is.

The recording uploaded to YouTube should be treated with greater caution: you are not handling an original copy or one that exists in a formal archive of television shows, but something that somebody else has uploaded to a website with few quality controls, claiming it to be original.

What might you do to check the authenticity of something like a TV recording uploaded to YouTube? Pause, and think about it. Here are some questions you might ask:

- How can I verify that this content is in fact a TV show from this time and date? Are there official archives or records I can use for comparison?
- Does it seem complete (rather than partial) in terms of length? Has anything been removed or altered, or garbled or corrupted in digitization and upload?
- Are there other partial or complete instances of this recording I can compare it to? Are there any transcripts or records in other media I can refer to?
- Are there any experts on the period I can ask, or secondary sources I can consult that feature this show or shows like it?
- Are there any surviving witnesses from this period who might remember the show or be able to comment on the recording?
- Overall, what other sources (both primary and secondary) offer the best opportunities for comparison, contextualization and verification?

Authenticity implies that the origin of a source is beyond reasonable doubt. If it's authentic, then it really is a period newspaper, a manuscript, a recording, an artefact, or data gathered in the particular circumstances claimed.

Doubts around authenticity arise when the journey of the source, from its origins into your hands, contains elements that are unclear, unknown or may involve confusion, loss or deception.

Note that authenticity does not guarantee either representativeness or relevance by itself. Secondary sources can be more reliable, detailed or useful than primary sources, and can gather together the findings of many primary sources or contain useful analysis. The most important thing is to be as certain as possible about what a source is in the first place.

Representativeness

We have already covered sampling at some length in the context of inductive reasoning. When it comes to research and analysis, one major challenge is basing your investigation on a **representative sample** – that is, one which represents the area you're trying to study as accurately as possible.

Representative sample: a sample of instances that have been carefully selected so that they represent the nature of the whole as accurately as possible

Another way of thinking about representativeness is to ask how far the evidence you are examining is typical of the field you are interested in. In historical research, written evidence from centuries ago will probably have been produced by relatively educated and privileged people – meaning that their typical experiences were exceptional in their society as a whole. The same is true of most fields relying on documentary evidence. Always ask: what does this evidence typify – and what might differing or unrecorded experiences have been like?

A few general points should be borne in mind when considering how representative any evidence you are looking at might be:

- In general, the bigger the better: small samples are more likely to misrepresent the whole than larger samples. Always beware of very small sample sizes.
- A sample can only be representative if its distribution mirrors that of the whole; across a country, for example, a representative sample of the population should take more people from densely populated areas and fewer from sparsely populated ones. Similarly, if you're studying a population with six women for every four men, any representative sample should preserve this same ratio of six to four.
- It's much easier for a sample to represent something that has a 'natural' distribution, like height or weight in a population; and much harder for a sample to represent something that has a very uneven or irregular distribution, such as wealth.
- Self-selection is a potential problem with samples: if you ask for volunteers to take part in a survey, you end up dealing with the kind of person who volunteers for surveys.
- There is no such thing as an entirely representative sample. Things will always get lost or distorted in the act of selecting a part to stand for a whole.

In general, beware of obviously **unrepresentative** evidence – arguments made on the basis of individual anecdotes, for example, or using very small numbers of results – and always try to investigate the limitations associated with any method of sampling. In particular, watch out for the assumption that observations based on a sample can uncritically be used as representations of the whole.

Relevant sources: those that strongly support a line of argument

Irrelevant sources: on close examination, these don't contribute to the main argument

Relevance

Relevant sources are those that strongly support a line of argument, while **irrelevant** sources are those that, on closer examination, don't contribute to the main argument. It sounds obvious, but you'd be surprised how often irrelevant evidence is used to support arguments, or to muddy the waters of critical analysis.

Here are three examples of arguments drawing on evidence to support a conclusion. How relevant do you think the evidence is in each case, and why?

According to government data dating back to the 1960s, rates of teenage pregnancy are close to an all-time low in the UK, suggesting that concerns over increasingly lax teenage attitudes towards sex may be unfounded.

According to reports in several of the UK's leading newspapers, teenage use of dating and hookup apps has risen to an all-time high, suggesting the prevalence of increasingly lax attitudes towards sex among teenagers.

According to reports from the hospitality industry, the number of young people drinking to excess in bars is close to an all-time low in the UK, suggesting media concerns over increasingly lax teenage attitudes towards sex may be unfounded.

The evidence presented in the first example is probably the most relevant of all, given that the records in question date back around 50 years, and that it seems reasonable to consider teenage pregnancy rates as one useful indicator of teenage attitudes towards sex.

The evidence presented in the second example – that teenage use of dating and hookup apps is at an all-time high – has some relevance to teenage attitudes towards sex. We might wonder, however, whether this evidence is sufficiently relevant to carry the argument on its own, given that dating and hookup apps have only been widely used for a few years, and it is hardly surprising that their use has increased over time. We might also question the assumption that using such apps automatically suggests 'lax' attitudes.

Finally, the fact that fewer young people are drinking to excess in bars is largely irrelevant to teenage attitudes towards sex: the evidence does very little to support the conclusion and is only loosely connected to the subject. A great deal of further evidence around drinking and sexual attitudes would be needed to support this conclusion.

When working with both primary and secondary sources, relevance is a key consideration. Irrelevant sources, no matter how good or interesting, can distract from the central questions at hand, or help conceal a weak or flawed argument. Never lose sight of the main points at stake and the obligation to clearly link evidence to argument.

Reputation, bias and authority

Using a primary source well means being sensitive to the circumstances of its production. A historical document may be useful precisely because of the biases it embodies: a nobleman writing in defence of their king; a politician delivering a self-justifying speech. The raw data from an experiment or piece of research is authoritative as a direct report of its results – but, unless you know the details of the research method, you are not in a position to make good use of this data.

Sometimes, when you examine the primary materials someone else has used, you will reach a different conclusion to them – or find that they have omitted, misunderstood or distorted something. This is why it's worth going back to primary sources yourself whenever you can. Only then will you properly understand what others have done in their secondary research, and what you might wish to do differently.

Reputation is the expert standing of a source and an important guide to quality

When it comes to secondary materials, you should aim to use sources that originate from an author, publication or source with a high **reputation** for quality – and that are up to date in their information and analysis. In practice, this tends to mean that you should look for articles published in peer-reviewed journals, books published by academic or high-quality publishing houses, or the considered opinions of authors or commentators known to be experts in a field.

Why does this matter? It takes a long time, and a lot of effort, to gain real understanding. Similarly, it takes a long time to master the approach needed to explore a field carefully and accurately, without leaping to false conclusions or acting on the basis of insufficient knowledge. Reputable journals, publishers and institutions aim to maintain standards of informed, impartial investigation.

Compare the following two paragraphs:

> The Earth's climate has changed throughout history. Just in the last 650,000 years there have been seven cycles of glacial advance and retreat, with the abrupt end of the last ice age about 7,000 years ago marking the beginning of the modern climate era – and of human civilization. Most of these climate changes are attributed to very small variations in Earth's orbit that change the amount of solar energy our planet receives. The current warming trend is of particular significance because most of it is very likely human-induced and proceeding at a rate that is unprecedented in the past 1,300 years. (NASA, 'Climate change: How do we know?')[20]

> The official position of the World Natural Health Organization in regards to global warming is that there is NO GLOBAL WARMING! Global warming is nothing more than just another hoax, just like Y2K and the global freezing claims in the 1960s and '70s were. Global warming is being used to generate fear and panic. Those behind this movement are using it to control people's lives and for financial gain. There are not many individuals, groups, or organizations willing to stand up against this fraud that is being perpetuated for fear of being persecuted, harassed, and ostracized by those who support global warming within the scientific and other communities. But fortunately, a few have decided to do the right thing and take a stand against this evil, proving just how unscientifically founded global warming is and exposing those who are behind it. (World Natural Health Organization, 'The global warming hoax')[21]

Which do you trust more? Both are information retrieved online in early 2017. The claims they present are very different, as, I would suggest, are the quality of the sources. NASA is an independent agency of the US Government employing some of the world's leading scientists, with a track record of excellence in research, achievement and collaboration with other leading scientific organizations across the world. The World Natural Health Organization was founded in 1983 by a bishop hoping 'to unite the world in truth concerning natural health care'. In this case, looking carefully at where these claims originate is an important indicator of both quality and **bias**.

Bias exists whenever a source has an agenda that distorts its perspective

You can (and should) read, watch, listen to and take in all kinds of secondary sources around any subject you're studying or interested in. But you also need to be extremely careful about whose views guide your own and who you turn to for direction. Always ask: what sources are, and are not, considered **authoritative** in your field – and upon what foundation do their claims of authority rest?

Authoritative sources are those that can most be relied on in a field

Currency, context and seminal works

Being open-minded doesn't mean giving all views equal weight.

In every field, there are **seminal** works (books, papers and arguments) that have helped define the debate around a particular concept or topic. Most non-scientists, for example, have heard of Albert Einstein, whose work in the first half of the 20th century helped define theories that still lie behind much scientific debate today – in particular, his work on space, time, energy and mass.

Seminal works are sources that help to lay the foundations of a field

life-TRANSFORMING ideas have always COME TO ME through books.

bell hooks

#TALKCRITICALTHINKING

Current sources are those that are up to date with the latest thinking and evidence

Replication is the requirement that results have been repeated in more than one experiment or investigation; widely replicated results are far more credible than those that have not been replicated

Physics has advanced considerably since Einstein published four seminal papers exploring these topics in 1905, but an awareness of his work remains important for students who want to understand many of the most important continuing concerns in their field. Similarly, there will be thinkers in most fields who have helped to establish key concepts and terms.

In general, good primary and secondary research around a topic will cover both some seminal past works, some works that are as **current** as possible, and some authoritative overviews providing context.

A final important question to ask of any individual source is whether its results or perspective are **replicated** elsewhere, or there is no similar research (or if research and analysis by others into this area have produced very different results).

Mapping the landscape of evidence

Think of your engagement with evidence as a gradual mapping process: building up knowledge of a particular landscape, piece by piece. Each source helps fill in a little more information – and helps you to better identify tensions, disagreements and gaps in your knowledge. Because you're never going to be able to read everything, or to conduct countless experiments, choosing carefully how to distribute your limited time and attention is a key consideration. Here's a summary of the key concepts:

Authenticity	Authenticity implies that the origin of a source is beyond reasonable doubt: that it is what it claims to be and that it can be traced from the present to its origins with confidence, ruling out the possibility of fakery, misattribution or alteration.
Authority	An authoritative source is one that you can safely accept as offering a high-quality, expert and accurate view on a topic. It will usually originate with a known expert, or a highly reputable publisher or outlet; or offer a definitive account of something that you have extremely strong reasons to trust as accurate.
Bias/Impartiality	The more biased a source, the more its author(s) are interested not in achieving knowledge as accurately as possible, but in advancing a particular view of the world. The more impartial a source is, the more it tries not to push one particular perspective at the expense of others – basing its argument on a fair and reasonable assessment of the facts. As long as you're aware of it, bias can itself provide useful evidence.
Currency	Is a source up to date in its field? If so, it is current: it has not been superseded by new thinking and offers a fair reflection of where things are today. Some fields are much faster moving than others.
Relevance	Sources are relevant when the information they provide is closely related to a line of argument in terms of its premises or conclusion. A source is irrelevant if it does not contribute to an argument, and may, instead, distract from the points under consideration.
Replication	Replication means repeating a result in other research, or a claimed fact being independently observed by others. In general, the more a result has been replicated, the more trustworthy it is. If someone is the only one arguing something, or the results have never been reproduced elsewhere, approach with caution.

Popular opinions can be wrong — but this doesn't automatically make unpopular opinions special.

Representativeness	How typical is the evidence you're examining – and what is it typical of? A sample is more representative when it better reflects the complexities of the whole it is being used to represent – and less representative when it does not. In general, smaller samples are less representative; and more uneven and complicated totalities are harder to represent. There is no such thing as a perfectly representative sample.
Reputation	When deciding what sources to use, reputation is a major consideration. Reputable sources tend to be those that appear in peer-reviewed academic journals, are published by serious publishers or are produced by known experts in their fields. Less reputable sources need to be treated with much greater caution and should not be relied on in the same way.
Seminal works	Seminal works are pieces of writing and research that are absolutely central to a particular field or topic, or that helped define its direction. Being aware of seminal works – and going back and looking at them directly if possible – is important for understanding the nature of debate and progress in most fields.

THINK ABOUT THIS: Which of the factors above do and don't apply to your current work and interests? What do you consider to be the best available resources to work from in your field – and where are they least satisfactory? Why is this? ....

....

....

....

....

....

CREATING A STRATEGY FOR CRITICAL READING

Some students may see reading, in the context of study, as the need to plough through and absorb daunting quantities of information. There is certainly hard work to be done in reading around any subject. But good reading is a qualitative rather than a quantitative business. It's not a question of getting through as much material as possible. Rather, effective reading entails expending your effort strategically.

The remainder of this chapter brings the first half of the book to a close by exploring what it means to:

- Plan your reading strategically.
- Critically evaluate what you read.
- Make meaningful connections between information and ideas.
- Actively develop your own understanding.

As we will see in Chapter 12, critical reading and writing are closely linked. Almost all good writing ultimately begins with good reading. If you can start reading early in your research, and keep your critical engagement high while you read, everything that follows will be far easier and more satisfying.

I really mean this — sustained, attentive reading time is precious.

Remember this when sitting down to explore a topic or text for the first time. Without context and understanding, information can seem arbitrary and impossible to engage with critically. Once you begin to see and to explore larger patterns, however, you'll find that further reading becomes easier rather than more difficult – and that you're able to remember more, explore materials more confidently, and start to develop your own perspective.

Reading strategy: taking a systematic approach to reading evidence and materials, in order to build up confidence and understanding, and make the most of your time

A successful **reading strategy** entails planning, preparation and the effective allocation of attention. You need to decide what you are going to read and in what order of priority. Doing this entails:

- Creating a longlist of relevant, useful books and resources.
- Turning your longlist into a balanced, realistic shortlist.
- Drawing on different study techniques to get the most out of your shortlist.

Making your longlist

Most courses and modules come complete with a reading list, which is likely to do much of the initial work of long-listing for you, and may also indicate priorities in terms of key texts, papers, resources and other materials. If you haven't been supplied with a reading list, many courses around the world publish lists online; finding a relevant list from a reputable institution should not be difficult. In general:

- You should *always* try to base your initial reading on *both* an official reading list produced by your institution or professor *and* an examination of one or more comparable reading lists, found online from other institutions or experts.
- If you have no reading list, or are approaching a topic for your interest or outside of a formal course, use the guidelines below to piece one together for yourself – with a particular emphasis on authoritative introductory resources that will help you make better reading decisions as you start to learn about your topic.

It's important to ensure you consider the possibilities available as widely as possible before whittling them down. Depending on your area of study, consider the approaches below for extending and supplementing your longlist according to your needs so that it includes:

- An **accessible introduction**: a text from a series specifically aimed at providing a brief, engaging (but reputable) introduction to the general area.
- A **core textbook**: a core textbook in the field, either defined as such in your reading list or mentioned across multiple reading lists from institutions online.
- A **mainstream book**: the right mainstream book can provide a relevant and engaging perspective on your area of interest.
- A **key journal**: the latest issues of a key journal or academic publication relevant to your field.
- A **mainstream magazine**: the latest issues of reputable mainstream publications relevant to your field.
- **Seminal research**: an influential historical paper or publication in your area of interest.
- An **authoritative online resource**: a recommended or influential online resource, such as a blog or website maintained by experts or used to host expert debate.

As a concrete example of the above, consider an undergraduate in the first year of their Economics degree (or studying for an introductory economics module). Here is a sample resource that might be relevant to them for each of the above categories, bearing in mind the fact that their final longlist should feature several items in each category:

- An **accessible introduction**: *The Rough Guide to Economics* offers an accessible overview of the field.
- A **core textbook**: the latest edition of Ben Bernanke's *Principles of Economics* is one example of a well-established general textbook.
- A **mainstream book**: Tim Harford's *The Undercover Economist* is an entertaining and informative introduction to many key concepts in practice. Great even if you hate economics!
- A **key journal**: *The Quarterly Journal of Economics* is among the most well-established journals in the field.

- A **mainstream magazine**: as the name suggests, our first-year economists might want to put *The Economist* magazine on their list.
- **Seminal research**: 'The Use of Knowledge in Society' is a seminal (and relatively readable) 1945 paper by Friedrich Hayek.
- An **authoritative online resource**: Nobel laureate Paul Krugman is a noted blogger and opinion columnist.

Your field of study or interest may be very different indeed to the above – indeed, it probably is. See if you can fill out, below, something corresponding to each category that's relevant to what you're working on at the moment:

- Accessible introduction: ....
....
....
....
- Core textbook: ....
....
....
....
- Mainstream book: ....
....
....
....
- Key journal: ....
....
....
....
- Mainstream magazine: ....
....
....
....
- Seminal research: ....
....
....
....
- Authoritative online resource: ....
....
....
....

In addition to the above, you can extend the range of your longlist by looking for resources through the following methods:

- Physically browsing the relevant section in your library to see which books are grouped alongside key texts, and may complement or contextualize them.
- Checking to see how many copies of a book the library holds: there tend to be multiple copies of important texts.

- Looking at online reviews and discussions from students in a similar position to yourself to see what they rate as most useful or relevant, and talking to students who have already been through the course about what most helped them.
- Looking out for developments and trends in your field that have been picked up in the 'quality' new media (and the research behind the stories).
- Searching catalogues and databases for key words, and looking for the top-ranked, most-cited and influential authors, papers and topics.

Can you think of anything else that might help you create as wide a range of potential resources as possible? Countless opportunities for consuming media of all kinds online are likely to exist, and these are not to be dismissed, so long as you're able to keep thinking in terms of quality, relevance and reliability. In particular, consider supplementing your initial reading with:

- Video and audio of lectures by experts in your field, as part of free online courses, taken from events or uploaded specifically to free learning platforms with a reputation for quality such as the Khan Academy.
- Interactive modules and resources created by experts, academic institutions, professional bodies or others with known expertise in the relevant field; this might include Massively Open Online Courses (MOOCs) from leading universities and video collections from academic publishers.
- Discussion and Q&A forums containing a high level of debate among students and practitioners in your field; this might include departmental websites at universities or particular forums mentioned on them.

In general, it's advisable to keep range and variety in mind when it comes to long-listing resources, and not to assume that any one kind of resource will give you the full picture, or that the existence of online materials such as lectures means there is no need to read texts at any length, either onscreen or in print.

Despite the increasing importance of video, audio and interactive platforms, most academic disciplines still require sustained reading and writing, especially when it comes to consolidating your knowledge of core concepts and information. Creating the time and space to read in a sustained, critical way is harder than ever amid all the opportunities that digital media present. Yet this very difficulty makes close textual engagement a more rather than less valuable skill in a digital age.

Today, the same information is at everyone's fingertips. It's the capacity to comprehend, contextualize and recombine it in meaningful ways that sets people apart both from one another and, increasingly, from what machines themselves can achieve.

Making your shortlist

If the point of a longlist is that it should be varied and comprehensive, then the point of a shortlist is that it should be useful: a practical tool that realistically addresses your current learning objectives. Creating and making good use of your shortlist means:

- Being clear about your current aims and objectives.
- Arranging your reading in a sensible order of priority.
- Being honest about your time and capacity.
- Prioritizing elements within each resource and approaching these with an appropriate study technique.

Let's go back to my example of a first-year Economics student and consider what it might mean for them to move from a longlist to a shortlist. For the sake of argument, we will assume that their longlist had 30 items on it in total, and that:

- This is the very start of their Economics studies, so they have little prior knowledge about the subject.
- They have two weeks to do some reading before the course begins, and fairly limited reading time available within the two weeks.
- Their aims and objectives at this stage are to grasp some of the basics of the field as fast as possible.

Here is a potential shortlist for the first two weeks of reading, in priority order:

1 Read all of *The Rough Guide to Economics* fairly rapidly, pausing to write notes on key concepts and also noting any difficulties or queries.
2 Read the Introduction and first chapter of the textbook *Introduction to Economics* closely, taking notes on key concepts and queries while doing so.
3 Try looking up resources such as Wikipedia articles around key concepts picked up in your notes, and skimming these with a critical eye to see how they are summarized and whose work is referenced.
4 Skim read the latest few issues of *The Economist*, picking out any articles of particular interest and cross-referencing key concepts with the books above.
5 If there's time, select another accessible introductory guide to economics from the longlist and start working through this – perhaps *Economics: A Very Short Introduction*.

This is probably quite enough for the time being and doesn't yet include any academic journals or research. These are best saved until you are more deeply engaged in a subject. In a different shortlist, applied later during a course, the first and most important thing to read might well be the original research paper in which a concept or experiment was outlined.

Accessing these online – easily one of technology's great gifts. Use it.

Do you agree with the list above? Does it echo your own experience, or seem too challenging or not challenging enough? Everyone reads in a slightly different style and has different preferences. Yet there are a number of different reading techniques that should form part of everyone's study approach.

Drawing on different reading techniques

In general, aim to be an **active reader**: someone who doesn't simply set out to absorb information, but rather who consciously deploys a variety of techniques as needed in order to get the most out of their time and resources.

Active reading: reading in an engaged frame of mind, with a focus on questioning, understanding and note-taking; and an ambition to see how a text can be useful to you

You can think of active reading as a conversation with a text. For the results to be meaningful, you must ask questions, tease out meanings and explore your own assumptions. One of the greatest mistakes many students make is to be too passive in their reading: taking in information without reflecting on it and failing to develop their own understanding and interests at the same time as engaging with others' work.

Reading and understanding aren't two different activities. If you're reading without understanding, stop. Go back and read what you didn't understand again, or seek some context elsewhere, or ask for help. Don't simply sit and let yourself be baffled.

Please do scribble all over this book!
(That's what these notes are supposed to encourage.)

Both good writing and good thinking are most likely to begin with active responses to reading: with notes, sketches, questions, queries, niggles, quotations, excerpts, paraphrases and materials that can then be turned into something more sustained and coherent.

SMART STUDY: Four different reading techniques to master

Here's a list of four suggested reading techniques to master, allowing you to move between different approaches as you have different reading aims and priorities:

- **Skim reading** allows you to move rapidly through information. It's best used when what you want is not deep understanding, but rather an overview of how information and themes fit together – and some pointers towards key concepts you'll return to later. In general, it's useful to skim through a text when you don't know specifically what you are looking for, or when you're trying to work out whether a text is relevant or not.
- **Scanning** a text is useful when you are looking for material relating to a particular word or theme. In general, it's useful to scan through texts when you know what you are looking for, but don't yet know where the best information will be found, or what it will be connected to. Scanning a text differs simply from searching it because it provides more opportunity to see how the text itself is structured.
- **Searching** a text using either an electronic resource or the index is effective when you are looking for a particular answer to a particular question, or for something self-contained. If you want to retain some sense of how things fit together, once you've located a key term, scan the area around it for context and related ideas.
- **Close reading** means carefully and closely reading a text, giving yourself enough time and space to understand and engage with its meaning, and to re-read elements as needed in order to fully grasp them. After skimming, scanning or searching a text, you may then wish to read one part of it closely. Don't skimp on this stage: it's this slow, deliberate engagement with key ideas that creates memory and understanding.

We'll practise putting all these techniques into action shortly. Before then, however, we need to look at the last and most important element of any reading strategy – note-taking and critical engagement.

THINK ABOUT THIS: What do you feel are your own best and worst reading habits? What kind of books and setting bring out the best in you? What do you find most difficult to read? Is there anything you can do to change this? ....

NOTE-TAKING AND CRITICAL ENGAGEMENT

Why is it important to take notes? In general, successful notes will help you do two things:

- Clarify your understanding of a text and help you assess it critically.
- Provide a clear record you can look back at and relate to other resources.

Achieving both of these means producing your notes in a systematic way and keeping them organized in a single location. This location can be digital or physical (or both) but needs to be linked to an environment in which you feel able to achieve focused and careful reading.

For some people, physically writing notes on paper can help consolidate understanding while shutting out distractions; for others, having a single document open on a computer can achieve the same focus; others prefer dedicated apps for managing clippings, information, productivity and collaboration. Even if you're working entirely online, don't underestimate your need for uninterrupted time and undistracted focus.

The first thing every single piece of note-taking should begin with is full details of the source you're using – both to enable you to find it again and to make it easy to cite if needed. Don't skimp on these details: ensure that, if it's worth taking notes on something, you start off by carefully recording everything you will need to cite it formally in your own work. This is vital for keeping your notes in order, for finding sources again if needed and for **citations**: referring to sources in an accepted academic style.

Citation: a reference to a source in an academic piece of writing, in which the details of the source should be fully and formally provided in the accepted format for your course

The required form for citations will vary from subject to subject, and between universities. You will always be told what citation style you are expected to adopt, and should easily be able to look this up online. As an example, the American Psychological Association (APA) format is commonly used across social sciences.[22]

Below is the basic APA reference-list format for listing an article in a periodical. The URL at the end is for the unique Digital Object Identifier (doi) assigned to identify articles and documents online:

> Author, A. A., Author, B. B., & Author, C. C. (Year). Title of article. *Title of Periodical*, volume number(issue number), pages. http://dx.doi.org/xx.xxx/yyyyy.

> Chatfield, T. (1996). How to make up article titles. *The Journal of Unconvincing Fictions*, 12 (3–4), 132–47. http://dx/doi.org/12.123/12345.

And here's the APA basic format for print books:

> Author, A. A. (Year of publication). *Title of work: Capital letter also for subtitle.* Location: Publisher.

> Chatfield, T. (1981). *Lies Lies Lies: An Entirely Fabricated Book.* London: Random House.

And here's the APA basic format for a newspaper article retrieved online:

> Author, A. A. (Year, Month Day). Title of article. *Title of Newspaper.* Retrieved from http://www.someaddress.com/full/url/

> Chatfield, T. (2015, October 21). My made-up online piece. *The Guardian.* Retrieved from www.guardian.co.uk/tomchatfield

Mastering citations is a case of precisely following the appropriate format. Note-taking, however, is more of an art – and you should feel free to adapt my guidelines to match your preferences and needs. In general, your notes should cover the following areas, being careful never to write notes simply for the sake of writing:

- A brief **synopsis** of the topic being addressed and its relevance to you.
- Your summary of the author's **conclusion** or overall point.
- Your summary of the **reasoning** offered in support of this conclusion.

- Your summary of the key **evidence** offered in support of the reasoning.
- Your **analysis** of how convincing you find the reasoning and evidence, together with any noteworthy gaps or problems.
- **Follow-up** questions to investigate; different ways in which you might make use of this source; and further reading and themes to explore relevant areas further.
- Any direct **quotations** you might wish to use in your own work.

The following is a worked example of how I might write notes on part of an article. For the sake of this example, imagine that I am conducting my initial research for an essay exploring the impact of human population growth and urban expansion on animal species, with a particular interest in evolutionary pressures and adaptation.

Part of a real article – great, surprising read.

First, here's the article itself. Read it closely and think about how you might approach the questions above before looking at my response.

Greater than the sum of its parts

Like some people who might rather not admit it, wolves faced with a scarcity of potential sexual partners are not beneath lowering their standards. It was desperation of this sort, biologists reckon, that led dwindling wolf populations in southern Ontario to begin, a century or two ago, breeding widely with dogs and coyotes. The clearance of forests for farming, together with the deliberate persecution which wolves often suffer at the hand of man, had made life tough for the species. That same forest clearance, though, both permitted coyotes to spread from their prairie homeland into areas hitherto exclusively lupine, and brought the dogs that accompanied the farmers into the mix.

Interbreeding between animal species usually leads to offspring less vigorous than either parent – if they survive at all. But the combination of wolf, coyote and dog DNA that resulted from this reproductive necessity generated an exception. The consequence has been booming numbers of an extraordinarily fit new animal spreading through the eastern part of North America. Some call this creature the eastern coyote. Others, though, have dubbed it the 'coywolf'. Whatever name it goes by, Roland Kays of North Carolina State University, in Raleigh, reckons it now numbers in the millions.

The mixing of genes that has created the coywolf has been more rapid, pervasive and transformational than many once thought. Javier Monzón, who worked until recently at Stony Brook University in New York State (he is now at Pepperdine University, in California), studied the genetic make-up of 437 of the animals, in ten north-eastern states plus Ontario. He worked out that, though coyote DNA dominates, a tenth of the average coywolf's genetic material is dog and a quarter is wolf.

The DNA from both wolves and dogs (the latter mostly large breeds, like Doberman Pinschers and German Shepherds) brings big advantages, says Dr Kays. At 25kg or more, many coywolves have twice the heft of purebred coyotes. With larger jaws, more muscle and faster legs, individual coywolves can take down small deer. A pack of them can even kill a moose.

Coyotes dislike hunting in forests. Wolves prefer it. Interbreeding has produced an animal skilled at catching prey in both open terrain and densely wooded areas, says Dr Kays. And even their cries blend those of their ancestors. The first part of a howl resembles a wolf's (with a deep pitch), but this then turns into a higher-pitched, coyote-like yipping.

The animal's range has encompassed America's entire north-east, urban areas included, for at least a decade, and is continuing to expand in the south-east following coywolves' arrival there half a century ago. This is astonishing. Purebred coyotes never managed to establish themselves east of the prairies. Wolves were killed off in eastern forests long ago. But by combining their DNA, the two have given rise to an animal that is able to spread into a vast and otherwise uninhabitable territory. Indeed, coywolves are now living even in large cities, like Boston, Washington and New York. According to Chris Nagy of the Gotham Coyote Project, which studies them in New York, the Big Apple already has about 20, and numbers are rising.

Source: Republished with permission of Economist Newspaper Group, from 'Greater than the sum of its parts', *The Economist*, 31st October 2015; permission conveyed through Copyright Clearance Center, Inc.

Here are my sample notes:

Article details	*The Economist* (2015) 'Greater than the sum of its parts', *The Economist.* Economist Group, 31 October. www.economist.com/news/science-and-technology/21677188-it-rare-new-animal-species-emerge-front-scientists-eyes (accessed 21 January 2017).
Synopsis	Dwindling wolf populations in southern Ontario have bred widely with dogs and coyotes. The resulting 'coywolves' are extraordinarily fit and are spreading through the eastern USA. This is a striking and relevant example of evolutionary adaptation in response to human-created environmental and population pressures.
Conclusion	Occasionally, animal species interbreeding can produce a strikingly successful new kind of animal; this has happened in the case of coywolves.
Reasoning	(1) Habitat and population changes due to human actions have brought coyotes, wolves and dogs into contact; and (2) a scarcity of sexual partners has, for over a century, led wolves to breed with the other two. The resulting mix of dog, coyote and wolf DNA turns out to (3) boost the size, speed and strength of coyotes, as well as (4) creating animals able to hunt in both open terrain and woodland. All of this has resulted in (5) highly successful new animals.
Evidence	Roland Kays of North Carolina State University, in Raleigh, reckons there are now millions of coywolves. Studies of 437 animals across ten north-eastern states and Ontario, by Javier Monzón while at Stony Brook University, showed a tenth of coywolf genetic material being dog, and one-quarter wolf. Boston, Washington and New York all have resident coywolves.
Analysis	It adds up to a compelling case study with strong evidence, although there's some admitted uncertainty and speculation around the origins of coywolves. Amazing that their range so far outstrips those of pure wolves and coyotes and that adaptation opens up vast new tracts of habitat.
Follow-up	Find other examples of such hugely successful adaptation and look into why interbreeding usually produces less vigorous offspring? Contrast with the usual story of species being wiped out? Good to read up other things about coywolves. Check out the original studies from Monzón, Kays and the Gotham Coyote Project. Also check background in textbook on evolutionary adaptation and interbreeding.
Quotations	Nice summary outline in second para: 'Interbreeding between animal species usually leads to offspring less vigorous than either parent – if they survive at all. But the combination of wolf, coyote and dog DNA that resulted from this reproductive necessity generated an exception. The consequence has been booming numbers of an extraordinarily fit new animal spreading through the eastern part of North America.' Nice line in sixth para: 'an animal that is able to spread into a vast and otherwise uninhabitable territory.'

What do you think? When you're ready, try the example below for yourself, in the space provided afterwards. For the sake of this exercise, imagine that you are studying a module during an undergraduate degree on Emergency Medicine, and have been asked to write a paper on the impact and potential uses of social media in emergency medicine. This is an edited extract from a 2011 paper in the *New England Journal of Medicine*.

Totally unlike your own field? Use your imagination!

Integrating Social Media into Emergency-Preparedness Efforts

The effectiveness of our public health emergency system relies on routine attention to preparedness, agility in responding to daily stresses and catastrophes, and the resilience that promotes rapid recovery. Social media can enhance each of these component efforts.

Since these new media are so pervasive in communication, it makes sense to explicitly consider the best way of leveraging these communication channels before, during, and after disasters. Networking sites such as Facebook can help individuals, communities, and agencies share emergency plans and establish emergency networks. Web-based 'buddy' systems, for example, might have allowed more at-risk people to receive medical attention and social services during the 1995 Chicago heat wave, when hundreds of people died of heat-related illness within a short period. Integrating these networks into a community's preparedness activities for public health emergencies could help to build social capital and community resilience, making it easier for both professional responders and ordinary citizens to use familiar social media networks and tools in a crisis.

These tools can also be used to improve preparedness by linking the public with day-to-day, real-time information about how their community's health care system is functioning. For example, emergency room and clinic waiting times are already available in some areas of the country through mobile-phone applications, billboard Really Simple Syndication (RSS) feeds, or hospital tweets. Routine collection and rapid dissemination of these measures of strain on a health care system can inform decision-making by patients and health care providers and administrators. Monitoring this important information through the same social channels during an actual disaster may help responders verify whether certain facilities are overloaded and determine which ones can offer needed medical care.

In many instances, by sharing images, texting, and tweeting, the public is already becoming part of a large response network, rather than remaining mere bystanders or casualties. During the first hour and a half of the 2007 massacre at Virginia Tech, students posted on-scene updates on Facebook. Online message boards generated by the American Red Cross have also been used during recent emergencies as a forum for sharing and receiving information about suspected disaster victims.

Social media are also becoming vital to recovery efforts after crises, when infrastructure must be rebuilt and stress management is critical. The extensive reach of social networks allows people who are recovering from disasters to rapidly connect with needed resources. Tweets and photographs linked to timelines and interactive maps can tell a cohesive story about a recovering community's capabilities and vulnerabilities in real time. Organizations such as Ushahidi have helped with recovery in Haiti [after the 2010 earthquake] by matching volunteer health care providers with distressed areas. Social media have been used in new ways to connect responders and people directly affected by such disasters as the Deepwater Horizon oil spill, flash floods in Australia, and the earthquake in New Zealand with medical and mental health services.

As with any new technology, there remain many hurdles between current use and optimal exploitation of social media. Although these media are used by people of both sexes and an expanding range of ages, it is important to recognize and explore the technology's limitations in reaching at-risk, vulnerable populations.

Furthermore, it is not always possible to know whether social media users are who they claim to be or whether the information they share is accurate. Although false messages that are broadcast widely are often rapidly corrected by other users, it is often difficult to separate real signals of a health crisis or a material need from background noise and opportunistic scams.

Careful consideration must also be given to issues of privacy and the question of who should monitor data from social media (and for what).

Now is the time to begin deploying these innovative technologies while developing meaningful metrics of their effectiveness and of the accuracy and usefulness of the information they provide. Social media might well enhance our systems of communication, thereby substantially increasing our ability to prepare for, respond to, and recover from events that threaten the public's health.

Here is a chart for filling out your notes. I have supplied the full initial article details:

Article details	Merchant, R.M., Elmer, S. and Lurie, N. (2011) 'Integrating social media into emergency-preparedness efforts', *New England Journal of Medicine*, 365: 289–91.
Synopsis	
Conclusion	
Reasoning	
Evidence	
Analysis	
Follow-up	
Quotations	

How did you find this exercise? If you ended up writing too much, remember the importance of being selective. There's no point reproducing most of an article or picking out every single piece of evidence. Focus on what's relevant and important to you. Here are a few thoughts on the article to compare to your own notes.

This article argues that social media can potentially enhance the public health emergency system in three main areas: preparedness, agility of response and resilience, and promoting rapid recovery.

In conclusion, it suggests making use of social media while developing meaningful measures of their effectiveness and accuracy. This is supported by a number of independent reasons: (1) that social networks can help share plans and establish networks in emergencies; (2) that real-time information can rapidly be distributed about the health care system and be monitored as an indication of load; (3) that the public itself can become active participants in a response network through social media; and (4) that people recovering from disasters can use social media to match needs with resources rapidly.

These potential advantages are significant, despite potential problems: (1) a potential lack of access to social media, especially among at-risk populations; (2) the unreliability of social media information; (3) privacy issues; and (4) who should monitor what, and how?

The articles uses as its evidence events such as the 1995 Chicago heat wave, when hundreds died, potentially preventably; the 2007 Virginia Tech massacre, when students posted on-scene updates on Facebook; and organizations like Ushahidi using social media to match volunteers with distressed areas after the 2010 Haiti earthquake.

Did you spot & comment on the date?

Much of this evidence is anecdotal and, as the article itself concedes, there is a need for meaningful measures of effectiveness. Importantly, this is an article from 2011 – which means it does not really qualify as current in terms of technology and social media. It's interesting to see an analysis from that time – and its overarching points about social media's potential enhancement of preparedness, response and stand of resilience – but thinking has significantly moved on in this area, together with the technology and its users.

In terms of follow-up, it would be interesting to compare this to more recent analyses, and to see what has and has not changed. Have these authors followed up on their own work, or have others reacted and responded to it recently? What have social media companies themselves done to create tools for emergency preparedness, and how far have problems and complexities unforeseen in 2011 arisen since then?

SMART STUDY: Linking your reading to other activities

Engaging critically with different kinds of source demands a range of skills specific to each kind.

Reading doesn't exist in a vacuum. This may sound too obvious to be worth emphasizing, but some people go through their studies without ever sharing or discussing the things they're learning about, and without ever stepping outside of set reading lists and textbooks. If you want to get as much as possible out of your reading, make sure you:

- Find other people with whom you can talk about what you're reading – whether by forming formal discussion groups with a few peers, talking to someone more experienced than you, mentoring someone less experienced, or just looking online to see who is engaging in a lively way with the field you're reading about.
- Look for those places within which lively debates and discussions exist: blogs, forums, in journals, in the mainstream press, in the media. Try to connect your own thinking with the question of what others care about, and why – even if (especially if) you disagree with them.

- Find a way of working that works for you – be honest about your life and habits: where and when you feel most able to focus; what kinds of books and resources help you to find your way into a new topic; and which most engage and excite you.
- Follow enthusiasms and serendipities: allow yourself to be curious and driven by curiosity.

THIS MATTERS. Curiosity drives much of the best research.

SUMMARY

For us to accept someone's reasoning, it must be not only coherent but also connected to the world by firm **evidence**. All study resources are typically divided into two categories, reflecting their distance from whatever is being investigated: primary and secondary.

- **Primary sources** derive directly from the place, time or phenomenon under investigation.
- **Secondary sources** are the product of someone else's work about or around an area of investigation.

When making use of sources, we must investigate whether they are:

- **Authentic**: authenticity implies that the origin of a source is beyond reasonable doubt: it is what it claims to be; it can be traced from the present to its origins with confidence, ruling out the possibility of fakery, misattribution or alteration.
- **Representative**: a sample or case study is more representative when it better reflects the complexities of the whole it is being used to represent – and less representative when it does not.
- **Relevant**: sources are relevant when the evidence they provide is closely related to a claim or line of argument; they are **irrelevant** if they do not offer any evidence or support.
- **Reputable**: reputable sources tend to appear in peer-reviewed academic journals, be published by serious publishers, or be produced by known experts in their fields; less reputable sources need to be treated with greater caution.
- **Biased** or **impartial**: the more biased a source, the more its author or authors are interested in advancing a particular view of the world; the more impartial a source is, the more it is based on an objective and reasonable assessment.
- **Authoritative**: an authoritative source is one that you can safely accept as offering a high-quality, expert and accurate view.
- **Seminal**: seminal works are those that have proved to be central to a particular field or topic, and helped to define its development.
- **Current**: a current source is one that has not been superseded by new thinking or information, and offers a fair reflection of where things are today.
- **Replicated**: in general, the more something has been replicated or independently observed elsewhere, the more we can trust it.

Creating a successful **reading strategy** entails planning, preparation and the effective allocation of intention:

- Make a **longlist** of as wide a range of potential resources as practicable, based, if possible, on a reading list or multiple reading lists relevant to your field.
- Turn your longlist into a **shortlist** relating to your current learning objectives, within which you have prioritized the order in which you will read a realistic number of resources.
- Draw on different **reading techniques** in order to get the most out of your time and resources. This kind of **active reading** means engaging, questioning, adapting and setting out to see how texts can be most useful to you. Techniques include **skim reading**, **scanning**, **searching** and **close reading**.

Your note-taking should always provide **full details** of each source you are using, enabling you to find it again and use it as an academic **citation**. When taking notes, use the following categories:

- **Article details**: always begin with these.
- **Synopsis**: this is a very brief outline of context and overall content.
- **Conclusion**: what is the main conclusion or intention of the article?
- **Reasoning**: what reasoning is used to support the conclusion?
- **Evidence**: what key evidence is used by the author(s)?
- **Analysis**: how convincing is what you've read, and how useful?
- **Follow-up**: what questions and investigations are prompted by this source, and what more would it be useful to know or investigate?
- **Quotations**: are there any particular parts of this source you might want to quote exactly in your future work?

Now watch the video 'Let's tear
some evidence into shreds'. It's on
YouTube. Tell me what you think via
#TalkCriticalThinking

INTERMISSION

How have you found this book so far? What impact has it had on your thinking, or the way you approach your work? If you've read the first half closely – and especially if many of the concepts in it were new to you – you may be surprised at how far you have come already. This intermission offers a moment for reflection and consolidation. Pause, glance back briefly across the first six chapters, then try to answer the following questions honestly.

What are three of the most useful points you feel you've learned so far from this book?

1 ....

....

2 ....

....

3 ....

....

Why are these three things useful? How do you feel they are relevant to you?

1 ....

....

2 ....

....

3 ....

....

What are three of the most difficult concepts you've found in the book so far?

1 ....

....

2 ....

....

3 ....

....

What is it about each of these that you find particularly difficult?

1 ....

....

2 ....

....

3 ....

....

There are some further exercises below. Like the exercises above, they are prompts designed to help you take charge of your own learning: to think strategically about your needs, and ask yourself how you might apply lessons from this book to your studies and everyday life. If there are things you feel I've got wrong, or points that have been addressed badly, this matters too. Try to work out what is lacking.

Have you come across any things in this book that you disagree with?

1 ....

2 ....

3 ....

Why do you disagree with these things above? What should have been said instead?

1 ....

2 ....

3 ....

How might you apply three of the things you've read about so far, to your work?

1 ....

2 ....

3 ....

How might you apply three things to your everyday life?

1 ....

2 ....

3 ....

Finally, to check your confidence and progress so far, answer these ten questions, scoring yourself in each case out of ten, where ten represents total confidence and zero represents no confidence at all.

1	I am able to pay close, detailed attention to information and ideas	______/10
2	I can summarize and explain information I've come across	______/10
3	I easily understand others' points of view and why they believe what they do	______/10
4	I can clearly express my own point of view	______/10
5	I am willing to change my mind and modify my beliefs when I learn new things	______/10
6	I am able to compare and to evaluate multiple sources of information	______/10
7	I can locate and research sources of relevant information by myself	______/10
8	I can clearly summarize and explain others' work, including its limitations	______/10
9	I am able to justify my own conclusions and to outline the evidence behind them	______/10
10	I am aware of and able to explain to others the limitations of my knowledge	______/10
Total score:		______/100

How did you do? As you may have noticed, these are the same ten questions that I asked in the very first chapter. If you answered them then, compare your scores. Hopefully, your score has increased.

If you scored 50 or below, I suggest that you re-read those sections of the first half of this book that you have least confidence in, before reading on. You can use the summary of the first half, below, to help find them. If you scored between 50 and 80, well done: consider revisiting and consolidating a couple of points before moving on, depending on your confidence. If you scored 80 or above, that's great. Give yourself a pat on the back and keep going.

Half way through!

Do come back to these pages later & re-read your own reflections.

PART II

BEING REASONABLE IN AN UNREASONABLE WORLD

GETTING TO GRIPS WITH RHETORIC

Vital!!! if you want to write well

How can you think critically about language and rhetoric?

↓

How can you think critically about fallacies and faulty reasoning?

↓

How can you think critically about cognitive and behavioural bias?

↓

How can you best overcome bias in yourself and others?

↓

How can you be a more critically engaged user of technology?

↓

How can you become a critically engaged writer and thinker?

I don't persuade a person because I use my words; I persuade a person because I use theirs

Richard Mullender

#TalkCriticalThinking

FIVE THINGS YOU'LL LEARN IN THIS CHAPTER

1 Three *different ways* we *use language*
2 How *persuasive messages work*
3 Why you should aim to be as *impartial* as possible
4 How to spot a range of *rhetorical devices*
5 How to evaluate *explicit emotional appeals*

The first half of this book set out what it means to be reasonable: to seek good reasons for accepting others' conclusions and to seek good explanations for the way things are. It also made the point that reasoning in this way neither comes naturally to people nor governs most of what we feel and do.

This bears repeating. There would be no need to study reasoning if we were naturally, inherently reasonable all of the time. There would be no need to study probability if, like computers, we calculated odds correctly as a matter of course.

We are not like this, however. Neither our most fundamental nor our most intense experiences of the world are best described in purely rational terms. It doesn't take a great deal of empirical observation to see that human motivations, interactions and interests are a mix of phenomena with deep roots in our evolutionary and social histories. We are creatures first and thinkers second – and rationally self-critical thinkers last of all.

Some people say that this makes us irredeemably **irrational**: that we act unreasonably most of the time, for motives inaccessible to us. I believe that this can put too much emphasis on a strictly logical definition of what is and is not reasonable – as well as making the unwarranted assumption that there is something inherently undesirable about being guided by emotion and sensation.

We are, certainly, highly **emotional** animals, driven by intensely felt attachments and a strong **moral** sense of what is right and wrong, just and unjust. But this is not an unfortunate disadvantage we would be better off without. This is the stuff of our humanity, our thinking as well as our feeling – and a field on which we can bring to bear our considerable powers of intellect, observation and empathy.

Unless we are able to richly and meticulously describe the **subjective** experiences through which we understand the world, we have no practical ability to put critical thinking into action, or to push back against those circumstances in which our **intuitions** may betray our best interests. Self-knowledge must not mean denying aspects of our nature in the pursuit of 'better' ways of thinking.

Irrational: predominantly guided by something other than logic or reason

Emotional: the strong, involuntary feelings that constantly colour our experience

Moral: the human sense of what is right and what is wrong

Subjective: an individual's unique personal experience and judgements, as opposed to an attempt to establish information that is independent of any individual

Intuition: the way in which we understand or decide things unconsciously, based on instinct and emotion and experience, rather than through a conscious process of reasoning

THE POWER OF LANGUAGE AND RHETORIC

Language is a marvellously flexible tool, and critical reasoning is only one small part of the uses we put it to. Most of the time, three related things are going on in our use of language:

- We are **communicating information** to one another: propositions that can be true or false and that claim to describe **objective** facts and the relationships between them.
- We are **expressing emotions and attitudes** that are neither true nor false in the same sense as the information above, but that reveal subjective experiences.
- We are **seeking to cause change** in others' behaviours or beliefs: by giving them orders, by making requests or by seeking to alter their attitudes, sentiments or opinions.

Objective: facts that exist independently of any individual perspective, and that remain true no matter what any individual happens to believe

Rhetoric: the art of persuasion through means other than reasoning

The last of these categories demands particular investigation if we are interested in the quest for reasonable arguments and explanations that characterize critical thinking. This is because it encompasses what is known as **rhetoric**: the art of persuasion through means other than reasoning.

If you happened to be studying in Europe 600 years ago, your education would have been founded on three pillars of learning taken from the classical world: grammar, logic and rhetoric. Together, these were known as the *trivium*, meaning the 'meeting place of three roads' in Latin. Grammar trained you to describe the world around you accurately. Logic trained you to draw reasonable conclusions from your knowledge. Rhetoric was the last and most significant of these foundational arts: persuading others of your conclusions and communicating ideas richly and successfully.

Rhetoric is the opposite of reasoning, so it must be bad, right? It's just a manipulative way of getting people to do things by playing on their emotions, right? Wrong. The assumption that rhetoric is the kind of clumsy manipulation that any smart person ought to see through is a myth, as is the idea that it is either a bad thing or an optional extra that we can choose to do or not to do. Our efforts to think usefully about rhetoric need first of all to respect its complexity, its universality and the ways in which it is woven into all acts of communication.

SMART STUDY: Dispelling four common myths about rhetoric

Myth	Acts of persuasion tend to be simple, crude things
Truth	Apparently simple acts of persuasion are often complex in their intentions and effects
Myth	Persuasion is a bad, misleading thing, and we would be better off aiming always to be purely logical and reasonable
Truth	Persuasion is neither a good nor a bad thing by itself – it's what you seek to persuade people of, and how, that defines it
Myth	Persuasiveness is a kind of optional extra that can be bolted onto a message or act of communication
Truth	Persuasion is an integral part of who we are and how we communicate, and is not something we can simply switch off
Myth	Smart people should be able to see through others' attempts at persuasion and come to their own conclusions
Truth	Actively applying critical thinking to persuasive messages can help you rethink your responses, but smart people are just as susceptible to manipulation as everyone else (sometimes more so, as they tend to be overconfident outside their own particular areas of expertise)

Ethos: establishing the trustworthiness of the source of an attempt at persuasion

Logos: the chain of ideas contained in an attempt at persuasion

Pathos: the emotional appeals made during an attempt at persuasion

As you might expect, classical Greece and Rome had a usefully systematic way of describing the combination of factors that a successfully persuasive message deploys. First formally set out by the philosopher Aristotle, these factors still offer a useful sense of the intricacies involved in any act of persuasion:

- **Ethos**: this comes first, and seeks to establish the trustworthiness of the author or source of the message. A message that succeeds in terms of ethos is one that speaks in an appropriate, reliable and respected register so far as its audience is concerned.
- **Logos**: once you've demonstrated that you can be trusted, logos describes the informational content you present to your audience. This is not necessarily the same thing as a rigorous argument. Rather, it describes the chain of ideas you would like your audience to follow towards your desired conclusion.
- **Pathos**: the way that something makes you feel. Pathos describes the emotional appeal of a message and the way it is delivered: it covers everything from fear and anger to patriotism and reverence, and is often the most important part of an act of persuasion. Emotional appeal is not inherently deceptive or unfair, and it is present even in the most seemingly impartial messages.[23]

Here's an exercise. Analyse the passage below in terms of *ethos*, *logos* and *pathos*, paying attention to the tone and what kind of audience this writing is aiming to persuade:

> As a senior clinician with several decades of hospital experience, I deplore the recent cuts to health care, which I believe represent not only an unacceptable reduction in the quality of care that staff are able to offer the public, but also an ideologically misguided attempt to achieve unattainable improvements in efficiency through market forces. The health system is not a conventional market, and its disproportionate duty of care towards the most vulnerable is a social good that exists outside of market forces. I myself have repeatedly had to tell acutely distressed families in recent months that all non-urgent care for their children must be delayed into the next tax year. Morale is at the lowest I have ever known. This is a crisis.

Did you find this a persuasive piece of writing? In what ways? How did it make you feel, or seem to be trying to make you feel?

In terms of *ethos*, the author begins by setting out their impressive credentials: an experienced doctor, trustworthy, speaking from concern and compassion rather than simply anger. In terms of *logos*, a number of parallel points are made that can be reconstructed into a fairly coherent argument, but whose effect when read is primarily to paint a vivid picture of a health system in crisis. In terms of *pathos*, the emotional appeal is kept at a restrained level, but still contains forceful vocabulary – 'deplore ... misguided ... most vulnerable ... acutely distressed ... crisis' – as well as particular references to the distress of families and their children, aimed at provoking empathy and compassion.

Finally, the ending – 'this is a crisis' – suggests both urgency and the timeliness of the message. There's one last Greek word that describes this component of persuasion's larger purpose: **kairos**, meaning 'the opportune moment'. Picking the right moment for words or action is vital to persuasion. Indeed, some of those professionally involved in industries of persuasion have argued that timeliness and preparation are the most important details of all: that someone is best 'pre-suaded' rather than simply persuaded, so that by the time you start the pitch itself, the main battle is already won.[24]

Kairos: the moment of opportunity at which persuasion is most likely to work

PUTTING PERSUASION IN CONTEXT

If you look back at the four components of successful classical persuasion, you'll notice that all of them rely on a successful grasp of context: establishing your trustworthiness in the eyes of a particular audience; bringing relevant content to their attention; striking the right emotional notes; and identifying the best moment in which to deliver your message.

This is hardly surprising. Knowing your audience is the foundation of any successful act of persuasion, and correctly grasping the context within which a message exists is the foundation of thinking critically about both its persuasive force and your best response.

Consider the following three texts, drawing on the same basic argument and ideas. Which of the three passages do you find most persuasive? Which is most effective at communicating its message?

1 Advances in genetic science are starting to permit parents to select for certain attributes in their offspring, based principally at this stage on embryo screening and selective implantation, but with an increasing body of research also surrounding germline modification and gene therapy. Any modification of human life at the genetic level is of great social and ethical as well as scientific significance, and demands both rigorous scrutiny and wide debate.

2 Genetic engineering now allows some parents to select some of their children's inherited characteristics, with more powerful and precise techniques on the way. This kind of science could have a huge impact on the future of humanity itself: it needs and deserves as wide a debate as possible.

3 Thanks to scientists playing god with the human genome, parents can now pick and mix the traits of their designer babies. This is a huge deal for the human race – or whatever you call what we might turn ourselves into. It's everyone's business – and we need to start talking about it right now, before it's too late.

(1) (2) (3) **MOST PERSUASIVE** .... **MOST EFFECTIVE** (1) (2) (3)

Linguistic register: the type of language typically used in a particular setting or context

The first one is written in the most formal, scientific style. The second one is a little more informal – a serious magazine article, perhaps – while the last one is more in the sensational style of a popular news report. Each of these different **linguistic registers** has its own particular impact. You may, for example, have found the first paragraph much more persuasive than the last, precisely because it avoids strenuously rhetorical effects and instead strikes a carefully reasonable tone. Alternatively, the level of detail in the first paragraph may have blunted its message compared to the clarity of the second passage. Or perhaps the emotional intensity of the last paragraph felt most appropriate, and the lack of emotion in the previous paragraphs misleading?

The third passage is certainly the most obviously rhetorical. Phrases like '*parents can now pick and mix the traits of their designer babies*' make things at once more vivid and sensational than in the first two accounts. This is rhetoric that asks you to be shocked – and to treat writing like this as a performance, closer to impassioned speech than to considered prose. Moreover, it's a kind of writing that is more interested in emotional impact that informational accuracy. In this case, the claim that 'parents can now pick and mix the traits of their designer babies' is actively misleading as an account of what is currently possible and available.

Note, however, that a lack of overt emotion and an authoritative tone can be just as rhetorically effective – and deceptive – as something emotionally intense. It is, for instance, perfectly possible to write complete nonsense in an academic register. Consider the following paragraph. Do you find it persuasive? What, precisely, is it arguing?

Advances in genetic engineering are starting to permit parents to select certain attributes in their offspring. Our accelerating capacity for tampering with human life at the genetic level is another sign of our impending departure from the conventional evolutionary hierarchy and its constraints, together with conventional so-called ethics. The urgent countervailing burden is now that we experiment radically upon ourselves unconstrained by such outmoded concerns so that we can ascend to the next level of species development, a place where only the fittest will be welcome.

....
....
....
....
....
....
....
....
....
....
....

This may sound authoritative and intelligent at first glance. If you read it more closely, however, you will see that it's effectively an argument in support of radical genetic experiments, ignoring all ethical concerns. If the author had simply written 'we should do genetic experiments on unborn children without worrying about any ethical concerns', the effect would be rather different. This brings us to an important point: Don't simply accept the linguistic register of a passage on its own terms. Work out to your own satisfaction what is being claimed and how it is being justified, while remaining alert to the ways in which any particular register itself has persuasive impact.

SMART STUDY: Three fundamental questions to ask about persuasion

Before you respond to any piece of evidence, information or argument, ask:

1 What type of writing am I reading?
2 Why is the author using this register and who is their intended audience?
3 According to what criteria or values can I judge and use this type of writing?

This will allow you to keep in mind the impact of a particular register and to ensure that you don't dismiss or accept what's being said unthinkingly. Whether you're reading an opinionated rant or a journal article, you need to work out who it is aimed at, what its authors' intentions are – and where your own needs and interests best fit into this context.

THINK ABOUT THIS: What techniques do you use to persuade different audiences in your life? How do your techniques of persuasion differ between friends, family and work? How do you set out in a written piece of work to persuade your readers that you know what you are talking about? ....
....
....
....
....
....

ANALYSING A MESSAGE IN DETAIL: EMOTION AND HUMAN STORIES

Look at the example below. Would you click on this link to find out more?

	YES	NO
This Kid Just Died. What He Left Behind Is Wondtacular.[25]	○	○

As you may have guessed, it's a headline from a popular website – from a 2013 article on Upworthy, in fact. In general, a journalistic headline is trying to persuade you that the article accompanying it is worth reading. In a digital age, headlines have taken on a still more important role than in the days of print, serving as the text for links that entice – or fail to entice – people into visiting a particular page, purely on the basis of this description. The most extreme examples of this are known as clickbait: headline descriptions only loosely related to actual content, trying to attract clicks at any cost and by almost any means.

This headline may not (quite) qualify as clickbait, but it's certainly pulling out all the rhetorical stops to generate emotional appeal of the kind that gets people sharing stories on social media. Take a look at it once again, and see how many emotive factors you can find in operation that might make you likely to click on it:

Do you ever share clickbait on social media — or sound like it yourself?

- ....
- ....
- ....
- ....
- ....
- ....

How many did you come up with? Here's a list of just some of the things I see going on:

Brevity and impact: most headlines and links aim for the maximum impact in the minimum number of words. Here, we learn about both a dramatic event (the death of a 'kid') and its amazing legacy in the space of ten words.

Suspense and anticipation: we are told to expect something interesting or amazing, but are given no precise details of what this is going to be.

Intensity and immediacy: the first four words present a highly emotive event – the death of a young person – in language that is at once particular ('this'), informal ('kid), immediate ('just') and bluntly impactful ('died').

Tragedy and triumph: as well as emotional impact, the two-part headline sketches an archetypical story in miniature – a tragic death, but also a heart-lifting message of hope. A satisfying narrative is being promised.

Originality and strangeness: the made-up word 'wondtacular' – a melding of 'wonderful' and 'spectacular' – both demands attention and suggests a resolution to the story that's not only heart-warming but also unique.

Universality: we are being promised a highly personal story, but in the most general of terms; no particular gender, age, nationality, location, name or detail of events is given. This could be almost anyone, and is thus relevant to almost everyone.

I'm not suggesting that all of the above goes consciously through your mind when you glance at a headline, link or status update online. In fact, it's precisely because none of this consciously runs through your mind that acts of emotive persuasion work so well. They draw on unconscious assumptions and sentiments, sketching the outline of a human story that will either entice us into empathy or push us towards condemnation. Take a look at the two rhetorical appeals below. Which do you find the most, and least, persuasive? Why?

....	Frightened children face freezing temperatures. Without
....	shelter and warm clothes they will struggle to survive. Every
....	minute counts. These children urgently need warm winter
....	clothing and blankets to protect them from the cold ... With
....	your help, we can make the world a safer place for children.
....	Please help us make sure no child is forgotten this winter.
....	(Unicef Syria Appeal, 2017)

....	They're not sending their best. They're not sending you.
....	They're sending people that have lots of problems, and
....	they're bringing those problems with us [*sic*]. They're
....	bringing drugs. They're bringing crime. They're rapists.
....	(Donald Trump on Mexican immigrants, June 2015)[26]

Two different kinds of persuasion are going on in these messages. The first uses a human story to create an intense emotional appeal to its audience's empathy, coupling the vivid image of frightened children facing freezing temperatures with the larger purpose of making the world a safer place for children. It aims to persuade its audience through compassion and identification, and make readers feel close to the children in question.

The second passage is also interested in powerful emotions, but in this case its aim is to make its audience feel distant from its subject: Mexican immigrants are not like 'you' but are criminals, rapists, people who bring their problems with them. It aims to persuade its audience through fear and aversion – to make 'us' feel that we are nothing like 'them'.

SMART STUDY: Rhetoric and emotional distance

In general, an emotionally engaging message either seeks to harness our sympathies or to harden our hearts, and it does this by the relationship it suggests between its audience and its subject. Are we, the audience, made to believe that something is near to us literally and metaphorically? Or are we told that it is alien to us and best kept far away in every sense? The closer you look at the emotional impact of language, the more you will see a version of these effects playing out – and, hopefully, the more alert you will be to attempts at manipulating you through suggesting either closeness or distance. In general:

- Rhetoric can bring us **closer** to a subject emotionally, and suggest that we should be **open** towards it.
- Or it can seek to make us feel **further away**, and suggest that it is something alien and threatening we should feel **closed** towards.

To a degree that we are not always aware of, much of the language we use continually establishes degrees of either closeness or distance between us and our subjects. We are constantly engaged in emotive suggestion and persuasion through our choice of words, and through our sensitivity to subtle gradations of feeling in every description. Here are several different ways of describing the same thing. Can you see what is going on in each case in terms of emotive persuasion?

> A number of protestors broke a window of a London office building.
>
> A bunch of crusty hippies smashed up the office window.
>
> Banking fat-cats watched as protestors burst into their air-conditioned splendour.
>
> A criminal element vandalized property in the City amid largely peaceful protests.
>
> Protests turned violent as anti-capitalists smashed their way into corporate offices.
>
> Peaceful idealists struck a symbolic blow against crony capitalism in London.

People are protestors, crusty hippies, a criminal element, peaceful idealists or anti-capitalists (or several or none of these things) depending on the particular story you wish to tell about them. They are bankers, or office-workers, or fat-cats, or crony capitalists. Each label implies something different. Pathos is not simply about making your audience feel sorry for people. It's about your view of the world – and about what world you want others to see.

The list above could go on and on. Can you extend it yourself with a few alternative perspectives? There is no limit to the different number of ways you can describe even one thing. Nothing is

How many other stories can you tell about the example above?

only what it seems – or rather, everything is what it seems to someone in particular, coming from a particular point of view.

- ....
- ....
- ....
- ....
- ....

AIMING FOR IMPARTIALITY

What is going on in terms of persuasion within the following article title?

> The role of the popes in the invention of complementarity and the Vatican's anathematization of gender[27]

For anyone who isn't specifically interested in this particular topic, the language of this headline is likely to be uninteresting – even incomprehensible. Does this mean it's a failure, given that most casual readers would be totally put off?

Not if we consider what a title like this is intended to achieve. As a synopsis of specialist information, it is clear and to-the-point. It is designed to appeal only to a small number of people, while warning others away. Achieving clarity, precision and detail in as few words as possible is its virtue. A title like this has succeeded if it persuades most people not to read the article, because its primary intention is to convey as precisely and clearly as possible the article's content, so that experts in the field know exactly what it is about.

If, instead, the article was titled 'Pope Gender Shock Scandal' it might persuade more people to read it, but this would completely fail to match the right readers to the topic. Indeed, writing rigorous titles for academic articles is quite an art. In many journals, house style forbids any title declaring a conclusion or an opinion (e.g. 'Environmental factors have greater influence on cancer than previously thought') and insists on a factual description of the investigation ('A reconsideration of the role of environmental factors in common cancers'). Why? Because a more striking title that sounds like a conclusion might:

- Generate unhelpful prejudice.
- Be used misleadingly out of the context of the research itself.
- Encourage casual readers to oversimplify the complexities of the research.
- Encourage an emotive popularity contest between competing research claims.

Avoiding prejudicial pitfalls and persuading people not to jump to unwarranted assumptions is a difficult art. Indeed, it takes every bit as much expertise and care as emotive persuasion. When it comes to your own writing, this skill is known as **impartiality** – achieving a clear, accurate and fair assessment of the relevant facts.

Impartiality: stripping away emotive bias from language and expressing yourself as objectively as possible

Achieving impartiality entails, as far as possible, stripping away emotional bias from language and expressing things from a more neutral perspective.

SMART STUDY SKILLS: Aiming at impartiality in your own work

There is no such thing as perfect impartiality, any more than there is such a thing as perfect objectivity, but there are some fundamental principles you should apply in order to present as clear, useful and fair-minded a perspective as possible in your own work:

If everybody always lies to you, the consequence is not that you believe the lies, but rather that nobody believes anything any longer.

Hannah Arendt

#TalkCriticalThinking

- Avoid the biases contained in highly emotive language.
- Express all the relevant facts of a particular situation clearly and carefully.
- Show your awareness of the relevant differing beliefs about the significance of these facts.
- Offer some evaluation as to the reasonableness of these different beliefs.

For each of the sentences below, try coming up with a more impartial formulation of the same information that describes the same thing:

Two idiots nearly got themselves killed by fooling around on the railway tracks outside the station yesterday; they only just got out of the train's way in time!

During the course of our investigation, we found evidence of some horrifying criminal activity in which macho gangs abused new initiates, for fun, until they were almost half-dead from repeated beatings.

Thanks to the ongoing cataclysm of climate change, future generations may never even hear the beautiful songs of what were once common garden birds.

How did you do? As you will have noticed, there is no single correct way to express things impartially, or any way of being completely neutral. Every different way of expressing something brings some implications beyond literal meaning. Sometimes, leaving out information can have as great an impact as including it. Here are my rewrites of the three sentences above:

1 Yesterday, two people trespassing on the railway tracks near the station narrowly avoided being hit by a train.
2 During the course of our investigation, we found evidence of gang initiations that left some new members severely injured from repeated beatings.
3 Climate change may mean that once-common garden birds vanish from this habitat over time.

Even a seemingly impartial description can have a hidden persuasive impact, however. Is 'climate change scepticism' a more scientific term than 'climate change denial'? Or is it a way of making an unscientific position sound more acceptable? Impartiality doesn't mean treating all claims as equally reasonable, or assuming that the best response lies in the middle between opposing claims.

With that in mind, here's an exercise embodying a particularly important research skill: combining information from several different places into a single account of your own. First, read these three related paragraphs on the same topic:

1 The Stanford prison experiment (SPE) was an attempt to investigate the psychological effects of perceived power, focusing on the struggle between prisoners and guards. It was conducted at Stanford University from 14 to 20 August 1971, and followed a group of students arbitrarily divided at the start into 'guards' and 'prisoners'.

2 The Stanford prison experiment is a textbook example of how to produce headline-grabbing but scientifically worthless – and ethically dubious – research. It's sadly typical of the field that it's still so widely discussed today, essentially because it makes for an interesting and shocking story rather than because it has merit.

3 The Stanford prison experiment was a milestone in psychological research and its insights into the more troubling aspects of human nature. Those who wish to learn how it is that ordinary human beings can inflict atrocities on one another, with barely a flicker of ethical concern, need look no further than the abuses and indignities its 'guards' inflicted on their 'prisoners'.

See if you can manage to write a summary that impartially conveys information from all three of these paragraphs: one which incorporates details from multiple perspectives without being unduly influenced by one particular view:

....

....

....

....

....

My own effort is below. How does it differ from your own? What is significant about the things that have been left out, or kept in?

> The Stanford prison experiment was a controversial attempt to investigate the psychological effects of perceived power, focusing on the struggle between prisoners and guards. It was conducted at Stanford University from 14 to 20 August 1971. Today, some critics consider it scientifically and ethically dubious – and famous largely because of its shock value – while others consider it a milestone in psychological research, offering insight into how easily people can be led by circumstances to mistreat one another while feeling little ethical concern.

Notice that my summary tries to convey a sense of the different opinions about the experiment while toning down their emotive language, and incorporating only necessary details. This doesn't mean it is free from all emotional and descriptive language. Rather, it aims to be in control of this, and to clearly indicate the diversity of opinions involved.[28]

What we must not do, when facing a range of opinions, is simply try to merge them into one undifferentiated account. We may have an opinion of our own to share, but this should be clearly labelled as such, together with other points of view. Achieving greater impartiality doesn't mean pretending there is only one perspective available. It means recognizing a diversity of perspectives, framing them carefully within those facts we know and not being afraid to identify the limitations of any particular perspective.

THINK ABOUT THIS: How does impartiality differ from neutrality? What does it mean to be impartial about a subject that provokes profound disagreement – climate change, abortion – where different perspectives are not necessarily equally backed by evidence? ....

....

....

....

....

....

RHETORICAL DEVICES

Rhetorical device: a persuasive technique used to enhance the appeal of a message

A **rhetorical device** is a persuasive technique used to enhance the appeal of a message. The following are some of the most significant rhetorical devices you'll encounter in your work and in everyday language.

Rhetorical questions

Rhetorical question: a question that is not meant literally and that does not require an answer, but which is used to make a point more forcefully

Here's an example of perhaps the most straightforward and yet effective persuasive device of them all, a **rhetorical question**:

> Do you really need me to tell you why stealing my food from the fridge is wrong?

We call this a rhetorical question because it isn't intended literally. I don't want you to answer my question. I'm not really asking a question at all. I'm simply using the form of a question in order to make a point more forcefully – in this case, that it's self-evident that you should not steal my food from the fridge, and that you should be ashamed for doing so.

Rhetorical questions are common in both everyday conversation and more formal acts of persuasion such as political speech-making. By inviting your audience to supply the answer to a question you have deemed too obvious to deserve debate, you can create a powerful pressure of assumption. Consider these examples:

- Do you really need me to spell it out?
- In what sense is going ahead as if nothing had changed a good idea?
- Should I stay silent just because it would be easier for you if I did?

In each case, an assumed answer is being forced onto the listener, while the speaker is not obliged to actually spell out what they think, thus protecting them from a straightforward objection. In general, rhetorical questions are a tempting but unhelpful way of writing. By concealing an assumption or a conclusion, they seek to shut down a debate – something they have in common with many rhetorical devices. If you can spot them, however, and know how to respond by identifying and engaging with the assumption in question, you can open up the debate again.

Jargon, smokescreens, buzzwords and euphemisms

Do you find the following passage persuasive?

> When debating the applicability of the employment legislation in question, as pertains to temporary staff employed on a short-term basis, there appears to be a prima-facie case for dismissing entirely the line of argument that there is no case to be answered – and for proceeding on the assumption that, at the least, nominal damages will be applicable.

Jargon: words and phrases familiar only to an expert audience, sometimes used legitimately between experts, but sometimes used in order to confuse non-experts and restrict their engagement

This is a classic example of **jargon**: forms of words familiar only to experts, sometimes used in order to exclude others by making it difficult to follow their sense. Jargon is acceptable when used to communicate precisely between experts, but not when it is intended only to impress or confuse those lacking expertise. In this case, a clearer way of saying the same thing might read: 'Looking at how employment law applies to temporary staff employed on a short-term basis, it seems reasonable based on first impressions to dismiss the argument that there is no case to be answered. Instead, we can proceed by assuming that at least a small sum of money will be awarded as damages.

In general, you should mistrust jargon unless it is being used in an appropriate context – and should especially beware of anyone packing their writing with unnecessary **buzzwords** designed to create an appearance of insight, understanding and expertise. What, for example, is actually being said in the following passage?

Buzzwords: fashionable words and phrases used to make something sound impressive and up to date; often a case of style over substance, with little thought beneath the surface

> The team met yesterday for some blue-sky ideation. We used tactile workshop tools and cues – crayons, bright paper pads, mood boards, heritage magazine issues – to create a safe space for radical concepts in the customer-relationships space inspired by the visual traditions of the 1960s and its ethos of radical changemaking.

I made this example up, but there's worse out there...

The answer is: not a lot, thanks to a mixture of buzzwords and jargon dressing up an everyday scenario as though it were something special. Here's what is actually going on: 'The team met yesterday to generate ideas. We used crayons, pads, notice boards and old issues of magazines to come up with a wide variety of ideas for customer relationships, inspired loosely by the 1960s.' But this doesn't sound as impressive, or allow you to charge clients as much money for your alleged expertise.

Jargon and buzzwords are about using inflated language to sound more impressive than you actually are, and to prevent others from engaging critically. When it comes to avoiding an uncomfortable point, a related form of irrelevant language is equally common: creating a verbal **smokescreen**. Here's an example you might encounter in the realm of politics, in response to a question that the speaker doesn't want to answer. Notice how they evade the question by generating a 'screen' of words related to the topic, but irrelevant to the particular point they wish to avoid:

Smokescreen: a process of verbal concealment, where someone attempts to avoid or hide a key point beneath a large volume of irrelevant words

> You ask me whether I have ever taken drugs? I would refer you to my long and honourable career in public service and to the considerable sacrifices I and my family have made for the public good – not to mention my many years of work alongside those suffering the ravages of drug addiction, and their families, for whom I have long been a compassionate and prominent voice of advocacy.

A final common category of verbal obfuscation is **euphemism**, meaning the avoidance of negative words in order to create a more positive impression than is actually warranted. Consider the following example. What is being described – and what is the euphemistic language trying to hide?

Euphemism: deliberately replacing a negative-seeming word or phrase with something more neutral, often in order to conceal the severity of what has happened

> The vehicle in question made an unscheduled rapid deceleration owing to brief distraction on the part of the driver, resulting in a sub-optimal experience for passengers, who suffered the inconvenience of minor damage to their physical persons.

In this particular case, the description entirely avoids words like 'crash', 'careless', 'accident' and 'injury' – instead replacing them with emotionally neutral jargon like 'unscheduled rapid deceleration'. In order to avoid this, we could rewrite the paragraph along these lines: 'The vehicle in question crashed thanks to careless driving, an accident that resulted in minor injuries to its passengers.'

Similarly, a company might describe itself as 'downsizing' its workforce rather than 'sacking' them; you might describe a meal as 'challenging' or 'interesting' rather than 'disgusting'; or you might say that the unexpected severe side-effects of a drug are 'unfortunate' rather than 'awful'. Euphemism is everywhere in business and politics – and anywhere else people want to hide the unpleasant implications of their words and actions.

SIX

JUDGE STRATEGY, NOT RESULTS. DON'T BE OBSESSED WITH SHORT-TERM SUCCESS. KEEP DOING THE RIGHT THING. EXPOSE YOURSELF TO SERENDIPITY AND OPPORTUNITY. CONSISTENTLY APPLY A SOUND APPROACH.

#TalkCriticalThinking

Hyperbole, litotes and paralepsis

Hyperbole deliberately exaggerates something for rhetorical effect, and its impact ranges from colourful everyday talk to highly emotive appeals. It's not intended to be taken literally. As with most rhetorical figures of speech, a skilful user of hyperbole can manage to enhance the emotional impact of their position without needing to justify its literal truth:

Hyperbole: deliberate exaggeration for the purpose of rhetorical impact

> You've said that about a million times already!
>
> It's all fake – everything they say is lies; they have no integrity or honesty whatsoever.

Litotes is the opposite of hyperbole and entails using understatement or a negative in order to emphasize a point. Again, it can be both a part of everyday language and a powerful persuasive device, often making use of a double negative to convey strength of opinion:

Litotes: deliberately understating or using a negative to make a point sound convincing while not seeming to claim it directly

> How was the event? Not bad, not bad at all.
>
> Should we trust her? Let me tell you, she will not easily be distracted, deflected or led astray.

Compare the effectiveness of the phrases above to straightforward statements with the same literal meaning:

> How was the event? Good.
>
> Should we trust her? Let me tell you, she will be focused, attentive and determined.

By being indirect, litotes manages to express a point of view without committing its user. Depending on context, it can thus help someone to sound more modest, more careful, more trustworthy or more determined, because it gestures towards other possibilities without needing to explain precisely what is being claimed.

Finally, **paralepsis** follows a similar rhetorical pattern. It involves introducing an idea while claiming that you don't, actually, want to discuss this idea. It's a wonderfully slippery device, and when used skilfully can cast all kinds of aspersions while shirking any responsibility for what is being said:

Paralepsis: introducing an idea while claiming you do not wish to discuss it, thus allowing you to make a claim while denying any responsibility for discussing it

> I don't want to dwell on the fact that my opponent has yet to come up with a single positive policy, or that her followers appear to be deserting her in droves. Instead, I want to focus on my own agenda.
>
> I have promised not to talk about his many, many business failures and inadequacies, nor about his sheer incompetence as a manager and as a leader. So I will not. I said I will not say it, so I will not say it.

If this seems too obvious a trick to work, think again. Rhetorical successes are often about what you can get away with saying, and how forcefully you can push people's emotional buttons, rather than about what stands up to a moment of reasoned scrutiny.

SUMMARY

Language has three common, overlapping uses:

- **Communicating information** that claims to be objectively true.
- **Expressing emotions** and attitudes that reveal subjective experience.
- **Seeking to cause change** in others' behaviour or beliefs.

The last of these categories encompasses the art of **rhetoric**: persuasion through means other than reasoning. Rhetoric is a complex, emotive art, and learning to recognize and make good use of it is an important aspect of critical thinking. We should remember that:

- Persuasion is not a good thing or a bad thing in itself; it's how it's used that matters.
- Persuasion is an integral part of how we communicate, not an optional extra.

One useful way of thinking about the combination of factors that make a message persuasive dates back to the ancient Greek philosopher Aristotle:

- **Ethos** establishes the trustworthiness and credentials of the author of a message.
- **Logos** describes the chain of ideas that the audience is intended to follow.
- **Pathos** describes the emotional appeal of a message and its delivery.
- **Kairos** describes the most opportune moment for a message to persuade.

Understanding persuasion means putting it in context and considering the **linguistic register** within which someone is operating – the type of language appropriate to a particular setting, together with its style and assumptions. Don't simply accept a certain linguistic register as proof of honesty and reliability, or as a definitive sign of unreliability.

In the most persuasive messages, we often find some or all of:

- A compelling human story
- An intensity of emotional appeal
- Elements of mystery and surprise
- The use of memorable or striking language.

Rhetoric also has distinct functions depending on whether it wants us to feel positive or negative towards its subject, something that often plays out in terms of distance:

- When seeking to create positive emotions, rhetoric often brings us **closer** to a subject emotionally, and suggests that we should be **open** to it.
- When seeking to create negative emotions, rhetoric often makes us feel **further away** from a subject emotionally, and suggests we should feel **closed** to it.

Learning to see beyond others' emotive language and achieve **impartiality** is an important and difficult skill. It entails stripping away emotional bias, as far as possible, and seeking to express things from a neutral perspective. To do this we must:

- Recognize the bias contained in highly emotive language.
- Clearly and accurately express the relevant facts.
- Remain aware of relevant differing beliefs about the significance of these facts.
- Offer some evaluation as to the reasonableness of different beliefs.

Rhetorical devices are persuasive techniques used to enhance the appeal of a message:

- **Rhetorical questions** are not intended literally and do not require an answer, but have an assumed answer that is used for emphasis.
- **Jargon** consists of words and phrases likely only to be familiar to experts, sometimes used to confuse or exclude non-experts.
- **Buzzwords** are fashionable words or phrases used to make something sound impressive, often with little meaning beneath their surface.

- **Smokescreens** are a kind of verbal concealment, using the discussion of irrelevant points to hide the fact that someone is avoiding a difficult subject.
- **Euphemism** entails deliberately replacing a phrase with negative connotations, by substituting something neutral or even positive-sounding in its place.
- **Hyperbole** deliberately exaggerates something for rhetorical effect.
- **Litotes** deliberately understates or uses a negative to make a point sound more convincing or likely to be accepted.
- **Paralepsis** introduces an idea while claiming it's not your intention to discuss it, allowing you to make suggestions without taking any responsibility for them.

Now watch the video 'The fine art of warping minds with rhetoric'. It's on YouTube. Tell me what you think via #TalkCriticalThinking

EIGHT

SEEING THROUGH FAULTY REASONING

How can you think critically about emotional and persuasive language?

↓

How can you think critically about fallacies and faulty reasoning?

How can you think critically about cognitive and behavioural bias?

How can you best overcome bias in yourself and others?

How can you be a more critically engaged user of technology?

How can you become a critically engaged writer and thinker?

WARNING: faulty reasoning is seductive... seeing through it is a central skill for study & life.

WHY IS IT
THAT SMART
PEOPLE
CAN BE SO
STUPID?
RAY HYMAN

#TalkCriticalThinking

FIVE THINGS YOU'LL LEARN IN THIS CHAPTER

1 How to spot *a faulty line of reasoning*
2 The difference between *formal* and *informal fallacies*
3 How to *identify* common *informal fallacies*
4 Where the *logic* of formal fallacies *breaks down*
5 How to understand *Bayes's Theorem* and *base rate neglect*

Bad reasoning isn't the same as basing your thinking on inaccurate information, or simply lying. Bad reasoning occurs when you make a faulty connection between premises and a conclusion – and yet this faulty connection is presented in the manner of a reasonable justification. Bad reasoning is thus a special kind of error. It's one in which the language, methods and tools of reasoning are misapplied.

Much of the time, careful reconstruction of an argument or consideration of an explanation will be sufficient to show its flaws. Sometimes, however, a faulty line of argument may appear to be correct or may exert considerable persuasive force. It may be mistaken for valid reasoning and treated as if it provided forceful justification for a conclusion.

This is a problem, for obvious enough reasons: the whole project of critical thinking threatens to break down if we cannot know whether a line of reasoning is sensible or merely seductive.

Fortunately, we can train ourselves to spot this kind of faulty reasoning by becoming familiar with its general forms, commonly known as **fallacies**. Fallacies are of interest in two ways. First, studying them allows us to explore the underlying ways in which reasoning is most commonly at fault. Second, studying them makes us more alert to the persuasiveness and deceptive appeal of this faulty reasoning – and better able to avoid it ourselves.

Fallacy: a flawed general type of argument that establishes a faulty connection between premises and conclusion, thus failing to give us a good reason to accept the conclusion

BEWARE!

Some fallacies are extremely seductive.

FALLACIOUS ARGUMENTS AND FAULTY REASONING

Some authors define fallacies in a strictly logical sense, while others extend them to cover a host of psychological vulnerabilities and poor approaches to reasoning. In this chapter, I have taken an inclusive approach, in the belief that it's valuable to think as broadly as possible about those occasions on which we are misled, misdirected or merely bamboozled.[29]

As we'll explore in the next chapter, the psychological roots of our susceptibility to faulty reasoning are every bit as fascinating as fallacies themselves – and intimately bound up with the business of being human. To start us off, here is a **fallacious argument** in action. Can you spot what is going wrong?

Fallacious argument: an argument whose conclusion does not follow from its premises, because its reasoning rests on an identifiable fallacy

> Everyone I've spoken to thinks that the president is doing a terrific job. You should stop moaning and accept that he's the right leader for this country!

Even if you instantly sensed that something isn't right with this line of argument, you may have found it difficult to pinpoint its flaw. This is because it is implicit rather than explicit. An unstated assumption is at work, and the problem lies here – in something that hasn't actually been said or directly acknowledged. Once we spell out the unstated assumption in question, the problem becomes clear enough:

> Everyone I've spoken to thinks that the president is doing a terrific job. The collected opinions of the people I've spoken to are sufficient for establishing the definitive truth. You should stop moaning and accept that he's the right leader for this country!

Appeal to popularity: a fallacious form of argument based on the assumption that whatever most people think must be true.

Notice that this unstated assumption – that popular opinion is sufficient for establishing truth – is general rather than particular. It's a form of fallacious argument known as an **appeal to popularity** and, once identified, is obviously inadequate to guarantee the conclusion (unless it can be shown that I have spoken in depth to a huge number of different people, and that their pooled opinions are indeed a definitive measure of presidential competence). Contrast this with a different fallacious approach to the same topic:

> Both the people I've spoken to think that the president is doing a terrific job. I've spoken to Burt and Ernie and they are always right. You should stop moaning and accept that he's the right leader for this country!

Appeal to irrelevant authority: a fallacious form of argument based on the perceived opinion of an authority without any expertise in a relevant area

In this case, basing an argument on the allegedly infallible opinion of two people is likely to constitute an **appeal to irrelevant authority**. Unless the people being appealed to are experts in this particular area, the argument can, at best, offer a very weak justification of its conclusion.

If Burt and Ernie happen to be the nation's most distinguished political commentators, appealing to their authority might count as a convincing reason to accept the conclusion. Assuming they're not, however, we are dealing with an argument that pretends to be offering certainty where, in fact, all it has to offer is weak support along these lines:

> Both the people I've spoken to think that the president is doing a terrific job. I've spoken to Burt and Ernie and they are moderately well informed. You should accept the possibility that Burt and Ernie have at least a small point and that maybe you should slightly modify your perspective in the light of this.

This is no longer a fallacious argument, because it's no longer confusing a weak, qualified claim with an unarguable truth. But the illusion of certainty is precisely what gives a fallacy much of its force. In many fallacies, a weak inductive argument is masquerading as a sound deductive argument – and this, it turns out, can be a comforting and convincing way to simplify the world.

Unwarranted hidden assumption: the faulty, unstated element of reasoning that a fallacy relies on, and that we aim to spell out in order to identify what is at fault

Every fallacy relies on an identifiable type of **unwarranted hidden assumption**: a generalization that pretends it can offer strong support to a conclusion which, in fact, is at best very weakly supported – or that entails a misunderstanding of deductive logic. Here are another two everyday fallacious arguments. See if you can spell out the unwarranted assumptions in each:

....	The leader of the opposition argued that morals in our country are going in the wrong direction. Then she was caught having an affair with a man 20 years her junior. So much for her argument!
....	During the course of our experiment, we saw that increasing the temperature in the room led to reduced performance among participants in Group 1. On that basis, the reduction in performance among participants in Group 2 during the course of the experiment must be due to an increase in temperature in the second room.

In the first example, the assumption is that 'if what someone does contradicts what they say, then what they say must be wrong'. This is clearly untrue. We may think less of someone's character if they are a hypocrite, but this has no necessary bearing on the reliability of what they are saying.

In the second example, the assumption is that 'because increasing temperature reduces performance, the only possible explanation of reduced performance is an increase in temperature'. This is untrue, as there are plenty of other reasons that performance could be reduced in addition to temperature: the faulty assumption entails a misunderstanding of logic.

Sometimes, it can be difficult to spot exactly what is going wrong with a piece of reasoning, or to explain convincingly to other people what the problem is. In these cases, using directly **comparable examples** can be a powerful method of clarification and illustration – constructing parallel arguments using precisely the same form of words and reasoning but a totally different topic.

Comparable example: a method for testing potentially fallacious arguments, and illustrating their flaws, by applying exactly the same reasoning in a different context

Let's consider the first example from this chapter once again, and its appeal to popular opinion:

> Everyone I've spoken to thinks that the president is doing a terrific job. You should stop moaning and accept that he's the right leader for this country!

We can test the forcefulness of this kind of reasoning with a comparable example, or three:

> It's the year 1066 and everyone I've spoken to thinks that the Earth is flat. You should stop moaning and accept that it is!

> Nobody I've spoken to knows what the word 'terpsichorean' means. You should stop moaning and accept that it doesn't have a known meaning!

> Everyone in this room says that two plus two equals five. So it does.

As you no doubt know, two plus two is four, the Earth is not flat and terpsichorean means 'related to dancing'. By taking exactly the same form as the argument under scrutiny, examples like this reveal the illegitimacy of its underlying assumption, and can help us, and others, to see through what could otherwise sound like legitimate reasoning.

THINK ABOUT THIS: Can you think of an appealing but fallacious argument you have encountered recently? Can you think of a directly comparable example that highlights its faulty reasoning? ....

....

....

....

....

....

FALLACIES, TRUTHS AND HIDDEN ASSUMPTIONS

It's worth emphasizing that an argument is not fallacious just because it is based on a false premise, and that a fallacious argument doesn't necessarily have either false premises or a false conclusion. Only one thing is definitively untrue in the case of a fallacious argument, and that's the claim that there is a convincing logical connection between premise and conclusion. Here, by contrast, is a valid deductive argument that happens to have a false premise:

> There are no capital cities in the world that begin with the letter 'P'. Paris begins with a letter 'P' so it cannot be a capital city.

The first premise is false and the conclusion is also false, but the form of the argument itself is perfectly valid: its conclusion does indeed follow logically from its premise. If we correct the factual error in the first premise, the reasonableness of this link between premise and conclusion is obvious:

> There are no capital cities in the world that begin with the letter 'X'. Xian begins with a letter 'X' so it cannot be a capital city.

An argument that has true premises can, however, be fallacious. For example:

> There are no capital cities in the world that begin with the letter 'X'. My friend lives in a city that is not the capital of China. That city must begin with the letter 'X'.

This is a fallacious argument, despite the truth of its premises. The conclusion does not follow from the premises, as we can see if we pick apart its supposed 'logic':

> There are no capital cities in the world that begin with the letter 'X'. My friend lives in a city that is not the capital of China. If no capital cities begin with 'X', then every non-capital city in the world must begin with 'X'. My friend's city must begin with the letter 'X'.

Clearly, this is nonsense (even if it makes your brain hurt slightly to check this). The fact that no capital cities begin with 'X' tells us only that non-capital cities can begin with any letter other than an 'X'. Finally, a fallacious argument can have both true premises and a true conclusion, because it's only the faulty connection between premises and conclusion that matters. For example:

> There used to be a capital city that began with the letter 'X'. Xian begins with a letter 'X'. So Xian must once have been a capital city.

In this example, every fact is true if taken individually. There did used to be a capital city in the world that began with the letter 'X', Xian does begin with this letter and it did use to be the capital of China. What is fallacious is the use of the word 'so' to suggest that this conclusion can reasonably be inferred from the first two premises. The information happens to be true, but the suggestion that one thing can be inferred from another is itself untrue, as a comparable example makes clear:

> I used to have a friend whose name began with the letter 'B'. Barack Obama's name begins with a letter 'B'. So Barack Obama must once have been my friend.

As we've already noted, if you're trying to work out whether an argument is fallacious or not, testing it by coming up with a comparable example can be very useful. In summary:

- An argument is not necessarily fallacious when it's based on a false premise or when it has a false conclusion.
- A fallacious argument can still have true premises.
- A fallacious argument can still have a true conclusion.
- The claim that there is a reasonable link between premise and conclusion is, however, always false in the case of a fallacious argument.

SMART STUDY: Two broad types of fallacies

Broadly speaking, fallacies fall into two categories, and knowing the difference between them is important if you want to correctly identify what is going wrong.

If you need to consider both the content of an argument and its relationship with external information, this is an **informal fallacy**. You'll need to demonstrate that its fault lies in some kind of factual inaccuracy, incompleteness or misjudgement. For example, 'Alice says that my band is world class – and she should know!' may or may not be a forceful argument, depending on just how expert a judge of bands Alice actually is.

If the error is purely related to the structure of an argument, you are dealing with a **formal fallacy**; and you can demonstrate the falsity of the reasoning using logic alone, without reference to external facts. For example, the structure of the following argument is invalid, so you can say it is fallacious without knowing anything about its content: 'All world-class brands have fans. My band has fans, making it a world-class brand!'

The following list of fallacies spans several sub-categories, but all of them are at root either formal or informal fallacies.

INFORMAL FALLACIES OF RELEVANCE (RED HERRINGS)

Giving fallacies a name is a useful aid to memory and recognition, but what matters most is learning how to skewer the abuses of reasoning with confidence. Elements of the categorization I've used here go all the way back to the ancient Greek philosopher Aristotle. This should, however, be treated as a broad thematic guide rather than something prescriptive or comprehensive.[30]

A surprising amount goes back to the ancient Greeks: people are still much the same.

A **fallacy of relevance** describes an argument that relies on premises that are either not relevant at all to its conclusion, or not sufficiently relevant to strongly support it. All fallacies of this type are **red herrings**, a term that originally described a strong-smelling fish used to lead hunting dogs away from a scent – and this now provides a neat metaphor for any intentional distraction away from what is actually at stake.

Fallacy of relevance: an argument relying on premises that are insufficiently relevant to its conclusion for us to accept this conclusion

Appeals to...

One of the commonest fallacies of relevance overlaps with the rhetorical phenomena we considered in the previous chapter, and consists of an '**appeal to**' emotive external factors. Here are a few examples. In each case, try to identify the nature of the appeal:

1 This is unquestionably the best small car available on the market: the president of Italy drives one! ....

2 She is the author of the biggest-selling poetry book of all time. Of course, she is the world's greatest living poet. ....

3 His research trial methodology was sloppy and its results dubious, but he has been having a rough time recently, so we should give him the benefit of the doubt. ....

4 At this difficult time, progressing with my plan is vital for our success. If you are not with me, we may need to have a frank discussion about your future at the company. ....

How did you do? These cases represent, respectively:

1 **Appeal to irrelevant authority**: invoking an authority that isn't actually able or qualified to prove your point (the president of Italy's choice of car doesn't provide a definitive answer to the question of which is the best small car).
2 **Appeal to popularity**: asserting that whatever is popular must be true or good (there is no simple or direct relationship between book sales and quality, as every author is painfully aware).
3 **Appeal to sympathy**: invoking sympathy as a sufficient reason for agreeing with something (although we may feel sorry for someone who has had a rough time, this should have no bearing on our assessment of the quality and accuracy of their work).
4 **Appeal to force**: using the threat of violence to compel agreement (the moment we force someone to agree with us through threats, we are abandoning the principle of reasoned debate, together with its interest in pursuing truth).

Argument by appeal: the fallacy of appealing to external factors such as authority or popularity to justify a conclusion, rather than using rigorous reasoning

In each case, an appeal is being made to something that is far less forceful (and more open to debate) than it is claimed to be. Emotive appeals are not necessarily without merit, but they often involve an element of wishful thinking, where a strong personal preference is misinterpreted as translating into a strong general reason that others ought to accept. There are many other types of appeal, including:

5 **Appeal to nature**: confusing what you believe is 'natural' with a fundamental truth that everyone ought to accept. *Nobody should wash their hair: hygiene is unnatural!*
6 **Appeal to tradition**: confusing something that people have done for a long time with something that must, therefore, be right. *There's nothing wrong with performing surgery without anaesthetic: people did it for hundreds of years!*
7 **Appeal to incredulity**: confusing the fact that you find something unbelievable with the likelihood that it is not true or possible. *Performing surgery through a tiny gap, like a keyhole, is simply a ridiculous idea – it can't be done!*

One special case of the 'appeal to' style of fallacy is an **appeal to ignorance**, which turns a lack of information into a potentially persuasive weapon. See if you can spot what is wrong with the following lines of argument:

....	There must be a God! Scientists have spent centuries trying to definitively prove that there isn't, and they have failed again and again.
....	There is no such thing as evolution. Scientists have spent centuries trying to prove its truth beyond all doubt, and they have failed again and again.

Both of these approaches may be rhetorically forceful, but they're not successful as arguments. Here is what is going on in each case:

- **Argument from ignorance: true unless proven false**. This is based on the claim that something must be considered true until it is proven to be false with absolute certainty. Any number of examples show that this is the wrong way of thinking about truth: *Your mother's skin must turn green when nobody is looking at her – nobody can show that this is untrue!*
- **Argument from ignorance: false unless proven true**. This is based on the related claim that something must be considered false until it has been proven true with absolute certainty. Again, it's easy to show that this is a confused form of argument. *There is still some doubt that charitable giving is of benefit to society, so you should accept that giving to charity does no good at all.*

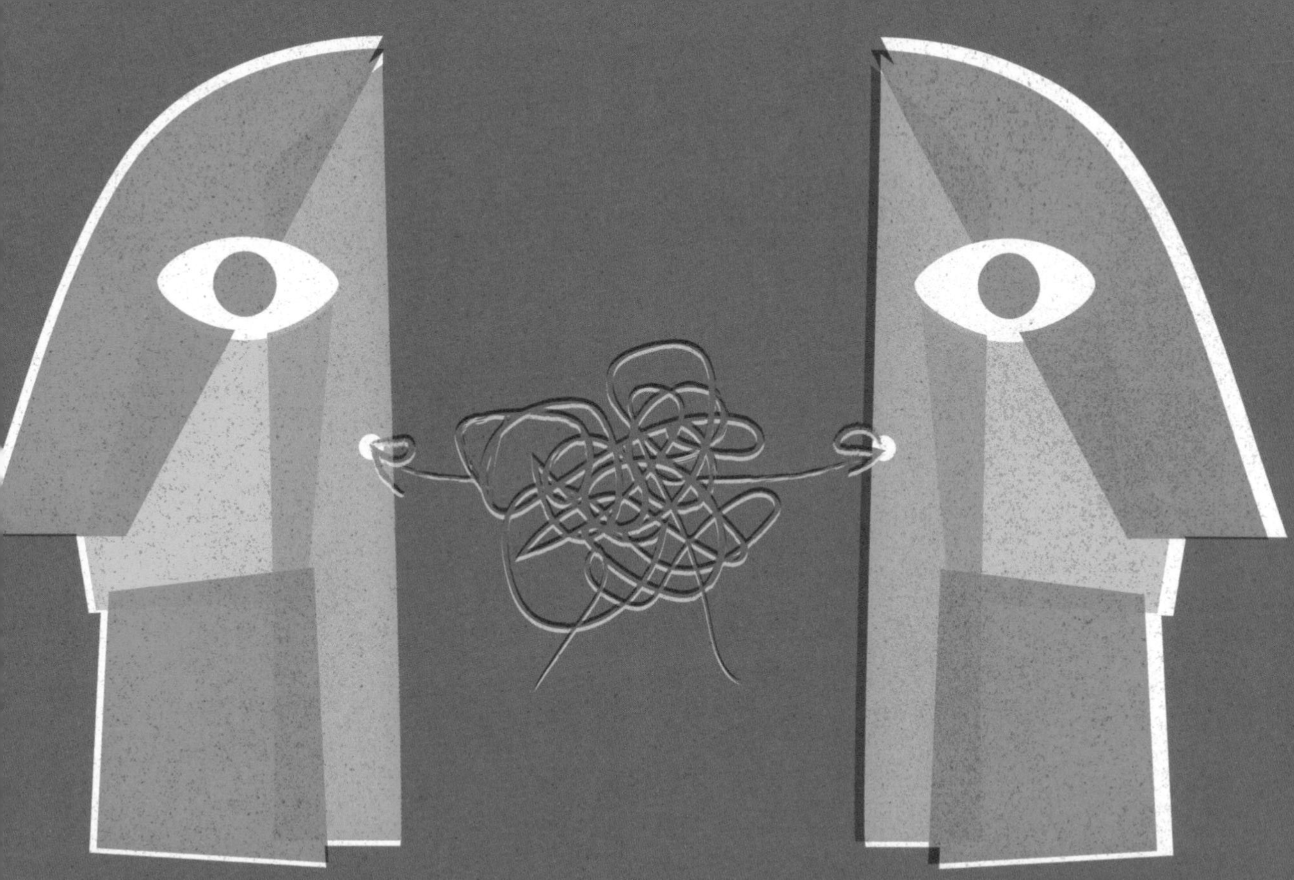

RATIONALIZATION MAY BE DEFINED AS SELF-DECEPTION BY REASONING.

KAREN HORNEY

#TalkCriticalThinking

In each case, the problem comes from treating the absence of certainty as a kind of certainty in itself, as if there were no such thing as probability or degrees of reasonableness. As we've seen from examining inductive arguments and evidence, absolute certainty is itself an impossible standard – and thus a dangerous tool in the arsenal of those who wish to promote their own views at any cost.

Ad hominem

Ad hominem: the fallacy of attacking the person making an argument rather than what they actually say

The second major fallacy of relevance is known as ***ad hominem***. This literally means 'to the person' and consists of attacking an argument based on claims about the person making that argument, as opposed to its actual content. Try to identify the slightly different ways this is done in the following three examples:

1 He claims that we need to raise taxes, but you can't trust that coming from someone like him: he's had three children by three different mothers. ....

2 You can't possibly accept her conclusion that vaccination is safe. Look at her job title: she's in the pay of the pharmaceutical lobby! ....

3 My doctor tells me to eat sensibly and exercise more. What does he know? He's overweight and barely able to walk. ....

Each of these represents a slightly different form of an *ad hominem* argument:

- **Abusive *ad hominem***: suggesting that you should reject a conclusion because the person presenting it has an undesirable quality. In the example above, it's implied that having children by different mothers makes someone untrustworthy and that what they say can thus automatically be ignored – something that's clearly a very tenuous claim about two things with no logical relationship.
- **Circumstantial *ad hominem***: suggesting that the circumstances of the person making a claim mean we must automatically reject anything they say. It may well be the case that we should treat what someone working in a field says about that field with caution, but this is very different to saying that there are strong grounds for simply dismissing it as wrong.
- **Appeal to hypocrisy**: suggesting that, if someone says one thing while doing something different, whatever they say in this area must be wrong. In the example above, there is no reason why a doctor who happens to be overweight should be wrong about diet and exercise. People are extremely sensitive to hypocrisy and often judge it harshly, yet hypocrites can be entirely correct, irrespective of what they may or may not do themselves.

As we'll see in the discussions of cognitive bias later in the book, the strength of our preference for consistency in others and ourselves can lead us to neglect other important factors – such as whether what is being said is actually true or acceptable, as opposed to merely consistent with other factors. The fact that someone is known to be aggressive and opportunistic may make sudden aggressive behaviour unsurprising coming from them, but the fact that they're not hypocritical doesn't make their actions any more acceptable.

SMART STUDY: Don't shoot the messenger

It may seem obvious that we should judge someone's arguments by their content, and not by what we know about the person making the argument – but this is often easier said than done.

For example, you might find it difficult to disagree with something written by a noted academic in your field, and be inclined simply to accept what they say without reading too closely. Or you might be more inclined to ignore what is said by someone with a very different perspective or background to your own.

Here's an exercise for resisting this kind of focus. When responding to an argument – or looking back over your responses to others' ideas – try removing any reference whatsoever to the originator of what you're engaging with: no names, no dates, no personal details. Decontextualize it entirely and see what you are left with. Then reintroduce a context and weigh up the relevant evidence as thoroughly as you can, but do so only after you've tried to clearly see what kind of claim is being made independently of its origin.

Irrelevant conclusions

Perhaps the purest fallacy of relevance is that of the **irrelevant conclusion** (known in Latin as ***ignoratio elenchi***). As the name suggests, this takes what appears to be a satisfactory piece of reasoning and then provides a conclusion that isn't connected to what came before. Also known as 'missing the point', the persuasiveness of this fallacy rests on the irrelevant conclusion seeming to address the question, while actually relying on a different, unacknowledged line of reasoning. Here are a couple of examples:

Irrelevant conclusion: presenting a conclusion that doesn't actually follow from the reasoning that supposedly supports it

> The article suggested that travel can broaden your empathy, if you deal directly with people outside of the tourism industry and don't bring too many preconceptions. But I've always thought it's a better idea to get to know your own country intimately.

> Are politicians becoming more partisan? Voting statistics show a clear trend over the last 50 years for an increasing percentage of votes to fall along party lines, with independent-mindedness in decline. We need to get big money out of politics.

Neither of these paragraphs is intellectually incoherent: you can work out what is being claimed and why. In the first example, the speaker seems to be making the point that it's misguided to talk about foreign travel broadening empathy in the first place, because people ought to be getting to know their own country better. In the second example, there's an implication that the presence of big money in politics has – somehow – caused politicians to become more partisan over time.

In each case, however, something that looks superficially like an argument is in fact a statement of opinion presented alongside a semblance of reasoning. The speaker is changing the subject midway between premise and conclusion, allowing them to imply a logical relationship where none exists.

Fallacy of ambiguity: shifting the meaning of terms during reasoning, or exploiting uncertainty in order to support an unjustified conclusion

INFORMAL FALLACIES OF AMBIGUITY (LINGUISTIC FALLACIES)

Fallacies of ambiguity occur when the meanings of words or concepts are subtly twisted during the course of reasoning, or when uncertainty over meaning is exploited to assert an unjustified conclusion.

Equivocation and amphiboly

In its simplest form, we may **equivocate** during an argument by using the same word in two different senses, creating an illusion of reason where none exists:

Equivocation: using a word in two quite different senses while pretending that they are the same in order to create the appearance of reasoning

> You are the light of my life. But all lights must be switched off – and so, too, must you.

As well as being distinctly strange and sinister, this argument makes no sense. The sense in which you are the 'light of my life' is nothing like the kind of domestic 'light' that gets switched on and off.

Amphiboly: using a phrase or sentence that can be interpreted as meaning more than one thing, without clarifying which

A slightly different abuse of ambiguity occurs when the structure of a phrase or sentence is itself open to multiple interpretations. This is usually known as **amphiboly** after the Greek word for 'indeterminate'. Much of the time, amphiboly is simply the opportunity for a joke:

> Towards the end of that day, I saw a wild deer in my car. I have no idea how he opened the door.

Sometimes, however (especially in the context of law and regulations), amphiboly can create significant problems in agreeing on the meaning of important information:

> The suspects were questioned individually by the police despite their objections.

In this case, it's not possible to know who was doing the objecting – the suspects or the police – and thus any line of reasoning based on the above is open to dispute.

A particular case of shifting meanings that deserves its own label can be seen in the example below, which entails changing the sense of one of the key terms during the course of the argument. Try to identify what is going on:

> A Scotsman never flees from a foe in battle. You say that Alan of the Riddell clan fled from his enemy just last week? Well, he is no true Scotsman!

Incredibly common way of rejecting criticism.

This particular example is known as the '**no true Scotsman**' fallacy, and it's especially common in business and politics. When faced with a counter-example to a cherished claim, it entails someone insisting that their claim still applies and that this counter-example doesn't 'really' disprove their cherished belief:

> All successful companies are helmed by an effective CEO. You say that you work for a massive, profitable company that doesn't have a CEO? Well, all truly successful companies have effective CEOs, so your company cannot be truly successful.

In this case, the speaker would rather invent the notion of a 'truly' successful company (as opposed to one that is merely successful) than alter their belief that an effective CEO is essential.

Composition and division

The fallacy of composition: mistakenly arguing that whatever is true of the individual parts must also be true of the whole

The fallacy of division: mistakenly arguing that whatever is true of the whole must also be true of its individual parts

Finally, the fallacies of **composition** and **division** entail erroneously assuming that whatever is the property of part of something must also apply to the whole, or vice versa. Here are a couple of examples.

> A few pieces of information about my social media habits are of no significance. Thus, a few pieces of information about the social media habits of each of one billion people are also of no significance.

> This book is amazing and insightful. Thus, every word in it must be amazing and insightful as well.

Note that, as is the case with many fallacies, the kind of reasoning above is not inherently or inevitably fallacious – it is simply flawed and simplistic, and only applicable in very particular circumstances (rather than as a general rule). Here are two further examples that illustrate just how foolish it can be to apply this kind of thinking, unthinkingly:

These are beautiful pictures. If I pile them all up in a huge random heap, the heap will also be beautiful.

This data set is rich and packed with fascinating opportunities for insight. Every individual piece of information within it must also be rich and packed with opportunities.

INFORMAL FALLACIES OF PRESUMPTION (MATERIAL FALLACIES)

Material fallacies, also known as fallacies of presumption, operate through premises that presume too much: that either begin by assuming the truth of their conclusion or avoid the relevant area of reasoning entirely. Some are invariably fallacious, while others are simply poor reasoning techniques that are best avoided, or at least treated with great caution.

Material fallacies: fallacies that either covertly assume the truth of a conclusion or avoid the real issues at stake

Begging the question and circular reasoning

Begging the question is a phrase often used outside of critical thinking simply to mean 'inviting a question about…'. Its original use, however, described an informal fallacy in which the conclusion of an argument is simply a rephrased repetition of one of its premises. For example:

Begging the question: putting the conclusion to be proven into your premises, thus producing something convincing-sounding that proves nothing

Universal justice is a great and noble aspiration – and it is thus excellent to pursue the ideal of just treatment afforded to all.

Quitting your job is the appropriate thing to do, because it is the proper action in these circumstances.

These may sound good, but they don't provide any actual reasoning. 'Universal justice' and 'the ideal of just treatment afforded to all' are essentially the same thing put slightly differently, so all that is really being said is 'Justice is great, because justice is great'. Similarly, the second example simply repeats itself, without offering anything beyond repeated assertion.

Begging the question is a specific type of **circular reasoning**, meaning – as the name suggests – reasoning that loops back on itself in order to demonstrate its own forcefulness. Typically, a circular argument might say that 'A is true because of B; and B is true because of A.' Here's a famous example:

Circular reasoning: an argument whose premise supports its conclusion, and whose conclusion supports its premise, making it a closed loop

I know that the Bible is the word of God, because we are told by God in the Bible that this is so.

This form of argument may seem deeply unscientific and unlikely to bother you in an academic context, yet it can feel surprisingly forceful when deployed at greater length:

Our research demonstrates that urban environments become more pleasant when there is less traffic, because a lower volume of cars and lorries is shown in our research to create an enhanced experience of cities.

Here, the conclusion (we've demonstrated that the environment is more pleasant when there is less traffic) is supported by the premise (our research shows that less traffic creates better cities) which in turn relies on the conclusion (that better cities have less traffic), and so on. We are trapped in a circle that verifies itself. The research in question may indeed demonstrate this conclusion, but all we are presented with in the sentence above is a repeated assertion.

Post hoc and fallacies of causation

The fallacy most commonly known by the first two words of its Latin name ***post hoc ergo propter hoc***, does exactly what is spelled out in the translation – 'after that, therefore because of that'. It

Post hoc ergo propter hoc: the fallacy of assuming that, when one thing happens after another, the first thing must be the cause of the second thing

assumes that, if one thing happened after another, the first thing caused the second. As with many informal fallacies, this may or may not be true in a particular case, but it is not a reasonable general rule to rely on:

> My uncle gave up smoking and drinking, and two days later he was dead. The shock must have killed him!

This is related to an error-prone way of thinking we explored in the first half of this book – that of forgetting that **correlation is not causation**. When two different phenomena closely follow one another, this does not mean that one causes the other. Similarly, it can be dangerously easy to **confuse cause and effect** unless you are able to rigorously test or investigate what is actually going on. Here are three examples respectively illustrating *post hoc*, confusing correlation with causation, and confusing cause and effect:

Correlation is not causation: the fallacy of assuming that, if two phenomena or sets of data closely follow one another, one must be caused by the other

Inverting cause and effect: the fallacy of confusing the direction of causation between two related phenomena, and thus mistakenly labelling an effect as a cause

> You came to visit and then my car broke down, so you must have broken my car.
>
> I've noticed that the grass in my garden and your hair are growing at the same rate; I'm worried that, if we cut your hair, the grass will stop growing.
>
> Our research suggests that buying newborn baby clothes is extremely likely to help people who want to have children, because most couples who buy newborn baby clothes go on to have a child within the next six months.

False dilemmas

False dilemma: fallaciously claiming that, in a complex situation, it is only possible for one of two things to be true

A **false dilemma** describes the fallacy of reducing a complex situation to a black-and-white choice between two options. Here's an example:

> You either accept that this course of action is in the best interests of our country, or you give hope to our enemies. Surely you don't wish to give hope to those who want to destroy us?

This sounds dramatic, but it's unlikely to accurately represent the full spectrum of possibilities available. It is, however, a powerful persuasive tool – and one that is used extensively across politics and business.

All false dilemmas are errors of oversimplification, meaning that the task of opposing them can be difficult. People don't always like being told that a simple, comfortable view of the world is wrong and that they face a much more complex choice than a direct *either/or* between two options.

SMART STUDY: Don't fall for false dilemmas

Beware of constructing false dilemmas in your own work (and life), especially where they might make things easier for you. It can be tempting to frame a research question, experiment or essay in terms of two comprehensive options – 'Are improvements in grades over time caused by smarter students or by better tuition?' – but this kind of framing is often likely to result in an oversimplification of what is actually going on.

In this example, improvements in grades might be due to both factors, or neither. A better research question would ask, 'What factors are associated with improvements in grades over time?', and start to build up an understanding of events with as few distorting assumptions as possible involved.

Loaded and complex questions

Loaded/complex question: asking a question about one thing that also includes an unstated assumption about another, in an attempt to force someone to accept this assumption

The **loaded question** fallacy buries some information surreptitiously in the wording of an argument in order to force an unwarranted assumption on someone. Here's an everyday example:

> Tell me, have you stopped being rude to everyone you meet yet?

This fallacy is also known as a **complex question** and it works by smuggling an unproven claim – in this case, that you are rude to everyone you meet – into a question about something else. This effectively forces you to accept the unproven claim if you accept the terms of the question. Here is a further example:

> Do you propose to take responsibility for the monstrous atrocities that have been committed by your government?

Once again, this kind of trick is especially common in politics and law – fields in which fluency in fallacies is a professional requirement. Try to work out what is going on in the following fictional legal cross-examination:

Bad Tom: Let me ask you this: is it not true that you personally benefited to the tune of several thousand dollars thanks to your regular raids on the petty cash supply?

Good Tim: No, it is not true. I never benefited!

Bad Tom: And yet you admit that you were regularly raiding the petty cash...

Unless you take the time to carefully rebut both the overall question and the separate conclusion within it, the questioner is able to proceed as if you had admitted to their unproven assumption. The correct response to such a fallacy is thus to identify, and to reject, the unproven claim itself: 'I never committed any kind of raid on the petty cash supply whatsoever, so this loaded line of questioning makes no sense.'

Faulty analogies and faulty generalizations

As the name suggests, a **faulty analogy** presumes a resemblance between one thing and another that does not in fact exist. Judging faulty analogies is not always easy, as all analogies are to a degree imperfect. The key question is whether there is a relevant similarity that illustrates an important point, or whether analogy is being used to suggest a similarity that doesn't hold up to closer scrutiny.

Faulty analogy: claiming two things are similar, even though they are not, in order to make an unreasonable conclusion look reasonable

Consider these two examples, which are typical of the way in which you might find yourself called upon to reflect on your studies and research. Which analogy is better, and why?

1 Extrapolating from the results of psychological testing in controlled conditions to real-life situations is difficult. Much like the difference between watching people play a driving video game versus driving around an actual city in their car, the complex interactions and unpredictability of real situations combined with higher stakes can create behaviours entirely unobserved in tests. ○

....

....

2 Extrapolating from the results of psychological testing in controlled conditions to real-life situations is similar to the difference between studying at college versus working in a job. One is a predictable environment where you know what is expected of you, while the other is complex and unpredictable and stressful in new ways.. ○

....

....

The first of these analogies seems reasonable, at least in a few key areas: it is drawing a distinction between a simplified simulation in which the stakes are low, and a complex reality in which things matter more.

The second analogy, by contrast, doesn't stand up to scrutiny. It seems to imply that studying at college is predictable and regulated in the same way as sitting a controlled psychological test, in contrast to 'working in a job'. But this analogy is both too vague and too weak to usefully illustrate an argument. Studying at college can be just as real and complex as working in a job, depending on the college and the job; the difference between them has nothing like the clear divide between a controlled test and everyday life.

Faulty generalization: using a small amount of evidence to justify a much larger observation that isn't actually warranted

Along similar lines, a **faulty generalization** draws a larger lesson, from particular events, which does not stand up to consideration. One example is the assumption that everyone has the same opinion as the people you know:

> I don't know anybody who likes the current government. They're hated by the entire nation!

We tend to label an argument fallacious when it actively sets out to deceive, or when it fails in a way that is pernicious, rather than simply being wrong. But we should also be especially alert to the implications of all generalizations and analogies – and the points at which even the best and (especially) the most commonly used ones break down and deserve to be challenged.

The slippery slope

Slippery slope: arguing on the basis that, if one small thing is allowed to happen, an inevitable and increasingly serious chain of further events will be set in motion

Slippery slope arguments are not inherently unreliable or necessarily intended to deceive. But they are a dangerous form of reasoning, in that they make it easy to dress up a claim that has little or no evidence in a persuasive way. They take their name from the image of an object teetering at the top of a slope, such that one small push will be all it takes to set it tumbling to the bottom. Here is one in action:

> If you let your son get away with stealing that chocolate unpunished, he will go on to steal something bigger, then something bigger, then something bigger again: there will be no turning back once this chain of events is set in motion.

This is clearly an absurd argument, and its absurdity hinges on an implication that allowing your son to get away with stealing chocolate is a genuine point of no return. The legitimacy of a slippery slope argument thus depends on whether the subject really is something that will escalate uncontrollably once started. Compare this argument:

> The precedent set in law by this judgement would be a slippery slope indeed, for if we permit one individual to successfully sue the manufacturer of their car for creating a car that it is possible to crash, there will be no turning back from thousands more lawsuits following.

This may be a reasonable argument. If it is indeed true that one judgement would set a precedent and trigger thousands more cases, we would do well to heed this warning. The burden of proof, however, should always fall on someone making such a dramatic claim. What they're aiming to prove is what's known as positive feedback – where a single event sets in motion an accelerating and inevitable chain of further events. Too often, what in fact is going on is that someone is using a slippery slope argument to give vent to their fears, and to express an objection to something minor as though it were major.

SMART STUDY: Six general guidelines for spotting informal fallacies

What should you be looking out for in general when trying to spot fallacies in others' work, and to avoid them in your own? Here are six questions it's worth asking before you accept anything as reasonable:

- Is an emotional, traditional or personal position being presented as a general truth without acknowledgement?
- Is someone judging a claim based on where it comes from, or who is making it, rather than its content?
- Is someone only pretending to use reasoning, while actually asserting whatever they believe as part of their premises?
- Is someone trying to distract or bamboozle you with what looks like reasoning, but which isn't relevant to their conclusion?
- If vivid analogies, metaphors or generalizations are being used, do they accurately describe the real world?
- Is it too good to be true? Is someone claiming to have found a simple, final answer to a complex question? If so, they're probably wrong.

Try asking all these of the arguments you see on social media. See how many survive the test.

TWO FORMAL FALLACIES: AFFIRMING THE CONSEQUENT AND DENYING THE ANTECEDENT

A **formal fallacy** is a failure of logic. Every formal fallacy is an invalid form of deduction: a pattern of illogical reasoning. As is the case with all deductive arguments, the fact that an argument has an invalid form tells us nothing about the truth of its premises or conclusion. We simply know that any invalid argument cannot guarantee the truth of its conclusion.

Formal fallacy: an invalid general form of deductive argument, in which the conclusion does not follow from its premises

We identified two formal fallacies in Chapter 3: **affirming the consequent** and **denying the antecedent**. Each of these effectively confuses one thing being true 'if' another is true with one thing being true 'only if' another is true. Here they are once again, in summary:

- **Affirming the consequent** is based on the mistaken assumption that, if B will necessarily be true when A is true, then the presence of B is sufficient to prove that A is also the case: 'If you love me, you'll reply to my email. You replied to my email, so you must love me.' It has the general form: 'If A, then B. B. Therefore, A.'
- **Denying the antecedent** is based on the mistaken assumption that, if B will necessarily be true when A is true, then observing that A is not the case must also mean that B is not the case: 'If you order steak, you'll enjoy your meal. You didn't order steak. So you cannot enjoy your meal.' It has the general form: 'If A, then B. Not A. Therefore, not B.'

For some further logical context, you can also find these two informal fallacies in my list of valid and invalid types of argument at the very end of the book.

The undistributed middle: a formal fallacy which mistakenly confuses something that applies to all members of a category with something that applies only to members of that category

THE UNDISTRIBUTED MIDDLE: A FORMAL FALLACY

Further logical confusion lies at the heart of a formal fallacy known as the **undistributed middle**. See if you can identify the precise problem with this example:

> All magicians have beards. My friend has a beard. So he must be a magician! *He isn't.*

Can you express exactly why the above argument is fallacious? It derives from the fact that saying 'all magicians have beards' is not the same thing as saying that 'only magicians have beards'. In the first case, we are describing a trait that magicians might share with many other people: a magician necessarily has a beard, but having a beard isn't sufficient to guarantee someone is a magician. In the second case, we are describing a unique trait that is guaranteed only to apply to magicians. Here's another, slightly more complex example:

> All mammals have eyes. My pet fish Bob has eyes. So Bob must be a mammal.

It's clear that this line of reasoning is nonsense, but it's slightly more difficult to spell out exactly why. The problem is that the information we need to know in order to decide whether the conclusion is true or not is absent. Is having eyes sufficient to guarantee that something is a mammal – or is it only necessary? We haven't been told. We know that mammals have eyes. We know that Bob the fish has eyes. But we do not know anything about the category 'all those things that have eyes'.

It thus remains possible that both mammals and Bob the fish are two unrelated instances of things that happen to have eyes. Hence the name 'undistributed middle', because the distribution of the key category, 'things that have eyes', is not specified. In general, the fallacy of the undistributed middle takes this form:

> All As are B. C is B. Thus, C is also A.

This can be tricky to grasp in the abstract, but it's alarmingly common in certain types of everyday thinking. For example, you may well have come across arguments along the following lines in the media:

> All potential terrorists who pose a grave danger to the safety of this nation originally come from one of the countries on this list. You originally come from one of the countries on this list. Thus, you are a potential terrorist who poses a grave danger to the safety of this nation.

It is alarmingly easy to slip into this kind of thinking.

This is an invalid argument, based on the unwarranted additional assumption that 'all people who come from the countries on this list are potential terrorists' (another way of putting this would be that only potential terrorists come from these countries). An undistributed middle term – 'all people who come from one of the countries on this list' – is surreptitiously and fallaciously assumed to be identical with one subset of individuals.

BASE RATE NEGLECT: ANOTHER FORMAL FALLACY

Here's an example of another formally fallacious way of thinking that is alarmingly common, not only in the media and politics, but also among those who ought to know better. This time, rather than entailing a confusion of necessary and sufficient conditions, it entails confusion around probability and statistics:

> Most ideological extremists are angry. Few non-extremists are angry. This person is angry. So she is probably an ideological extremist.

The problem is that, without first investigating the relative numbers involved in each category, we cannot actually say anything meaningful about the probabilities involved. For example, if

99.99 per cent of the population are non-extremists, then this means that – even if every single extremist were angry – they would still almost certainly be outnumbered by non-extremists who just happen to be angry.

This is called the **base rate neglect** fallacy because it ignores the underlying proportions of whatever is being discussed. It's perhaps most familiar in everyday life as a form of stereotyping against a minority group: 'My house was robbed. It must have been someone from that small bunch of immigrants: most of them are criminals.' Such thinking is often unlikely, statistically, to be true, because – no matter what the level of criminality among a small minority – there will be far more criminals in total who don't belong to that small group.

Base rate neglect: ignoring the underlying frequency of one element in an analysis, and thus potentially reaching an incorrect conclusion about the likelihood of a certain result

We also see this effect in fields such as finance or business when people focus on making a big profit on costly but rarely purchased items, thus neglecting the more important question of total sales:

> 'I make $200 per sale on fridges, and just $5 per sale on printer cartridges. I should focus on selling fridges, right?'
>
> 'No, because you only sell two fridges a week, while you can sell a hundred cartridges every day.'

The simplest version of this fallacy takes the following general form:

> Most As are C. Few Bs are C. X is C. Probably, X is also an A.

THINK ABOUT THIS: Why do you think it is so easy to neglect base rates when thinking about something involving large and small groups? How might you explain the problem to someone else in order to help them understand it? ....

....

....

....

....

....

FROM BASE RATE NEGLECT TO BAYES'S THEOREM

Most significantly for the purposes of study and research, a form of the base rate fallacy can occur whenever you need to analyse rare or unlikely events.

Consider the following paragraph, about taking a test for a rare (fictional) medical condition known (naturally) as fictionalitis. Given the following information, what is the chance that I am indeed suffering from this condition?

> I am being tested for a rare medical condition, fictionalitis, known to affect one person per million. I have no symptoms, but have been reading about it online and want to reassure myself. The doctor tells me that, if I do indeed have fictionalitis, the test will always correctly identify it. If I don't, the test is still 99.9 per cent accurate. Great! I take the test, and five minutes later she tells me the result. It's positive. The test has identified me as having fictionalitis. How unlucky can you get?

◯ **UNLIKELY**.. **VERY LIKELY** ◯

Intuition suggests that I should be very worried by this result. The most common reaction, even among some experts, is to say that there is a 99.9 per cent chance I am suffering from fictionalitis. This is wrong, because it neglects the extremely low base rate associated with the disease itself, and the effect of this base rate when combined with the accuracy of the test. In fact, there is around a 99.9 per cent chance that I do not have fictionalitis. How can this be?

False negative: a negative test result produced in error, when whatever is being tested for is in fact present (e.g. a pregnancy test saying you are not pregnant when you actually are)

To answer this, let's look at what would happen if we tested one million people for fictionalitis. We know that just one person out of the million is actually likely to have this condition, and that the test will be positive for them. This particular test has no **false negatives**, meaning cases where someone who has fictionalitis gets a negative test result. This thus gives us one guaranteed positive result per million people. But this is only the start.

False positive: a positive test result produced in error, when whatever is being tested for is in fact absent (e.g. a pregnancy test saying you are pregnant when you actually are not)

We also know that the remaining 999,999 people will not have the condition, and that the test is 99.9 per cent accurate for them. This means that it will produce a negative result for 999 people out of every 1,000, but that it will also wrongly produce a positive result once per 1,000 people, known as a **false positive**. Testing 999,999 people will thus produce approximately 1,000 additional positive results, all of them false.

In total, this leaves us with 1 + 1,000 = 1,001 positive results per million people. We know that only one of these actually applies to someone suffering from fictionalitis, but we don't know which one: if we did, we wouldn't need to use a test in the first place. There is no way of distinguishing between our 1,000 false positives and one true positive result.

Overall, we must conclude that my positive result has a 1,000 out of 1,001 chance of being a false positive: almost exactly a 99.9 per cent chance that I do not have fictionalitis.

True positive: a positive test result that correctly corresponds to the presence of whatever you're testing for

Does this still seem strange? The statistics involved are easier to grasp if we use something based on rates we already have some sense of on an intuitive level. Take this question:

> I am an author. How likely is it that I have sold over ten million books?

Pretty obviously, it's very unlikely that I have sold over ten million books. Even though only one out of every few thousand people is a professional author, only a very tiny proportion of these authors have sold ten million books (please note: in real life, I am not one of these people). You would never assume that just being an author means I must have sold millions upon millions of books. It's far, far more likely that I am simply an author.

Bayes's theorem: a method for calculating the probability of an event based on our knowledge of previous events

Yet this scenario is essentially the same as our medical one. Only a tiny proportion of 'positive results' – people who are authors – will actually enjoy the rare 'condition' of selling millions of books. The chance that I am both an author and have sold ten million books is much less likely than that I am simply an author. Once you find out I'm an author, by far the most likely scenario is that I'm in the 'hasn't-sold-ten-million' category.

Base rate: the initial, underlying likelihood that something we are investigating is the case (e.g. the base rate of disease X in this population is one case per 2,000 people per year)

The most important method used to deal with problems like this is known as **Bayes's theorem** after its inventor, the 18th-century philosopher and minister Thomas Bayes. Bayes was interested in what he called 'a problem in the doctrine of chance' – how exactly we should update our probabilistic beliefs in the light of new evidence.[31]

Bayes's theorem begins with the observation that we always begin with a basic expectation – the **base rate** – of how likely something is. In the case of our medical example, our basic expectation is that a person selected at random from the population has a one-in-one-million chance of suffering from fictionalitis. Given no further information, you would thus say that my chance of suffering from fictionalitis is one in a million: a probability of 0.000001.

Having established this base rate, we can now conduct an investigation in order to obtain new information. In this case, our investigation takes the form of a test. If we are lucky enough to have a test that is always accurate, then the information it provides – a positive or a negative result – allows us to update our belief to a certainty one way or the other. Mostly, however, what we need to do is work with different degrees of uncertainty.

In our initial scenario, a negative result does give us certainty. The test I have described never produces a negative result when someone in fact does suffer from fictionalitis (this isn't true of many tests in the real world). But a positive result simply improves our level of confidence. To calculate this improvement precisely, we can take the information we have just learned – my positive result in this particular test – and use our knowledge of all the probabilities involved to update our expectations. Specifically, we take the following:

$$\text{Chance that any one person has fictionalitis} = \frac{1}{1{,}000{,}000} \text{ or } 0.000001$$

$$\text{Chance that someone with fictionalitis has a positive test result} = \text{certainty} = 1$$

$$\text{Chance of getting a positive result for any reason} = \frac{1001}{1{,}000{,}000} = 0.001001$$

Bayes's theorem has the following general form, where A is the first factor we are interested in (having fictionalitis) and B is the additional factor whose impact we wish to consider (having a positive test result):

$$\text{Chance (A given B is true)} = \frac{\text{(Chance of A} \times \text{Chance of B given A is true)}}{\text{Chance of B}}$$

Putting our figures into this provides the updated chance that, given the positive result, I do indeed have fictionalitis:

$$\frac{\text{(Chance any one person has fictionalitis} \times \text{Chance of someone with fictionalitis getting a positive result)}}{\text{Chance of getting a positive result for any reason}}$$

$$= \frac{(0.000001 \times 1)}{0.001001} = 0.00099900099 \text{ (approximately 1 in 1,000, as we saw)}$$

These numbers look complicated because they have many decimal places. We can, however, use some much simpler numbers to work through a different example. See if you can fill in the blanks below:

There are 1,000 students studying on a Critical Thinking course, and I know that 50 of them have borrowed a copy of my textbook from the library. Unfortunately, I left some notes for a new book I'm writing about *Really Critical Thinking* inside one of these copies while working in the library. I have just bumped into one of the students from the course. If she has a textbook, what is the chance that her copy contains my notes?

Chance of (A) any one student having my notes = ☐

Chance that (B) any one student on the course has a copy of my textbook = ☐

SEVEN

MOST THINGS REVERT TO THE MEAN. AN EXCEPTIONAL RESULT IS LIKELY TO BE FOLLOWED BY A LESS EXCEPTIONAL ONE. THINGS TEND TO RECOVER OVER TIME – OR TO FALL BACK FROM A HIGH. DON'T GIVE CREDIT FOR WHAT WAS LIKELY TO HAPPEN ANYWAY.

#TalkCriticalThinking

Chance that (B is true given A) the student with my notes has a textbook = [ ]

Chance of A given B = $\frac{\text{(Chance of B given A} \times \text{Chance of A)}}{\text{Chance of B}}$ = [ ]

You should arrive at the figures that there is: a base rate chance of 0.001 of any student having my notes (1 out of 1,000); a 0.05 chance of any student having my textbook (50 out of 1,000); and that it is a certainty that the person with my notes has a textbook. We can thus say that, if the person I have bumped into has a textbook, there is a (0.001 × 1)/0.05 = 0.02 chance that this textbook contains my notes.

This is clear enough when you think about it another way. Because there is no chance that any of the 950 people without textbooks have my notes, the moment we receive the information that the person I'm talking to has a textbook, we can see that there is a 1-in-50 chance (0.02) that she has the notes.

Here is a slightly more complex example, this time adjusting the roles of the first factor we're interested in (in this case, having a copy of my textbook) and the additional factor whose impact we wish to consider (having my notes):

> There are 1,000 students studying on a Critical Thinking course, and I know that 50 of them have borrowed a copy of my textbook from the library. Unfortunately, I left nine sheets of notes for another book I'm writing about *Extremely Critical Thinking* inside nine copies from the library – and one last sheet of notes bundled up with one of the printouts I gave to every student without a textbook. I just bumped into one of the students from the course, and she says that she has one sheet of my notes to return to me! Given this, how likely is it that she also has a copy of my textbook?

Chance that (A) any student has a copy of my textbook = [ ]

Chance that (B) any student has a sheet of my notes = [ ]

Chance that (B is true given A) any student with a textbook has a sheet of notes = [ ]

Answer = $\frac{\text{(Chance of B given A} \times \text{Chance of A)}}{\text{Chance of B}}$ = [ ]

In this case, the chance that any student has a copy of the textbook remains 0.05 (50 out of 1,000). The chance that any student has a sheet of my notes is now 0.01 (10 out of 1,000 – because there are ten sheets of notes in total). The chance that any student with a textbook has a sheet of notes is 0.18 (9 out of 50, because there are nine sheets somewhere in the 50 books). And so the final probability that she has a copy of the textbook, given that we know she has a sheet of notes, is (0.05 × 0.18)/0.01 = 0.9 or 90 per cent.

This is a much higher figure than in the first example. Why? Because we are now updating our knowledge in the light of information that narrows things down considerably: knowing someone has a sheet of notes makes it very likely that they also have a textbook.

Once we have arrived at this figure, we can again see that it makes intuitive sense. There are ten sheets of notes, nine of which are in textbooks and one of which is not. Therefore, someone with a sheet of notes will, nine times out of ten, turn out to have a textbook as well. Most real-life examples of Bayes's theorem are not nearly so neat or intuitive, but they follow the same basic pattern. Trust the numbers, not your first impressions – and beware of the confusion associated with any extremely rare event or condition.

SUMMARY

A **fallacy** is a recognisable general type of faulty reasoning. Effectively engaging with a fallacious argument means identifying its **unwarranted hidden assumption**. If necessary, a **comparable example** can help both to clarify whether an argument is fallacious and to illustrate persuasively why it is flawed.

Fallacious arguments cannot guarantee the truth of their conclusions, but they are not the same thing as arguments with false premises:

- An argument is not necessarily fallacious when it is based on a false premise or when it has a false conclusion.
- A fallacious argument can still have true premises.
- A fallacious argument can still have a true conclusion.

There are two broad categories of fallacies:

- **Informal fallacies** are faulty or flawed forms of reasoning that relate to the content of premises, and must be determined with reference to external information.
- **Formal fallacies** are logically invalid forms of argument, and the fault in their reasoning can be determined purely by reference to logical structure.

Three general types of informal fallacy are:

- **Fallacies of relevance (red herrings)**: these rely on premises that are either irrelevant or not sufficiently relevant to reasonably support a conclusion.
- **Fallacies of ambiguity (linguistic fallacies)**: these occur when the meanings of words or concepts are twisted during the course of reasoning, or uncertainty and ambiguity are used to support an unjustified conclusion.
- **Material fallacies (fallacies of presumption)**: these have premises that assume too much and that represent some of the most common techniques of poor reasoning, even when they are not necessarily fallacious.

Four common formal fallacies are:

- **Affirming the consequent**: this is based on the mistaken assumption that, if B will necessarily be true when A is true, then observing B is sufficient to prove that A is also the case: 'If you love me, you'll reply to my email. You replied to my email, so you must love me.' It has the general form: 'If A, then B. B. Therefore, A.'
- **Denying the antecedent**: this is based on the mistaken assumption that, if B will necessarily be true when A is true, then observing that A is not the case must also mean that B is not the case: 'If you order steak, you'll enjoy your meal. You didn't order steak. So you cannot enjoy your meal.' It has the general form: 'If A, then B. Not A. Therefore, not B.'

- **The undistributed middle**: this is based on the unwarranted assumption that knowing X about members of a category is the same as knowing that X applies only to members of that category. For example: 'All magicians have beards. My friend has a beard. So he must be a magician!' Even if it is true that 'all magicians have beards', this is not at all the same thing as saying that 'only magicians have beards'. In general, the fallacy takes the form: 'All As are B. C is B. Thus, C is also A.'
- *****Base rate neglect**: this is based on the logical-seeming claim that, if most As are C and few Bs are C, then any randomly picked C is more likely to be an A than a B. Why is this fallacious? Because until we know how big category A is, relative to category B, we cannot in fact say anything about how likely a randomly picked case is to belong to either group. For example: 'Most diplomats are bilingual. Few ordinary Londoners are bilingual. If I meet someone bilingual in London, they're likely to be a diplomat.' This is a fallacious argument, because it neglects the fact that there are very few diplomats in London relative to the overall population.

*One of the TOUGHEST things in the book

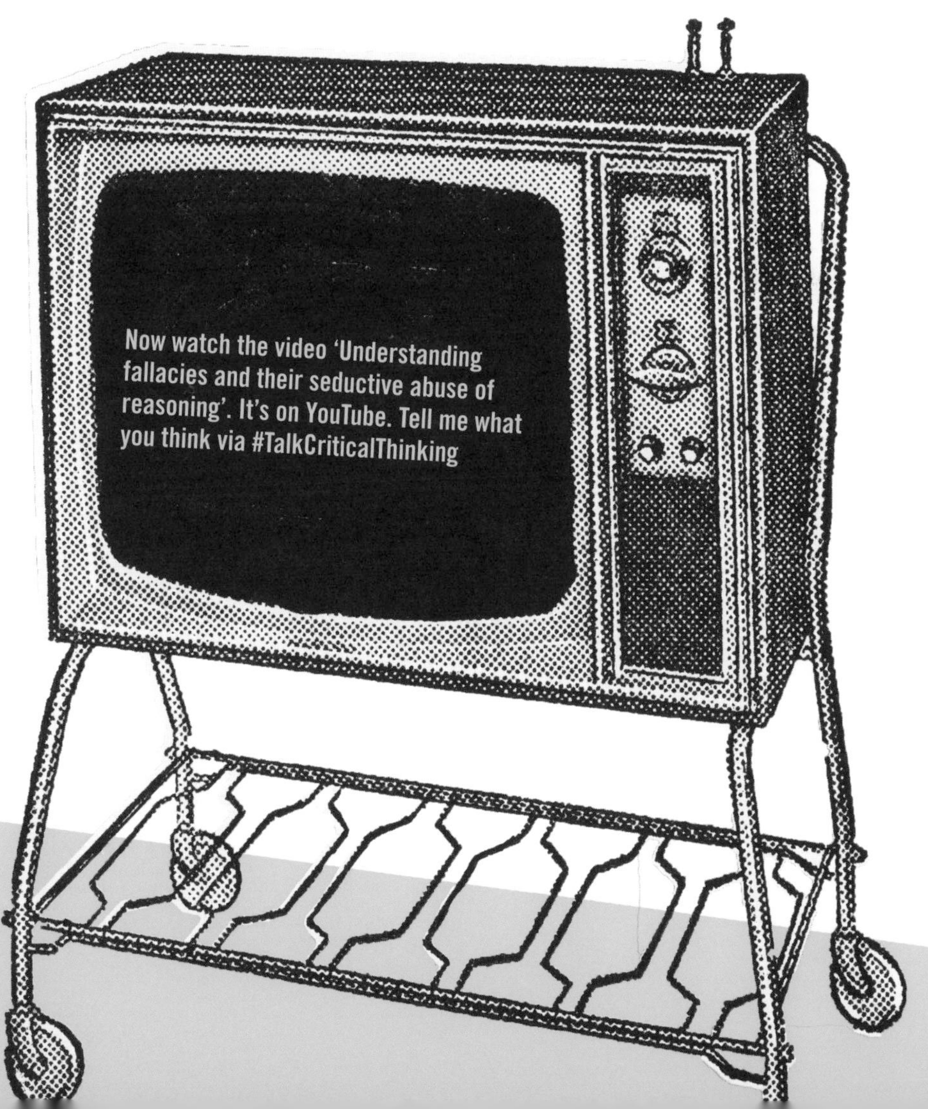

Now watch the video 'Understanding fallacies and their seductive abuse of reasoning'. It's on YouTube. Tell me what you think via #TalkCriticalThinking

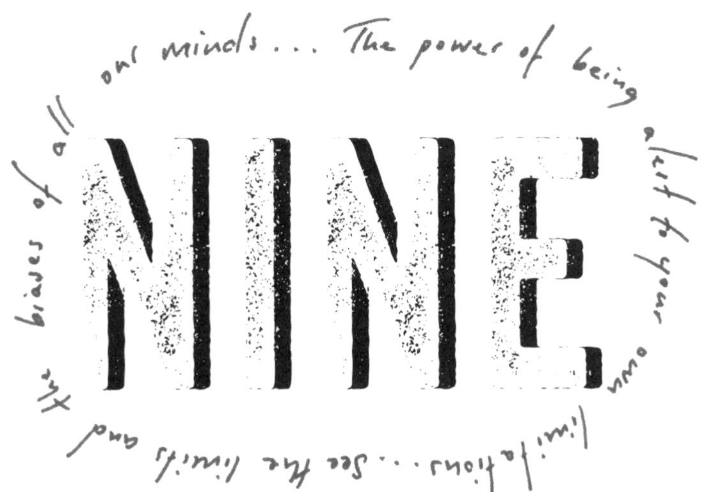

NINE
The power of being alert to your own limitations... See the limits and the biases of all our minds...

UNDERSTANDING COGNITIVE BIAS

How can you think critically about emotional and persuasive language?

How can you think critically about fallacies and faulty reasoning?

How can you think critically about cognitive and behavioural bias?

How can you best overcome bias in yourself and others?

How can you be a more critically engaged user of technology?

How can you become a critically engaged writer and thinker?

You cannot reason people out of positions they didn't reason themselves into.

Ben Goldacre

#TalkCriticalThinking

FIVE THINGS YOU'LL LEARN IN THIS CHAPTER

1 *Why* we spend most of the time using *short cuts* in our *thinking*
2 *Four everyday short cuts* used in thinking
3 What we mean by a *cognitive bias*
4 Common types of *cognitive bias* and how they *affect our judgement*
5 Why *people are bad judges* of their own expertise

Human beings don't deal in neutral information about the world. We exist inside our own perceptions, glimpsing our shared reality only through the lens of individual experience. We also cannot possibly take in all the information around us, understand everything, or spend our time considering all possibilities and perspectives. Mostly, we need to be able to act and interact with confidence, in a timely manner, deploying the slow and resource-intensive business of conscious attention only where it really adds value.

Our conscious awareness is thus highly selective, and geared towards behaviours that enabled small groups of humans to co-operate around common causes across hundreds of thousands of years of evolution. In outline:

- We prefer speed and simplicity to slowness and complexity.
- We are most influenced by the immediate and the local.
- We tend to see things in terms of patterns and narratives.
- These patterns and narratives reflect us and what we already know.
- We extend these patterns into our accounts of the past and the future.
- We are highly selective about how and what new information we notice.

Do you trust this person or not? Do you take a risk in this situation or play it safe? What do you enjoy, and why? Feelings flush our bodies and brains before we are consciously aware of what is going on, allowing us the possibility of decision and preference in the first place. To be without emotion would mean being paralysed by even the tiniest dilemma.

Heuristic: a cognitive short cut or 'rule of thumb', allowing for quick decision-making and judgement

In psychological terms, emotional reactions often inform a kind of mental short cut or rule of thumb, allowing us to make quick, effective decisions without using up too much time or energy-intensive consideration. Short cuts like this are known as **heuristics**, and our thinking is packed with them – practical, approximate methods that don't guarantee success, but that are essential in everyday situations.[32]

Cognitive bias: a particular situation in which mental heuristics introduce a predictable distortion into our assessment of a situation, resulting in a flawed judgement

A key to understanding many mental short cuts and habits is their replacement of a complex question with something amenable to a quick, simple and instinctual solution. When such solutions work well, which is most of the time, we don't even notice what has happened. Sometimes, however, our mental short cuts will misfire in a particular situation: they will produce a **cognitive bias**, meaning a flawed judgement that does not represent a correct assessment. These biases are impossible to eliminate, but not to comprehend or to mitigate, if we are sufficiently meticulous and strategic in our approach.

THINK ABOUT THIS: Before reading any further, pause and ask yourself: which biases in your own thinking, if any, are you most aware of? Which biases or distortions do you most commonly find yourself coming up against in others? Do you share these too? ....
....
....
....
....
....

FOUR TYPES OF HEURISTIC

Below are explanations of four of the most significant heuristics explored so far by researchers. Other heuristics exist, but what matters most is familiarizing yourself with the underlying psychological mechanisms that these point towards – together with the fact that, most of the time, these mechanisms are remarkably effective and efficient in delivering appropriate judgements.

1 The affect heuristic

Here's a simple choice. You are in hospital suffering from a rare disease that is fatal if left untreated, and have to choose between two experimental treatments. In trials involving 20,000 patients, which treatment would you prefer to take?

- Treatment A, which resulted in the deaths of 4,900 people ◯
- Treatment B, which was 70 per cent effective at saving lives ◯

What was your natural response upon being presented with this choice? If you were reading and thinking carefully, you probably realized that Treatment A is a better option than Treatment B. This is because, while Treatment B saves 70 per cent of lives, Treatment A saves fractionally over 75 per cent of lives: 4,900 is fractionally less than 25 per cent of 20,000, and the rest of the patients must have been saved.

For a lot of people presented with similar options, however, the vivid and concrete information that 4,900 people died while taking Treatment A outweighs a purely mathematical assessment of the percentages. This is known as the **affect heuristic** and describes the fact that people tend to rely on the emotional intensity of their responses to different options as a guideline to deciding between them – even when this emotional response is potentially misleading.

Affect heuristic: a tendency to use the strength of positive or negative emotional reactions as a decision-making short cut

As researchers such as the psychologist Paul Slovic[33] have explored, there are broader implications for the fact that people tend to let their likes and dislikes dictate the conclusions they form. If, for example, you identify yourself as a conservative thinker, then you are more likely to judge conservative arguments positively and opposing arguments negatively. Conversely, if you have a strong positive identification with liberal politics, then you will tend to let this preference dictate your beliefs – and treat liberal ideas as convincing and positive, and opposing ideas as unconvincing and negative.

Does this sound too extreme or simplistic to be true? Think of it as a tendency to see the world as tidier than it actually is. If you perceive something to be good, it is natural to underplay its costs and disadvantages. If you perceive something to be dangerous or negative, it is natural to underplay its benefits and advantages. And if you are struggling to choose between alternatives, emotional impact tends to substitute for other factors.

Imagine that you have decided to donate $10 each month to a marine conservation charity and are choosing between two different organizations in an effort to donate to as worthwhile a cause as possible. Which of these approaches would you pick?

- Hi! Could you give $10 each month to charity in order to help raise awareness of environmental degradation in the Pacific Ocean? ○
- Hi! Could you give $10 each month to protect a family of dolphins at risk from environmental degradation in the Pacific Ocean? ○

While the question of how your money might most effectively be spent is a tricky one, I suspect that the second approach is more enticing on a purely emotional level. This may seem both obvious and manipulative: sponsoring dolphins is designed to be more appealing than raising general awareness. Yet this emotional appeal is difficult to keep distinct from the overall decision-making process. A potentially difficult question that is complex to resolve (what's the best way to spend my monthly charitable donation?) is replaced by a simpler question that is quick and easy (what do I prefer: raising awareness or protecting dolphins?).

2 The availability heuristic

Consider the following:

- Do you think that more English words begin with the letter K than have the letter K as their third letter? ○
- Or do you think that more English words have the letter K as their third letter than begin with the letter K? ○

Have a think about it – what's your answer? If this is the first time you have encountered this question, you are likely to guess that more words begin with K. This is wrong. There are in fact approximately three times more words in English with K as their third letter than those with K as their first letter. But it is much more difficult to think up words based on their third letter than it is to think up words beginning with that same letter – and this relative difficulty is used to provide a quick answer to the question.[34]

This is known as the **availability heuristic** and describes the tendency to assume that something is likely or significant in direct proportion to how easily it comes to mind. Perhaps most famously, people tend to over-estimate the likelihood of death or injury from causes such as terrorism because these generate very high levels of media attention and awareness – and to under-estimate the likelihood of death or injury from less striking causes, such as heart disease or traffic accidents (Americans are about 35,000 times more likely to die from heart disease than terrorism).[35]

Availability heuristic: a tendency to be disproportionately influenced by whatever most easily or vividly comes to mind when making a decision or assessing options

In other words, one extremely vivid story that attracts large amounts of publicity can have more impact on people's perceptions than any information about likelihood or significance. If a celebrity dies of a rare form of cancer, many people will subsequently tend to think of that disease ahead of other, much more common cancers.

In general, the ease or difficulty with which particular information comes to mind is taken as a direct indication of its likeliness. This is one of the reasons that frequently repeating something makes people more likely to treat it as true (the neologism 'truthiness' captures this vague sense of familiar rightness even in the absence of evidence). Consider the following two questions and try to answer them honestly as they apply to you by over-writing the truest option:

1 On average, do I spend more time, less time or about the same amount of time as an average person reading books and articles?
2 On average, do I spend more time, less time or about the same amount of time as an average person using my mobile phone?

How did you answer? Did you rate yourself above average in either or both habits? In general, people tend to over-estimate the time and effort they put into activities compared to other people because they are more aware of their own actions than others'. Our own habits loom large because they are more easily available to us. What we don't know, meanwhile, we automatically discount.

In one experiment on married couples, each partner was separately asked to estimate their own contribution to shared domestic tasks as a percentage: tidying, shopping, washing and so on. The total of both partners' estimates was greater than 100 per cent in most cases. Each partner systematically over-estimated their contribution because their own actions came much more easily and vividly to mind.[36]

Once again, the availability heuristic involves swapping a tricky factual question ('in what precise proportion do you and your partner divide various domestic tasks?') for a far easier question about ease and emotion ('how easily can you bring to mind your own domestic contribution versus your partner's?').

Recency bias: a tendency to over-estimate the significance of more recent things, because they come more easily and vividly to mind

Plenty of interesting phenomena exist as a result of the availability heuristic, but one that's worth noting in particular is **recency bias**, meaning a tendency to over-estimate the significance of recent events simply because they come more easily to mind. Here's a question to think about:

Who might you name as five of the greatest musicians of all time?

- ....
- ....
- ....
- ....
- ....

Have you thought of a few names of great musicians? How many were born in the last 50 years? How many were born in the last century, or two centuries? If you had to make a list of 20 or 50 musicians, how many would you even be able to name from more than a few hundred years ago?

Recency bias inherently applies when we think about questions like this, because we tend to know much less about the distant past compared to more recent history. Questions about musicians are subjective and usually asked for entertainment purposes, but the same doesn't apply to fields such as politics, technology, economics and history. If we wish to understand our world as fully as possible, taking the long view is a vital counterpoint to the disproportionate attention we tend to pay recent events simply because they are fresh in our experience.

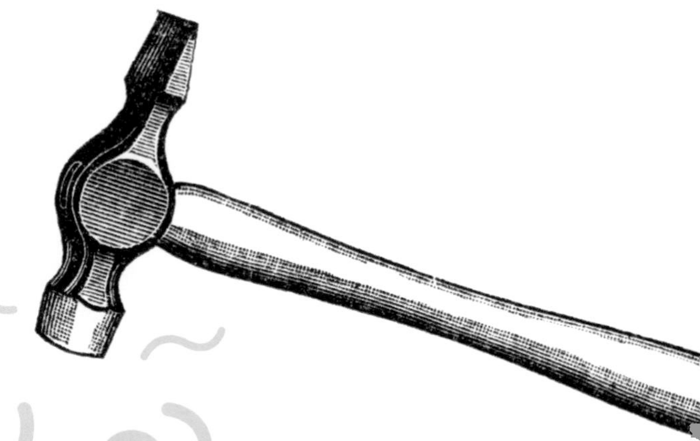

THE TEST OF ALL BELIEFS IS THEIR PRACTICAL EFFECT IN LIFE.

HELEN KELLER

#TalkCriticalThinking

3 The anchoring heuristic

Read the following carefully, filling in the blank space at the end of the paragraph with any number you see fit:

> I used to enjoy shopping at the Tasty Wine Shop at number 997 High Street, next to the Meaty Butchers at 999 and the Green Green Grocers of Home at 995. I liked to buy a case of tasty wine every now and then, as recommended by the owner. Tragically, he died suddenly last year at the age of
>
> After that, I enjoyed shopping at the Select Wine Shop at number 12 High Avenue, next to the Veggie Emporium at 10 and the Hair Today Gone Tomorrow Salon at 14. I liked to buy a case of select wine every now and then, as recommended by the owner. Tragically, he also died suddenly just last week at the age of

This may seem a strange exercise, but give it a go. There's no right or wrong answer – simply select any figure you like for the age in each of the paragraphs. Done? Good. Which number is bigger and which is smaller? If you came up with a larger age for the first paragraph than the second, you may have been experiencing a version of the **anchoring effect**.

Anchoring effect: the ability of a starting value or frame of reference to influence your subsequent judgements, even when it has no relevance to what you're considering

Anchoring occurs when something acts as an 'anchor' for your judgement, influencing it in a particular direction without you consciously noticing what is going on. The two paragraphs in my example are almost identical, except that the street addresses in the first paragraph – 997, 999 and 995 – are considerably higher numbers than the street addresses in the second paragraph – 12, 10 and 14. Self-evidently, street addresses have no direct relationship with the age at which someone suddenly dies, even if that person is fictional. Yet research suggests that even completely unrelated 'anchors' can influence our judgement, and do so without us consciously noticing.[37]

Why is this? The first thing to note is that no judgement occurs in a vacuum. Across a host of fields, we assess things by a process of comparison rather than in absolute terms. The Earth is big compared to the scale of the human body, but small compared to the Milky Way galaxy. If I asked you to add to a list I was making of really big things, and I began by saying 'the planet Jupiter, the Sun, the age of the universe', you would almost certainly make a different contribution than if I said 'the Empire State Building, the Great Wall of China, the Great Pyramid of Giza'.

You may not order the lobster – but it made the chicken look cheaper!

This is an appropriate reading of context and is essential to our everyday functioning, but it's not a mechanism we can simply switch off, even when it may be unhelpful. Our judgement always tends to be particularly influenced by the first information we receive. As most people who work in sales know, it can help to begin a negotiation by asking for an unrealistically high price in order to make a higher number seem more reasonable, or to initially show someone something that's much too expensive for them, simply to make everything that comes after feel cheap. Restaurants and supermarkets play a similar trick: the prominence of very expensive items makes merely pricey items seem affordable.

Focusing effect: the tendency to focus excessively on one striking aspect of something, thus failing to give full consideration to a full range of other relevant factors

We see a version of this in what's known as the **focusing effect**. This describes a tendency to focus too much attention on one immediately obvious feature of something, leading to an unbalanced assessment. Imagine you are talking to a friend about their desire to move house and they tell you the following. Do you trust their judgement?

> I'm fed up with living in cold, damp England. You barely see the sun at all for three months of the year. I'm going to head to California and try to find a job. Sunshine, sea, beautiful people, movies. It'll be a better life for me out there, I know it! No more trudging around in the gloom wearing a jacket and two jumpers.

Obviously, you will need to know much more before offering your friend any worthwhile advice. But on the basis of the paragraph above, you might suspect that they are focusing too much on one of the most immediately obvious features of life in California – the weather – and thus failing to give other factors due consideration.[38]

In this, the familiar pattern we see in other heuristics is repeated. A tricky question involving complex information ('should I move to California?') is swapped for an easier question about ease and emotion ('how does the first thing that comes to mind when I think about California make me feel?'). And even if the person who has performed the swap notices what is going on, they may not be able to escape its disproportionate influence.

4 The representativeness heuristic

Here is one of the most infamous psychological case studies of recent decades, involving a fictional bank employee called Linda.[39] Read it and then select one of the two options in the final sentence:

> Linda is 31 years old, single, outspoken and very bright. She majored in philosophy. As a student, she was deeply concerned with issues of discrimination and social justice, and also participated in anti-nuclear demonstrations. Which is more probable?
>
> - Linda is a bank teller ◯
> - Linda is a bank teller and is active in the feminist movement? ◯

Which option did you go for? As you may remember from the first half of the book, it is a logical certainty that Linda is more likely to be a bank teller than she is to be a bank teller who is active in the feminist movement. This is because the second possibility is entirely contained within the first. Every bank teller who is active in the feminist movement must be a bank teller, but there are also plenty of other female bank tellers who are not active in the feminist movement.

If you went for the second option, or found yourself drawn to it, you were experiencing what is known as the **representativeness heuristic** – an elaborate way of saying that people are often more influenced by how convincing a representation of something is offered, than by how strictly likely it is. The possibility that Linda is a feminist bank teller feels more plausible than the possibility that she is simply a bank teller, and this plausibility creates a preference that can outweigh mathematical probability.

Representativeness heuristic: the tendency to be influenced by the plausibility of a story or characterization, at the expense of underlying questions of its probability

There's plenty of debate around whether the Linda problem illustrates an irrational blindness to probability, whether it is in fact natural to interpret 'most probable' as synonymous with 'plausible' in the context of the question, or whether some other perfectly reasonable process of inference creates the effect.[40] What we can say with some confidence is that our preference for coherent, consistent narratives can lead us to have false confidence in the accuracy of certain judgements. Here's another example:

> I'm a young Englishman with a healthy tan who likes to spend time outdoors, stay physically fit and drink strong tea with two sugars. Is it more likely that I work in:
>
> - Agriculture, forestry and fishing sector ◯
> - Mining, energy and water supply ◯
> - Health and social work? ◯

What do you think? A wise answer based on my description might begin with a question: 'well, how many people in England work in each of those sectors?' A less wise answer might go, 'it sounds like you work in a physically demanding outdoor job like agriculture, or utilities'.

As it happens, more than four times as many people in the UK are employed in health and social work than are employed in all of the other categories listed in my example combined.[41] In the absence of other relevant information, this suggests that I am most likely to be involved in health and social work. The representativeness heuristic, however, describes our tendency to assess such a scenario not by seeking out meaningful data, but by seeing how closely someone conforms to a **stereotype**. The better a description fits with our expectations of what a representative individual is most likely to look like, the more likely we are to match them together.

Stereotype: a commonly held, simplified and idealized view of the typical characteristics of something or someone of a particular type

Once again, a kind of substitution is in action. We are swapping an effortful investigative question ('how many people are employed in each of these sectors?') for an easier question about emotion and expectation ('what stereotype does a person like this seem most closely to correspond to?'). Stereotyping is almost universal in our dealings with people we do not know personally, and even with many people that we do know. It's also just the tip of the iceberg where **social biases** are concerned: biases that specifically affect our judgements about other humans, and that can combine with structural social inequalities to create some of our world's most urgent injustices.[42]

Social biases: a general term for instances of bias in our judgments about other people, groups of people, or social and cultural institutions

SMART STUDY: A summary of four key heuristics

We have looked at four heuristics, each embodying a different cognitive shorthand:

1 The **affect heuristic** – the strong influence of emotional intensity as a guide to judgement, even when this may be misleading ('the beautiful celebrity in that advert looks so happy: the product must be special!').
2 The **availability heuristic** – the strong influence of how easily something comes to mind as a guide to judgement, even when misleading ('I heard about that beautiful celebrity who was lactose intolerant: I must be too!').
3 The **anchoring heuristic** – the strong influence of the first information we encounter on our subsequent judgement, even when misleading ('my new car costs $45,000, which makes $1,000 extra for red seats a real bargain').
4 The **representativeness heuristic** – the strong influence of how closely something conforms to our expectations ('this wine costs a lot, comes in a posh bottle and is being served to me by a French person in a white jacket: it must be something special!').

Remember, heuristics are both natural and essential. It's only when they misfire and result in a misleading judgement that they constitute a cognitive bias. This is most likely to happen when you are rushed, inexperienced, bombarded with information, being deliberately manipulated (hence the advertising, media, sales and marketing examples above) – or when you allow prejudice and generalizations to define your attitude towards other people and cultures.

WHEN TO TRUST HEURISTICS AND WHEN TO DISTRUST THEM

Heuristics allow quick decision-making and judgement, via the simplification of a complex question into something more intuitive. On the whole, they work extremely well, are essential to our lives – we couldn't function without them.

When are heuristics and intuitions at their most reliable? They are most effective in situations resembling the conditions in which humans have evolved over hundreds of thousands of years to handle, or when we as individuals have developed meaningful skills for managing over the course of our lives:

1 We are interacting with people whom we know on a **local, human scale**.
2 We are dealing with **clear choices** about which we have **reliable information**.
3 We're making decisions about a field in which we possess **relevant expertise**, developed on the basis of the repeated and meaningful exercise of skill.

By contrast, heuristics and intuitions are considerably less reliable when we encounter the kind of complex situations that have only existed very recently in our evolutionary history, or that we have had no opportunity to practise and develop meaningful skills for handling:

- We are dealing with largely **unknown** people at a **distance**.
- Either we are required to decide on the basis of **inadequate** information or we are faced with an **overwhelming** number of options and inputs.
- We're making decisions about a field in which we possess **no relevant expertise**, having had no opportunities to practise while receiving meaningful feedback.

These describe a great deal of what we do online!

Consider the following situations: should we trust intuitions based on mental heuristics in any of these cases? If so, why?

1 You met online. You've never actually met in real life, but what he says when you exchange messages makes you feel you know him completely and he looks so kind in his photos. Now he has suddenly told you he needs money, fast. Your gut tells you that you can trust this kind, loving man. Should you go with that feeling?
2 The stock market is surging. You've worked as a trader for five years and your gut is telling you that it's going to keep on rising. Should you trust this feeling?
3 You're playing in a golf tournament. You've been a pro golfer for two years and spent the decade before that practising every hour of every day to get your game to where it is today. Something is niggling in the muscles of your back. You don't know what it is; nothing seems to be wrong with your play – yet – but your gut tells you that you're at risk of injury. Should you trust it and stop play?

In the first example, it's pretty obvious that you shouldn't trust your gut feelings. An attractive image and kind words may make you feel that you know someone, but online encounters are very different from real life. Our warm feelings towards the way someone looks and sounds can overcome rational doubts, but they shouldn't.

In the second case, it's less obvious what to do. If someone has worked as a trader for five years, they are nominally an 'expert'. Yet the sheer complexity and unpredictability of stock markets means that almost all of this expertise is meaningless when it comes to knowing what will happen next. All the evidence suggests that we are no good at predicting systems of this scale, complexity and unpredictability, and that any 'gut' sensation of confidence we may have is largely an illusion, best ignored.

In the final example, golf – like most sports – is a field in which meaningful individual expertise is very real indeed. Real skill exists, situations can revealingly be comprehended and compared on a human scale, and ability rather than blind chance dominates outcomes. Over a decade of practice is thus likely to yield profound intuitive knowledge of both the sport and your own body, making this kind of intuition best respected.

SMART STUDY: Why should you care about heuristics?

There are two main ways in which becoming more aware of how heuristics work can be useful in your life and work.

First, becoming more aware of the short cuts your everyday thinking relies on will give you more insight into your preferences, and more appreciation of the degree to which these do not need defending or justifying in strictly rational terms.

Second, this awareness will also help you be alert to – and put strategies in place to resist – both deliberate and accidental causes of cognitive bias.

As we noted at the very beginning of this book, this resistance often begins with slowing down: taking a moment to think twice about what is going on and bringing into critical focus the kind of mental short cuts both you and others may be using without even noticing.

BIASES BASED ON HOW THINGS ARE PRESENTED

This is the first of three sections dealing with different types of cognitive bias: biases specifically born from predictable distortions introduced by the short cuts we use when making judgements. To begin with, here's a question for you to answer quickly. Which of these two products would you prefer to buy if you glanced at them in a supermarket?

- Beef mince: organic and delicious, 90 per cent fat-free! ○
- Beef mince: delicious, organic, with 10 per cent fat. ○

You probably noticed that this is simply the same thing described in two different ways: beef mince that is 90 per cent lean meat and 10 per cent fat. You probably also noticed, however, that the formulation '90 per cent fat-free' is more enticing than '10 per cent fat'. This is known as a **framing** effect. Like two different frames that make the same picture appear different, the fat content of the beef has a different emotional impact depending on how it's described – and, as we've seen, people make most of their judgements on the basis of emotional impact rather than statistical analysis.

Framing effects: the way in which presenting the same scenario in different ways can affect judgement and alter preference, based on perceptions of loss and gain, positive and negative

Framing effects are especially important because no information can ever be presented without some kind of framing – and yet, in most instances, you only get to see one framing device, and thus don't appreciate that there may be many different ways of thinking about the same thing. Here are some examples of how we might **re-frame** information, given a moment to pause and select a different emphasis. What might be the intentions behind the framing and re-framing in each of these cases?

Re-framing: deliberately selecting a different way of presenting information in order to challenge the emphasis created by a particular initial framing

....	Crime is at its lowest for four decades, with just 370 violent crimes per 100,000 people this year / *Although crime is at its lowest for four decades, there are still 370 violent crimes each year for every 100,000 people.*
....	In the educational case study we investigated, the level of absence among year 5 students was 10 per cent / *In our educational case study, year 5 students had a 90 per cent attendance record.*

.... One in every ten politicians reported receiving hate mail at their office / *Ninety per cent of politicians had never received hate mail at their offices.*

.... There are still 10 miles left to run in the marathon; I'll never make it / *I've run 16 miles of this marathon and am still going; I'll make it!*

You might think that these alternatives are pretty obvious. But, when presented with information framed in a particular way, most people simply accept it, not noticing that every presentation comes complete with assumptions they might wish to dispute. What about these two opportunities. Which does your instinct favour?

- Fancy a gamble? You've got a 10 per cent chance of winning $95 and a 90 per cent chance of losing $5. ○
- Buy a lottery ticket for $5? There's a 10 per cent chance of winning $100![43] ○

Which option did you go for this time? If you prefer the second, read them both carefully one more time. These options are also identical, at least in mathematical terms. Each one gives you a 10 per cent chance of finishing $95 richer than when you started, and a 90 per cent chance of finishing $5 worse off. If you don't believe me, read them again. The outcomes really are identical.

For many people, however, the second option is much more appealing. Why? The first option presents you with a 90 per cent chance of 'losing' $5. The second option asks you to 'buy' a lottery ticket for $5, complete with a 90 per cent chance of winning nothing. Both of these describe the same process, but it comes framed in two very different ways: in one, you see yourself as risking a loss with only a slim chance of gain; in the other, you are purchasing the chance of a gain.

The psychological force of this form of framing is known as **loss aversion** and it is one of the fundamental insights to come from **prospect theory**: an observation-based theory of how people deal with different prospects in terms of perceived risk, gain and loss.

Loss aversion: the observation that losses are more painful than equivalent gains, and that people thus tend to be biased towards loss avoidance when making decisions

Developed by Daniel Kahneman and Amos Tversky in the late 1970s, prospect theory has proved extremely significant in the short history of behavioural economics – and earned its developers a Nobel Prize – as it contradicts the standard economic notion that people will assess risk based on final outcomes. In contrast to this, it suggests that people assess risk based on the psychological impact of the perceived losses and gains involved, and that this dominates their decision-making.[44]

Prospect theory: an observation-based theory describing how people choose between different degrees of known risk, and between different potential losses or gains

Perhaps prospect theory's most significant insight is that people are more sensitive to losses than they are to gains – a sensible enough strategy in evolutionary terms – and that a strong aversion to perceived loss can disproportionately influence decision-making. Consider the following example: which of these options do you prefer?

- Pay an insurance premium of $20 to guard against a 1 per cent chance that you will lose or damage your $1,000 pair of designer sunglasses. ○
- Don't pay for any insurance and accept the 1 per cent risk of losing your $1,000 glasses and not being able to afford to replace them. ○

Assuming you can afford it, I suspect you would be tempted to pay $20 in order to eliminate the anxiety of losing such a valuable pair of sunglasses. Is this reasonable? It's difficult to say, in the sense that it makes perfect psychological sense to pay a small fee in order to eliminate the anxiety associated with a large potential loss.

Once we consider the fact that you face many similar decisions during the course of your life, however, it becomes more difficult to justify this preference:

> Assuming that you make many decisions of this type, being prepared to pay $20 to guard against a 1 per cent risk is equivalent to paying out 20 x 100 = $2,000 for every $1,000 of loss that you can, on average, expect to incur over time.

How do you feel about buying the insurance now? It ultimately depends on how much value you place on peace of mind. What we can say, however, is that what seems entirely reasonable and unproblematic in a one-off case makes far less sense as a general strategy. This is the basis for much of the insurance industry's profitability, because each payment is treated as a one-off opportunity to eliminate risk, rather than one instance of a lifelong series of decisions.

At the other end of the spectrum, we see a related effect connected to the slim chance of avoiding a near-certain loss. For example, would you accept the following offer?

> While shopping, you managed to lose a bag containing $1,000 in cash that you had been saving up for a long-awaited forthcoming vacation. Oh no! If you're willing to spend $75 on a taxi to help you retrace your steps as quickly as possible, however, there is a slight chance – about 4 per cent – that the bag is still sitting under a bench in a park on the other side of town.

Do you take the taxi? Once again, this feels like a one-off decision about peace of mind. Are you willing to pay $75 in order to have at least a chance of getting a large sum of money back? Perhaps. The appeal is easy to understand. A 4 in 100 chance that you will get $1,000 back may well feel worth $75 – especially as it will allow you to say to yourself afterwards, 'well, I did everything I could'.

The moment we start to evaluate this as part of an ongoing strategy for decision-making, however, it once again becomes hard to justify. Paying $75 for a 4 per cent chance of recovering $1,000 is, in the long term, equivalent to paying out about $1,875 for every $1,000 you recover. This is not a good deal. Broadly speaking:

- People often seem to over-value, from a purely mathematical standpoint, the opportunity to eliminate a small risk of loss (hence insurance).
- People also seem to over-value, again from a purely mathematical standpoint, even the slim chance of avoiding a near-certain loss (hence desperate gambles).

Prospect theory continues to undergo debate and revision, not least around what actually causes the phenomena it is based on (and what role regret and anticipation have in our decisions). In outline, however, it represents a significant shift in modern Economics towards the observation of how real people actually make decisions, not to mention the question of how we might either help people make better decisions or more skilfully manipulate them into making the decisions we prefer.

BIASES BORN FROM OVER-SIMPLIFICATION

Confirmation bias describes a human tendency that featured heavily in the first half of this book: the tendency to pay attention only to things that confirm our pre-existing ideas. Consider the following story, which is my version of a famous illustrative tale:

> A man walks into town claiming to be a brilliant marksman. 'Prove it', you say – and so he walks outside, points his gun at a blank wall in the distance and fires several dozen shots at random into the brick. When he has finished, he walks up to the wall, gets out a marker pen and carefully draws a target around the largest cluster of holes. He turns to you with a grin. 'I told you I was a great shot', he says. 'Just look how many bullets I got on target at that distance!'

Confirmation bias: the tendency to pay attention only to things that confirm our pre-existing ideas, and to ignore or seek to explain away evidence that contradicts them

Told like this, the story seems absurd to the point of ridiculousness. The man shot first and then drew on the target afterwards – of course he isn't any kind of marksman. Yet most of us are, on occasion, guilty of this kind of thinking, which in this particular instance is known as the **sharpshooter fallacy** or the **clustering illusion**.

The sharpshooter fallacy/clustering illusion: the tendency to see a pattern where none exists, by imposing it after the event on evidence while ignoring whatever doesn't fit

People tend to find patterns even when these aren't justified by evidence, and to do so by paying attention to similarities while ignoring differences. Unless we are extremely cautious, we are apt to see what we either want to see or expect to see, or are inclined to view as noteworthy, while ignoring information that is not meaningful to us in this way.

Consider the case of someone who sees something that looks like the face of Jesus in a slice of burnt toast, and declares it to be a miracle. This kind of thing has happened on more than one occasion (hence the inimitable BuzzFeed headline '22 People Who Found Jesus In Their Food').[45] Images of the miraculous toast are shared and discussed; it may even be sold for a large amount of money. What is going on? Two things are occurring that, when taken together, account for most events hailed as miraculous or revelatory:

- The very large number of cases in which nothing that strikes the human mind as particularly noteworthy are ignored ('one billon pieces of burnt toast look a bit like all kinds of different things')
- A claim that people are predisposed to deem noteworthy is offered as the single correct interpretation of a chosen instance ('these marks resemble Jesus' face and must be miraculous').

Here's a more serious example for you to think about. How might confirmation bias be present in this particular experiment and in the larger claims made for its results?

....	Our study suggests that homosexual people who actively
....	wish to change their sexual preference through a
....	programme of counselling can do so. Volunteers for our
....	experiment sought counselling and many reported a
....	change in their sexual preference following this process,
....	confirming our belief that homosexuality is not 'natural'
....	and can be overcome with help and willpower. We believe
....	that those who did not report an initial change would
....	come around to this view with time and effort.[46]

Many things are wrong with the above investigation. First, the fact that it used volunteers actively seeking to change their sexual preference through counselling suggests that such people may have begun with a strong investment in a particular outcome, and both a pre-existing desire and belief in its desirability. Second, the experimenters themselves seem to share this assumption, given that they are setting out to seek confirmation of this same belief with willing volunteers, and seem intent on interpreting any and all results in accordance with their predetermined assumptions.

Experiments such as this may seem laughably poor as investigations of what is actually going on – as indeed they are – yet they are by no means uncommon among people determined to find a certain pattern in events. Once we have decided that a certain pattern exists, we can find confirmation for it everywhere and anywhere. One striking example of this is the **just world hypothesis**, which describes a belief commonly embodied in phrases like 'what goes around comes around'. In other words, everything balances out in the end: good things happen to good people, bad things happen to bad people, and all is ultimately for the best.

Just world hypothesis: the belief that everything balances out in the end and that the world is fundamentally arranged in a way that is fair

Can we be sure that such a view of the universe is not correct? Not definitively. What we can say, however, is that its cruder forms create a troubling incentive to assume that people who suffer ill fortune somehow deserve their suffering – and that, if all things are for the best, we need not worry too much about trying to change them.

As we saw in the first section of this chapter, plausibility often counts for more on an intuitive level than probability. Similarly, our confidence in the information we possess is often more closely related to its **coherence** than its accuracy or likelihood. Take the following two stories. Which do you find more convincing?

Coherence effect: the tendency to judge information not by its accuracy or likelihood, but by how internally coherent a story or a worldview it embodies

	MOST PLAUSIBLE
Me and my friend, we were driving along. Everything was fine. Suddenly, I found myself steering off the road into a tree. I didn't see it until we hit it. Except, my friend told me to watch out for a tree. So perhaps I did see it.	○
My friend Jason and I were driving along when he said something to me, about this picture he just got on his phone. Well, I didn't want to look because I was driving but I turned my head slightly, and then I suddenly saw an animal in the road, like a rabbit, and I steered just a little to avoid it and the wheel caught a bit of gravel on the verge and, next thing I know, bang! We hit a tree.	○

The second of these paragraphs is certainly a more vivid and coherent account of events, including a firm narrative of cause and effect. Does this make it more reliable? No. Once we think of it as a more elaborate and more specific explanation of the same events as the first paragraph, then we can see that it is less likely to be entirely true: the very vagueness of the first description means it is less likely to include unreliable elements, while the apparent coherence of the second story relies upon all its details being accurately recalled and connected.

As you'll probably have noticed, however, the coherent narrative structure of the second paragraph makes it easier and more satisfying to grasp than the first paragraph. Coherence – something that is easily grasped as a whole and that hangs together persuasively – is experienced as evidence of credibility, while uncertainty and inconsistency make something seem less credible.

SMART STUDY: Never trust a good story

Stories are perhaps the most fundamental patterns we see in the world: chains of cause and effect, action and consequence, in which the most significant factor is not evidence or reasoning but plausibility.

If you want to be a truly alert critical thinker, you need both to respect and to be deeply sceptical of the power of a good story. Anecdotes are a vivid form of persuasion and illustration, but they're no basis for research. Compelling narratives offer us explanations, reasons and purposes, but these are things we ourselves create and they are far from neutral.

How can you avoid what's sometimes known as the 'narrative fallacy'? Try seeing how many different stories you can tell based on the same facts, and whether you can make the same information fit into two entirely contradictory accounts. If you can, congratulations – you've decisively demonstrated that you need to find out more!

This is significant not only in settings like a court of law, where the credibility of a witness is all about consistency, but also in those circumstances where we value our own consistency above evidence that we ought to change our minds.

Have you ever bought a ticket for an event – a play, a concert, a film – and found that you're not enjoying it all, but nevertheless stayed throughout the entire thing because you didn't want to waste your money by leaving? This is an example of what is sometimes called the **sunk cost fallacy**, so-called because the money you spent on a ticket is 'sunk' and cannot be got back, whatever happens.

Sunk cost fallacy: the tendency to continue expending energy on something you are emotionally invested in beyond the point at which it makes sense to abandon it

You might as well leave if you're not enjoying the experience, rather than adding the psychological cost of a bad night out to the monetary cost of a ticket. But a desire to maintain consistency with your own past decisions keeps you in place.

A more dangerous version of this is the tendency to keep going with a project even after it becomes increasingly obvious that it is likely to fail. Rather than endure the contradiction of admitting that something you believed would succeed is a failure, you keep pouring in effort long after it would have been more sensible to give up. As to whether this is actually fallacious – or whether it's entirely understandable on the basis of reputational damage and social expectation – that is a matter for ongoing debate.[47]

BIASES BORN FROM A LACK OF INSIGHT

In 1999, the psychologists Justin Kruger and David Dunning tested students at Cornell University in three fields: logic, grammar and humour.[48] Students sat four tests in total and were then asked to estimate where they thought their scores ranked them compared to other students. The result was intriguing. Competent students produced a fairly accurate estimation of their own expertise. The weakest of the students, however, consistently and substantially over-estimated their own performance: they thought that they were approaching the top third of results, when in fact they were in the bottom quarter.

Why did this happen? The authors noted that, once weak students had been given some instruction in their areas of weakness, their ability to estimate their own lack of ability improved. In other words, people who know very little about something have little capacity to accurately assess their own lack of skill, because they don't have much of a sense of just how much they do not know. It takes some knowledge to realize how much you do not know.

Dunning–Kruger effect: the tendency of people with little or no ability in an area to greatly over-estimate their ability, resulting in ignorance breeding unwarranted confidence

This phenomenon is known as the **Dunning–Kruger effect** in its discoverers' honour. It stems from the fact that some degree of practice and skill is needed for people to be able to compare themselves to others, meaningfully. In the absence of this, all of us have a tendency to over-estimate our abilities. Ignorance breeds overconfidence, while it takes dedicated practice to create caution.

If this were all psychology suggested about expertise, we might take some comfort: people who know what they're doing can, indeed, tend to have a realistic assessment of their own abilities. It's those who don't even notice that they don't know anything that we need to watch out for. Unfortunately for experts the world over, however, a second well-evidenced effect is also commonplace.

Overconfidence effect: the strong tendency for most people – and especially experts outside their domain of expertise – to have excessive faith in their judgements and abilities

This is known as the **overconfidence effect** and describes a powerful psychological tendency for people to have more confidence in their judgements than those judgements actually warrant. In a classic study conducted during the academic year 1968–9, the decision analysts Marc Alpert and Howard Raiffa asked groups of Harvard students to estimate a number of different figures: quantities ranging from the egg production of the USA in a given year and total car imports, to the toll collections of the Panama canal and the number of doctoral students enrolled at Harvard Business School.[49]

These were not numbers students were familiar with, and so they were asked to suggest a possible range of values for each answer, such that there was a 98 per cent chance that the true value lay somewhere within the range they had chosen. You can try it for yourself, first of all. For each of the following questions, select a range of possible results such that you are almost certain – 98 per cent certain, to be precise – that the correct answer will lie somewhere within your selected values:

What was the total egg production of the USA, in millions, in 1965?	
How many foreign cars were imported into the USA in 1967, in millions?	
How many doctoral students were enrolled at Harvard Business School in 1969?	

These questions will still be more difficult for you to guess than students in 1968/9, given five decades' distance in time, so you should have been even more cautious and broad in your chosen range. Here are the results. How did you do?

Total egg production in 1965:	64,588 million
Foreign cars imported in 1967:	697,000
Doctoral students enrolled in 1969:	235

If you're anything like the students who originally took the test, at least one of these values is likely to lie outside your chosen range. As it turned out, instead of just 2 per cent of the actual results lying outside students' guesses (as you would hope, given they were aiming at 98 per cent accuracy), the range of possibilities provided by students proved incorrect in 40 per cent of cases – a failure rate 20 times greater than the one they were asked to aim for.

What does this show? As subsequent research has repeatedly suggested, people are wildly overconfident about the accuracy of their own predictions; and this overconfidence extends to estimating their own abilities at pretty much any activity where there is little exposure to a truly representative sample of others' activities: driving, cooking, starting a successful business, love-making.

And some of the worst people of all for this kind of mis-reckoning? Experts. While experts may be adept at predicting performance within their own fields, this doesn't extend to restraining themselves outside the limits of their expertise. Someone who is justifiably confident in one area – the minutiae of macroeconomic theory, for example – is more likely than a non-expert to be unjustifiably confident in other areas.[50]

How often, for example, have you seen a famous author or performer asked for their opinion about a field they have no expertise in, such as politics or international aid? How often have experts offered predictions in areas whose profound uncertainty – the future price of oil, distant geopolitical trends – should make the only honest answer 'we cannot know'? Few things can be harder to say for someone professionally obliged to appear more confident than others.

SMART STUDY: Buster Benson's cognitive bias cheat sheet

One of the most useful resources I've found on cognitive bias is a 'cheat sheet' designed by technologist Buster Benson, which synthesizes a master list of cognitive biases into four categories. It's a great, practical tool for triggering reflection on your own work, habits and thinking. Below is my summary of Benson's key points; you can read more about the original online.[51]

1 **There is too much information out there** – so we only tend to pay attention to notable changes, strikingly odd things, repetitions, and confirmations of our existing beliefs.
2 **There is not enough meaning out there** – so we tend to fill in the gaps with patterns, generalizations, assumptions, simplifications, and projections of our current mindset.
3 **We don't have enough time** – so we tend to assume that we're in the right, that we are competent, that whatever is easy or available is best, and that we should finish what we start.
4 **We can't remember or track everything** – so we recall our own experiences selectively, generalize on the basis of examples and archetypes, and rely on technology as a form of external memory.

BEHAVIOURAL ECONOMICS AND THE RESEARCH CONTEXT

It's important to note that the research underpinning the observations in this chapter is continuing to develop; that it is much-debated and disputed in places; and that I have only scratched its surface. Please don't treat my account as an impartial guide to the fundamentals of human nature – there's no such thing. Think of it as a rapid tour of the last few decades of research, and as the starting point for further reading and thinking of your own.

There are many accessible and enjoyable books in this area, as well as some unusually readable scientific papers, among which three in particular deserve highlighting. They are all by Daniel Kahneman and Amos Tversky, who between them have defined many of the central themes of what has become known as **Behavioural Economics**.

Behavioural Economics: the application of psychological insights and methods to economics, exploring through experiment and observation the real-life decisions people make

What is Behavioural Economics? It has become one of the most fashionable branches of psychological research in recent years, but its basic proposition is simple enough: applying the methods and insights of psychological research to the field of economics. It is, in other words, interested in observing how real people actually make decisions relating to risk, loss, gain and perceived value, rather than relying on mathematical models of what a reasonable person ought to do. In this, it has become a leading example of the observation-based exploration of systematic biases in human thought and action.

If you only read three academic papers in the field, make it these – and make sure you do so critically, asking yourself how far you agree with what they argue, and how far there remains room for further research and debate within this young discipline:

- 'Judgment under uncertainty: heuristics and biases' (*Science*, 1974)
- 'Prospect theory: an analysis of decision under risk' (*Econometrica*, 1979)
- 'The framing of decisions and the psychology of choice' (*Science*, 1981).[52]

EIGHT

SEEK REFUTATION OVER CONFIRMATION. ANY IDEA CAN ENDLESSLY BE CONFIRMED IF YOU'RE ONLY LOOKING FOR THINGS THAT SUPPORT IT. SEEK OUT CHALLENGES AND CONTRADICTIONS, AND PUT YOUR ARGUMENTS TO A GENUINE TEST.

#TalkCriticalThinking

SUMMARY

Careful, conscious scrutiny is a time-consuming and resource-intensive process, and so humans have evolved to rely on a large number of largely unconscious, instinctual and emotive approaches to making rapid yet broadly accurate judgements.

We call the cognitive short cuts that allow quick decision-making and judgement **heuristics**. They usually involve replacing a complex question with something amenable to a quick, simple solution.

Four types of heuristic are of particular interest and feature prominently in the literature of **Behavioural Economics** – a young field that uses the methods and insights of psychology to investigate real-life decision-making behaviours, based on experimental observation:

- The **affect heuristic** describes a tendency to use the strength of positive or negative emotional reactions as a decision-making short cut.
- The **availability heuristic** describes a tendency to be disproportionately influenced by whatever most easily or vividly comes to mind when making a decision or assessing options.
- The **anchoring effect** describes our reliance on an initial value or frame of reference in reaching a judgement, even when it is of no relevance to the question we are being asked to judge.
- The **representativeness heuristic** describes a tendency to be influenced by the plausibility of a story or characterization, at the expense of assessing its likelihood.

Becoming more aware of the heuristics that everyday thinking relies on can help us base our investigations of human experience on a realistic assessment of how judgements are reached. This awareness can also help us be alert to – and put strategies in place to resist – both deliberate manipulations and accidental sources of error.

Most of the time, heuristics are effective and reliable in everyday situations, especially when they involve dealing with people we know and situations of which we have plenty of experience.

When they result in an incorrect judgement, however, this is an example of **cognitive bias** – a predictable distortion of judgement or thought. Significant cognitive biases include:

- **Framing effects**: presenting the same scenario in different ways can affect judgement and alter preference, based on perceptions of loss and gain, positive and negative.
- **Re-framing**: deliberately selecting a different way of presenting information in order to challenge the emphasis created by a particular initial framing.
- **Loss aversion**: the observation that losses are more painful than equivalent gains are perceived as beneficial, and that people thus tend to be biased towards loss avoidance.
- **Confirmation bias**: the tendency to pay attention only to things that confirm our pre-existing ideas, and to ignore or seek to explain away evidence that contradicts them.
- **Sharpshooter fallacy/clustering illusion**: the tendency to see a pattern where none exists, by imposing it after the event on evidence while ignoring whatever doesn't fit.
- **Just world hypothesis**: the belief that everything balances out in the end and that the world is fundamentally arranged in a way that is fair.

- **Coherence effect**: the tendency to judge information not by its accuracy or likelihood, but by how internally coherent a story or worldview it embodies.
- **Dunning-Kruger effect**: the tendency of people with little ability in an area to greatly overestimate their skill, meaning ignorance breeds unwarranted confidence.
- **Overconfidence effect**: the tendency of most people – and especially experts outside their domain of expertise – to have excessive faith in their judgements and abilities.

Now watch the video 'The mental short cuts that define your world'. It's on YouTube. Tell me what you think via #TalkCriticalThinking

ESSENTIAL!
↓
Practical techniques for:
1. Thinking more clearly.
2. Escaping the most common errors in research.

OVERCOMING BIAS IN YOURSELF AND OTHERS

How can you think critically about emotional and persuasive language?

↓

How can you think critically about fallacies and faulty reasoning?

How can you think critically about cognitive and behavioural bias?

How can you best overcome bias in yourself and others?

How can you be a more critically engaged user of technology?

How can you become a more critically engaged writer and thinker?

Science is GREAT, but INDIVIDUAL scientists are DANGEROUS. They are human; they are marred by the biases humans have. Perhaps even more.

Nassim Nicholas Taleb

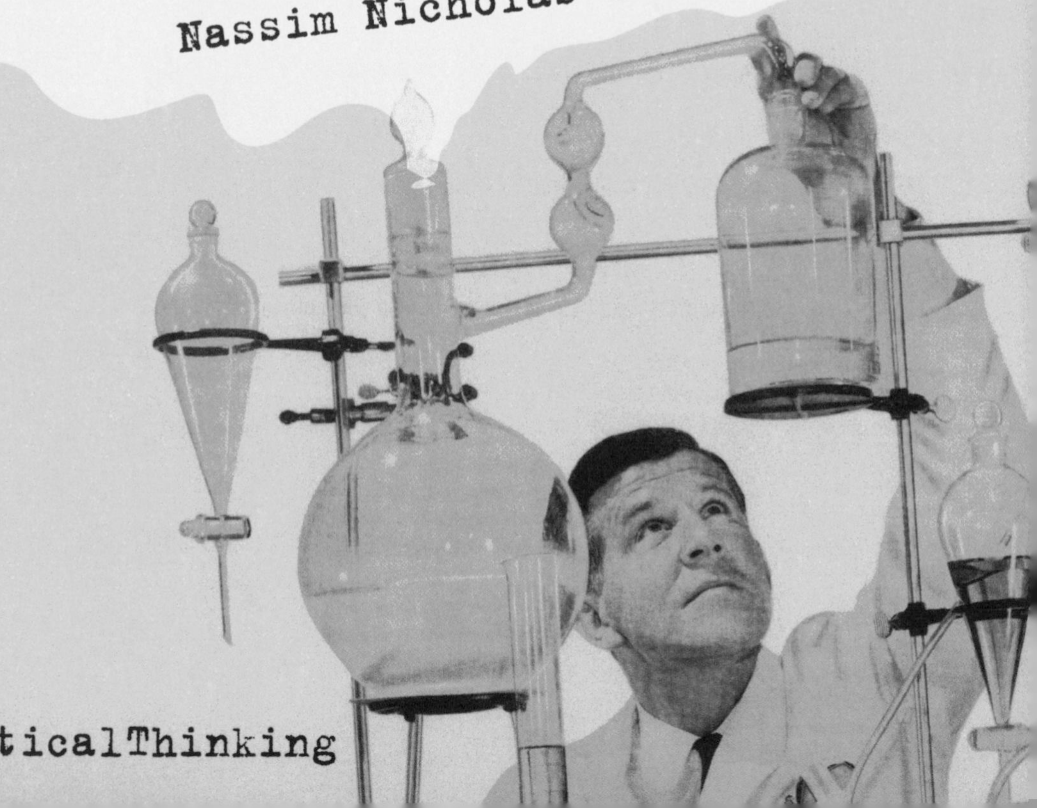

#TalkCriticalThinking

FIVE THINGS YOU'LL LEARN IN THIS CHAPTER

1 When it's important to *distrust your intuitions*
2 How *not to be* misled by *random events*
3 How to make sure you *do more than* judge things by results
4 How not to over-estimate the *predictability of events*
5 When you can *trust your intuition*

The time, attention and energy required to think critically is scarce and easily spent elsewhere. This chapter thus turns to a practical question: what do you need to know in order to distrust your intuition effectively?

Ensuring you are as familiar as possible with rhetorical appeals, fallacies, heuristics and cognitive biases is a good start. But there are also some practical fundamentals to be learned, relating to the ways in which reality itself tends to differ from our expectations. In particular, I am interested in how we can get better at overcoming three types of **misclassification** that lie at the root of many cognitive confusions:

The Overcoming Bias blog makes for brilliant browsing around this — do check it out.

- We attach undue significance to a random event or coincidence.
- We overlook the significance of things that have not happened.
- We assume that things are simpler and more predictable than they actually are.

ATTACHING EXCESSIVE SIGNIFICANCE TO RANDOM EVENTS

The law of small numbers

Here is some information for you to interpret. What might we reasonably conclude from the following, assuming that it is accurate?

> In a study of performance across all primary schools in the country, we found that the smallest schools were heavily over-represented among the worst performers, with a significant majority of the worst-performing schools across the nation falling into the category of 'small or very small schools' compared to the average size.

Have a think: the possibilities are almost endless. Perhaps small schools are more likely to be under-funded, or less able to attract and retain excellent teachers? Perhaps they are considered less desirable by ambitious parents, or tend to be found disproportionately in more disadvantaged areas? Perhaps they lack certain benefits that might come from having a large and diverse body of students, or lack organizational planning and efficiencies that larger schools are better able to institute? What do you think?

Here is a second piece of information for you to assess. Assuming the following is also entirely accurate, what might explain this?

> In a study of performance across all primary schools in the country, we found that the smallest schools were heavily over-represented among the best performers, with a significant majority of the best-performing schools across the nation falling into the category of 'small or very small schools' compared to the average size.

Again, the possibilities are almost endless. Perhaps small schools are more likely to attract and retain excellent teachers, or to be considered more desirable by ambitious parents? Perhaps they benefit from a close-knit community and intimate scale, and a more individual focus on students? Perhaps they are considered more desirable by ambitious parents, or are better able to spend their funds effectively? What do you think?

At this point, you may be confused. Is it possible for both this and the previous information to be true at the same time: can small schools be disproportionately represented among both the best and the worst in the country? Yes. There is indeed a perfectly reasonable explanation for the fact that small schools are likely to be over-represented among both the best and the worst in the country. But we can only appreciate this if we abandon the assumption that small schools must be either 'a good thing' or 'a bad thing', and instead start to think about the way in which reality is structured.

As you may remember from the first half of the book, using a large sample is important for getting realistic results. This is because variations of all kinds are likely to be more extreme when you use a small sample. Imagine there are a handful of extremely large schools in the country – a dozen 'super' schools with 1,000 or more students. Even if, by chance, a handful of exceptionally talented students happen to be attending one of these schools at the same time, the large number of total students means that the average performance at the school will barely increase.

By contrast, there are likely to be many small schools with only a few hundred pupils. A handful of exceptionally talented students attending one of these schools – or some other exceptional temporary circumstances – will have a far larger impact on average performance than at the largest schools. Like tiny boats bobbing around rapidly in the ocean, very small schools will show far more variation and sensitivity to external influences than very large schools, which, like enormous cargo ships, will barely move, even in the largest waves.

Overall, we should thus automatically expect any selection of large and small groups to be over-represented at both its extremes by the smallest groups, because these smaller groups are by far the most likely to be pushed towards an extreme by whatever influences are out there. There is no pattern to explain. This is simply the way numbers behave in the real world. When you're studying the same factors in each case, large samples will show less extreme variations than small samples. These facts are sometimes known as the **law of large numbers** and the **law of small numbers**, respectively.

Law of large numbers: the larger a sample, or the more often a consistent measure is repeated, the more likely its results are to tend towards the expected outcome

Law of small numbers: the smaller a sample, or the fewer times something is measured, the more likely its results are to differ from the expected outcome

Try it for yourself. For each of the following, how far do you agree with the given interpretation of the evidence?

1 We investigated the accounts of over 10,000 small businesses and found that those offering highly skilled professional services, such as accounting, were most likely to be profitable, while those offering less skilled support services, such as events management, were least likely to be profitable. This suggests that a business's required level of professional skills, and the resulting barriers to entry and competition in the field, are significantly related to likely profitability.

DISAGREE .... **SOMEWHAT AGREE** .... **AGREE**

2 We investigated the accounts of over 10,000 small businesses and found that those with three or fewer employees were significantly more likely to report double-digit increases in profitability than their largest competitors. This suggests that having a very small number of employees is significantly related to enhanced prospects of profitability.

DISAGREE .... **SOMEWHAT AGREE** .... **AGREE**

The first of these statements presents relatively robust evidence that profitability is connected to professional skills. Reviewing 10,000 small businesses by category is, depending on the methodology used, likely to produce meaningful comparisons, as long as each category is represented by a comparable range and quantity of businesses.

The second of these statements is less convincing. Without looking at the overall data, we cannot say for sure what is going on, but the law of small numbers suggests that the smallest businesses are naturally likely to contain more extremes of both profit and loss than the largest ones. Unless there is further compelling evidence, such as very few of the smallest businesses reporting large losses, we should assume that this result comes from nothing more remarkable than chance.

SMART STUDY: Three principles for dealing with small numbers

1 Whenever you are dealing with data, always be aware that small samples will naturally show greater variability than large ones.
2 Whenever you see an exceptional result – if, for example, you find a very high- or low-performing outlier among a number of institutions you're examining – always consider the possibility that very small numbers are involved.
3 Don't seek to explain something that doesn't need explaining. Focus, wherever possible, on larger and longer-term trends, and data sets sizeable enough to suggest significance.

Reversion to the mean

Here's an example of a second significant statistical illusion in action:

> I'm pleased to report that our research has produced an impressive practical result. We looked at the performance of 2,000 students across a variety of subjects and invited 50 of the weakest to undergo our study skills training. After these 50 students had successfully completed our training materials, we looked at their performance again the next term and were delighted to see a substantial and significant improvement made, on average, by our 50 subjects.

Should we be impressed by this result or sceptical about the benefits provided by the training? The answer, unfortunately, is that we should be very sceptical of these benefits, thanks to a phenomenon known as **reversion to the mean**.

Reversion to the mean: the tendency of an exceptional result to be followed by a less exceptional one, assuming a normal distribution of results over time

Reversion to the mean describes a fact that is obvious enough when you think about it, but highly deceptive when you don't: after an extreme result, you should expect the next result to be less extreme.

Consider your own academic performance. If one week you get the best results that you have ever got, it's likely that next week's result will not be quite as good – unless something has profoundly affected your underlying abilities. Similarly, if you are having the worst week of your life, you can rest assured that the next week is likely, statistically, to be better.

This can be a sneaky way to make an intervention look effective.

In my example, above, the same applies to the 50 worst-performing students out of 2,000. Even if they are much weaker than average in terms of underlying ability, it is unlikely that the 50 worst students in one term will also be the very worst 50 students the next term. There is thus only one direction that their average performance can go over time – up.

For similar reasons, you might think twice about buying shares in a company that's currently enjoying the highest share price it has ever known, because a decrease from an exceptional level is more likely than a further increase.

Why do we call this reversion to the mean? The 'mean' in this case is the average level that something hovers around over time. If you take a measurement and find that the result is unusually high or low, it is likely that the next time you take a measurement, it will be closer to the average. If you pick someone at random out of a crowd and find that they are very tall, the next person you pick at random is likely to be shorter. Similarly, if you are told that I have picked two people at random from a crowd, and that the second person was very tall, it is likely that the first person was shorter.

As my first example suggested, it is important to make allowances for this both when designing experiments and thinking about the world. How might reversion to the mean play a role in the following scenario?

> I'm a teacher and I have one rule I have found to be effective: punishment is good at stopping underperformance, but praise is no good at reinforcing excellence. How do I know? If someone does very badly and I know they could do better, I punish them – and next time they usually improve. But if someone does well, praising them rarely seems to do any good: even if I congratulate them profusely, they still tend to do worse the next time.[53]

Can you see what is going on here? The teacher in question is observing their students' performance accurately. But this teacher is also, unfortunately, drawing the wrong conclusion. In general, very poor performers will naturally do better the next time no matter what their teacher does, and very good performers will do worse the next time. This is simply because it is in the nature of performance to revert to the mean. The information is accurate, but the interpretation is not.

As a final example, can you see the flaw in the following study, and suggest how you might compensate for it?

> We wished to examine the impact of therapeutic group sessions in helping people who self-identified as problem drinkers to reduce their alcohol intake over time. In collaboration with a local health centre, we identified a dozen of the heaviest drinkers out of 100 self-identified problem drinkers known to the centre. These dozen people all participated in weekly meetings for two months, facilitated according to our group process. At the end of the two months, it was found that the alcohol intake of our group members had on average decreased significantly when compared to the overall average for the 100 known to the centre.

Much like my initial example of student performance, the problem with this study is that it begins by selecting one dozen of the heaviest drinkers out of 100. Although weekly therapy may well have helped these people, and problem drinking is not the same kind of phenomenon as academic performance, reversion to the mean still suggests that one dozen extreme cases are likely (on a purely statistical basis) to become less extreme over time, on average, compared to the rest of the group. In other words, we can't be sure that the observed effect is real.

How could we improve this experiment? The most obvious method would be to randomly split the 100 people into two groups: a control group (receiving no therapy) and a treatment group (undergoing weekly group sessions). This would produce far more persuasive evidence of causation if the treatment group showed significant improvement.

REMEMBER THAT TO EXPLAIN IS MUCH EASIER THAN TO PREDICT. MOST THINGS ARE MORE COMPLICATED THAN YOU THINK, EVEN IF YOU THINK YOU UNDERSTAND THIS SENTENCE.

HAIM SHARPIRA

#TalkCriticalThinking

SMART STUDY: Don't forget about reversion to the mean

1 Remember that an exceptional result in one direction will naturally tend to be followed by a less exceptional result in that direction.
2 Also remember that an exceptional result is likely to have been preceded by a less exceptional result in that direction.
3 Make allowances for reversion to the mean in any assessment: if you can, either use control groups or ensure that you are studying a full spectrum of subjects.

Fundamental attribution errors

The nature of the interpretative failures discussed above – the problem of small numbers, and reversion to the mean – should seem familiar after the previous chapter's discussion of heuristics and cognitive biases. People are not always good at accepting that many things happen simply because of chance or environmental factors, rather than because somebody or something has specifically caused them.

Fundamental attribution error: the tendency to disproportionately view events as the result of deliberate actions and intentions, rather than as a product of circumstances

A general name for this tendency is the **fundamental attribution error**, a phrase describing our tendency to read events as the result of specific actions or interventions, rather than as a more general result of underlying circumstances.[54] Here's an everyday example:

> I've been stuck behind this driver for the last 5 miles; I can't believe how slowly he's going. He must be distracted, or really incompetent, or just a terrible driver!

Many of us have been in a situation like this (at least, I have been in a situation like this many times). And, often, it is eventually followed by an observation like this:

> Ah, no – now I finally see it – there's a bunch of cyclists on the road ahead of him and it's almost impossible to overtake on this winding road.

Can you see what happened? In this case, I instantly leapt to an explanation of the slow driver's behaviour based on presumptions about his personality and attitude. I assumed that he was choosing to drive slowly, and that someone else in his position – like me – would do things quite differently. I blamed him for my frustratingly slow driving experience, by assuming that he was directly responsible for it and thus deserving of my scorn.

Yet, as I discovered, circumstances neither of us could control were in fact causing the slow driving. I would have been forced to drive exactly the same way in his position. And I would probably have had other drivers behind me cursing my driving in turn, for as long as they couldn't see the cyclists.

Why do we do this, and why does it matter? As so often, our tendency is to see the world as tidier and more coherent than it actually is: a place of single causes and narrative chains of events, where people can be held directly responsible for everything they do. Consider the following explanations and analyses. Which do you find more convincing? Which would be more convenient to believe if you were in charge of the prison system in question?

> The abuse experienced by prisoners was, we believe, attributable to the actions of a small minority of guards who were psychologically unsuited to their roles and who maliciously abused the power they had been given. Far more rigorous psychological testing and profiling should, we believe, prevent the recurrence of such events.

> The abuse experienced by prisoners was, we believe, attributable to a situation that over time dehumanized prisoners and left guards wielding arbitrary and often unaccountable power over them. Only changes to the nature of the system itself will, we believe, prevent the recurrence of similar events.

One of the more disturbing possibilities that resisting the fundamental attribution error raises (and one reason that we are not always keen to resist it) is that perfectly ordinary people can be led to act in strange, sadistic and inhumane ways as a result of their circumstances. This is not to say that personality has no role to play, but that its role may be less than we like to think. David McRaney writes well about this in *You Are Not So Smart* – see the further reading. However tempting it is to put the blame on people who, unlike ourselves, are bad or weak or foolish, the fact is that even when it comes to our own lives and actions, we have less control and insight than we might like to think.

There's a neat term that addresses this point, developed by the philosophers Thomas Nagel and Bernard Williams: **moral luck**. Moral luck pinpoints the curious fact that we often judge someone harshly in moral terms for something that is not under their control, even though we, at the same time, accept the idea that someone should only be held responsible for things they can control.[55] For example, how would you judge my actions in the following story?

Moral luck: the paradoxical observation that we ought to blame people only for things they can control, yet in practice we often judge them as a result of lucky or unlucky outcomes

> I was driving along the wet road slightly above the speed limit, just like everyone else around me. Some water had pooled at the side of the road, my wheels hit it at exactly the wrong angle and I crashed at high speed into a small car, killing its driver.

Many people would say that, in this situation, I am to blame for a terrible accident and should be punished. This is fair enough, but what about all the other drivers on the road who were travelling at the same speed as me? Is it fair to punish me severely for something that could have happened to anyone else on the road who was similarly unlucky? Would it not be fairer to deal with everyone on an equal basis, given that everyone was driving at the same speed? Then again, how far does anyone driving on a road actively choose to drive at the same speed as all the other drivers?

We can keep asking questions like this all day (and many philosophers have done). The point is that, once you start to ask what we can and cannot hold people responsible for, luck and circumstances loom larger than is comfortable. Does someone born into poverty and violence deserve to have their actions judged by the same criteria as someone born into wealth, peace, privilege and nurture? Should we judge people by the end results of their actions or by their attitude and intentions?

There is no simple answer to questions like these. As we'll explore in the next section, however, judging only by end results is often a misleading way of thinking about the world.

THINK ABOUT THIS: Can you think of an example of fundamental attribution error from your own life? Are there things you feel that you control that, in fact, you mostly don't?................

....

....

....

....

....

FAILING TO CONSIDER THINGS THAT DIDN'T HAPPEN

Alternative histories and outcome bias

The title of this section describes an important blind spot in our observations and habits: the tendency to judge all decisions by how things eventually work out, neglecting the possibilities entailed along the way. Here is a simple illustration of the phenomenon, borrowed from the author Nassim Nicholas Taleb:[56]

> Imagine that an eccentric millionaire offers you a prize of one million dollars for playing a game of Russian roulette. One bullet is put at random into a revolver with six chambers and you must pull the trigger. Five times out of six, you get a million dollars. One time out of six, you die. Now imagine that you have the opportunity to play this game once a year for the rest of your life. Does that sound like a good deal?

Alternative histories: all the other possibilities that did not play out in real life, but could have happened instead of the events we actually observed

Obviously enough, playing such a game is a terrible (and terrifying) idea. Yet it neatly illustrates what Taleb calls the principle of **alternative histories** and their invisibility in our everyday thinking.

In this delightful example, five out of six histories lead to riches, while one out of six leads to death. In the real world, we only get to see one of these histories – we don't get to see several realities play out in parallel. If someone survives, we notice them and their money: we assume they must be doing something right. If someone doesn't survive, we are far less likely even to register their existence. It's only if we consider all the alternatives in parallel that we can come up with an accurate model of what embracing this strategy represents: one death for every five survivors.

Understanding this is crucial once we start weighing up what it would mean to use the same strategy year after year. If enough people play a game like this over time, we end up with a small number of very rich people and a lot of graves. But only the rich people are interesting and noticeable and so, unless we make a deliberate effort to factor in the alternative histories, the immense risks of adopting this strategy may go unconsidered.

The game is illustrative rather than literal, but the point it makes is all too real. By focusing on striking outcomes rather than processes – on the few people who end up worth millions of dollars, rather than the many who didn't make it – we not only tolerate but can also end up emulating strategies every bit as unsound as Russian roulette.

Outcome bias: the tendency to assess the quality of a decision once the result of that decision is known, rather than by considering whether it made sense at the time

This is known as **outcome bias**. Once an outcome is known, we tend to see the past as a story leading inevitably towards that outcome, overlooking the uncertainties and possibilities that existed at the time. Yet the quality of a decision depends not on its end result, but on its engagement with circumstances at the time. For example, which of these decisions seems better to you?

	BEST
• Captain Alex surveyed the overwhelming odds against his troops on the battlefield, and gave the signal to retreat: better that we live to fight another day than throw our lives away in a skirmish, he said.	○
• Captain Bob surveyed the same odds and, with implacable hatred of the enemy rising in his throat, ordered every trooper in his company to throw themselves into an all-out attack.	○

I would say that Captain Alex sounds a good deal more impressive as a military commander than Captain Bob. But what if the following was the result: would this change your thinking?

	YES	NO
• Having given the signal to retreat, Captain Alex's troops withdrew with minimal losses and rejoined the main army.	○	○
• Captain Bob's company, meanwhile, threw themselves into the assault with such ferocity that they punched right through the enemy line and – although almost every single one of them died in the process, including Captain Bob himself – by sheer luck they managed to cripple the enemy's forward supply lines. Captain Bob was awarded a posthumous decoration of the highest order for his bravery.	○	○

Thanks largely to luck, Captain Bob is now a (dead) war hero. Yet his decision remains worse than Captain Alex's, irrespective of its outcome. If everyone in an army behaved like Captain Bob, they would pretty soon run out of troops.

I discussed one form of this particular failure of imagination at the very start of the book: **survivorship bias**, in which successes are counted but failures are ignored. Corporations and wealthy individuals are particularly susceptible to this form of bias, thanks to the invisibility of alternative histories in these fields. Everyone has heard of Google and Apple, but nobody has a list of the thousands of similar startups that failed early, or of the millions of potential companies that didn't even get started. Successful survivors are prominent and endlessly analysed, even though they're also so rare that few meaningful lessons can be learned by looking only at them.

Survivorship bias: the tendency only to pay attention to survivors and success stories, creating a distorted picture that ignores failures and those who dropped out

Here are three further examples of outcome bias and neglected alternative histories. For each, can you see what might be going wrong with the analysis and which unseen possibilities aren't being considered?

1 The corporation gambled everything on that hostile takeover bid, and it played off handsomely. Committing to a bold strategy of aggressive takeovers is the recipe for success right now, and we need to continue pursuing it.

2 It's clear that doing a lot of rowing can give people a superb, balanced physique: just think of all those rowers we saw out on the river at 6am, all of them in magnificent shape. If you want to get into great shape, you should start training right now!

3 Military scientists have now examined numerous bombers returning from active combat. Based on the damage caused by enemy fire, they have drawn up a plan for protecting our aircraft by more heavily armouring bombers in those areas that consistently suffered the worst damage from anti-aircraft fire.

In order to see how this kind of thinking is flawed, we can look at each of these scenarios in turn, spelling out those factors that remain hidden when we look only at results – but that become clear once we consider the alternative histories along the way:

1 The company gambled everything on that hostile takeover bid. Across our sector, historically, 90 per cent of similar takeover bids have ultimately lowered the value and productivity of the companies involved. Even though it appears to have worked out well, for now, it was a poor strategy – and the person who took the decision should be reprimanded for recklessness despite their success.
2 It's clear that those people rowing on the river all have excellent physiques and are very fit. It also seems clear that highly motivated, naturally athletic people with physiques suited to the sport are far more likely to be out on the river rowing at 6am than other kinds of people. Simply taking up rowing is unlikely to turn you into them.
3 As the statistician Abraham Wald pointed out during the Second World War, damage of this type actually shows which areas of a plane can safely receive damage while enabling it to return from combat! What's truly significant is the fact that all the surviving planes were not hit at all in certain areas, because any hits in those areas caused an aircraft to crash. Thus, what the military need to do is to reinforce their planes in precisely those areas that have not been damaged at all among survivors.[57]

Hindsight and publication bias

Hindsight bias: the tendency to see the past, in retrospect, as more predictable than it actually was – and to treat unforeseen events as though they were foreseeable

Hindsight bias is closely related to outcome and survivorship bias, and describes how people act as though something were predictable and inevitable after it happens, even though they did not predict it.

Hindsight bias is especially pernicious because we cannot help but adjust our perceptions after an event. In retrospect, the doomed celebrity's life becomes a study in alienation, depression and the addiction that finally killed them. In retrospect, the murderer's childhood and relationships are clearly seen to indicate their mental disturbance. And so on.

The problem is that unless we can be honest about how and why we didn't see things coming, we have no way of improving our ability to anticipate or mitigate against the next event – and yet the distortion of hindsight is built into the fabric of our memories. The answer? Keeping honest and complete records helps, as does refusing to play the game of retrospective certainty. But accurate and exhaustive record-keeping can be more challenging than you might expect, even when it comes to academic research. Consider the following example:

> There have been over 1,000 medical studies investigating the relationship between diet and heart disease. In one widely reported investigation, modest daily consumption of dark chocolate was associated with a significant improvement in several of the cardiac health factors of a treatment group when compared to the control, suggesting an exciting new avenue of exploration for further research.

Is it actually the case that chocolate is good for the heart? Perhaps. Given that over a thousand studies have investigated the relationship between diet and heart disease, however, it's more likely that at least a few will have produced unlikely results by chance – simply because of the weight of numbers.

In general, a few striking positive results will always emerge from any frequently studied field, simply as a matter of chance. Rather than being treated as possibilities in need of further investigation, though, these same results often attract prominent publication and publicity, while studies that fail to demonstrate any significant effects are much less likely to be published or publicized. This phenomenon is known as **publication bias**.

Publication bias: the tendency of academic journals to be more likely to publish research with positive or striking outcomes than other, equally valid research lacking such outcomes

You might think that philosophers, scientists and researchers should be immune to this kind of bias. In many fields, however, there are simply too many incentives around outcomes and impact. In response to this, an increasing number of journals and scientists are calling for the prominent publication of research that suggests a lack of causation or significance – and for researchers to ensure that the methods and results of their investigations are fully and openly published, preventing them from **cherry-picking** striking results out of context.

Cherry-picking: deliberately selecting a few striking results or strong effects from within a larger piece of research while suppressing the rest, thus misrepresenting the investigation

One campaign devoted to this thoroughness and transparency is AllTrials, an international initiative aimed at redressing the under-reporting of negative results in trials, and at providing practitioners and the public with as full and accurate a global record of research as possible. This kind of approach embodies one of the most important techniques for mitigating against bias: building collective systems and modes of practice that compensate for our weaknesses.[58]

SMART STUDY: Three principles for learning from non-events

1 By putting too great an emphasis on outcomes and positive findings, we often fail to learn from non-events and ignore the significance of alternative histories. In order to redress this, it's important for you to assess the quality of decisions and strategies, irrespective of their outcomes.

2 Survivorship bias and our natural interest in exceptional cases can blind us to the more mundane majority of cases that don't end in success or a striking result. In order to remedy this, it's also important for you to pay as much attention as possible to negative findings and rates of failure within a field.

3 In the short term, luck and random variation often dominate outcomes. In the long term, sound strategies and skill are more likely to succeed. Similarly, it's only by looking at long-term and large-scale trends that you can hope to find meaningful patterns.

OVER-ESTIMATING REGULARITY AND PREDICTABILITY

To return to a term we encountered in the first section of this chapter, what exactly do we mean by 'mean'? The **mean** is what is most commonly meant when the word 'average' is used. It's simply the total of every result divided by the overall number of results. Sometimes, this is useful and makes perfect sense:

> The average weight of a full-grown male Alsatian is between 30 and 40kg.

And sometimes it is obviously nonsensical:

> The average human being has one testicle and one ovary.

There are, however, other kinds of average – and it's worth diverting down this route to see just how much can be concealed beneath notions of the 'average'.

Let's say that the average height of a British man is around five feet and ten inches, or 175cm. If you happen to be British, male and five feet ten inches tall, you might assume that roughly half of the male population is taller than you and roughly half is shorter than you. You would be correct to think this. Similarly, you might guess that there are more people of approximately your height than of any other height: that very tall and very short people are rare. Once again, this intuition is correct.

Normal distribution (bell curve): also known as a **Gaussian distribution**, this is a continuous distribution with a peak in the middle of a range of results that curve away symmetrically

This is because height is a natural phenomenon with a **normal distribution**, sometimes also known as a **bell curve** – when you draw it as a graph, the curve is shaped like a bell. Also known as a **Gaussian distribution**, this is a continuous distribution with a peak in the middle of a range of results that curve away symmetrically each side; it is frequently used in the natural and social sciences to represent an idealized likelihood of results for a variable that has not yet been measured.

Imagine that you are offered a job as an analyst at a boutique financial services company that employs 15 full-time workers, including the post that you are potentially walking into. You know that the average salary at the company is £60,000 and that you will start work halfway up the company, with seven employees more junior to you and seven above you. Does this mean you can expect to start on £60,000 and that most people at the company will be earning about the same as you?

No. This would be true if the distribution of salaries at the company followed the same pattern as attributes like height, intelligence and weight. But financial distributions are anything but natural. Here is a list of actual earnings at this particular imaginary company:

Five researchers/assistants	£25,000 each
Office manager	£30,000
Two analysts	£35,000 each
Two senior analysts	£40,000 each
Marketing manager	£50,000
Chief technology officer	£75,000
Chief financial officer	£100,000
Chief operating officer	£100,000
Chief executive officer	£270,000

Mean: a 'traditional' average – the total of every result divided by the number of results

We can talk about averages in three different ways at this company and each one will give a completely different answer:

- The **mean** is the total earnings divided by the number of people: £900,000 of wages in total divided by 15 people, making £60,000. Only four people out of 15 actually earn more than average by this measure, but they earn so much that it pulls the mean upwards.

- The **median** is the salary in the very middle – with seven people above and seven below. This figure is £35,000 – considerably less than the mean but dividing the workforce exactly in half.
- Finally, the **mode** is the most frequently occurring value, which happens to be the £25,000 earned by five researchers/assistants. The most common wage is, in this situation, also the lowest wage.

Median: the middle result in a series, when it is set out in order

Mode: the most frequently occurring value in a series

What can we learn from this? For a start, simply talking about the 'average' when it comes to things like income doesn't tell the whole story. Depending on which kind of average you select, you can suggest three very different stories. Imagine the CEO of the company delivering three different messages aimed at three different audiences:

1 I would like to refute the allegation that we do not pay our staff well by noting, first of all, that the average salary across our small firm is £60,000 per year.
2 I would like to reassure our investors that payroll is not excessive, and that if you pick an employee at random from our main office they are most likely to earn £25,000.
3 We aim for fair remuneration that is neither excessive nor stingy, around a sensible median of £35,000 – in line with similar high-performers in our industry.

Notice that not one of these figures even hints at the £270,000 the CEO is taking home. To grasp this, we would need to ask questions about the overall distribution of the numbers in question, and to realize that any natural inclination to assume a normal distribution is dangerously misleading in this case. This point is clear when you compare visual representations of different distributions. Here is a graph of male heights for a representative sample of 50,000 men:

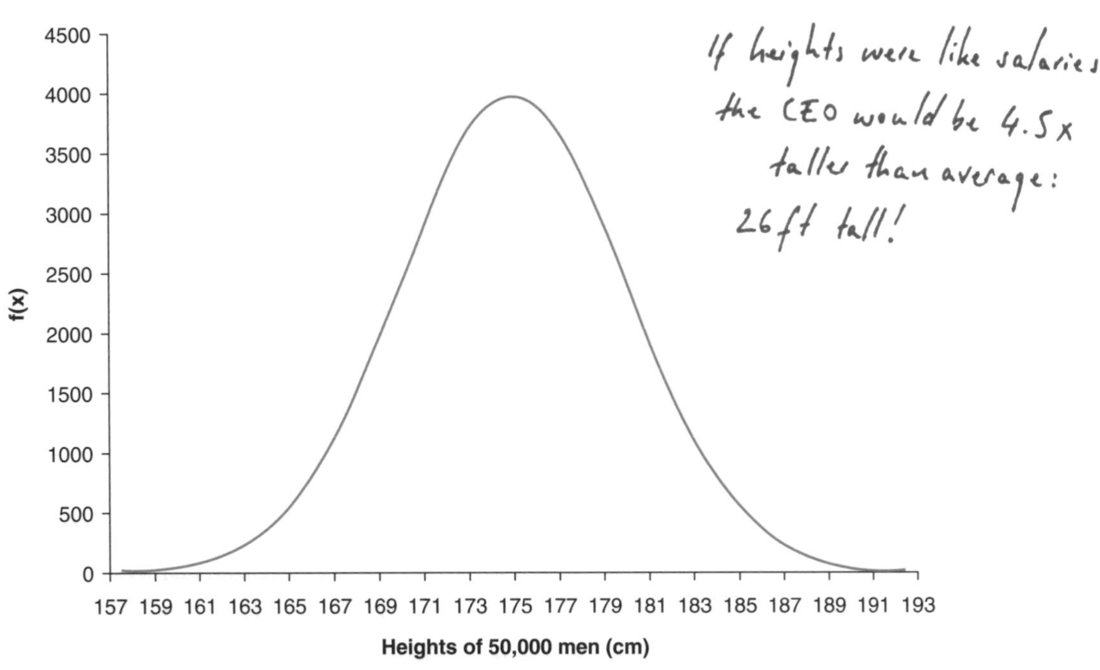

And here is a graph of post-tax earnings in the UK:

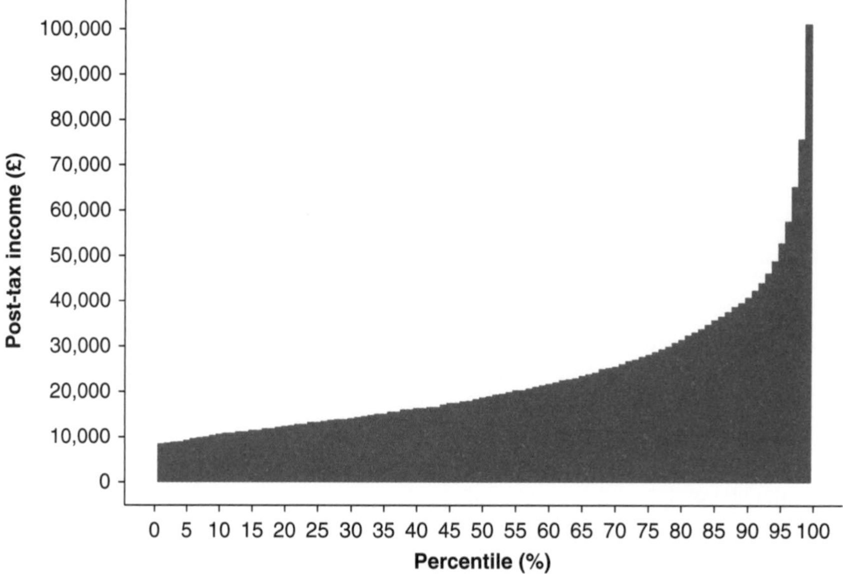

In the first graph – a normal, 'natural' distribution – the mean, the median and the mode are approximately the same. Knowing something about average height is likely to provide you with some pretty accurate intuitions about people's height in general. In the second graph, however, the mean, median and mode are very different. In this situation, any intuitions about what is normal, natural or predictable are likely to be misleading. A few extreme results outweigh the rest in terms of the mean; a long tail of lower results define the mode and median.

For each of the following scenarios, try to assess whether talking about a 'traditional' average in the form of the mean is likely to be useful or misleading:

		USEFUL	MISLEADING
1	Our research set out to test current political knowledge across a sample of 50 undergraduate students. On average, students scored just three out of ten correct answers when asked to name as many current members of the cabinet as possible.	◯	◯
2	Total global wealth is estimated at $250 trillion – an average of approximately $33,300 for each of the world's 7.5 billion people. Humanity as a whole has never been better off.	◯	◯
3	We are researching flood defences for the new coastal development. The average high tide in this region is 1.5m above mean sea level. For assured safety, we propose a defence structure based on a maximum of three times this level: 4.5m above mean sea level.	◯	◯

Using an average in the first case is reasonable. Knowing the average score tells us something useful about the level of knowledge among students, although it would still be better to see the complete range of scores. The second example, however, is misleading. The world's wealth is distributed extremely unevenly – and the fact that it averages $33,300 needs to be seen alongside the fact that approximately half of this wealth belongs to just 1 per cent of the population. In other words, 1 per cent of people own more than the remaining 99 per cent put together.

Finally, the third example – about flood defences – is not just misleading, but dangerous. Average high tides are not an appropriate measure for this kind of defence. What's needed is a historical record of extremes, plus a great deal of caution. I happen to have based these sample figures on the North Sea coast of Britain, where regions with an average high tide of 1.5m above mean sea level have seen several floods of over 5m above mean sea level during the 20th century.

Impact of extremes: the fact that just one extreme event, even if rare, can have a more significant impact than any number of ordinary events

This last case illustrates another important point about patterns and predictability: the **impact of extremes**. When something roughly fits a normal curve – heights, intelligence, common causes of death – things like variation and risk can meaningfully be estimated. But when infrequent, unpredictable events far outweigh any number of 'normal' events in their long-term consequences, our ability both to predict and to mitigate against risks is far less. Just one exceptional flood can cause billions and billions of dollars in damage. Just one day of sufficiently exceptional temperatures, high or low, is all it takes to wipe out an entire crop.

Illusion of predictability: the illusion that an observed pattern will necessarily be repeated, or that current notions of normality will always apply

Regularity, normality and averages are often a worse-than-poor guide to this kind of phenomenon, because they can breed complacency and misunderstanding. They create an **illusion of predictability**: the deceptive sense that something complex and susceptible to sudden change can be handled in the same way as genuinely predictable things.

Here's another graph to consider. It represents the stock price of a real, historical company over time. Would you buy stock in this company at the point at which the graph ends?

If you decided to buy stock – great idea! Here's the graph extended over a little more time. If you decided to buy, you've now doubled your money. Would you like to buy more?

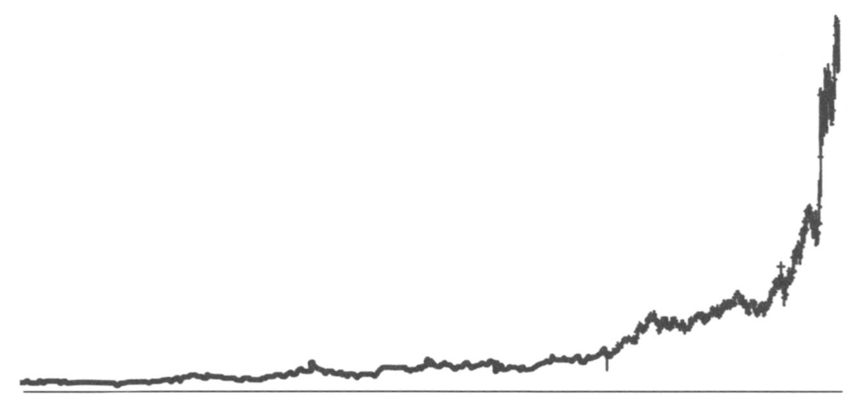

Oh dear. I hope you sold your stock. Here's the final graph, complete with scale:

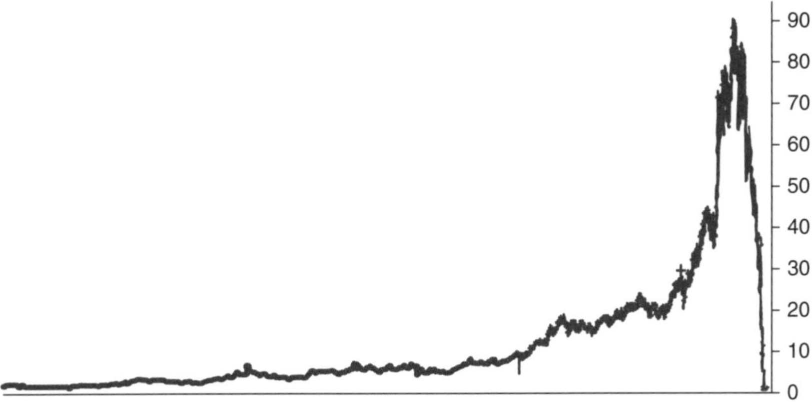

As you can see, it ends at approximately zero. The company was called Enron, and in November 2001 it became bankrupt following a famously reckless period of expansion, risky investments and concealment of debts. Almost every week for months, the company seemed to be doing better and better. It was praised for its dynamism and ambition. It was a global financial success story. And then, suddenly, it wasn't. Everything changed.

Should people have seen Enron's crisis coming and done something to stop it? Yes. Yet they didn't. Nothing was done until it was too late. And at the root of this lies a way of thinking that we all share, to some degree: mistaking trends for truths, taking too short a view and failing to anticipate how suddenly and entirely the world can change.

Almost everything many of us take for granted – prosperity, security, growth, technology, life itself – will at some stage be entirely disrupted by an unanticipated surprise. It's a question of when, not if. Predictable patterns and our sense of normality are, in the long term, illusions. Consider the following few questions:

- Why do economies keep on growing, and will they do so forever?
- Will computers keep on getting faster and faster?
- What capabilities will machines have in 10, 20 and 50 years' time?
- Will the world keep on getting richer and more developed indefinitely?
- What will the most destructive conflict of the 21st century look like?

Well, it's as good as certain that nothing goes on indefinitely

These questions are not answerable with any certainty, and this is the point: acting as though they are predictable or likely to follow any current trend is at once lazy, dangerous and certain to be proven wrong sooner or later.

SMART STUDY: How to avoid short-term thinking

- Plan for surprises, not continuity. Don't assume you know what you are looking for in research, or that any trends you currently observe will continue indefinitely.
- Remember that one-off extreme events are often more significant than thousands upon thousands of ordinary events.

- Averages and normal distributions make intuitive sense, but don't accurately describe most of what happens in complex systems.
- The longer something has lasted, the longer it is likely to go on lasting: it has already weathered a great number of shocks and surprises. Look deeply into the past if you hope to take any enduring lessons into the future.

THINK ABOUT THIS: Can you think of something that will still exist in 100 years' time? Or a thousand? What about something significant that will be gone within 50? ....

....

....

....

....

....

HUMANS: GOOD AT SOCIAL SITUATIONS, BAD WITH NUMBERS

To finish the chapter on a slightly more cheerful note, here's a puzzle for you to attempt. Imagine there are four playing cards in a row in front of you. Each of them has the name of a drink written on one side and a number on the other – but you can only see the upturned sides. You are allowed to turn over as many or as few of the cards as you like in order to answer this question:

> The legal age for drinking alcohol is 18 and these cards represent drinkers in a bar: on one side is the age of the person and on the other side is what they are drinking. What card or cards must you turn over in order to check whether everyone is obeying the law, while turning over as few as possible?

The upturned sides of the four cards show a 23, a 16, a beer and a coke, as in the diagram below:

23	16	Beer	Coke

What do you think? Most people have little difficulty in spotting the fact that you only need to turn over two of the cards to check that everyone is obeying the law: the 16 and the beer. This is because you need to confirm that the person drinking the beer is aged 18 or over, and you need to confirm that the 16-year-old does not have an alcoholic drink. You can leave the other two cards alone. It doesn't matter what the 23-year-old is drinking, because they can legally drink alcohol if they wish; and it doesn't matter how old the person drinking the coke is, because it's not alcoholic.

You may remember a version of this puzzle from Chapter 4, when we encountered it in a slightly different form: the Wason Selection Task, involving a rule about colours and numbers. You may also remember that around 90 per cent of people get the Wason Selection Task wrong on a first attempt. By contrast, exactly the same puzzle is easily solved by most people when set out in the

NINE

BEWARE ANCHORING EFFECTS. MAKE VERY SURE YOU DEFINE YOUR TERMS OF REFERENCE IN ADVANCE, AND DON'T ALWAYS LET SOMEONE OR SOMETHING ELSE DO IT FOR YOU.

#TalkCriticalThinking

form above. Why? Because we are highly evolved to handle social settings and familiar social rules. They engage our emotions and intuitions. They are easily imagined in concrete terms – unlike statistics and abstract logic, which take considerable effort to process and which don't align with our intuition. In other words:

- We are very well adapted, in general, to assessing small-scale social situations rapidly and accurately, so long as we know the conventions governing them.
- We are relatively poorly adapted, in general, to assessing large-scale complex problems involving statistics, and are often misled by intuition when facing them.

All of which leads to perhaps the most important recommendation of all:

- When facing the kind of situation in which you have reason to believe your intuitions are unreliable: stop, slow down and seek cognitive reinforcements.

SUMMARY

What do you need to know in order to **distrust your intuitions effectively**? Watch out for three types of misclassification:

- We wrongly assume that something that **happened by chance** is significant.
- We overlook the significance of **those things that did not happen**.
- We assume that things are **more regular and predictable** than they actually are.

First, attaching excessive significance to random events:

- The **law of small numbers** suggests that, the smaller a sample or the fewer times something is measured, the more likely its results are to differ from the expected outcome. By contrast, the **law of large numbers** suggests that, the larger a sample or the more often a consistent measure is repeated, the more likely its results are to tend towards the expected outcome.
- **Reversion to the mean** describes the fact that an exceptional result is most likely to be followed by a less exceptional result, and an outstanding performance by a less outstanding performance.
- The **fundamental attribution error** is a tendency to disproportionately view events as the result of deliberate actions and intentions, rather than as a product of circumstances.
- **Moral luck** describes the paradox that we ought only to blame people for things they control, and yet in practice we often judge them by the result of fortunate or unfortunate events that lie beyond their control.

Second, failing to consider things that didn't happen:

- **Outcome bias** describes a tendency to assess the quality of a decision by looking only at its result, rather than by considering whether it made sense at the time.
- **Survivorship bias** describes a tendency only to pay attention to survivors and success stories, creating a distorted picture that ignores failures.
- In order to avoid falling into the traps above, we need to consider **alternative histories**: the range of different possibilities that exist at a particular moment in time, together with their likelihood. Over time, alternative histories will 'catch up' with those following an unwise decision-making strategy.
- **Hindsight bias** is a tendency to see the past, in retrospect, as more predictable than it actually was, and to treat unforeseen events as though they were foreseeable.

- In academia, **publication bias** describes the temptation for journals to publish research with positive or striking outcomes in preference to other, equally valid research that demonstrates a lack of significance or causation.
- **Cherry-picking** in research means deliberately selecting a few striking results or strong effects from within a larger piece of research while suppressing the rest, thus misrepresenting the strength of the effects under investigation.

Third, over-estimating regularity and predictability:

- We need to be alert to the **impact of extremes**: the fact that just one extreme event, even if rare, can have a more significant impact than any number of ordinary events.
- We need to beware the **illusion of predictability**: the belief that an observed pattern will necessarily be repeated, or that current notions of normality will always apply.

Finally, we need to be aware of where our abilities and vulnerabilities lie:

- We are very well adapted, in general, to **assessing small-scale social situations** rapidly and accurately, so long as we know the conventions governing them.
- We are relatively poorly adapted, in general, to **assessing large-scale, complex problems involving statistics**, and are often misled by intuition when facing them.

Now watch the video 'Why your brain wasn't made to handle maths'. It's on YouTube. Tell me what you think via #TalkCriticalThinking

ELEVEN

THINKING CRITICALLY ABOUT TECHNOLOGY

How can you think critically about emotional and persuasive language?

↓

How can you think critically about fallacies and faulty reasoning?

↓

How can you think critically about cognitive and behavioural bias?

↓

How can you best overcome bias in yourself and others?

↓

How can you be a more critically engaged user of technology?

↓

How can you become a critically engaged writer and thinker?

↓

How can you challenge your tech habits & assumptions?

THE MOST IMPORTANT THING ABOUT A TECHNOLOGY IS HOW IT CHANGES PEOPLE.

JARON LANIER

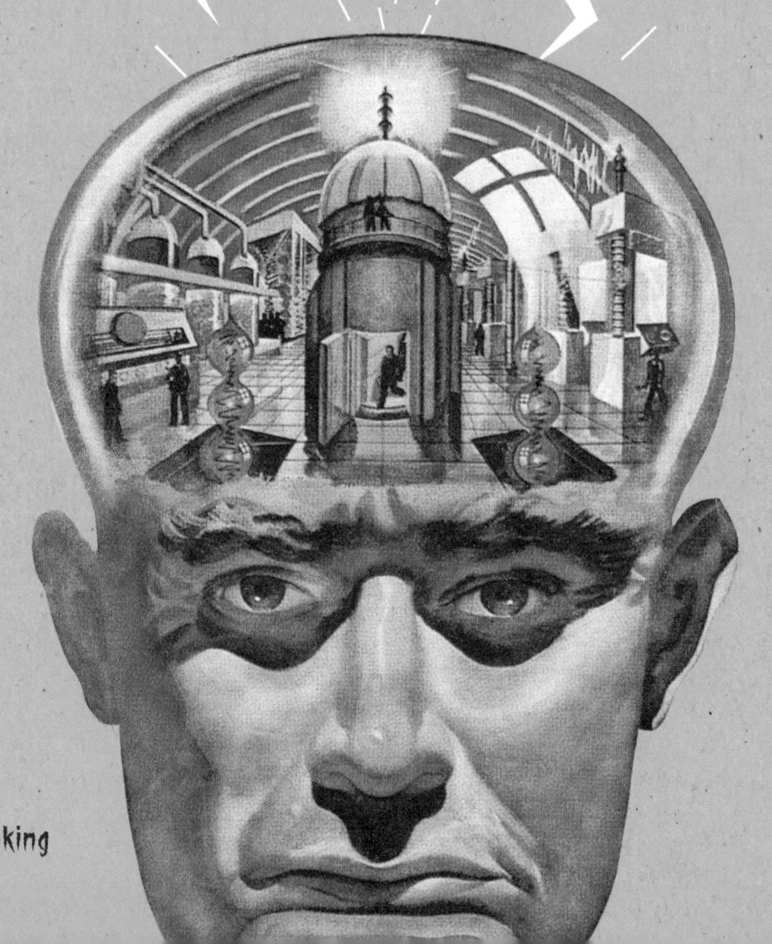

#talkcriticalthinking

FIVE THINGS YOU'LL LEARN IN THIS CHAPTER

1 The difference between *data*, *information* and *knowledge*
2 How to become more *aware of bias* within information systems
3 How to *conserve your own attention*
4 Practical *strategies for online search* and *discovery*
5 How to *identify* your own *most valuable skills* in a digital age

When we think critically, we are engaged in a process of reasoning rooted in scepticism – in the possibility that what we think we know is inaccurate, and that by actively seeking refutation and inviting counter-arguments we can collectively improve our understanding. This is especially important when it comes to analysing human thought and behaviour, and the ways in which we are vulnerable to bias, manipulation and misunderstanding.

This chapter turns to an equally important challenge: thinking critically about technology, and in particular those technologies created to help us preserve, access and process information. Much like us, technologies have their biases and blind spots, and these overlap with our own biases in complex ways. Far from being neutral tools, our technologies encode certain habits, assumptions and ways of seeing the world; ways that, unless we are careful, help define our actions and attitudes without us even noticing what is going on.

We live in a digital age, meaning we are surrounded by vast amounts of information available almost instantly and everywhere. We have more information more readily available at our fingertips than any previous era could even conceive of, together with more ways of interrogating, organizing, processing and creating new things with it.

Yet this does not automatically mean we know or understand more. It may even mean that we know less about some things: that we are presented with so many fragmentary or contradictory accounts that our ability to differentiate between them, or arrive at any overall understanding, is compromised. Equally, it has never been easier to collaborate and share, to ask others for help and advice, and to build common resources.

Profound and novel challenges come with this territory. This chapter explores some of them and suggests practical techniques for engagement. As we'll see, many of these challenges relate to a tension between what it means on the one hand to acquire, debate and disseminate knowledge and, on the other hand, to interact constantly with and through information systems. Some of these tensions are set out below:

Acquiring, debating and disseminating knowledge	Everyday use of information systems
Slow, effortful process	Fast process with an emphasis on ease
Truth and accuracy prioritized	Emotional and social impact prioritized
Popular beliefs don't dictate legitimacy	Popular beliefs extremely important
Persuasion primarily through reasoning	Persuasion primarily through rhetoric
Critical thinking about systems and frames	Uncritical acceptance of systems and frames
Actively inviting debate and dissent	Seeking confirmation and group consensus

Do you recognize any of these from your own life and relationships with and through technology? Do you agree, or disagree, with the tendencies they suggest?

In practice, aspects of both the above categories apply to almost all of our use of technology, whether for work or leisure. Even in academic research, we are highly influenced by social and emotional impacts, by popular beliefs and by the incentives particular systems create. We are social animals and, from language and writing onwards, the tools we have created for preserving and sharing information are social at root. The underlying question is thus: how effectively are we able to pursue knowledge while also interacting through shared, sociable information systems, and benefiting from their opportunities?

FROM DATA TO KNOWLEDGE VIA FAKE NEWS

Raw data: raw facts or figures awaiting processing

Words like 'data', 'information' and 'knowledge' are often used interchangeably. When it comes to thinking critically about technology, however, it pays to be more precise. Here is some **raw data** for you to consider:

8091, 8848, 8167, 8611, 8586, 8485, 8163, 8126, 8188, 8516.

What do you make of these numbers? Not much, probably. Data like this consists of raw facts that haven't yet been processed or organized. As a first step in processing this data, I'm going to arrange the numbers in some kind of order:

8848, 8611, 8586, 8516, 8485, 8188, 8167, 8163, 8126, 8091.

Does this mean anything to you now? Once again, probably not. By itself, simply arranging numbers in ascending or descending order doesn't make them useful or comprehensible. They could refer to anything. Now, however, I'm going to provide a context:

The heights of the ten tallest mountains in the world in metres are: 8848, 8611, 8586, 8516, 8485, 8188, 8167, 8163, 8126, 8091.

Information: data that has been processed or structured within a context that makes it meaningful

Now we're getting somewhere. Instead of a mere sequence of numbers, you are looking at some specific **information**: data that has been processed, arranged or structured within a context that makes it meaningful.

The word 'information', I should note, can itself have quite different meanings depending on context. The sense I'm using it in might be described as 'data plus meaning' and should be distinguished from its sense in information theory, a hugely important field spawned by Claude E Shannon in 1948, upon which much of modern information technology is founded. Follow the footnote to this paragraph for further reading around this fascinating topic.[59]

Knowledge: Verified information that we have good reason to believe is true

So, we have some information about something particular: the heights of very tall mountains. Is there anything further to be said or done? Yes. Information makes claims about the way things are, but it does not necessarily give us any reason to accept these claims as true. **Knowledge**, by contrast, is information that we have good reason to believe is true: a much rarer and more difficult thing to acquire.

Verification: a reliable process for testing the truth of information

Knowledge requires information, but it also requires something further: **verification**. Verification is the process of testing information against reality. As we've seen in the first half of this book, this, in practice, is likely to entail either an empirical investigation (climbing ten mountains while holding some advanced measuring equipment) or careful research into the evidence gathered by others (books, articles, websites, photos, videos and so on).

How might you set about verifying the heights I have supplied for the world's ten tallest mountains? As in almost any contemporary scenario that doesn't involve conducting an experiment, you would do this primarily through digital information systems: by going online, by searching websites and references, by sifting the world's vast quantities of shared information.

What then? A quick search suggests that the figures in my list are broadly accurate. They are, for example, the ones offered by Wikipedia on its 'List of highest mountains on Earth' page (at least at the time of writing, in April 2017). Yet this is only the start of the story. As further reading and research reveal, this list of heights is broadly accurate, but there are also considerable complexities entailed in determining them.[60]

Anyone who claims never to use Wikipedia is (probably) a liar.

What are these complexities? Try it for yourself, now. Go online and see how many different results you can find when you read around the following questions:

- What is the world's tallest mountain called?
- How tall, exactly, is the world's tallest mountain?
- Is there more than one suggested figure out there?
- If so, which one is better – and why?

As you may have noticed after comparing a number of different websites, the mountain known variously as Mount Everest, Sagarmāthā and Chomolungma (in English, Nepali and Chinese) is described as 8,848m tall by China and Nepal, but as 8,850m tall by the US National Geographic Survey. Others, meanwhile, debate whether earthquakes may have changed its height; and whether its official height should or should not include the snow cap over the underlying rock.

Given all this, is it possible for us to 'know' either that this mountain is 8,848m tall or that it is 8,850m tall, or neither? No. What we need is **transparency**: to offer an honest, accurate summary of the findings and limitations of our process of verification. After researching a number of reliable sources and looking into some of the intricacies of mountain measurement, we might write something like this:

Transparency: ensuring you offer an honest account of the nature and the limitations of your research and verification processes

> Because of the variation between surveys, the continued existence of older measurements alongside more recent ones, and the difficulties of precisely determining the sea level from which height should be measured, a number of different figures exist for the heights of some of the world's tallest mountains, and we cannot be sure that any of these figures is precisely accurate. Mount Everest (also known as Sagarmāthā and Chomolungma) is the tallest mountain in the world in terms of height above sea level, and is currently recognized by Nepal and China as 8,848m tall and as 8,850m by the US National Geographic Survey. K2 (also known as Mount Godwin-Austen or Chhogori) is the world's second-tallest mountain and its height is usually given as 8,611m, although a 2014 GPS survey suggested that a height of 8,609m may be a more accurate measurement.[61]

And so on. What began with some seemingly simple information – the heights of the world's ten tallest mountains – has become something much more qualified and complex.

Is this a problem? It would certainly be much tidier to stick with the original list of figures. Yet knowledge doesn't often look like this. Precisely because it entails testing information against reality, knowledge tends to be messy and open-ended. It involves questions about what it is possible for us to know, how we know it, and where and how different sources of information disagree.

Authority: the claim that one source in particular has primacy over others and can offer the 'official' account of something

It also entails rival claims of **authority**: over who gets to decide on official truths. The governments of China and Nepal, at the time of writing in 2017, both officially recognized Everest/ Sagarmāthā/ Chomolungma as 8,848m tall. Others, like the US National Geographic Survey, disagree and may make the case that their own claims are more authoritative.

One of the most significant features of a digital age is that informational conflicts are the stuff not only of scientific and intellectual dispute, but also of everyday political and social life: an arena within which not only nation states and corporations but also individuals are constantly competing.

Who do you trust to tell the truth? Your friends? Media giants? Independent witnesses? Google? Siri? How can you know the information you're receiving hasn't been manipulated or faked? Is information about you – true, false or somewhere in between – being shared and processed somewhere right now, shaping the world's opinion of who you are? How do you know somebody is who they claim to be in the first place?

These are the everyday questions of the 21st century and, as you'll have noticed, they take us a long way away from the confident verification of knowledge. Yet the tools that permit information warfare, fake news, disinformation, snooping, hacking and media manipulation are also those through which we can pursue insight, understanding and knowledge – just so long as we don't expect it to be easy, or any victory to be final. Here's a brief outline of the ground we've covered so far:

Authority	The claim that, based on its source, one particular account of the way things are should have primacy over others
Information	Data that has been structured, processed, arranged or placed in a particular context in order to make it meaningful
Knowledge	Information that has been verified and that we thus have good reason to believe describes the way things actually are
Raw data	Raw figures or facts awaiting processing and organization
Transparency	Honestly and clearly showing the nature of your process of verification, and acknowledging its limitations
Verification	Performing a reliable process in order to investigate the accuracy and reliability of information

It's time to try some verification for yourself. Read the passage below and then try to verify its claims by doing some research online. Then, write out your own – more accurate and transparent – version in the space below:

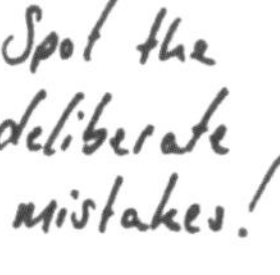
Spot the deliberate mistakes!

> 'Houston, we have a problem…', as astronaut Jim Lovell famously said at the moment that would come to define NASA's 1969 Apollo 13 mission, which has subsequently become a byword for grit and ingenuity in the face of a crisis.

As you've hopefully discovered, the line 'Houston, we have a problem' was spoken in the film of *Apollo 13*, but wasn't said in exactly that form during the mission itself, which took place in 1970 (not 1969). My own updated version of the paragraph is below, including a reference to probably the best source for verifying this information: NASA itself.

> 'Houston, we've had a problem here.' According to NASA's official account, these were the words astronaut John Swigert spoke at 9:08pm on 13 April 1970, the moment Apollo 13 experienced the accident (an oxygen tank explosion) that would subsequently make it a byword for grit and ingenuity in the face of a crisis.[62]

Your own version may have been quite different, but the key point is that you have conducted an investigative process resulting in the improvement of the local **information environment**. Like someone editing a Wikipedia page to make it slightly more accurate, detailed or transparent – or someone publishing a high-quality scientific paper – this kind of verification and updating is a contribution, however minor, to the world's possibilities of verified knowledge.

Information environment: a way of talking about the overall realm of information shared between people, organizations and systems, together with its properties

There is much more information in the world than there is knowledge, and there is even more raw data, waiting for someone or something to use (or abuse) it. But this only makes it more important to scrutinize every claim as closely as we can, and to seek to contribute to an information environment of greater reliability, transparency and quality. In general, remember that:

- Data itself is made, not found: it is manufactured by measurement, as the result of a particular process. It is never simply a neutral, infallibly accurate record.
- Information is also actively created, by the deliberate arrangement and contextualization of data. Information often exists in the absence of knowledge.
- Knowledge requires information, but it also requires something more: a reliable way of testing this information against reality.
- All knowledge relies on particular decisions about how we can measure, test and know things in the first place. It is framed within certain assumptions.
- It is thus important that we are as transparent as possible about these assumptions, because no knowledge is ever final, neutral or exhaustive.

SMART STUDY: Ten tips for spotting online misinformation

The following tips were released in April 2017 by Facebook in partnership with the independent UK fact-checking charity Full Fact, to help users engage with the complicated problem of spotting fake news and misinformation. It's a useful guide to the basics of online verification, and suggests ten techniques you can apply in both everyday browsing and more in-depth investigations:[63]

- **Be sceptical of headlines**: false news stories often have catchy headlines in all caps with exclamation points. If shocking claims in the headline sound unbelievable, they probably are.
- **Look closely at the URL**: a phony or look-alike URL (web address) may be a warning sign of false news. Many false news sites mimic authentic news sources by making small changes to the URL. You can go to the site to compare the URL to established sources.
- **Investigate the source**: ensure that the story is written by a source that you trust with a reputation for accuracy. If the story comes from an unfamiliar organization, check its 'About' section to learn more.
- **Watch for unusual formatting**: many false news sites have misspellings or awkward layouts. Read carefully if you see these things.
- **Consider the photos**: false news stories often contain manipulated images or videos. Sometimes the photo may be authentic, but taken out of context. You can search for the photo or image to verify where it came from.
- **Inspect the dates**: false news stories may contain timelines that make no sense, or event dates that have been altered.
- **Check the evidence**: check the authors' sources to confirm that they are accurate. Lack of evidence or reliance on unnamed experts may indicate a false news story.
- **Look at other reports**: if no other news source is reporting the same story, it may indicate that the story is false. If the story is reported by multiple sources you trust, it's more likely to be true.

- **Consider: Is the story a joke?** Sometimes false news stories can be hard to distinguish from humour or satire. Check whether the source is known for parody and whether the story's details and tone suggest it may be just for fun. [Also, check whether it is April Fool's Day (1 April)!]
- **Note that some stories are intentionally false**: think critically about the stories you read and only share news that you know to be credible.

THINK ABOUT THIS: What things can you be absolutely certain you know? How is it that you know these things? Can you be sure your knowledge is totally accurate? Is it at all possible you are confused, mistaken or inaccurate, or that you might change your mind about these things?

SOCIAL PROOF AND SYSTEM BIASES

There are two main ways we can obtain information about the world: through our senses, which process both immediate and mediated information; and also through our beliefs about what other people are thinking or doing. Consider the following scenario:

> You are standing in a crowd in a theatre, when suddenly people all around you start to panic and frantically begin trying to get to an exit.

Here, the evidence of your senses tells you what is going on – the movement of bodies, the environment's feel, sights, smells, tastes, sounds – but it is the social interpretation you put on this information that guides your understanding and actions. Other people in the crowd clearly appear to believe there is a threat, or at least some urgent reason to seek an exit. On this basis, you're likely to adopt the same assumption as the one that (you assume) is motivating them, and you will also start to run towards an exit.

Social proof: this describes a situation in which other people's apparent beliefs act as the proof on which you base your own beliefs

If you accept there is a threat, you have acted in accordance with **social proof**, also known as **informational social influence**: a situation in which other people's behaviour and their apparent beliefs are treated as proof that you ought to believe the same thing.[64] In the scenario above, two important questions are at stake:

1 Are you correctly interpreting other people's beliefs?
2 Are these beliefs reasonable in the first place?

If both of these things are true, then social proof is a reliable – and valuable – source of information. If you are correct both that other people are panicked and trying to reach an exit, and that a genuine threat means that it is reasonable for them to do this, then it is also reasonable (and indeed highly desirable) for you to adopt the same belief.

If, however, something has gone wrong with either your interpretation of others' collective actions, or with the reasonableness of the process that has led to these collective actions, then you have a problem. And it's a problem that you are likely to make worse by your own subsequent actions

The Internet is like alcohol... It accentuates what you would do anyway

Esther Dyson

#talkcriticalthinking

because, if you embrace social proof, you will become just another part of the crowd, increasing its influence. Consider the following scenario:

> A group of people are standing in the street, pointing upwards and looking intently at the sky. You're not sure what they are looking at but, intrigued, you join in as well, trying to find out what all the fuss is about.

You may well have encountered such a situation before, and noticed that there doesn't actually have to be anything worth looking at for it to happen. All it takes is one person to start looking up intently, another person to stop and try to work out what they are looking at, and before long a crowd of people has gathered – providing more compelling social proof with each additional member.

At the same time, all it takes to dispel this false consensus is one person to speak out with sufficient confidence and authority, provided others believe them when they say 'actually, there's nothing up there to see, I'm sure of it'.

In general, we tend to be most influenced by social proof when we are uncertain of our own information and judgement: when there is no truly authoritative voice, information source or common knowledge available to us. Uncertainty of this kind may occur when:

- We have **too little information** to make what we feel is an informed decision ourselves, so we rely on others' actions and perceived beliefs as a guide.
- We have **too much information** to meaningfully assess all our options, and so once again we become reliant on other people as a guide.
- We lack **relevant expertise** or **access to trusted expertise**, and thus rely on majority belief as our best guide to a field in which we have little confidence.
- We are in a **polarizing social context**, such as an intensely tribal or emotive group, creating a strong pressure to conform to the majority's opinion.

As you may have noticed, all four of the conditions above occur frequently in our interactions with others through digital information systems. In fact, social proof is built into the architecture of many of the online services we use every day: from social sharing, likes, rankings, votes, reviews and traffic-based measures of authority, to online advertising, sales, media, impact factors and citations.

When it comes to search algorithms, for example, the most important factor in recommendations and rankings is the aggregated observation of millions upon millions of people's choices. Why? Both because it works and because there is simply too much information for any kind of universal content-based assessment. What matters is what most people do, together with what most people like, discuss, review favourably, purchase, return to and find most familiar and easy. Moreover, giving people what they want, telling them what they want to hear and matching them to information they are predisposed to believe is an excellent business model, together with collating and re-selling the details.

Is this a bad thing? Not always, no. It often yields excellent and reliable results. As Google was among the first companies to discover, how much people use a resource – and what kinds of resources people connect to one another – is perhaps the most reliable measure of a certain degree of quality, usefulness and appeal. But a host of challenges, trends and predictable distortions also come with this terrain.[65] I have grouped these tendencies loosely together under the heading **system biases**.

Systems biases: predictable biases and distortions that can exert a powerful influence within networked information systems

Much like the list of fallacies earlier in this half of the book, these tendencies are well worth remembering if you're interested in what it means to make better use of, and help to improve, information systems. They're not exclusive to information systems – and they're by no means present in every way to organize information – but they do hopefully suggest a useful selection of structural influences worth heeding in our digital age.

Network effects

In the early 1980s, the inventor of the Ethernet system for connecting computers into local networks, Robert 'Bob' Metcalfe, developed a sales presentation with a bold claim at its heart: that the value of a network increased in proportion to the square of its number of users, while its cost only increased in proportion to the number of connected machines. In other words, beyond a certain number of users, the value of a network begins to increase exponentially above the cost of adding new users.[66]

It was the perfect message for selling more Ethernet cards. Its was also prescient. By the mid-1990s, the effects of what had come to be known as Metcalfe's law was seen not only in networked hardware but also in the data and software networks running on that hardware. Metcalfe was popularizing a phenomenon that had long been known to telecoms engineers, known as the **network effect**: the fact that the most useful network is generally the one that is used by most people, and it becomes more and more useful as more people join in.

Network effects: the tendency of a service to become more useful and valuable as more people use it – and potentially more dominant and harder to opt out of

You would never use a phone – no matter how good – if you could only use it to contact three numbers. Similarly, past a certain level of scale, a dominant network can become the only good choice because it's the place most likely to connect you to what you want. Why use a search engine that only indexes a fraction of the information you're interested in? Why use a social network if none of your friends are on it?

Network effects help explain the 'winner takes all' tendency of large, open networks like the internet, where companies like the 'big five' of Apple, Google, Amazon, Microsoft and Facebook can dominate competitors in almost every region, making it extraordinarily difficult for small or local players to compete. They also embody a central tension related to social proof in an information age: something may not be that good, or that accurate, and still lock people into using it because they feel they have no choice.

As we'll see, network effects underpin many of the other trends discussed in this section, because they underpin the gathering and conversion of massive amounts of information into powerful, predictive and profitable patterns. Network effects also relate to a unique feature of information systems when it comes to competition and monopolies. Buying manufactured goods in a marketplace where only one company makes them is likely to produce far worse results than if several companies are competing for your custom. But information resources based on data are likely to be better if a company has more data, and best of all (at least in principle) if one company holds all the data – and can thus search everything, connect you to everyone, and analyse every factor exhaustively.

This runs entirely contrary to conventional thinking about marketplaces. Should a tiny number of private companies be able to hold almost all our data? You may argue that this is what's best for consumers in terms of usefulness and user experience – but only if you're prepared to ignore those aspects of social and civic life that private companies are not incentivized to respect.

Impact over insight

This describes the degree to which emotional impact – and the corresponding likelihood that content will be shared and discussed, and attract attention – matters more than the integrity of the content itself. This is most true of online business models based on measuring and selling attention, together with all the data associated with engagement.

Always true of media, to some extent – but much more so today

For instance, a sensational video featuring entirely fictional claims about a politician might get millions of views (and even influence the outcome of an election) on the basis of its emotional impact, irrespective of the truthfulness of its claims. Impact often counts for much more than insight in the emotionally driven arena of social media and sharing.

Quantity over quality

This describes the degree to which volume of traffic, number of users or other quantitative measures are treated as directly correlated with quality, rather than as relating to it in a much more qualified way.

For example, you might decide to purchase something because it is a bestseller and thus 'must' be excellent, rather than recognizing that, while there must be something about a bestseller that has caused it to sell so well, this is likely to relate to a host of factors in addition to quality (it may be that the seller is massively discounting in an effort to get rid of stock, for instance, or has been manipulating recommendation algorithms).

Echo chambers

This describes the tendency of people to seek out only information, sources and relationships online that support their own worldview. Given the vast quantity of options out there, people are able to endlessly find confirmation of whatever views they hold, and to avoid interactions that might challenge them.

For instance, someone might be extremely surprised by an election result, because almost all the news and views they consumed supported the candidate who lost. In an echo chamber, all you hear is voices very like your own, echoing from wall to wall.

Filter bubbles

Where an echo chamber is based on someone's active choices, a filter bubble is imposed by information systems themselves on the basis of customization and personalization, meaning that someone might not even realize they are seeing the world from within such a bubble. The term was coined in 2011 by Eli Pariser in his book of the same name.[67]

For example, a search engine may modify its results based on your individual preferences and history, producing only the kind of results that you are likely to approve of. Similarly, a social media feed may deliberately show only things you are likely to like – or to feel strongly about – based on a detailed analysis of your profile and history.

As with echo chambers, the potential problem is that this creates a biased information environment that supplies only resources selected to conform to your prejudices, or to the prejudices and priorities of the corporations mediating your access to information. One rich question provoked by this observation is under which circumstances an information environment can best create serendipitous connections, plurality and the puncturing of filter bubbles – something discussed in the study skills at the end of this section.

Polarization

This describes the potential result of grouping together a number of people with similar views and interests, as often happens in social media and online groups when people self-select according to a particular concern. In such groups, the lack of a broad diversity of opinion can, over time, make the group as a whole gravitate towards extreme positions, because genuinely opposing voices do not exist and groups tend to encourage coherence and consistency.

For example, discussions within an online group of activists might, over time, move towards a more extreme position, with less willingness to compromise, if it only contained members from a narrow spectrum of views. This can also encourage societal polarization, because people with differing views engage less with one another and instead spend a majority of their time engaging only with like-minded people. Note that there's nothing inevitable about social media causing polarization, and there is plenty of ongoing dispute as to its role.[68]

Tyranny of the minority

This describes the way in which a highly vocal, inflexible minority can come to dominate policy and decisions. For example, if a group of 100 people are planning a meal and 90 of those people are flexible about what they eat while ten people absolutely refuse to eat anything that isn't 100 per cent organic, the group will be obliged either to provide a 100 per cent organic meal or to split up acrimoniously.

In general, an inflexible and persistent minority has the power to disproportionately influence outcomes when it exists alongside a more tolerant and flexible majority – a fact that can lead to extreme positions that are actively endorsed only by minorities who nevertheless dominate debates and negotiations.

Algorithmic bias and inscrutability

I've already observed that all data is made rather than found – something that becomes highly significant once you move into the realm of big data and the machine-learning algorithms trained with this data. Two potential problems are worth particular attention.

First, algorithms can swallow and regurgitate any biases contained in the original data. Second, the inscrutability of most machine-learning processes can make this process difficult to either critique or reverse engineer, unless you have an expert understanding of the original data and its limitations – something that many end users of algorithms entirely lack.

For example, research published in April 2017 in the journal *Science* suggested that algorithms analysing large bodies of English-language text tended to acquire gender and racial biases embedded in this language. Such results are just the tip of the algorithmic iceberg and suggest an area in which critical analysis is needed if we are not to accidentally train AIs to enforce existing social inequalities, prejudices and exclusions.[69]

Not to mention companies using them to advance their own agendas unchecked.

Structural recency bias

As we saw in Chapter 9, recency bias entails over-estimating the significance of recent events at the expense of longer-term trends. For instance, someone might put great emphasis on a recent electoral result when trying to explain the state of the economy, neglecting long-term trends. Several factors make this kind of bias especially influential when it comes to information online.

Try escaping the hysterical/speed of news & social media once in a while — & see how different the world starts to feel.

Many sites, search engines and social media services emphasize freshness and novelty as a criterion for relevance. This combines with the dominance of information streams as a way of presenting information, with an emphasis of trending topics and the present moment.

The internet itself has only been widely used for a few decades, with vastly more information produced each year than in all previous years put together, weighting the information environment itself against the longer term – and this is before you consider the failure to maintain or to make accessible many older digital resources. Finally, because people themselves are free to search for anything they like, they are naturally more likely to seek out recent things that come more easily to mind.

SMART STUDY: How to resist system biases in ten easy(ish) steps

1. Don't let emotional impact dominate your online actions: if the topic is an important one, focus on verification and the provenance and basis of others' claims.
2. Dig into edit histories and follow up references: try to find out how and where information that may be widely accepted actually came into being.
3. Go beyond the easy and instant: always aim to browse beyond the first page of search results, the most-cited sources and the most popular solutions.
4. Allow yourself to engage deeply and serendipitously with themes and topics that interest you, rather than simply trying to cover the 'greatest hits' in a field.
5. Go big and small: deliberately use small networks and services in parallel with large ones. Draw on a diversity of individual recommendations, reviews and curated links.
6. You can use social media to break out of your echo chamber: deliberately follow people and sources from different perspectives and backgrounds to your own.
7. Don't get institutionalized: it may be where your friends spend all their time, but don't end up using just one service more than you do everything else put together.
8. Become more aware of your filters: see how search results and recommendations may be being customized based on your history or preferences, and how you can turn this off.
9. Live beyond the moment: dig into the past, take the longer view, deliberately search back through years rather than months. Resist the perpetual pressure of the present.
10. Always ask of data: which things are and are not being measured, *how* is this being done, and *what* might be the biases and limitations of the resulting claims?

TIME, ATTENTION AND OTHER PEOPLE

Critical thinking requires you to slow down: to think twice and to ask whether your intuitions and instincts can be trusted in a particular situation. Time pressure is one of the great complaints provoked by technology, and for a simple enough reason: when very limited human time comes up against limitless opportunities for connection and interaction, there's a clear mismatch – and a battle of willpower and habit that almost everyone will have experienced.

We can think of this in terms of **suffusion** and **scarcity**. One of the most significant scarcities in an age of information suffusion is human time and attention itself. And the pressure on this resource plays out through two related challenges:

- Everyone and everything is constantly competing online to win attention, and there isn't nearly enough to go around, either individually or collectively.
- Constant connectivity can flatten every moment of time into the same kind of experience, and this isn't good for either human cognition or well-being.

Take something as simple as email. Too often, I find that my own email inbox is a to-do list that has been written for me by other people: a list of tasks that I haven't chosen, that don't correspond to my priorities and preferences, and yet that I feel I need to work through methodically on a daily basis.

How did this happen and what can I do about it? Emptying my email inbox can feel like the most essential and satisfying of tasks, yet sending more email simply means getting more email back in return, while filling up everybody else's inboxes along the way. What I actually want isn't a clear inbox. It's peace of mind. It's meaningful communication with friends and colleagues. It's having enough space in my head for other things.

> **THINK ABOUT THIS:** What do you think are your own best and worst habits when it comes to technology? How might you do more of the best and break out of the worst? ....
> ....
> ....
> ....
> ....
> ....

It seems to me that we face two entwined questions every time we reach towards a screen. What does the system we're using want us to do? And what do we ourselves want? If we're not careful, we will only ever answer the first of these questions. And if that sounds a little dramatic, here is some advice in two key areas for managing your time and relationships with (and through) technology.

Daily habits and priorities

Pick 'n' mix from these hints however you like.

Prioritize by importance, not ease: don't fall into the trap of putting off the things that really matter just because other things are easier to accomplish immediately. Make sure the things that matter most have enough time set aside for them.

Batch your tasks: rather than constantly switching between tasks, try to arrange at least some of your day into focused chunks of attention allocated to one task at a time. For example, set aside an hour at the start or end of a day (or both) for email and messages, and don't check these in-between – if you can manage to resist the temptation for that long.

Pull, don't push: interruption is the bane of focus – when working, you should aim to 'pull' rather than 'push' notifications, meaning you check them when it suits you, rather than have them constantly arrive in the background of whatever else you're doing.

Embrace boundaries: don't turn all your time into the same kind of time. Don't be online every minute of the day, and try not to bring the same kind of connectivity into every moment and place in your life. You'll work better if places like the library and the study are only for work. You'll relax better if places like the kitchen and bedroom are not for hours of browsing and messaging.

Communications and other people's time

Be brief, helpful and clear in the messages you send to others, using helpful subject lines and a clear structure. Most emails and messages don't require more than four sentences.

If they're longer, use bullet points and white space to keep things clear, and ensure that important points aren't overlooked inside a hunk of text. Do others the courtesy of reading their messages closely.

Avoid long chains wherever possible in email, messages and discussions: resolve things, then move on. Don't stay copied in when you don't need to be and don't constantly seek reassurance.

Time is an excellent filter: delay your replies to non-urgent messages, updates and emails. You may find that some of them don't need replying to at all. If something is truly urgent, get it dealt with instantly; otherwise, let others wait until you are ready.

SEARCH, DISCOVERY AND CATEGORIES OF KNOWLEDGE

You are about to start work. What do you do? You turn to a digital device: a laptop or desktop computer, a smartphone, a tablet. Then you start typing or – increasingly frequently – speak your request out loud.

If you're beginning a piece of work, you probably type a query into a search box – a search engine, like Google; a library catalogue; a database of academic papers; a general online resource, like Wikipedia; or a specialized online resource, such as government records, health data and newspaper archives. Probably, you'll make your way to most specialized online resources via an initial search query. Also probably, you won't think very much about any of this.

But what does it mean to search effectively? The answer seems so obvious it is hardly worth stating. A search is successful if you find what you were looking for. Yet in order to fully describe this process, we need to consider the nature of both **search strategies** and **discovery strategies**: techniques that enable us not only to find particular information but also, more importantly, to find out what kind of thing we ought to be looking for in the first place.

- **Search strategies** are about finding things that we already know about, or that we are aware we need to find out about.
- **Discovery strategies** are about finding out what kind of things we need to know, opening up a field for investigation and exposing ourselves to diverse perspectives.

This allows us to account for four different categories of knowledge and ignorance:

- **Identified knowledge** ('known knowns'): those things we know that we know and are typically just one click or careful search term away.
- **Identified ignorance** ('known unknowns'): those things we know that we do not know and are thus explicitly setting out to investigate: a careful search strategy can help us home in on these.
- **Unidentified knowledge** ('unknown knowns'): those things that are known but have not been formally identified as knowledge in our investigation: a successful discovery process allows us to identify a range of different sources of knowledge.
- **Unidentified ignorance** ('unknown unknowns'): those things we do not know we do not know and are thus likely to find out about belatedly, if at all.

These four categories can be mapped in a diagram based loosely on the psychological testing technique known as a **Johari window** (named after its two inventors: Joseph Luft and Harrington Ingham, who first developed it in 1955 at Western Training Laboratories as an illustration of relationships in terms of awareness):[70]

	Certain (known)	Uncertain (unknown)
Identified (known)	Identified knowledge 'known knowns'	Identified ignorance 'known unknowns'
Unidentified (unknown)	Unidentified knowledge 'unknown knowns'	Unidentified ignorance 'unknown unknowns'

To begin with, let's consider what it means to research something in a non-academic context. Imagine that you have been asked to help out one of your less technologically confident cousins with the following task (and that you're keen to help, rather than irritated to be asked):

> Thanks so much for agreeing to help! I'm looking to buy a new laptop for around £500, but I don't know what to get. I want something light with a good battery life. I don't care so much about how powerful it is. It's for work and I travel a lot. Someone suggested I check out the new Lite99 model from FictionalLaptops? But really, I'm happy to go along any lines you suggest. It would be really kind if you could send me over two or three recommendations.

How would you set about helping this person? Have a think. First of all, you need to consider as clearly as possible the purpose of your research. The key points are:

- You are looking for a new laptop priced at around £500.
- The laptop should be light and have a good battery life.
- It doesn't need to be especially powerful.
- It should be appropriate for work and travel.

You have also been asked to evaluate one specific question:

- Does the new Lite99 model laptop from FictionalLaptops fit these criteria?

Finally, at the end of your research, you need to:

- Deliver two or three recommended laptops that best fit the above criteria.

Simple enough? Let's deal with the specific query about the Lite99 model first. In order to answer this, you will need to verify the price and specs of the Lite99 laptop. In order to do this, in turn, you will need to find the Lite99 laptop via a reliable, authoritative source: its manufacturer's website or the website of a reliable online sales outlet, or a review or discussion in a reliable online article or forum – or, ideally, all of the above for comparison.

How will you set about doing this? Here, we are operating in the realm of a **search strategy** aimed at tapping into **identified knowledge** (the criteria you know you need to fulfil; the specific Lite99 laptop you have been asked to check out; what kind of a final result you want to deliver) and **identified ignorance** (researching how good the Lite99 laptop is; researching what laptops meet the criteria you have been given). Starting with the Lite99 laptop itself, you might thus begin by:

- typing the two search terms, *Lite99* and *FictionalLaptops*, into a web search engine, looking through the results and opening up several suitable pages
- typing the two search terms, *Lite99* and *FictionalLaptops*, directly into the search box of a site like Amazon to see its price, details and reviews
- typing the two search terms, *Lite99* and *FictionalLaptops*, into the search box of a particular expert site you trust for an informed discussion.

By looking through and comparing this information, you should be able to answer your research question about the existence and specifications of the Lite99.

Now, you face a more open field of inquiry – one which requires you to begin a discovery process aimed at turning up **unidentified knowledge**. These are the key questions: what do you need to know about that you don't yet know about, and how can you begin to discover this?

The first step is to deploy a range of deliberately vague search terms, designed to cast a wide-enough net to turn up potential key information about laptop makes, models, features, prices and quality. Over time, your discovery strategy might end up looking something like this:

↓ **Begin with varied, general search queries** – producing a wide selection of pages and articles about laptops in the right kind of price range.
↓ **Develop initial ideas about more and less trustworthy sources** of opinion about laptops: online magazines, discussion forums, expert reviews, and so on.
↓ **Browse the most reliable and expert resources for key considerations** to look out for when buying laptops in this price range – more and less desirable makes, the specs of suitable laptops, decisive factors, things to watch out for.
↓ **Follow up with more specific search queries** – these might include manufacturers of laptops that seem promising, names of high-quality review sites.
↓ **On the basis of this second search, start to directly research** multiple models of promising laptops across manufacturer, sales and review sites.
↓ **Move towards highly specific search queries** – precise model names, typed in inverted commas in order to find exact results, across review and sales sites.
↓ **Using the above queries, engage in depth** with the most promising models, comparing features, date of production, price and availability, and user and expert reviews.
↓ **Keep a record and produce an initial draft** of what, in this case, you judge to be the best balance of price, features and quality meeting the original criteria.
↓ **Edit your initial draft down, focusing on the most relevant materials** by deciding which laptops from your longlist achieve the best balance of criteria.
↓ **Write up your results clearly and helpfully** in a summary form: a friendly email, providing recommendations, links to manufacturers and where best to buy.

Written out like this, it looks like an extremely complex process. Yet you probably do more sophisticated things than this all the time when it comes to online shopping or investigating other people on social media. If you're a reasonably experienced online shopper, you could probably complete the above task to a high standard in under an hour.

Let's now try applying the ten steps above to something in your own field of study. Use the table on the following page to fill in each box in turn as you research a particular question, topic or theme.

While doing this exercise, you may notice that we haven't yet dealt with the last and most mysterious category of knowledge and ignorance in our initial classification: the **unknown unknowns**.

Imagine, in the laptop-recommending scenario, that just as you are about to send off your expertly written email of laptop recommendations, you mention what you're doing to another family member. They raise their eyebrows and say this:

> You ought to know that your cousin absolutely refuses to use any laptop without a back-lit keyboard. Don't even think about recommending a model without one!

What to do now? You check your shortlist and find that only one model on it has a back-lit keyboard. Sighing, you start looking through the longlist again.

 Cntd. on the page after next...

What do you want to research? Try to come up with one question	
List varied, general search queries to begin	
Based on these, list an initial range of trustworthy sources	
List key considerations and questions based on the best sources	
Follow this up with several, more specific searches	
List the main points coming from these searches	
Search for in-depth sources on the most important specific points	
Explore the best in-depth sources you have found during these searches	
Start to record all key points from the above in an organized way	
Once you've collated this key information, edit it for relevance	
Write up the information above in a clear and useful form	

Just in time, you have gained knowledge about something important that you didn't even know you didn't know. We can contrast this with your earlier search and discovery process, during which you mapped out information within what seemed like a reasonable field of inquiry. Your unknown unknown has come from outside this – it's something that, in retrospect, you might have found out by talking directly to your cousin about their laptop expectations. This is often the case:

- Engaging and speaking with other people directly is one of the most important ways you can stop yourself from narrowing your focus too soon – and from falling into the trap of assuming that what you have found onscreen is all there is to be known, or that can be known.

Here's a more serious example to consider. It is the early 1950s and you are presented with the following outline of a hugely significant research project. Given the advantage of hindsight, what unknown unknowns might you want to be wary of here?

UNKNOWN UNKNOWNS

....	In order to test the limits and consequences of the most significant new weapon in the history of warfare – the atomic bomb – and train our troops to deal with its deployment on the battlefield, we will be combining large-scale military exercises with live atmospheric nuclear tests. Tens of thousands of troops will be positioned at a distance of seven miles from live atomic explosions, observed carefully, put through manoeuvres and marched through the blast zone afterwards.

This brief account resembles what happened during the Desert Rock exercises in America between 1951 and 1957. The identified area of ignorance under investigation was the question of how troops might be trained for conflicts involving atomic bombs, and what their immediate effects might be. The unidentified area of ignorance that proved most significant, however – the 'unknown unknown' – was the severe long-term consequences of exposure to radiation. In the 1990s, thousands of people were eventually compensated for the consequences of radiation exposure under the Radiation Exposure Compensation Act: a statute that, according to the US Department of Justice, had by 2016 approved over two billion dollars in payouts to over 31,000 people (Desert Rock was not the only source of exposure to radiation).[71]

Why is it worth mentioning these things in the particular context of technology? As in the example above, unknown unknowns – those forms of ignorance we have not yet identified – are often what matter most in the long term. Too narrow a consensus on immediate opportunities and challenges can blind us to them, as can an unwillingness to draw on diverse expertise and acknowledge uncertainty – factors that a focus on technology-based 'solutions' can exacerbate.

THINK ABOUT THIS: Can you think of any unknown unknowns that have caught you out – things you didn't know or think to ask about that, if you could go back in time, you would tell your younger self to watch out for? ....

....

....

....

....

....

SMART STUDY: Don't get trapped by unknown unknowns

1 Expose yourself to a diversity of sources and opinions early in the research process, without focusing too soon on a single, narrow line of investigation.
2 Continue exposing yourself to serendipitous and unplanned information sources, especially via contact with a diversity of other thinkers, researchers and critics.
3 Maintain a healthy disregard for prevailing opinions and orthodoxies.
4 Remain open-minded and flexible, and invite debate, dissent and critique from others.

PRACTICAL TIPS FOR SEARCH, DISCOVERY AND BEYOND

To close the chapter, I've collected a range of practical tips spanning search, discovery and beyond. You may be familiar with many of these; some may seem so obvious they aren't even worth mentioning. Yet I suspect there will be at least one or two you haven't encountered before.

At the end of this section is a table for you to write out five suggestions you've taken from this list that you think might be useful to you. As ever, this is the most crucial element in the learning process: taking generic advice and translating it into practical habits. & keep trying!

I don't live up to my own advice much of the time.

Be precise when you're certain

The more precisely you know what you're looking for, the more it pays to be as precise as possible in your search terms: an effective search will produce a small number of relevant, high-quality results.

Put precise phrases inside quotation marks to find only those exact words in that exact order. For example, searching for 'Protein measurement with the folin phenol reagent' will only produce results featuring precisely this phrase – the title of one of the most-cited scientific papers of all time.

If you're not sure about the exact phrasing of a quotation or title you're looking for, either search for a few words you are sure of, or search without quotation marks for the most unusual few words you're interested in. For instance, if you cannot remember the exact title of the paper above, searching for the terms *measurement folin phenol paper* will easily locate the original paper.

Using more unusual words or longer phrases will produce fewer results. In the example above, typing *folin phenol paper* locates the paper in question instantly, while typing *protein measurement* does not do so as effectively.

Use discovery to unlock search

A successful discovery process will help you to 'unlock' new areas of investigation, by providing you with some of the key terms, phrases, themes and authorities that indicate relevant and informed discussions.

Once you start to acquire these key words and concepts, you'll be able to search for and compare information far more effectively; until you do, you may find yourself unable to locate high-quality resources.

For example, if you want to learn about the history of digital computers in detail, you might start off with some generic search terms, but once you discovered the names of some of the earliest computers, searching specifically for terms like *Electronic Numerical Integrator and Computer 1946*, you would be likely to 'unlock' more detailed, specific resources.

Use advanced search to narrow down results

Most search engines will feature a number of 'advanced' options that allow you to narrow down searches by criteria such as date, language, exact phrase, range of numbers, region, last updated, where terms appear and type of file.

You can also access similar options to narrow down results across media such as images and videos, based on format-specific criteria such as date, duration or quality. In general, always narrow down a search as much as you can.

Search within results and pages

Remember that you can search within web pages using a browser's own integrated 'find' function (Ctrl + F in Windows, Cmd + F on a Mac) to take you instantly to a key word or phrase. Don't waste time scanning and scrolling when you can simply type and click.

You can also use a browser search to go straight to a particular word within a page of search results, and choose to display a larger number of search results on one screen in order to make it easier to scan and search them. Once you've found a useful online resource or website, use its internal search function to find particular pages.

SMART STUDY: Using operators within search queries

Not many people realise the range of what's possible here.

Operators are special characters and commands you can integrate into search terms, giving you a short cut to advanced techniques. Think of them as a programming language for search engines. Below is a selection of the most useful, based largely on Google (although several are standard). Microsoft's Bing has an impressive selection of advanced operators too:[72] explore for yourself and see what you find.

- Exclude certain words by putting a minus sign in front of them. For example, typing *famous Toms –Cruise* would return search results that featured the words 'famous' and 'Toms' but not 'Cruise'.
- By default, entering multiple terms into a single search looks for results containing all of them. You can instead put *OR* between terms in order to display results featuring either one term or another. For instance, typing *Paris OR Amsterdam* would return results featuring either 'Paris' or 'Amsterdam'.
- If you don't know exactly what you are looking for, or how to spell something, you can use the * symbol as a 'wildcard' in place of a word or letter. For example, searching '*richest * in history*' would return results for this four-word phrase featuring any word at all in place of *. Similarly, searching *techno** would return results featuring any word beginning with 'techno', such as 'technology', 'technocrat' and 'technological'.
- Search for results within a particular website by putting *site:XXX* in front of your query. For instance, typing *site:bbc.com horses* would return results for the word 'horses' only from within bbc.com.
- Use *inurl:XXX* to search only within a web address itself (a web address is also known as a URL), or the qualifier *intitle:XXX* to search only within a page title. For example, searching *intitle:FAQ* will bring up all pages with 'FAQ' in the title.
- Use the tilde symbol ~ to search for synonyms. For instance, typing *~college* will find results not only about colleges, but also about words with a similar meaning, such as 'universities'.
- Search a particular range of results by typing two full stops followed by a space. For example, typing *nobel peace prizes 1920.. 1960* will produce a list of results for Nobel Peace Prizes ranging between 1920 and 1960.

- See the cached version of a site – an older, snapshot version of the site stored on Google's servers rather than the current 'live' version – by typing *cache:XXX* where X is the site address. For example, *cache:bbc.com* will show the latest snapshot of the BBC site taken and stored by Google.
- Search for related sites by typing *related:XXX*. For instance, *related:NYtimes.com* will list sites similar to the *New York Times* (top of the list when I searched in 2017 were USA Today, CNN and the LA Times).
- Search for sites that link to a particular URL by typing *link:XXX*.

Use social search, ask for help – and give it

Search social media directly for topics and themes to find links to discussions, articles and further ideas.

Don't be afraid to put queries out there on social media, in the comments of relevant pages, in forums and discussions, or on dedicated services like Quora. It never hurts to ask, and might lead to a discussion or information worth a thousand searches.

If you know the answer to someone else's question, help and share your experiences. What goes around comes around. Plus, explaining something to others can be one of the best ways of making sure you know it yourself.

If you know a lot about something, why not edit shared resources like Wikipedia and make things a little better for others? Anyone can do it: it's quick and easy, and it can help consolidate your own learning and understanding.

Life beyond Google: use a variety of tools and services

Putting lists of digital resources into a textbook is often a waste of time, as they can change rapidly over time and vary greatly between disciplines, institutions and regions. This is therefore a deliberately general list of types and categories.

Above all, ensure you familiarize yourself with how to search specialist academic, library and journal resources at your institution as soon as possible. Ask a librarian for help if needed. Don't be shy or slow to start using these. They're expensive, vital resources, and your course is likely to have particular recommendations and requirements. Are there databases you need to search for papers? From PubMed and Web of Science to Google Scholar, ORCID and JSTOR and far beyond, make sure you're confident with the core tools for your field.

Librarians are amazing. Make good use of them!

Your institution will also have subscriptions to a variety of study resources such as dictionaries, records, archives, online manuscripts and so on, varying by subject. Explore these on faculty and library pages, and work out whether they might enhance your studies, or prove useful and interesting in their own right.

Google is great, but don't rely on it exclusively. Use other search engines for general queries to get a variety of results; and when you're looking for something particular, ensure that you use more specialized tools.

Once you've found a useful site or resource, search inside it. Use its own search functions and go directly to it when needed.

Don't forget, you can search within individual pages or articles, using the search function in your web browser: go directly to relevant key words, rather than waste time scrolling through and looking for them manually.

TEN

EVERY OPTION YOU'RE GIVEN CAN BE WRONG. BEFORE YOU CHOOSE, ASK FIRST – IS THE BEST OR MOST MEANINGFUL RESPONSE EVEN ON OFFER? PERHAPS THE BETTER CHOICE IS TO REJECT THE DEAL. LOOK OUTSIDE THE FRAME.

#TalkCriticalThinking

Searching the pages of scanned books can be especially useful for uncovering reliable, original versions of texts and quotes. Google Books is probably the best tool for this, outside of libraries and subscription services.

Search images, books, videos, news and locations as needed to get more useful results. Sometimes, images will be far easier to look through and choose between than written results. Sometimes, you may wish to search within news results. Sometimes, videos from a reliable source will demonstrate or explain something much more clearly than text, especially if you're looking for a practical 'how to'.

Collate, organize and be ambitious

Collate, curate and manage the content that matters to you through a variety of tools, productivity apps, web-clipping services and specialist software: from Pinterest, OneNote and Evernote, to academic reference tools like EndNote and Reference Manager – and (as ever) far beyond these few current examples.

Keep good records, be organized and use technology to make your life easier – not to make additional work (or displacement activities) for yourself. Use productivity apps and tools, but remember: don't turn something into a habit unless you're sure it's genuinely worth your time.

Don't confuse copying and pasting with original work. Type your own final work from scratch, keeping it separate from your records, curation and clippings. Take ownership of what you create, and make sure it's all your own.

Repetition and refinement are your most important skills. Don't go with the first result on the first page by default. Don't go with the first draft of anything you produce. Go beyond, read around, cultivate variety. Nothing is easier to spot than work that has never gone beyond the first page, the top few results, or the easiest and most obvious things that came to hand.

I MEAN THIS. Go beyond, do more, think a little harder.

Finally, ask yourself: what are the most useful **five tips** from the above lists for you, and how might you apply them in your own work, studies and practice? Fill out the list below:

	GENERAL ADVICE		HOW WILL IT WORK FOR ME?
1		•	
2		•	
3		•	
4		•	
5		•	

THINK ABOUT THIS: Do you feel optimistic about the future of technology? Which technologies are you most excited about, looking ahead? Which are you worried about, or do you dislike?

SUMMARY

In a digital age, there is a tension between what it means to acquire, debate and disseminate knowledge and to interact constantly with and through information systems.

- **Acquiring, debating and disseminating knowledge** tends: to be slow and effortful, to prioritize truth and accuracy, to persuade primarily through reasoning, and to actively invite debate and dissent.
- **Interacting constantly through shared information systems** can put an emphasis on speed and ease, on emotional and social impact, on popularity rather than truth, and on confirmation and consensus.

Given that elements of both of these tendencies are present in most uses of technology, an important underlying question is:

- How effectively are we able to pursue knowledge while also interacting through shared, sociable information systems, and benefiting from their opportunities?

To think precisely about this process, it is useful to make a distinction between data, information and knowledge:

- **Raw data** is figures or facts, awaiting organization.
- **Information** is data that has been structured, processed, arranged or placed in a particular context in order to make it meaningful.
- **Verification** entails performing a reliable process in order to investigate the accuracy and reliability of information.
- **Knowledge** is information that has been verified, and that we thus have good reason to believe describes the way things actually are.
- **Transparency** entails honesty and clearly showing your process of verification and acknowledging its limitations.
- **Authority** describes the claim, based on its source, that one particular account of the way things are has primacy over others.

More information does not automatically create more knowledge. In fact, it creates considerable challenges when it comes to creating knowledge and understanding. Particular vulnerabilities and biases to be alert to in information environments include:

- The power of **social proof** and its conflation of **authority** with **popularity**.
- An emphasis on **impact over insight**, and on **quantity over quality**.
- The prevalence of **echo chambers**, **network effects**, **filter bubbles** and **polarization**, together with the **tyranny of the minority**.
- **Recency bias**, together with an emphasis on **speed** and **freshness** as proxies for significance and merit.

All of these challenges are connected to time and attention, and to our reliance on cognitive heuristics (mental short cuts) when called on to make decisions constantly and rapidly within an environment where we are continually exposed to others' opinions.

When conducting any investigation, we need to account for four different general types of knowledge and ignorance, and to do so by deploying both an effective **search strategy** (finding something specific that we know we are looking for) and a **discovery strategy** (discovering what it is we ought to be looking for):

- **Identified knowledge** ('known knowns'): those things we know that we know and that are typically just one click or careful search term away online.
- **Identified ignorance** ('known unknowns'): those things we know that we do not know, and are thus explicitly setting out to investigate or discover.
- **Unidentified knowledge** ('unknown knowns'): those things that are known but have not been identified as a source of knowledge by us.
- **Unidentified ignorance** ('unknown unknowns'): those things we now know we do not know and will thus find out about belatedly, if at all.

Gaining knowledge within this last category of 'unknown unknowns' is difficult and demands the deliberate cultivation of a **diversity of sources**, an **open planning period**, continued exposure to **serendipitous information**, and remaining **open-minded, flexible** and resistant to **prevailing opinion**.

In other words:
Talk to varied other people about stuff!

Now watch the video 'Beating the bias built into machines'. It's on YouTube. Tell me what you think via #TalkCriticalThinking

PUTTING IT ALL TOGETHER: CRITICAL THINKING IN STUDY, WORK AND LIFE

Advice for better writing & thinking.

Choose your own onward path.

How can you think critically about emotional and persuasive language?

↓

How can you think critically about fallacies and faulty reasoning?

↓

How can you think critically about cognitive and behavioural bias?

↓

How can you best overcome bias in yourself and others?

↓

How can you be a more critically engaged user of technology?

↓

How can you become a critically engaged writer and thinker?

INSPIRATION

(hopefully)

Writing is making sense of life. You work your whole life and perhaps you've made sense of one small area.

Nadine Gordimer

#TalkCriticalThinking

FIVE THINGS YOU'LL LEARN IN THIS CHAPTER

1 A recipe for *good writing*
2 What *good* academic *writing looks like*
3 *Things to avoid* in your writing
4 The importance of *cultivating better habits*
5 *Ten commandments for critical thinking*

If you want to think critically, to work well and to engage successfully with others, you need to care about words and the ideas they contain. You need to expose yourself to others' views, and to express your own, as richly as possible. This takes a great deal of practice. But it's worth doing – and I want to begin this final chapter by suggesting some ways in which you can make it happen. We'll then move on to the question of what you aspire towards more broadly: of what more effective thinking might mean for you and which habits are most likely to take you there.

GOOD WRITING IN GENERAL

One of the most invigorating habits I try to encourage in myself is reading widely and serendipitously. I love getting lost in interesting books: science fiction, non-fiction, philosophy, thrillers with a twist. If I can, I like going out and doing this in a café, library or coffee shop – somewhere I can sit for a while outside my ordinary routines, watching the world.

The joy of a good read!

I find this focus the perfect antidote to the mess of emails, social media updates and fragmentary tasks that await me onscreen. It also fuels my mind. Getting lost in other people's words creates a sense of energy and possibility without which I wouldn't write, work or think as I wish. Hence my first recommendation for good writing:

It's an amazing thing!

(1) Good writing begins with good reading: this isn't the same thing as reading only 'good' books. It means reading widely, closely, passionately, eccentrically, with pleasure and ambition. It means following recommendations, but also developing your own taste and cultivating curiosities. What do you enjoy reading most in general? What do you enjoy reading that's related to your area of work? These are the kinds of questions that will drive your deepest engagement with writing, and help you develop the appetite and capacity for reading that underpins all successful writing.

THINK ABOUT THIS: Try asking this question of anyone you know and respect: friends, family, colleagues – *If you were to recommend just one book to me, what would it be?* Some of the recommendations I've received from asking this have had a huge impact on my thinking. Here, for example, is a book that two friends independently told me I had to try: *Popper*, by Bryan Magee (Fontana Modern Masters series, 1985). It's just over 100 pages long and a brilliant read. I would like to recommend it to you in turn.

(2) Avoid avoidance: ask any professional writer about the greatest challenges they face and they are likely to mention the blank space that stares back before you've begun a project. Getting going is often the toughest bit. How do you start on something big, something uncertain, something that demands knowledge you don't yet have? The best answer is – it doesn't really matter. You simply need to get going. You need to produce something that breaks the silence. It's the process of writing itself that teaches you what you have to say.

Hence the advice I offered in Chapter 6: be an active reader, produce notes and annotations and scribbles as you write, and start generating words of your own as early as possible. It doesn't matter that these words won't be perfect. It matters that you are starting to think in the form of writing: to get ideas outside your own head. Always be aware of your own avoidance tactics – whether these are doing something else entirely, 'organizing' yourself in ways unrelated to writing, or pretending you need to have read everything before you can begin. Don't tolerate avoidance. Don't let the perfect be the enemy of the good. Get going.

(3) All good writing is also rewriting: producing any serious, sustained piece of writing requires you to become your own reader: to look back over your own work with a critical eye. You need to deploy all your skills of close, critical reading to engage with your own work. And, if you're doing it right, you should enjoy the process.

Adding these comments is the last thing I'm doing to this book — & it feels great — almost done!

This may sound strange, given that self-criticism can be paralysing. But I honestly believe that rewriting and editing your own work is extraordinarily satisfying, if done in the right frame of mind. When I'm rewriting something, I like to print it out in order to take it off-screen and work on it with a pen in hand, often over a cup of coffee (coffee features heavily in my own writing process). I do this because it frees me up to encounter my own words as a reader. I don't like doing all my writing and editing in one place, onscreen, because this can get claustrophobic and overwhelming.

This may be different for you, but I would urge you to try different places and methods for re-engaging with your own work – and always to build some time and space for rewriting into any sustained project. Revisiting and clarifying what you have to say is the place where decent work turns into good work, and where something half-formed begins to take on the final form of whatever you actually want to say. Sudden insights and leaps of understanding also tend to need time and space to appear – a moment of silence, a walk or a pause, a change of scene.

(4) Practice: this is simple enough, yet can't be said too much. Nobody reads or writes well without doing so often. Don't be daunted by this: rather, throw yourself in. Get reading, get writing, get trying. Repeat, learn, enjoy. It's a mistake to assume that learning takes the form of understanding something first, and then working on the basis of this understanding. Most of the time, skill and understanding emerge over time as a result of practice – as a result of repeatedly doing something and gradually piecing together insights as you go.

GOOD ACADEMIC WRITING IN PARTICULAR

Writing well in an academic context is a particular skill. Although you may both inform and entertain your reader along the way, you are aiming, above all, to prove certain things: to prove that you understand what is expected of you, that you have researched and understood the necessary materials, and that you are organized and competent enough to structure a reasonable response. What you don't show will get you no credit. The following is a guide to successful academic writing in nine steps:

(1) Make sure you understand what is being asked of you: What question are you addressing? What length and what deadline are you working to? What will a successful essay or project do, and what criteria are you being graded by? If you don't know these things, you cannot succeed. It is your job to select and to address a suitable question, and to understand what a good answer looks like.

This may sound obvious, but perhaps the most common study error of all – at every level – is failing to think sufficiently about the question you are addressing, or making unwarranted assumptions about what is and is not required. Before you go any further, make sure you:

- Paraphrase in your own words exactly what the question you're addressing means.
- Confirm how much you are aiming to write, and by what deadline it is due.
- Check how you are going to be marked or graded, and what exactly you are expected to include in your essay or project. Make a list of all this.
- Seek out at least one successful example of a previous project or essay in the same field, so that you have a sense of what you are aiming towards.
- Ask for clarification as early as possible if you are unsure about any of the above. Don't waste time wondering, worrying or getting yourself confused.

(2) Plan your reading, conduct your research, gather information: we looked at this in detail in Chapters 5 and 6. Make sure that your planning and reading form a strategic and an active process. Don't delay the process of writing notes and starting to sketch ideas. Be highly engaged from the start: generate notes, suggestions and the beginnings of arguments. Here's a brief recap of the advice on reading strategies from Chapter 6:

PLEASE take this advice! Don't delay, start writing early, no matter how sketchily.

- Create or adopt a longlist of a wide range of possible resources.
- Turn your longlist into a shortlist relating to your current learning objectives, within which you have prioritized a realistic number of resources.
- Draw on different reading techniques in order to get the most out of your time and resources: use skim reading, scanning, searching and close reading as appropriate.
- Ensure that all of the above entails note-taking, active engagement and constantly asking how a particular resource is useful to you.
- Don't forget: all note-taking should always provide full details of each source you are using, enabling you to find it again and use it as an academic citation.

(3) Structure your content/draw up an outline: structuring your content is not a question of thinking until you come up with the perfect sequence of ideas out of the blue. It's an opportunity to write things down, cross things out, experiment with possibilities, and cut and paste and shift concepts freely until their best sequence emerges.

Start by writing everything down, and then gradually get rid of whatever turns out to be irrelevant. Iterate, edit, improve. The best arguments and explanations tend to emerge from the most comprehensive processes of structuring and re-structuring. Guide your process of revision and iteration with reference to the following key questions:

- What are the most important things I want to say?
- In what order does it make most sense to say them?
- Which evidence best supports these points?

These are easy questions to ask and difficult ones to answer. You won't get it right in one attempt – or in two. Keep asking and keep revising your outline, until you get there.

(4) Come up with a good introduction: once your outline is broadly defined, you're ready to start writing for real. Starting with the introduction is a good idea, even if it's only a draft that you revisit later. A good introduction should instantly demonstrate three things to your reader and, by doing so, should help you focus on precisely what you need to do:

- Show that you understand what is being asked of you.
- Show that you're aware of the wider context within which your work exists.
- Show that you're about to offer a clear, logical and evidence-based account.

(5) Write the main body of your work logically and clearly: write according to your outline and keep the big picture in view. You are aiming to convey a sense of control and coherence, and to make it clear at all times what is going on. In a longer piece of work, use headings and section divisions to keep the structure useful and obvious.

Keep in mind what you yourself have found helpful as a reader of other people's work. Clarity matters much more than trying to sound clever or 'academic'. In general:

- Give each point its own paragraph, or two paragraphs if it's complex. Don't use needlessly long paragraphs: ten lines are plenty. Avoid extremely short paragraphs, too.
- Structure your individual paragraphs by opening them with a clear statement or question, and ending them with either a summary or a link to the next paragraph.
- Don't get bogged down in one point, or fail to leave enough time or space to cover everything that's needed. Keep referring to your outline to maintain perspective.
- Make sure that the reading experience flows smoothly rather than jumps between unrelated ideas: use linking phrases, or headings and sections.

(6) Your conclusion must answer the question you set out to investigate: refer back to your introduction when writing the conclusion, and if necessary re-draft them both in parallel. Especially in an essay, it's extremely important how you tie the whole scheme together. This doesn't mean forcing yourself into a definitive statement which your evidence doesn't fully support. Don't be afraid to be cautious and qualified in what you conclude, or to reflect on the complexities you've discovered. An engaging conclusion is often reflective rather than definitive.

(7) Finish your first draft and set aside the time to revise it: write your first draft in full, feel proud, give yourself a pat on the back, and then make sure you've set aside a block of time for re-reading and revision. You should reserve at least a couple of days for re-drafting your work, and something more like a week for longer essays and projects. Plan backwards from your deadline and build this time into your schedule.

This should be the most satisfying part of all. When you revise your work, you're not just checking spelling and grammar and formatting (although this is important), but are taking the opportunity to encounter yourself as a writer and refine your own style and arguments.

(8) Don't forget to provide references and a bibliography: make sure you know exactly what is required by your department or course on this front. If you're organized, and if you keep good records while doing your reading and research, this should be no problem – especially with software to assist you.

Don't fall down here because you haven't thought about it until too late, or because you haven't bothered to look up what the requirements are. Get on top of these details, get them out of the way and don't let them detract from the proper business of reading, writing and thinking.

(9) It's not just about a grade; it's about feedback and a conversation: you've gone to all the effort of writing something at length. Try to get the most out of anyone and everyone who has read your work – whether it's friends, family, tutors and professors, or peers online. Read closely and carefully any feedback you get, and try to think honestly about how you can use it to do better the next time. Ask:

- What are my strengths and weaknesses?
- Who or what could I learn from, or use as a model for doing better?
- What is my strategy for improvement?

These are the questions that in the long term define excellence and success. It's not about getting it right instantly, or plucking a brilliant insight out of thin air. Like most things worth doing, writing is about finding a way of working that allows you to improve.

SMART STUDY: What NOT to do in your writing

- Don't try to sound too clever or 'academic'. Don't try to sound like somebody or something you are not. Clarity is the best policy: for you and for your reader.
- Don't go with your first draft. Leave yourself time to read and re-read what you have written, to edit your work and to make sure it isn't full of unnecessary errors.
- Never copy and paste anything unless it's a quotation, and always put all quotations within quotation marks. Never pass off others' work as your own or use their points without acknowledgement.
- Don't offer your opinions to the exclusion of others. Present a range of others' opinions in your evidence, ensure you are generous and thorough in representing their beliefs, then carefully summarize your own position afterwards.
- While working on a long project, don't get bogged down, stressed out and lost in detail. If you're losing perspective, take a break – step away from the screen, do something else and then revisit your work when you're ready.
- Be clear, be precise but don't be pedantic, and don't let pedants beat you around the head with grammatical 'rules' that are usually no such thing. It's fine to split infinitives and to end sentences with prepositions, for example. Be lively and generous in your style, not dry and nervous.

I hate pedantic books of pretend 'rules' for language.

THINK ABOUT THIS: What are some of the best, most impressive and most engaging things you have read across a variety of genres? What were the authors doing in each case that worked so well? Can you go back and find any particular sentences or phrases that embody their style?

WRITING AND REWRITING IN PRACTICE

Given the central role of rewriting in my scheme, this section contains some practical exercises in rewriting. I have deliberately avoided a more in-depth 'rules of style' approach, because many of these so-called rules are, at best, subjective preferences rather than any kind of absolute standard.

SMART STUDY: Seven practical principles for rewriting

1. **Be brief**: look for unnecessarily wordy phrases that can be replaced by simpler, shorter ones – and for waffle and unnecessary qualifications that detract from your points.
2. **Be clear**: look for long, complex sentences that would be better off as several shorter ones.
3. **Clarity isn't the same as precision**: it's much more important to say clearly what you mean than to obsess about defining every term precisely.
4. **Stay on point**: look for unnecessary or distracting content that can be removed entirely.
5. **Guide your reader**: use signposting words and links to clarify the flow of your ideas.
6. **Revise radically**: don't be afraid to shift around sentences and paragraphs as much as needed to improve structure and flow.
7. **Re-read yourself closely**: it's a waste of time to skim your own writing when you're editing. Re-read yourself slowly and closely. It may help to print your work out and go through it line by line with a pen in hand.

Replacing unnecessarily wordy phrases with shorter ones is an important skill and worth turning into a habit. Have a go at rewriting the following paragraph with this in mind. To make things easier, I've underlined particular phrases you might want to rewrite:

> This essay will undertake an in-depth exploration of sociological analyses of divorce, focusing itself in succession upon a range of causative theoretical analyses of rising divorce rates in western societies. These include steadily iterative alterations in legal systems, economic and technological paradigm transformations, shifts in normative assumptions within the moral and social domains, and the rise of a post-religious public consciousness.

....

....

....

....

....

....

....

How did you do? Here's my version, below, with the new phrases underlined. As you'll see, I've simplified the paragraph by avoiding jargon words wherever possible. The result is considerably more readable, while losing little in terms of sense.

> This essay will explore sociological analyses of divorce, focusing on a range of explanations for rising divorce rates in western societies. These include changes to legal systems, economic and technological developments, shifts in moral and social norms, and the rise of secularism.

Second, here's an exercise in splitting up excessively complex sentences into several shorter ones. Again, this is an important skill for helping others to follow your train of thought. Your own ideas are rarely as clear to other people as they are inside your own head, and manageable sentences are an important way of breaking up ideas into digestible chunks. Try turning the following very long sentence into three shorter, clearer sentences:

In any library in the world, I am at home,

unselfconscious, still, and **absorbed.**

Germaine Greer

#TalkCriticalThinking

> Amid a climate of fiscal and political pressure, the shortfall in qualified teachers presents the current generation of students with both a severe challenge and a potential opportunity in terms of collectively putting pressure on government to redress some of the most unpopular and demoralizing aspects of a new teacher's working life – expectations around intensive testing and monitoring being one such especially prominent area.

Here's my version, below. Yours may well differ. What matters is that you keep the same sense while improving clarity. If you've changed the language more than me, that's fine – there is still plenty of room for improvement in what I've written.

> Amid a climate of fiscal and political pressure, the shortfall in qualified teachers presents the current generation of students with both a severe challenge and an opportunity. These students are potentially in a position to put collective pressure on government to redress some of the most unpopular and demoralizing aspects of a new teacher's working life. One such prominent area is the expectations around intensive testing and monitoring.

Third, here is an exercise to help you practise staying on point by deleting unnecessary material. It's amazing how often a first draft contains words that can be removed completely without loss – especially towards the beginning, when writing is often at its most uncertain. See how much you can improve this passage by deleting unnecessary material:

> When assessing causes of successes and failures in business, it is clear that the most significant factors causing these things are often ones that lie beyond the control of businesses themselves: factors such as market conditions, competition and chance events. It thus follows that we should be prepared in principle as researchers to treat all accounts of heroic individual business leaders building success through skill with a healthy initial degree of scepticism. This is an important point to remember.

How did you do? Below is my own edit of the paragraph, with unnecessary material struck through, followed by a revised version with this material removed. How does this compare to your own edit? Can you manage to come up with something even shorter than me, while preserving the meaning?

> When assessing causes of success and failure in business, ~~it is clear that~~ the most significant factors ~~causing these things are~~ often ~~ones that~~ lie beyond the control of businesses themselves: ~~factors such as~~ market conditions, competition, ~~and~~ chance events. It ~~thus~~ follows that we should ~~be prepared in principle as researchers to~~ treat all accounts of heroic ~~individual~~ business leaders building success through skill with ~~a healthy initial degree of~~ scepticism. ~~This is an important point to remember.~~

> When assessing causes of success and failure in business, the most significant factors often lie beyond the control of businesses themselves: market conditions, competition, chance events. It follows that we should treat all accounts of heroic business leaders building success through skill with scepticism.

My new version of the paragraph is 44 words long, as opposed to 79. That is almost half as short, with no real loss of meaning. The new version presents its points without waffle, and crisply sets up ideas to be explored: in particular, I've trimmed away qualifications and repetitions. This creates a more direct style in which points aren't softened behind phrases like 'a degree of' and 'in principle' – qualifications that may sound thoughtful and careful on first reading, but that contribute little of value.

Are there similar verbal tics that you find recurring in your writing: stock phrases that add little in terms of meaning, but that may make you feel safer? Don't confuse being vague and indirect with being intellectually rigorous. It's quite an art to express complexity and uncertainty crisply, but it's worth doing. For this final exercise, see if you can find a briefer and clearer way of summing up the following paragraph, without distorting its meaning:

Respecting complexity isn't the same as waffling vaguely around it.

> On the basis of our analysis of historical data dating back 50 years, it is not unreasonable to suggest that there may be a causal relationship between, on the one hand, underlying levels of volatility and, on the other hand, market performance, albeit one involving complex feedback mechanisms.

How far did your simplification go? Here is my version, which reduces 48 words to just 23 – less than half the length of the original:

> Our analysis of 50 years of historical data suggests a possible causal relationship between volatility and market performance – albeit one involving complex feedback.

This may read as a more confident analysis than the first version, but it simply lacks the padding sometimes used to make an analysis sound more expert than it actually is. Don't be fooled by this in others' work and don't let yourself get away with it. Inside every first draft is a neater, shorter, crisper piece, waiting for you to chip away the words you don't actually need.

GETTING THE WORK DONE: WHAT IS HOLDING YOU BACK?

As I commented at the start of this chapter, much of the struggle associated with writing (and work in general) lies in overcoming those things that stand between you and getting on with it – the factors that block or inhibit you. This is equally true of students and professionals: it's just that professionals have, hopefully, developed more habits and techniques for getting past these blocks. (They also get paid, which helps.)

If you're stressed, afraid, unengaged, angry, or can't concentrate as you might like to – why is this? Is there something you can do differently that would make things feel better? Are there other things that you care about, that you want to write about and explore? In general, you need to do two related things when dealing with questions like this:

- Be honest about what's holding you back.
- Be practical about asking what you can (and can't) change.

Habits: by focusing our attention on those things we do often and largely unconsciously, we can transform our behaviour by creating the conditions for new and different behaviours

Entire books have been written about routines and productivity, some of which are excellent,[73] but in this section I want to focus on what it means to acquire **habits** conducive to critical reading, writing and thinking.[74]

The first time we do something, we are usually making an active choice and engaging critically with what we want or need. We carefully select a new mobile phone, an item of clothing, a place to study, a place to live, a commuting route, furnishings for our bedroom. After we have done this, our choice begins to slip beneath conscious awareness. It becomes habitual: something we do or use without thinking. It may also turn out, over time, to be something we shouldn't have taken on, or that we would be better off doing differently.

Reassessing your habits can be hard work, but it's well worth doing. Your habits define how you spend most of your time and energy. As we've seen in the previous chapters, active engagement is a precious and limited resource: something you need to apply sparingly and selectively. There is no such thing as a perfect routine, but there are better and worse ways of structuring your time – and unless you are prepared to engage with what you do on this structural level, you are unlikely to work, think or live as well as you might.

Don't get obsessed with bad habits — think about good ones too.

Hence the significance of setting aside some time and space to examine your habits. Are there things you habitually do that you wish you didn't, or that disproportionately diminish your energy, engagement, attention or pleasure? Are there other things you habitually do (or would like to do more often) that restore you to your better self – that invigorate and enhance your identity, your engagement with the world and others, your sense of possibility?

As we draw towards the end of the book, see if you can think of three things you would like to do less often, three things you wish you did more frequently, and three things you cannot change but would like to worry about less.

Three things that I would like to spend less time doing are:

1 ....

....

2 ....

....

3 ....

....

Three things that I would like to spend more time doing regularly are:

1 ....

....

2 ....

....

3 ....

....

Three things that I cannot change but should worry less about are:

1 ....

....

2 ....

....

3 ....

....

You may be surprised at how the simple act of writing these out can help you challenge and change your attitudes – and how giving yourself permission not to worry about some things can create opportunities elsewhere. When are you at your best? How can you aim to be that way more often: to put yourself in the kind of situation that allows you to live most fully? These may sound like self-indulgent questions, but they're also practical tools for working and thinking more effectively, and for defining the direction in which you ultimately wish to aim.

CRITICAL THINKING AND YOU

Here, for the last time, are ten questions for scoring your own critical thinking. Ten represents total confidence and zero represents no confidence at all. Fill them out and tot up your total.

1	I am able to pay close, detailed attention to information and ideas	______ **/10**
2	I can summarize and explain information I've come across	______ **/10**
3	I easily understand others' points of view and why they believe what they do	______ **/10**
4	I can clearly express my own point of view	______ **/10**
5	I am willing to change my mind and modify my beliefs when I learn new things	______ **/10**
6	I am able to compare and to evaluate multiple sources of information	______ **/10**
7	I can locate and research sources of relevant information by myself	______ **/10**
8	I can clearly summarize and explain others' work, including its limitations	______ **/10**
9	I am able to justify my own conclusions and to outline the evidence behind them	______ **/10**
10	I am aware of and able to explain to others the limitations of my knowledge	______ **/10**
Total score:		______ **/100**

If you've worked through this book in order, this should be the third and final time you answer these ten questions. What is your final score, and how does it compare to previous self-assessments? How far have you progressed? In what areas do you have most, and least, confidence? Whatever your answers, congratulations on making it this far! On the following page is a final exercise, designed to help you consolidate your learning, plan what comes next and celebrate what you have discovered.

As I thinker, I am most confident in ...

while I am least confident when ...

One of the most valuable insights of this book, for me, is ...

while I was least interested in learning about ...

Looking back, it is most important for me to revise ...

while I want to investigate more about ...

My strategy for continuing to improve and develop is ...

TEN COMMANDMENTS FOR CRITICAL THINKING

These aren't really commandments, of course. They're something between recommendations and heartfelt advice, and I hope they are a useful note on which to end.

(1) First and foremost, slow down: does what's in front of you matter and require deep thought? If so, pause. It deserves a strategy. If not, don't worry too much. Get on with it, get it out of the way.

(2) Conserve mental energy: you have limited willpower, limited mental energy and limited attention. Try to build habits and a working environment that help you focus. This almost certainly means not having email or social media open in the background. Don't let others dictate your time and attention.

(3) If in doubt, wait: time itself is a powerful filter. Pauses and silence are the friends of better thought. Leave those difficult messages for a few days, even a week, and suddenly what you need to say will feel much clearer – or you may decide not to say anything at all.

(4) Know your limits: don't pretend to know what you don't know. Practise saying: *I don't know; I need to find out more.* Seek out others' expertise where yours runs out. And remember: expertise is specific. Don't assume that someone who knows about Physics has a clue about Economics.

(5) Beware sunk costs: once you've put time, effort, cash or care into something, it's tempting to stick with it no matter what, in order to justify your input. Don't. You'll never get that expenditure back, so try not to consider it at all when looking ahead. Don't over-value what you have, just because you have it. If it's not working out: cut your losses. Be brutal – don't get shackled to your past.

(6) Judge strategy, not results: judging by results is dangerous. Stupid strategies can end well; sound strategies don't always work. A bad strategy with a good outcome was still a bad strategy, while a good strategy that didn't work is still worth repeating. This is the only way to play the odds in the long term. Don't be obsessed with short-term success. Keep doing the right thing.

(7) Most things revert to the mean: an exceptional result is likely to be followed by a less exceptional one, whether good or bad. Don't be fooled. Just like the economy after a crash, things tend to recover over time, or to fall back from a high. Don't give someone or something credit for whatever was likely to happen anyway. Look to the long term, the big numbers and the underlying trends.

(8) Seek refutation over confirmation: any idea can endlessly be confirmed if you're only looking for support – you can convince yourself the Earth is flat if you never look more than a mile away. Seek out challenges and contradictions, and put your arguments and beliefs to a genuine test. If an idea or a theory cannot be tested or disproved, it isn't worth much.

(9) Beware your frames of reference: would you walk one mile for £20? Imagine: you're about to buy a kettle for £40 and then discover it's on sale for £20 in a shop 1 mile away. You probably take a walk. Now, you're buying a car for £6,000 and you discover it's on sale for £5,980 (also) a mile away. You probably stay put. Why? Your perceptions are always relative, never absolute. Make very sure you define your terms of reference and don't let someone else do it for you.

(10) Every option you're facing can be wrong: before you choose, ask – is the best or most meaningful response even on offer? A website says you must either enter your personal details or not get access. Perhaps the better choice is to reject the deal. A politician says we must either raise taxes or lower immigration, but that's no reason for you to accept either. Look outside the frame. Ask whether you're really being given a choice. Ask, is there a different, better way of thinking?

Spotting hollow choices can give a good indication of where other people most fear critical thought.

SUMMARY

Good writing begins with good reading: reading widely, passionately and actively. Write notes, plan your strategy and start filling the page and the screen sooner rather than later. All good writing is also **rewriting**. Learn to read your own work closely, with a critical eye. When writing in an academic context, follow these steps:

- Ensure you understand what is being asked of you.
- Plan your reading, conduct your research and gather information.
- Structure your content and draw up an outline.
- Come up with a good introduction.
- Write the main body of your work in a logical sequence.
- Write a conclusion that clearly answers the question you began with.
- Finish your first draft and set aside the time to revise it.
- Don't forget to provide references and a bibliography.
- Embrace feedback and conversations. Learn and improve.

When it comes to getting the work done, ask yourself:

- What **holds me back** psychologically from writing and engaging?
- What are the most **significant practical obstacles** to working in the way I would like to work, and achieving what I would like to achieve?
- What is my **strategy** for overcoming these obstacles?

Pay close attention to your habits: both those things you wish you did less & those you would like to do more often. There is no such thing as a perfect routine, but there are better & worse ways of structuring your time, & unless you are prepared to engage with what you do on this structural level, you are unlikely to work think or live as well as you might.

Now watch the video 'Ten commandments for critical thinking'. It's on YouTube. Tell me what you think via #TalkCriticalThinking

AND FINALLY...

We live in an age of smart tools and big data: vast and rapidly shifting volumes of information that can only be rendered comprehensible to us by machines, and that are in turn integral to training machine-learning systems.

Under the right conditions, these systems are narrowly brilliant at optimizing and recognizing patterns, and making inferences on the basis of these patterns. Their full potential can only be guessed at, but it is already changing our world: capturing more and more of the terrain we used to think of as uniquely human, from natural language and image recognition to making medical diagnoses and writing music.

Humans, in contrast to our creations, are dazzlingly adept at making rapid inferences from very small amounts of data. We are highly adaptive, creative and critical thinkers across many domains, simultaneously. We are both biased and empathetic. We collaborate, we negotiate, driven by the twin engines of our feelings and our capacity for understanding.

These two things – feeling and understanding – belong only to the human realm, at least for now. Between them, they drive everything we do. They cannot be separated, because they are aspects of one and the same process. As I have sketched out in this book, we are today beginning to understand more about the intricacies of our own minds and motives – and this also means that we are becoming increasingly expert at manipulating each others' minds through every means at our disposal.

Behavioural Economics, Cognitive Psychology, Neuroscience, Social Psychology: the insights of all these fields are being fed directly into business models aimed at eliciting certain behaviours for profit, and into political models aimed at producing certain outcomes for power. This isn't paranoia: this is simply what it means today to be alive, connected to the world and to other people through ever-denser networks of information.

We are far from helpless in the grip of these manipulations, but we are also – often – perilously under-informed or indifferent to the biases built into the systems we inhabit. What does a free, successful and critically engaged life look like in the 21st century? It begins with the freedom to make reasoned judgements on the basis of relevant, accurate information. But it also begins with you, your time and your attention: how you choose to spend it, with whom and in pursuit of which aims.

If you don't think for yourself, someone else will do it for you.

Many of the jobs of 30 years' time don't exist yet. But, if we're lucky, the questions that will enable us to make them worthwhile do, including the question of which values we wish our creations to relentlessly pursue on our behalf. I believe it has never been more important to think critically, together, about the way the world actually is and what we ourselves are in the process of becoming.

Good luck with your work, your life and your thinking – and thank you for reading.

READING GUIDE

OTHER BOOKS ABOUT CRITICAL THINKING

Bowell, T. and Kemp, G. (2015) *Critical Thinking: A Concise Guide* (4th edition). London: Routledge. A detailed, clear exploration of the field that's especially impressive in dealing with argument reconstruction and assessment in detail.

Cottrell, S. (2011) *Critical Thinking Skills: Developing Effective Analysis and Argument* (2nd edition). London: Palgrave Macmillan. An attractive, accessible and wide-ranging introduction to both critical thinking skills and their wider study context, packed with great exercises.

Fisher, A. (2011) *Critical Thinking: An Introduction* (2nd edition). Cambridge: Cambridge University Press. A highly readable introductory textbook suitable for both A-level students and early undergraduates.

van den Brink-Budgen, R. (2010) *Critical Thinking for Students* (4th edition). Oxford: How To Books. A basic introduction to concepts, useful for its lucidity when it comes to claims, explanations and assumptions. Most appropriate for AS or A-level students.

Warburton, N. (2007) *Thinking from A to Z* (3rd edition). London: Routledge. A short, sweet alphabetical guide to key concepts in critical thinking.

LOGIC AND REASONING

Copi, I.M., Cohen, C. and McMahon, K. (2016) *Introduction to Logic* (14th edition). London: Routledge. A classic that's both expansive and accessible, and comprehensive when it comes to both the rules of logic and its wider context and significance.

Hodges, W. (2001) *Logic* (2nd edition). London: Penguin. A well-designed introductory textbook with a clear style and exercises aimed at helping undergraduates master the fundamentals.

RESEARCH METHODOLOGIES

Kumar, R. (2014) *Research Methodology: A Step-by-Step Guide for Beginners* (4th edition). London: Sage. A lucid and comprehensive guide, especially strong on data, sampling and processing.

Thomas, G. (2013) *How to Do Your Research Project: A Guide for Students in Education and Applied Social Science*. London: Sage. Does exactly what it says in the title, in a personable and accessible way, with great illustrations, detail and relevant examples throughout.

CRITICAL READING AND WRITING SKILLS

Wallace, M. and Wray, A. (2011) *Critical Reading and Writing for Postgraduates* (2nd edition). London: Sage. Sophisticated and in-depth, as the title suggests, but with an accessibility that makes it valuable for any undergraduate looking to improve.

Warburton, N. (2007) *The Basics of Essay Writing*. London: Routledge. A clear and friendly introduction, with detailed practical advice covering often-overlooked essentials.

THINKING CRITICALLY ABOUT TECHNOLOGY

Floridi, L. (2014) *The Fourth Revolution: How the Infosphere is Reshaping Human Reality*. Oxford: Oxford University Press. One of the finest and most wide-ranging popular explorations of the human consequences of the information age, from a leading academic thinker.

Gleick, J. (2011) *The Information: A History, A Theory, A Flood*. London: Fourth Estate. An intellectual history of the machine age in one dazzling narrative, at once a history of ideas and human invention – one of my own favourite books about how our digital age was born.

Hendricks, V.F. and Hansen, P.G. (2016) *Infostorms: Why do we 'Like'? Explaining Individual Behavior on the Social Net* (2nd edition). New York: Springer. One of the best in-depth explorations I've found of the forces underlying online social behaviours, and how to model and understand them.

Lanier, J. (2010) *You Are Not a Gadget: A Manifesto*. London: Penguin. A delightful provocation and meditation on the relationship between humanity and technology, as fresh today as when it was written.

COGNITIVE BIAS AND BEHAVIOURAL ECONOMICS

Ariely, D. (2009) *Predictably Irrational: The Hidden Forces that Shape Our Decisions*. London: HarperCollins. One of the first and best mainstream books in the field, written as a first-person tour of research and its implications by a founding expert.

Kahneman, D. (2011) *Thinking, Fast and Slow*. London: Penguin. There is no better mainstream guide to behavioural economics than this modern classic. Essential reading from the Nobel laureate who helped define the field.

McRaney, D. (2012) *You Are Not So Smart*. London: Oneworld. Lively, well referenced and wide-ranging, this tour through 48 common cognitive biases is a great starter text.

BECOMING MORE COMFORTABLE WITH STATISTICS, UNCERTAINTY AND PROBABILITY

Blastland, M. and Spiegelhalter, D. (2013) *The Norm Chronicles: Stories and Numbers about Risk*. London: Profile Books. One of the liveliest recent examinations of risk in everyday life, and what it means to think with playful rigour about possibilities, from skydiving to terrorism.

Field, A. (2016) *An Adventure in Statistics: The Reality Enigma*. London: Sage. Unconventional, long, illuminating and beautiful, this combination of illustrated novel and stats textbook covers almost everything a social scientist needs to know for stats.

Huff, D. (1973) *How to Lie with Statistics*. London: Penguin. Short, sweet and simple, it's not far off 50 years old, but if you can pick up a second-hand copy this remains a wonderful introduction to thinking critically about others' abuse of numbers.

Taleb, N.N. (2001) *Fooled by Randomness*. London: Penguin. The first book in Taleb's *Incerto* series is a fine place to introduce yourself to his idiosyncratic genius. Infuriatingly brilliant.

TWO INTERESTING BOOKS TO HELP YOU THINK ABOUT THE WORLD

Blackburn, S. (1999) *Think*. Oxford: Oxford University Press. A dazzling introduction to philosophy of mind that will fit into your pocket – and fill your head with dizzying questions.

Feynman, R.P. and Leighton, R.B. (2011) *Six Easy Pieces: Essentials of Physics Explained by Its Most Brilliant Teacher*. New York: Basic Books. Even if you know nothing about physics, the vigour and rigour of Feynman's explanations are a case study of genius at work – few people have probed more deeply into the mysteries of the universe, or explained them with such insight and force.

GLOSSARY

Abductive reasoning: sometimes known as 'inference to the best explanation', this seeks to establish the best possible explanation for something believed to be true

Ad hominem: the fallacy of attacking the person making an argument rather than what they actually say

Alternative histories: all the other possibilities that did not play out in real life, but that could have happened instead of the events actually observed; considering alternative histories is an important technique for accurately assessing strategies rather than only judging by results

Amphiboly: using a phrase or sentence that can be interpreted as meaning more than one thing, without clarifying which

Ampliative reasoning: another way of describing inductive reasoning, intended to show that such reasoning works by 'amplifying' premises into a broader conclusion

Anchoring effect: a heuristic; the ability of a starting value or frame of reference to influence your subsequent judgements, even when it has no relevance to what you're considering

Argument: an attempt to persuade someone through reasoning that they should agree with a particular conclusion

Argument by appeal: appealing to external factors such as authority or popularity to justify a conclusion, resulting in a weak or entirely fallacious argument when such factors have no direct relevance to the conclusion they are alleged to support

Argument from ignorance: a fallacious form of argument based on the unjustified claim that something cannot be considered true unless it has been proven with absolute certainty

Assertion: a statement of fact or belief, provided without support or justification

Assumption: something relevant to an argument that has been taken for granted by the person presenting it, rather than spelled out

Attention vs distraction: the tension between allocating focused engagement to the task in front of you versus allowing yourself to be distracted

Authoritative: those sources that are considered most trustworthy and reliable in a field

Base rate: the basic, underlying likelihood that something we are investigating is the case: for example, the likelihood that someone selected at random has a particular medical condition, based upon our knowledge of how common that condition is within the population at large

Base rate neglect: the formal fallacy of ignoring the the base rate in your analysis, especially when this base rate is extremely low, and thus reaching an incorrect conclusion: for example, assuming that if someone is an author then they are likely to have sold millions of books, ignoring the fact that very few people sell millions of books even if they are authors

Bayes's theorem: a method for calculating the probability of an event based on our knowledge of previous events – allowing us to avoid the fallacy of base rate neglect and to correctly assess the odds of, for example, someone having an extremely rare disease in the event of a positive test result from a test that is not always accurate. (If the disease is very rare, a positive test result is not likely to indicate that someone genuinely has the disease unless the test is as accurate as the disease is rare.)

Begging the question: an informal fallacy; putting the conclusion that is to be proven into your premises, thus producing something convincing-sounding that proves nothing

Behavioural Economics: the application of psychological insights and methods to economics, exploring through experiment and observation the real-life decisions people make

Bias: approaching something in a one-sided way that creates a distorted account of the way things actually are

Black swan event: an event that defies both previous experience and expectations based on that experience, making it almost impossible to predict

Buzzwords: a rhetorical device; fashionable words and phrases used to make something sound impressive and up to date; often a case of style over substance, with little thought beneath the surface

Causation: asserting causation is to claim that one thing is the direct cause of another

Cherry-picking: deliberately selecting a few striking results or strong effects from within a larger piece of research while suppressing the rest, thus misrepresenting the investigation

Circular reasoning: an informal fallacy; an argument whose premise supports its conclusion and whose conclusion supports its premise, making it a closed loop that proves nothing

Clarification: spelling out what is meant by a particular phrase, idea or line of thought

Clustering illusion: *see* **Sharpshooter fallacy**

Cogent: an inductive argument that has a good structure, but whose conclusion we should not necessarily accept as true (similarly to a valid deductive argument)

Cognitive bias: a particular situation in which mental heuristics (short cuts) introduce a predictable distortion into our assessment of a situation, resulting in a flawed judgement

Coherence effect: a cognitive bias; the tendency to judge information not by its accuracy or likelihood, but by how internally coherent a story or a worldview it embodies

Comparable example: a method for testing potentially fallacious arguments and illustrating their flaws, by applying exactly the same reasoning in a different context

Complex question: *see* **Loaded question**

Conclusion: the final point that someone making an argument is trying to convince you of; the final proposition in any argument, supported by its premises

Confirmation bias: the universal human tendency to use new information to confirm existing beliefs, rather than seeking to improve and clarify understanding

Conscious bias: when someone deliberately presents a one-sided view of something or explicitly holds a one-sided opinion about something (as opposed to **unconscious bias**)

Control group: a group, usually selected at random from within a test population, that does not receive any kind of experimental intervention and can thus provide a comparison to the **treatment group**

Correlation: two trends that follow each other closely are correlated; the exact degree of correlation between two sets of information can be calculated through a variety of statistical methods

Correlation is not causation: a phrase warning against the fallacy of assuming that, if two sets of data closely follow one another, one must be caused by the other – where in fact correlations are common and exist for a wide variety of reasons, while direct causal relationships are relatively rare

Counter-example: an example whose discovery makes it necessary to rethink a particular position, because it directly contradicts a generalization previously believed to be true

Critical thinking: setting out to actively understand what is really going on by using reasoning, evaluating evidence and thinking carefully about the process of thinking itself

Current: sources that are up to date with the latest thinking and evidence are said to be current

Description: simply reporting information without any attempt at evaluating, commenting on or using the information to persuade

Dogmatism: to be dogmatic is to believe that certain principles or ideas are both absolutely true and immune to any form of critical scrutiny or discussion

Double-blind: a research trial in which neither the subjects nor the researchers know who is in the control group and who is in the treatment group

Dunning–Kruger effect: a cognitive bias; the tendency of people with little or no ability in an area to greatly over-estimate their ability, resulting in ignorance breeding unwarranted confidence

Empiricism: a way of thinking about the world rooted in the precise observation of what you can verify with your own senses and can investigate through experience and observation

Equivocation: the fallacy of using a word in two quite different senses while pretending that they are the same in order to create the appearance of reasoning

Euphemism: deliberately replacing a negative-seeming word or phrase with something more neutral, often in order to conceal the severity of what has happened

Exaggeration: over-stating your case, often as a rhetorical tactic

Explanation: a suggestion for the reason or reasons that something came to be the way it is; a good explanation should account for all known facts as economically as possible

Explicit premises: those claims that someone has explicitly set out in support of their conclusion

Extended argument: an argument in which the final conclusion is supported by one or more premises that are themselves intermediate conclusions, supported by previous premises

Extraneous material: information that is not relevant to an argument and that, during analysis and reconstruction, should thus be left out

Fallacious argument: an appealing yet flawed argument that establishes a faulty connection between premises and conclusion, thus failing to give us good reason to accept the conclusion; usually classified as being either an informal (a dubious assumption that does not stand up to external evaluation) or a formal fallacy (an internal error of deductive logic)

Fallacy of composition: mistakenly arguing that whatever is true of the individual parts must also be true of the whole

Fallacy of division: mistakenly arguing that whatever is true of the whole must also be true of its individual parts

False dilemma: an informal fallacy; claiming that, in a complex situation, it is only possible for one of two things to be true

False negative: a negative test result produced in error, when whatever is being tested for is in fact present

False positive: a positive test result produced in error, when whatever is being tested for is in fact absent

Falsification: the contradiction of something previously accepted as true or obvious; seeking to test a theory by attempted falsification is a central aspect of the scientific method, as it provides a more rigorous standard of proof than seeking confirmation

Faulty analogy: an informal fallacy; claiming two things are similar, even though they are not, in order to make an unreasonable conclusion look reasonable

Faulty generalization: an informal fallacy; using a small amount of evidence to justify a much larger observation that is not actually warranted

Feasibility: the question of whether a proposed research question can meaningfully be addressed given the time, resources and information at your disposal

Focusing effect: a cognitive bias; the tendency to focus excessively on one striking aspect of something, thus failing to give full consideration to a full range of other relevant factors

Formal fallacy: an invalid form of argument representing an error in deductive logic, meaning that arguments in this form cannot be relied on to arrive at valid conclusions

Framing effects: a heuristic; the way in which presenting the same scenario in different ways can affect judgement and alter preference, based on perceptions of loss and gain, positive and negative

Fundamental attribution error: a cognitive bias; the tendency to disproportionately view events as the result of deliberate actions and intentions, rather than as a product of circumstances

Gaussian distribution: *see* **Normal distribution (bell curve)**

Heuristic: a cognitive short cut or 'rule of thumb', allowing for quick decision-making and judgement

Hindsight bias: a cognitive bias; the tendency to see the past, in retrospect, as more predictable than it actually was, and to treat unforeseen events as though they were foreseeable

Hyperbole: deliberate exaggeration for the purpose of rhetorical impact

Illusion of predictability: a cognitive bias; the illusion that an observed pattern will necessarily be repeated, or that current notions of normality will always apply

Illustration: a particular instance of a general point

Impact of extremes: the fact that just one extreme event, even if rare, can have a more significant impact than any number of ordinary events

Implicit premises: not spelled out by the person stating an argument, but *assumed* as part of their reasoning and need to be included in reconstruction

Implicit qualification: when a general statement is not literally intended, some implicit qualification needs to be assumed, indicating the frequency with which it applies

Independent premises: premises that support a conclusion individually and don't rely on each other

Inductive reasoning: a form of reasoning in which the premises strongly support a conclusion, but where we can never be absolutely certain that it is true

Inductive strength or **inductive force**: a measure of how likely we believe an inductive argument is to be true

Inductively forceful: an inductive argument that has both a good structure and true premises, and whose conclusion we thus have good reason to accept as true (similar to a sound deductive argument, although without its certainty)

Informal fallacies: faulty or flawed forms of reasoning that contain a flawed assumption, but one whose flaws must be determined with reference to external information

Information environment: a way of talking about the overall realm of information shared between people, organizations and systems, together with its properties

Intermediate conclusion: a conclusion arrived at during the course of an argument; it is then used as a premise for building towards the final conclusion

Invalid reasoning: incorrectly applying deductive reasoning, so that your conclusion does not logically follow from your premises

Inverting cause and effect: the informal fallacy of confusing the direction of causation between two related phenomena, and thus mistakenly labelling an effect as a cause

Irrelevant conclusion: an informal fallacy; presenting a conclusion that doesn't actually follow on logically from the reasoning that supposedly supports it

Irrelevant sources: sources that, on close examination, don't contribute to the main argument

Jargon: words and phrases likely to be familiar only to an expert audience, sometimes used in order to confuse non-experts or to exaggerate difficulty and complexity

Just world hypothesis: a cognitive bias; the belief that everything balances out in the end and that the world is fundamentally arranged in a way that is fair

Law of large numbers: the larger a sample, or the more often a consistent measure is repeated, the more likely its results are to tend towards the expected outcome

Law of small numbers: the smaller a sample, or the fewer times something is measured, the more likely its results are to differ from the expected outcome

Linked premises: premises supporting a conclusion when taken together, but not individually

Litotes: a rhetorical device; deliberately understating or using a negative to make a point sound convincing while not seeming to claim it directly

Loaded question: an informal fallacy, also known as a 'complex question'; asking a question about one thing that also includes an unstated assumption about another, in an attempt to force someone to accept this unstated assumption no matter what their answer

Logic: the study of the principles distinguishing correct from incorrect reasoning

Loss aversion: a cognitive bias; the observation that losses are more painful than equivalent gains, and that people thus tend to be biased towards loss avoidance when making decisions

Margin of error: an expression of the degree to which results based on a sample are likely to differ from those of the overall population

Mean: a 'traditional' average: the total of every result, divided by the number of results

Median: the middle result in a series, when it is set out in order

Metacognition: thinking about thinking itself; the higher-order skills that allow you to successfully keep on learning, improving and adapting

Mode: the most frequently occurring value in a series

Moral luck: the paradoxical observation that we ought to blame people only for the things they control, yet in practice often judge them as a result of lucky or unlucky outcomes

n = 1: a sample size of one indicates an anecdote rather than a serious investigation; any inductive argument based on a single instance is likely to be very weak

Necessary condition: a condition that must be met if something is to be true, but that cannot by itself guarantee the truth of that something

Network effect: the tendency of a service to become exponentially more useful and valuable as more people use it, as well as potentially more dominant and harder to opt out of

Non-argument: any element of a piece of writing that does not attempt to persuade you of a conclusion through reasoning, and thus doesn't qualify as part of an argument

Normal distribution (bell curve): also known as a 'Gaussian distribution', this is an idealised continuous distribution with a peak in the middle of a range of results that curve away symmetrically

Null hypothesis: the exact opposite of the hypothesis you're testing; seeing whether you can falsify a null hypothesis is a common way of ensuring rigour in research

Objectivity: trying to understand something from a neutral perspective, rather than relying on a single opinion or the first information that comes to hand

Observational error: errors due to the accuracy of your measuring system, usually reported as ±X, where X is the potential difference between measured and actual values

Occam's razor: the principle that, when choosing between explanations, the simplest one is usually best, while more assumptions make something less likely to be true

Outcome bias: a cognitive bias; the tendency to assess the quality of a decision once the result of that decision is known, rather than by considering whether it made sense at the time

Overconfidence effect: a cognitive bias; the strong tendency for most people – and especially experts outside their domain of expertise – to have excessive faith in their judgements and abilities

Over-generalization: suggesting that something is more generally true than it actually is, often as a rhetorical tactic; making a far broader claim than is the case in reality

Paralepsis: a rhetorical device; introducing an idea while claiming you do not wish to discuss it, thus allowing you to make a claim while denying any responsibility for discussing it

Placebo: a deliberately ineffective treatment, such as a sugar pill, supplied to a control group in order to give them the potential psychological benefits of thinking they are receiving a treatment, thus allowing researchers to rule out this psychological impact as a potential cause of any health effects

Post hoc ergo propter hoc: the informal fallacy of assuming that, when one thing happens after another, the first thing must be the cause of the second thing

Prejudice: holding a belief without consideration of the evidence for or against it; deciding in advance of hearing an argument what you believe to be the case

Premise: a claim presented by an argument in support of its conclusion

Primary sources: sources derived directly from the subject, period or phenomenon under investigation

Principle of charity: the philosophical principle that one should always begin with the assumption that someone else is truthful and reasonable, and try to reconstruct their argument in its strongest form, in order to ensure your own analysis and response is as rigorous as possible

Probability: the study of how likely something is to happen, or to be true

Prospect theory: an observation-based theory developed by Nobel laureates Daniel Kahneman and Amos Tversky describing how people make decisions under different conditions of known risk, and select between different potential losses or gains

Publication bias: the tendency of academic journals to be more likely to publish research with positive or striking outcomes than other, equally valid research lacking such outcomes

p-value: short for 'probability-value'; the probability that an experiment's results came about through pure chance, expressed in the form of a decimal between one (certainty) and zero (impossibility); one common threshold for declaring a result significant is 0.95, meaning there is a 95 per cent or better chance that the observed outcomes or trend did not arise purely by chance

Qualitative research: exploratory research based on assessing the qualities or nature of something, rather than by measuring it

Quantitative data: research based on precisely quantifying a particular variable or variables in order to generate usable statistics

Ranking inductive arguments: determining which inductive arguments are more or less convincing relative to one another

RCT: short for a 'randomized controlled trial', in which subjects are allocated at random to a control group or to a treatment group (or groups)

Reasoning: thinking about things in a sensible or logical way, and then presenting this thinking so as to permit meaningful debate, disagreement and collaboration

Recency bias: a cognitive bias; the tendency to over-estimate the significance of more recent things, because they come more easily and vividly to mind

Red herrings: a term that originally described a strong-smelling fish used to lead hunting dogs away from a scent, and that now provides a useful metaphor for any intentional distraction away from what is actually at stake

Re-framing: deliberately selecting a different way of presenting information in order to challenge the emphasis created by a particular initial framing

Relevant sources: those that are closely related to a line of argument

Representative sample: one that very closely resembles the larger group it is taken from, allowing accurate general claims to be made about that group; no sample can ever be perfectly representative

Reputation: the expert standing of a source and an important guide to its reliability

Reversion to the mean: the tendency of an exceptional result to be followed by a less exceptional one, assuming a normal distribution of results over time

Rhetoric: the attempt to persuade by appealing to emotions rather than to reason

Sample: the particular cases you are using to stand for the entire category about which you wish to make an inductive generalization

Sampling bias: biases introduced by imperfect methods of selecting a sample

Scepticism: not automatically accepting as true something you hear, read or see

Scientific method: the systematic empirical investigation of the world through observation, experiment and measurement, together with the development, testing and reformulation of theories

Secondary sources: the product of someone else's work about a particular subject, period or phenomenon

Seminal: these works are sources that helped to lay the foundations of a field

Sharpshooter fallacy: also known as the clustering illusion, the tendency to see a pattern where none exists, by imposing it after the event on evidence while ignoring whatever doesn't fit

Single-blind: a research trial in which the subjects do not know whether they are in the control group (in which case they are receiving a placebo) or the treatment group (in which case they are receiving the actual treatment) but those conducting the experiment do know this

Slippery slope: arguing on the basis that, if one small thing is allowed to happen, an inevitable and increasingly serious chain of further events will be set in motion

Smokescreen: rhetorical device; a process of verbal concealment, where someone attempts to avoid or hide a key point beneath a large volume of words talking about something else

Social proof: also known as 'informational social influence', this describes a situation in which other people's apparent beliefs act as the proof on which you base your own beliefs

Sound argument: an argument that is both valid and has true premises, meaning its conclusion must also be true

Standard of proof: the threshold beyond which you have decided to accept something as proven, meaning you will not accept something as true if this standard is not met

Statistical significance: the probability that a particular result was achieved entirely through chance, as opposed to having a noteworthy cause; setting a threshold for significance is the usual way of establishing a particular standard for proof in an experiment

Stereotype: a cognitive bias; a commonly held, simplified and idealized view of the typical characteristics of something or someone of a particular type

Straw man: a rhetorical device; an absurd simplification of someone else's position that is obviously wrong or stupid, and that is only expressed so that it can easily be defeated

Style: the way something is written; different topics and audiences require very different styles

Sufficient condition: a condition that, if met, is sufficient to guarantee the truth of something else; for example, in a test whose pass mark is 60, getting 70 is sufficient to guarantee that you have passed

Summary: a brief outline of key information, often setting out the main points covered in a longer piece of work

Sunk cost fallacy: a cognitive bias; the tendency to continue expending energy on something you are emotionally invested in beyond the point at which it makes sense to abandon it

Survivorship bias: a cognitive bias; the tendency only to think about successful examples of something, failing to consider the bigger picture in which the vast majority of all cases are failures or have not endured

Treatment group: a group of subjects who are receiving active treatment; the difference between their results and those of the **control group**, if any, should indicate any impact from the treatment

Unconscious bias: when someone's opinions or decisions are distorted by factors that they are not even aware of (as opposed to **conscious bias**)

Uncritical thinking: automatically believing what you read or are told without pausing to ask whether it is accurate, true or reasonable (as opposed to **critical thinking**)

Unrepresentative sample: a sample that does not resemble the larger group it is taken from, meaning that claims derived from it will be distorted

Unsound argument: an argument that does not meet the standard of soundness, either because it is invalid or because one or more of its premises is untrue, or both; thus, you cannot rely on its conclusion being true

Unwarranted conclusion: a conclusion that is not supported by its premises

Unwarranted hidden assumption: the faulty, unstated element of reasoning that a fallacy usually relies on, and that we aim to spell out in order to identify what is at fault

Valid reasoning: correctly applying deductive reasoning in drawing out the logical conclusion of your premises

A SYNOPSIS OF FIVE VALID FORMS OF ARGUMENT

Only **deductive** arguments can be valid or sound. **Inductive** arguments are **strong** if they provide good reasons to accept their conclusions, but this is always a question of degree, and they can only ever suggest that something is extremely likely.

Combining the following five basic valid forms of deductive argument, while familiarizing yourself with common related fallacies and abuses of their forms, should allow you to test the logical validity of much more complicated arguments.

Never forget that a **valid** argument only guarantees its conclusion is true if its premises are also true. Otherwise, it simply repeats whatever assumptions have been made in its premises. A **sound** argument is both valid and has true premises, meaning its conclusion must be true. But coming up with premises that you are certain are true is much harder in real life than in case studies.

1 *MODUS PONENS*: AFFIRMING THE ANTECEDENT

Modus ponens is the abbreviated Latin for 'the mood that affirms' and describes a valid deductive argument in this general form, also known as **affirming the antecedent**:

Premise 1: If A, then B. *If you go out without a jacket, you will get cold.*

Premise 2: A. *You are going out without a jacket.*

Conclusion: **Therefore, B. *Therefore, you are going to get cold.***

Affirming the antecedent needs to be carefully distinguished from a similar but invalid form of argument – the fallacy of **affirming the consequent**, which takes the following form:

Premise 1: If A, then B. *If you go out without a jacket, you will get cold.*

Premise 2: B. *You are cold.*

Conclusion: **Therefore, A. *Therefore, you must have gone out without a jacket.***

In effect, the fallacy confuses B being true 'if' A is true with B being true 'only if' A is true.

2 *MODUS TOLLENS*: DENYING THE CONSEQUENT

Modus tollens is abbreviated Latin for 'the mood that denies' and describes a valid argument in this general form, also known as **denying the consequent**:

Premise 1: If A, then B. *If you go out without a jacket, you will get cold.*

Premise 2: Not B. *You are not cold.*

Conclusion: **Therefore, not A. *Therefore, you cannot have gone out without a jacket.***

An invalid form of argument that corresponds to denying the consequence: a formal fallacy known as **denying the antecedent**. It takes this form:

Premise 1: If A, then B. *If you go out without a jacket, you will get cold.*

Premise 2: Not A. *You have not gone out without a jacket.*

Conclusion: **Therefore, not B. *Therefore, you cannot be cold.***

Once again, this confuses B being true 'if' A is true with B being true 'only if' A is true.

3 HYPOTHETICAL SYLLOGISM/CHAIN ARGUMENTS

The term 'syllogism' describes any deductive argument in which a conclusion is inferred from two premises, while 'hypothetical' describes the fact that each premise takes the form of 'if... then'. A hypothetical syllogism thus has this form:

Premise 1: If A, then B. *If the business makes a loss, the CEO will be sacked.*

Premise 2: If B, then C. *If the CEO is sacked, the business will need a new CEO.*

Conclusion: **Therefore, if A, then C. *If the business makes a loss, it will need a new CEO.***

A more general term for this kind of argument is a 'chain argument', because it describes a chain of cause and effect – one that we can stretch beyond the two premises of a syllogism if we want: A is sufficient to guarantee B, B is sufficient to guarantee C, and so on.

Remember, though, that validity is by itself no guarantee of truth – and this particular form of argument is often exploited by the insertion of less-than-true premises:

> If you don't pay for my holiday, I'll be stressed and sad; if I'm stressed and sad, I'll fail my exams; if I fail my exams, I won't get a job; if I don't get a job, I'll never be a productive member of society. Therefore, unless you pay for my holiday, I'll never be a productive member of society.

4 DISJUNCTIVE SYLLOGISM: THE *EITHER/OR* ARGUMENT

A disjunctive syllogism is based on stating that either one thing or another must be true, meaning that, if one thing is not true, the other must be: the absence of A is sufficient to guarantee B, and the absence of B is sufficient to guarantee A. It has this general form:

Premise 1: Either A or B. *Either the CEO has been sacked or the business is profitable.*

Premise 2: Not A. *The CEO has not been sacked.*

Conclusion: **Therefore, B. *Therefore, the business must be profitable.***

Like chain arguments, this *either/or* form of argument is often exploited for the purpose of misleading persuasion. Consider this particular disjunctive syllogism:

> Either the defendant is guilty of the crime or he has learned how to be in two places at the same time. Given that the latter cannot be the case, the former must be: he is guilty as charged.

This is a valid argument. Notice, however, that its validity rests on the assumption that there are no other possible situations beyond the two it describes: either the defendant is guilty, or he has learned how to be in two places at the same time. Is this likely? Probably not, but the prosecuting lawyer would like you to think so.

5 CONSTRUCTIVE DILEMMA

This last form of argument leaves us not with a single conclusion, but with two possibilities. In effect, it combines two of the previous forms of argument – a disjunctive syllogism (either A or B) and affirming the antecedent (if A, then B). It's also vulnerable to the same kind of abuse as these arguments: oversimplifying a situation in which it's useful to pretend there are only two options. It takes this form:

Premise 1:	Either A or B. *Either the old CEO has been sacked or the business is profitable.*
Premise 2:	If A, then C. *If the old CEO has been sacked, the business will need a new CEO.*
Premise 3:	If B, then D. *If the business is profitable, the old CEO will get a bonus.*
Conclusion:	**Therefore, C or D. *So, either the business needs a new CEO or the old CEO will get a bonus.***

If you like this bit of the book, consider getting one of the logic textbooks in the further reading section — there's plenty more to learn!

ENDNOTES

WHAT IS CRITICAL THINKING (AND WHY DOES IT MATTER)?

1 Wasik, J. (2012) 'Hacked by a phisher? How the grandparent scam works', *Forbes*, 6 September. Available at: www.forbes.com/sites/johnwasik/2012/09/06/hijacked-by-a-phisher-how-the-grandparent-scam-works (accessed 28 January 2016).

2 Kahneman, D. (2012) *Thinking, Fast and Slow*. London: Allen Lane.

3 The term 'confirmation bias' itself was coined by Peter Cathcart Wason in 1968, although the tendency it described had long been known to students of human nature. See Wason, P.C. (1968) 'Reasoning about a rule', *Quarterly Journal of Experimental Psychology*, 20 (3): 273–81.

CHAPTER 1

4 Baumeister, R.E., Bratslavsky, E., Muraven, M. and Tice, D.M. (1998) 'Ego depletion: is the active self a limited resource?', *Journal of Personality and Social Psychology*, 74 (5): 1252–65.

CHAPTER 2

5 *The Oxford Companion to Philosophy* begins its entry on the principle of charity with this useful summary: 'In its simplest form, it holds that (other things being equal) one's interpretation of another speaker's words should minimize the ascription of false beliefs to that. For example, it suggests that, given the choice between translating a speaker of a foreign language as expressing the belief that elephants have wings and as expressing the belief that elephants have tusks, one should opt for the latter translation.' See Honderich, T. (ed.) (2005) *The Oxford Companion to Philosophy* (2nd edition) New York: Oxford University Press.

CHAPTER 3

6 The Vegan Society (n.d.) 'Definition of veganism'. Available at: www.vegansociety.com/go-vegan/definition-veganism (accessed 24 April 2017).

7 A brief note on logic and computers: Digital computing is founded on the insight that it's possible for a combination of tiny switches, called a transistor, to embody a valid logical proposition. You can, for example, create a transistor so that it will produce a positive output if it receives a positive input from another transistor; or so that one transistor switches on only when two others are both on; or so that one transistor switches on when another is off. This simple logical vocabulary is the basis of all computer algorithms – and it is, incredibly enough, sufficient to produce everything that modern computers achieve. It just takes billions of switches and a grasp of logic.

8 In formal logic, there are nine elementary valid arguments that can be used to form most others: *modus ponens, modus tollens*, hypothetical syllogism, disjunctive syllogism, constructive dilemma, absorption, simplification, conjunction, and addition. An excellent textbook outlining these and much else is Copi, I.M., Cohen, C. and McMahon, K. (2010) *Introduction to Logic* (14th edition). New York: Routledge.

CHAPTER 4

9 The American pragmatist philosopher Charles Sanders Peirce (1839–1914) introduced the term 'ampliative reasoning' to clarify the way in which the conclusions of inductive arguments extend what is asserted in their premises. See Houser, N. and Kloesel, C.J.W. (eds.) *The Essential Peirce* (1992/1998). Indiana: Indiana University Press.

10 For an excellent explanation of both sampling and its statistical context, see Field, A. (2016) *An*

Adventure in Statistics, London: Sage, and Chapter 10 in particular.

11 'That the sun will not rise tomorrow is no less intelligible a proposition, and implies no more contradiction, than the affirmation, that it will rise. We should in vain, therefore, attempt to demonstrate its falsehood. Were it demonstratively false, it would imply a contradiction, and could never be distinctly conceived by the mind.' In Hume, D. (1772/1993) 'Cause and effect: part I', *An Enquiry Concerning Human Understanding*. London: Hackett.

12 This is an example perhaps most famously discussed in Taleb, N.N. (2007) *The Black Swan: The Impact of the Highly Improbable*. New York: Random House.

13 Wason, P.C. (1968) 'Reasoning about a rule', *Quarterly Journal of Experimental Psychology*, 20 (3): 273–81. As noted earlier, Wason also gave us the phrase 'confirmation bias'.

CHAPTER 5

14 A classic text in translation from the Latin is Bacon, F., Sir (1620) *Novum Organum* (ed. J. Devey, 1902). New York: P.F. Collier. This can be read in full online at http://oll.libertyfund.org/titles/bacon-novum-organum. The term 'empirical' itself comes from the Latin noun *empiricus*, describing the school of physicians who believed in basing their expertise upon experience (as opposed to those who believed in basing their expertise upon the Hippocratic tradition of sacred medical writings).

15 The American pragmatist philosopher Charles Sanders Peirce (1839–1914) coined the term 'abductive reasoning' in addition, as noted in a previous footnote, to that of 'ampliative' reasoning. It was Peirce who established the three-part distinction between deduction, induction and abduction to which my account in this book is indebted, together with the theory that these three modes of reasoning between them map out the scientific method: abductive reasoning first suggests a hypothesis, the researcher then deduces what must logically be true if this hypothesis is true, then induction finally makes predictions that permit the testing and refining of the initial hypothesis.

16 The friend was William Stukeley, who published his account in *Memories of Sir Isaac Newton's Life* (1752); the manuscript was released online by the Royal Society and has subsequently appeared, among other places, in Chown, M. (2017) *The Ascent of Gravity: The Quest to Understand the Force that Explains Everything*. London: Weidenfeld & Nicolson.

17 There are many accounts of the history of gravitation research; a thorough recent book is Chown, M. (2017) *The Ascent of Gravity: The Quest to Understand the Force that Explains Everything*. London: Weidenfeld & Nicolson.

18 This phrase was first used by the philosopher Gilbert H. Harman in 1965, and was intended to offer a more precise definition than Peirce's sense of abduction. 'I prefer my own terminology because I believe that it avoids most of the misleading suggestions of the alternative terminologies,' he wrote. 'In making this inference one infers, from the fact that a certain hypothesis would explain the evidence, to the truth of that hypothesis. In general, there will be several hypotheses which might explain the evidence, so one must be able to reject all such alternative hypotheses before one is warranted in making the inference. Thus one infers, from the premise that a given hypothesis would provide a "better" explanation for the evidence than would any other hypothesis, to the conclusion that the given hypothesis is true.' Harman, G. (1965) 'The Inference to the best explanation', *The Philosophical Review* 74: 88–95.

19 I borrowed this example from a wonderful short book on statistics: Huff, D. (1973) *How to Lie with Statistics*. London: Penguin.

CHAPTER 6

20 NASA (n.d.) 'Climate change: How do we know?' Available at: https://climate.nasa.gov/evidence (accessed April 2017).

21 World Natural Health Organization (n.d.) 'The global warming hoax'. Available at: www.wnho.net/global_warming.htm (accessed April 2017).

22 One of the clearest and most useful APA Style guidelines resources I have found online is offered by the Purdue Online Writing Lab at https://owl.english.purdue.edu/owl/resource/560/01/ (retrieved July 2017)

CHAPTER 7

23 Aristotle's *Treatise on Rhetoric* dates from the 4th century BC; one of the most authoritative modern editions is the Loeb Classical Library (1989). For an accessible and entertaining account of classical rhetoric in both ancient and modern contexts, see Leith, S. (2011) *You Talkin' To Me? Rhetoric from Aristotle to Obama*. London: Profile Books.

24 See the fascinating book, Cialdini, R. (2016) *Pre-suasion*. London: Simon & Schuster.

25 This was the original headline used by Upworthy on 20 May 2013 for the article now titled 'This amazing kid got to enjoy 19 awesome years on this planet: what he left behind is wondtacular'. Available at: www.upworthy.com/this-amazing-kid-got-to-enjoy-19-awesome-years-on-this-planet-what-he-left-behind-is-wondtacular (accessed April 2017).

26 See Washington Post staff (2015) 'Full text: Donald Trump announces a presidential bid', *The Washington Post*, 16 June. Available at: www.washingtonpost.com/news/post-politics/wp/2015/06/16/full-text-donald-trump-announces-a-presidential-bid (accessed April 2017).

27 From Case, M.A. (2016) 'The role of the popes in the invention of complementarity and the Vatican's anathematization of gender', University of Chicago Public Law & Legal Theory Working Paper, No. 565.

28 If you're interested in reading about the Stanford prison experiment in more detail, one rich resource is the Stanford Prison Experiment website at http://www.prisonexp.org/ (accessed July 2017) which encompasses detailed information about the original experiment, and materials from the 2007 book and 2015 film it inspired, all put together by the experiment's originator, Philip Zimbardo.

CHAPTER 8

29 As we will see later in this chapter, the ancient Greek philosopher Aristotle was the first to list fallacies and his work continues to underpin many common approaches. A useful discussion of ancient and modern approaches to fallacies can be found on the Stanford Encyclopedia of Philosophy website at https://plato.stanford.edu/entries/fallacies/ (accessed July 2017)

30 Aristotle identified 13 fallacies in *Sophistical Refutations*, one of the six books that make up his collected works on logic, the *Organon*. A full text can be accessed online at http://classics.mit.edu/Aristotle/sophist_refut.1.1.html (accessed July 2017).

31 The Royal Society have made the original 1763 text of Bayes's essay available online, as part of its *Philosophical Transactions*. See Bayes T. (1763) 'An Essay towards solving a Problem in the Doctrine of Chances'. *Philosophical Transactions*, 53: 370–418. doi:10.1098/rstl.1763.0053

CHAPTER 9

32 The American political scientist and economist Herbert A Simon (1916–2001) was the first to use the term 'heuristics' to describe mental short cuts for decision-making, in the 1950s. Simon discussed heuristics in the context of what he called 'bounded rationality', which described the limitations of individual decision-making in terms of the complexities of a problem, the capacity of the mind and the time available. Hence the practical importance of achieving satisfactory solutions through rules of thumb, rather than focusing only on the best possible theoretical solution. See Simon, H.A. (1955) 'A behavioral model of rational choice', *Quarterly Journal of Economics*, 69 (1): 99–118.

33 Finucane, M.L., Alhakami, A., Slovic, P. and Johnson, S.M. (2000) 'The affect heuristic in judgment of risks and benefits', *Journal of Behavioral Decision Making*, 13 (1): 1–17.

34 This example first appeared in Tversky, A. and Kahneman, D. (1973) 'Availability: a heuristic for judging frequency and probability', *Cognitive Psychology*, 5 (2): 207–32.

35 For this, other statistics and a useful explanation of the psychological mechanisms in play, see Anderson, J. (2017) 'The psychology of why 94 deaths from terrorism are scarier than 301,797 deaths from guns', *Quartz*, 31 January. Available at: https://qz.com/898207/the-psychology-of-why-americans-are-more-scared-of-terrorism-than-

guns-though-guns-are-3210-times-likelier-to-kill-them/ (retrieved July 2017).

36 Ross, M. and Sicoly, F. (1979) 'Egocentric biases in availability and attribution', *Journal of Personality and Social Psychology*, 37 (3): 322–36.

37 See Ariely, D., Loewenstein, G. and Prelec, D. (2003) '"Coherent arbitrariness": stable demand curves without stable preferences', *Quarterly Journal of Economics*, 118: 73–106. doi https://doi.org/10.1162/00335530360535153

38 My choice of example is influenced by Schkade, D.A. and Kahneman, D. (1998) 'Does living in California make people happy? A focusing illusion in judgments of life satisfaction', *Psychological Science*, 9 (5): 340–6.

39 The 'Linda problem' first appeared in Tversky, A. and Kahneman, D. (1974) 'Judgments under uncertainty: heuristics and biases', *Science*, 185 (4157): 1124–31.

40 For an example of objections to the Linda problem see Hertwig, R. and Gigerenzer, G. (1999) 'The "conjunction fallacy" revisited: How intelligent inferences look like reasoning errors', *Journal of Behavioral Decision Making*, 12: 275–305. doi:10.1002/(sici)1099-0771(199912)12:4<275::aid-bdm323>3.3.co;2-d

41 For the period October to December 2016, the Office of National Statistics Labour Force Survey reported 375,000 people working in agriculture, forestry and fishing; 528,000 people working in mining, energy and water supply; and 4,143,000 people working in health and social work. See 'EMP13: Employment by industry', released on 15 February 2017, online at www.ons.gov.uk/employmentandlabourmarket/peopleinwork/employmentandemployeetypes/datasets/employmentbyindustryemp13 (retrieved July 2017).

42 One recommended place to start reading around prejudice, stereotyping and exclusion is hooks, b. (1981) *Ain't I A Woman: Black Women And Feminism*. Boston, MA: South End Press.

43 The key initial paper that introduced framing effects, including a version of this particular example, is Tversky, A. and Kahneman, D. (1981) 'The framing of decisions and the psychology of choice', *Science*, 211 (4481): 453–5; while a useful later paper analysing different types of framing effect is Levin, I.P., Schneider, S.L. and Gaeth, G.J. (1998) 'All frames are not created equal: a typology and critical analysis of framing effects', *Organizational Behavior and Human Decision Processes*, 76 (2): 149–88.

44 See Kahneman, D. and Tversky, A. (1979) 'Prospect theory: an analysis of decision under risk', *Econometrica*, 47 (2): 263.

45 See Knutson, A. (2013) '22 People Who Found Jesus In Their Food', *BuzzFeed*, 29 March. Available at: www.buzzfeed.com/arielknutson/people-who-found-jesus-in-their-food (retrieved July 2017).

46 My (fictional) example is not based on any one study, but its general points echo the criticisms made in its 2009 report by the American Psychological Association Task Force on Appropriate Therapeutic Responses to Sexual Orientation, which conducted 'a systematic review of the peer-reviewed journal literature on sexual orientation change efforts (SOCE)' and concluded that 'efforts to change sexual orientation are unlikely to be successful and involve some risk of harm, contrary to the claims of SOCE practitioners and advocates'. See American Psychological Association (2009) *Report of the Task Force on Gender Identity and Gender Variance*. Available at: www.apa.org/pi/lgbt/resources/policy/gender-identity-report.pdf (accessed July 2017).

47 For a detailed exploration of this, see Amankwah-Amoah, J. (2014) 'A unified framework of explanations for strategic persistence in the wake of others' failures', *Journal of Strategy and Management*, 7 (4): 422–44.

48 Kruger, J. and Dunning, D. (1999) 'Unskilled and unaware of it: how difficulties in recognizing one's own incompetence lead to inflated self-assessments', *Journal of Personality and Social Psychology*, 77 (6): 1121–34.

49 Alpert, M. and Raiffa, H. (1982) 'A progress report on the training of probability assessors'. In D. Kahneman, P. Slovic and A. Tversky (eds) *Judgement Under Uncertainty: Heuristics and Biases*. Cambridge: Cambridge University Press. pp. 294–305.

50 Some of the complexities of expert overconfidence are explored in Lin, S.-W. and Bier, V.M. (2008) 'A study of expert overconfidence'. *Reliability Engineering and System Safety*, 93: 775—7. This includes the observation that experts are by no means always overconfident in their own fields and that previous effects suggesting this may be due in part to noisy data.

51 See Benson, B. (2017) 'Cognitive bias cheat sheet, simplified: thinking is hard because of 4 universal conundrums', *Medium*, 8 January. Available at: https://medium.com/thinking-is-hard/4-conundrums-of-intelligence-2ab78d90740f (accessed April 2017).

52 Tversky, A. and Kahneman, D. (1974) 'Judgments under uncertainty: heuristics and biases', *Science*, 185 (4157): 1124–31. Also online at http://psiexp.ss.uci.edu/research/teaching/Tversky_Kahneman_1974.pdf; Kahneman, D. and Tversky, A. (1979) 'Prospect theory: an analysis of decision under risk', *Econometrica,* 47 (2): 263. Also online at www.princeton.edu/~kahneman/docs/Publications/prospect_theory.pdf; Tversky, A. and Kahneman, D. (1981) 'The framing of decisions and the psychology of choice', *Science*, 211 (4481): 453–8. Also online at http://psych.hanover.edu/classes/Cognition/Papers/tversky81.pdf.

CHAPTER 10

53 A version of this story is told by Daniel Kahneman in his delightful autobiographical essay on the Nobel Prize website at www.nobelprize.org/nobel_prizes/economic-sciences/laureates/2002/kahneman-bio.html (retrieved July 2017).

54 The phrase 'fundamental attribution error' was coined in 1977 by the social psychologist Lee Ross to describe people's tendency to attribute others' behaviour to their intentions and character, even if that behaviour was clearly a result of circumstances. See Ross, L. (1977) 'The intuitive psychologist and his shortcomings: distortions in the attribution process'. In Berkowitz, L. (Ed.) *Advances in Experimental Social Psychology*, 10. New York: Academic Press. pp. 173–220.

55 See Williams, B. (1981) *Moral Luck*. Cambridge: Cambridge University Press; and Nagel, T. (1979) *Mortal Questions*. New York: Cambridge University Press.

56 See Taleb, N.N. (2007) *Fooled by Randomness: The Hidden Role of Chance in Life and in the Markets*. London: Penguin.

57 Among many other places, this story is told well in Ellenberg, J. (2014) *How Not to be Wrong: The Hidden Maths of Everyday Life*. London: Penguin.

58 See the AllTrials website for full details at www.alltrials.net

CHAPTER 11

59 Shannon's foundational paper in information theory was published in two parts in 1948: Shannon, C.E. (1948) 'A mathematical theory of communication', *Bell System Technical Journal*, 27 (3): 379–42; and Shannon, C.E. (1948) 'A mathematical theory of communication', *Bell System Technical Journal*, 27 (4): 623–66; subsequently republished under a new title, together with additional materials by Warren Weaver, in Shannon, C.E. and Weaver, W. (1949) *The Mathematical Theory of Communication*. Champaign, IL: University of Illinois Press. For an excellent, accessible introduction to information theory, see Floridi, L. (2010) *Information: A Very Short Introduction*. Oxford: Oxford University Press. And for a dazzling popular history of information that remains one of the most compelling non-fiction books I have ever read, see Gleick, J. (2011) *The Information: A History, A Theory, A Flood*. London: HarperCollins.

60 See Wikipedia, 'List of highest mountains on Earth', at https://en.wikipedia.org/wiki/List_of_highest_mountains_on_Earth (accessed April 2017).

61 For a news story on the heights of Everest according to Nepal, China and the USA, see BBC News, 'Nepal and China agree on Mount Everest's height', 8 April 2010, online at http://news.bbc.co.uk/1/hi/world/south_asia/8608913.stm. For an account of surveying the height of K2, see 'Steep questions: how tall is K2?', GPS World, 29 July 2015, online at http://gpsworld.com/steep-questions-how-tall-is-k2. For a useful summary of the measuring and error margins involved in surveying mountains, see 'How do you measure a mountain?' on the official OS blog, 2 August 2011, online at www.ordnancesurvey.co.uk/blog/2011/08/how-do-you-measure-a-mountain (including useful links in the comments section). (All of the above accessed 15 April 2017.)

62 See the official NASA history *Apollo Expeditions to the Moon*, Chapter 13.1, 'Houston, we've had a problem', by J.A. Lovell, online at https://history.nasa.gov/SP-350/ch-13-1.html (accessed April 2017).

63 Retrieved from 'The Full Fact Toolkit' at https://fullfact.org/toolkit in April 2017.

64 For an excellent in-depth analysis of social proof in the context of technology, see Hendricks, V.F. and

Hansen, P.G. (2016) *Infostorms: Why do we 'Like'? Explaining Individual Behaviour on the Net*. New York: Springer.

65 It remains worth reading Brin and Page's original 1998 paper presenting Google and its prototype model for 'effectively dealing with uncontrolled hypertext collections where anyone can publish anything they want'. See Brin, S. and Page, L. (1998) 'The anatomy of a large-scale hypertextual web search engine'. In: Seventh International World-Wide Web Conference (WWW 1998), April 14–18, Brisbane, Australia. Available at: http://ilpubs.stanford.edu:8090/361/ (retrieved July 2017).

66 Metcalfe himself tells the story in Metcalfe, R. (2007) 'It's all in your head', *Forbes*, 20 April, online at www.forbes.com/forbes/2007/0507/052.html (retrieved July 2017): 'Using a 35mm slide… I argued that my customers needed their Ethernets to grow above a certain critical mass if they were to reap the benefits of the network effect. 3Com sold $1,000 cards that connected desktop computers into a network. Here was the payoff: The cost of installing the cards at, say, a corporation would be proportional to the number of cards installed. The value of the network, though, would be proportional to the square of the number of users. Multiply the number of networked computers by ten and your systemwide cost goes up by a factor of ten but the value goes up a hundredfold.'

67 Pariser, E. (2011) *The Filter Bubble: What the Internet is Hiding from You*. New York: Penguin.

68 For example, see Boxell, L., Gentzkow, M. and Shapiro, J.M. (2017) 'Is the internet causing political polarization? Evidence from demographics', NBER Working Paper No. 23258, March.

69 See Greenwald, A.G. (2017) 'An AI stereotype catcher', *Science*, 356 (6334): 133–4; and for a lively broader discussion of these emerging issues, see O'Neil, C. (2016) *Weapons of Math Destruction: How Big Data Increases Inequality and Threatens Democracy*. New York: Penguin.

70 See Luft, J. and Ingham, H. (1955) 'The Johari window, a graphic model of interpersonal awareness', in *Proceedings of the Western Training Laboratory in Group Development*. Los Angeles, CA: UCLA.

71 The Wikipedia entry on the Nevada Test Site, where Desert Rock and other operations took place, has useful details and links to follow for further reading at https://en.wikipedia.org/wiki/Nevada_Test_Site (accessed July 2017).

72 See Microsoft's Advanced Operator Reference page for Bing at https://msdn.microsoft.com/en-us/library/ff795620.aspx

CHAPTER 12

73 For example, I highly recommend Allen, D. (2015) *Getting Things Done: The Art of Stress-free Productivity*. London: Piatkus.

74 For an excellent book on habits, see Duhigg, C. (2012) *The Power of Habit: Why We Do What We Do, and How to Change*. New York: Random House.

INDEX

'Research is what I'm doing when I don't know what I'm doing'
— Wernher von Braun